Case Studies in

Systematic
Software
Development

Prentice Hall International Series in Computer Science

C. A. R. Hoare, Series Editor

Case Studies in
Systematic
Software
Development

EDITED BY

Cliff B. Jones
Department of Computer Science
University of Manchester

AND

Roger C. F. Shaw
Praxis Systems plc

PRENTICE HALL
New York   London   Toronto   Sydney   Tokyo

First published 1990 by
Prentice Hall International (UK) Ltd
66 Wood Lane End, Hemel Hempstead
Hertfordshire HP2 4RG
A division of
Simon & Schuster International Group

Printed and bound in Great Britain at the
University Press, Cambridge

Library of Congress Cataloging-in-Publication Data

Jones, C. B. (Cliff B.), 1944–
    Case studies in systematic software development /
Cliff B. Jones, Roger C. F. Shaw
        p.   cm. – (Prentice Hall International series in
computer science)
    Includes bibliographical references.
    ISBN 0–13–116088–5 : $33.95
        1. Computer software – Development – Case studies.
I. Shaw, Roger C. F.   II. Title.   III. Series.
QA76.76.D47J659   1989
005.1 – dc20   89–39813 CIP

British Library Cataloguing in Publication Data

Jones, Cliff B. (Cliff Bryn), *1944–*
    Case studies in systematic software development. –
    (Computer systems. Software. Development.
    Mathematical models)
    1. Computer systems. Software. Development.
    Mathematical Models
    I. Title   II. Shaw, Roger C. F.
    005.1

ISBN 0–13–116088–5

1 2 3 4 5   94 93 92 91 90

Contents

Foreword

VDM is currently the most widely spread method for the systematic, via rigorous, to formal development of software, from programs to programming systems.

Background

VDM, as first conceived, around 1973–1975, at the IBM Vienna Laboratory, derived its foundational and methodological constituents from many academic sources: notably from the works of, and inspired by such researchers as, Jaco de Bakker, Rod Burstall, Tony Hoare, Peter Landin, John McCarthy, Robin Milner, John Reynolds, Dana Scott, Christopher Strachey, and many others. The inspirational background offered here was cast into a whole to form 'classical' VDM by the Viennese industrial researchers (the late) Hans Bekić, and Wolfgang Henhapl, Peter Lucas, Cliff Jones and myself.

Three VDM R&D phases – and two schools

Since VDM research and development left Vienna, around 1975–1976, a number of independent, mostly compatible directions have been pursued. Roughly three phases of VDM R&D can be identified: (1) the 'classical' Vienna VDM (1973–1978) – as manifested for example in the book: *The Vienna Development Method – the Meta-Language* published in 1978 by Springer Verlag as its 61st Lecture Notes in Computer Science volume (LNCS61), and *Formal Specification and Software Development* mostly by Cliff Jones and myself (Prentice Hall International (PH), 1982); (2) the parallel, complementing VDM as witnessed by the books: *Software Development – a Rigorous Approach* (SDRA) by Cliff Jones (PH), 1980, *Towards a Formal Description of Ada* (Springer Verlag, LNCS98), and *Systematic Software Development using VDM* (SSD/VDM) by Cliff Jones (PH, 1986); and the more independent, not always fully compatible lines of VDM R&D as witnessed by the book *MetaSoft Primer* by Andrzej Blikle (Springer Verlag, LNCS288, 1987), and by the article 'The RAISE Language, Method and Tools', by Mogens Nielsen *et al.*, and appearing in Springer Verlag's new journal: *Formal Aspects of Computing*, Vol. 1, No. 1, 1989.

Phase 2 can be characterized as composed of a Danish (LNCS98) and an English (SDRA and SSD/VDM) 'school'. The difference in emphasis between the two schools is really superficial: styles of notation differ, modes of defining functions and operations either mostly directly, and mostly applicatively (the Danish school), or (the English school) by means of pre-/post-conditions, and, for operations, on a slightly different imperial state notion.

– a unification

The British Standards Institute's current VDM standardization effort is successfully amalgamating these two schools. The present book follows this consolidation.

Whereas phase 3 work may be called post-VDM, and whereas it is too early to speak of this work's wide acceptance, the present book offers material that can be readily adapted in any mature industrial environment.

The present book

For widespread acceptance of formal methods in industry, realistic case studies, carefully documented, must be presented. The various case examples presented here ought to convince most dogmatic 'anti-formalists' that VDM is a sound, industry-ready method for developing large scale, primarily sequential, deterministic software – software that can be trusted.

Although VDM was first conceived while developing a compiler for PL/I, it is refreshing to see its wider use in such diverse areas as databases (Chapters 2–3), proof systems (Chapter 4), explaining and implementing the crucial, 'originally' logic programming notion of unification (Chapters 5–6), storage management, whether in an operating system, a database management system or a program's run-time system (Chapters 7–8), non von Neumann computer architectures (Chapter 11), user interface systems (Chapter 12), or graphics (Chapter 13). Of course, a classical programming language definition must be given (Chapter 9) – and that chapter may be a good starting point for students, but a semantic analysis, in the form of a definition, of what constitutes 'object-orientedness' in programming languages is also presented (Chapter 10).

A warning, and a promise

It is my sincere belief, one which has been tempered by many years of sad industrial experience, that the present, large software houses may easily become extinct if they do not provide a means – for the hundreds of young candidates that graduate yearly – to pursue software development in the only exciting and professionally responsible way it should be developed – namely formally. Young, upstart, companies which offer this opportunity to the recent academically trained software engineers and programmers will attract the coming (large) generations.

An old generation clings to such 'dogmatisms' as: (1) `formal definitions are unreadable`, (2) `it is hard to prove programs correct`, (3) `the technology is not available`.

This book proves otherwise: (1) the definitions are easy to read – and one should only entrust serious software development to professionals anyway; (2) it is not that hard to reason about correctness – and who would want incorrect software if it could be correct?; and (3) the technology, VDM, has been here for quite a while – it is industry's task to develop industry-scale tools.

Industry no longer has any excuse not to put the results of academic research into daily practice. This volume certainly proves that academic research is industrially useful.

To specify formally, and to formally develop software, is to create insight into, and theories about, otherwise complex systems.

This book, with its balanced examples proves that point: it is refreshingly relaxing to develop beautiful software embodying elegant theories formally – and VDM is presently the strongest contender!

Dines Bjørner
Holte, 25 September 1989

Preface

Although young by the standards of most engineering disciplines, software development tackles tasks of enormous complexity. In seeking a systematic approach to control this complexity, the software industry is recognizing the need for a variety of new practices. High on their list is an acceptance that 'formal methods' are necessary if large systems are to be developed to higher standards than currently prevail. Formal methods is a term which is used to cover both the use of mathematical notation in the functional specifications of systems and the use of justifications which relate designs to their specifications. One of the most widely known and used formal methods is called the 'Vienna Development Method' (more often referred to as 'VDM'). VDM was developed in an industrial environment but has also evoked considerable academic research.

VDM provides both a specification notation and proof obligations which enable a designer to establish the correctness of steps of design. It is a development method in the sense that it offers notation and framework for recording and justifying specifications and design steps. VDM does not, however, claim to be a normative method in the sense that it results in the choice of a standard or best design: the designer provides the insight. Chapter 1 discusses how VDM concepts fit into the broader subject of 'software engineering'.

VDM grew out of earlier research but became a coherent whole in the mid 1970s. Since then it has been developed and discussed in a literally hundreds of publications. A clear sign of its maturity for industrial use is the availability of a variety of textbooks which set out to teach the use of both the specification and design justification parts of the method. Furthermore, courses are available from commercial organizations and two international conferences (organized by the European Community, 'VDM-Europe' group) have been dedicated to VDM.

It is the experience of the authors and editors of the current volume (amongst many other people) that methods like VDM enable them to describe major computer systems. Such experience is difficult to convey in a book and a textbook on a method such as [Jon90] is certainly an inadequate medium. Although the examples in this volume are not large by industrial standards, they should provide a much clearer indication of how to tackle major systems than is possible in any book whose main task is teaching the method from scratch. It has long been obvious that there is a significant need for such material: both of the editors have taught courses where the step from the textbook examples to an industry-sized specification has to be bridged by some sort of case study.

Much case study material has – in fact – been available in the literature. Unfortunately, the papers are not always easily located and the notation (often because of such mundane issues as printing devices) varies from one publication to the next. Experience of teaching VDM to industrial audiences constantly reminds one of the importance of a uniform style of presentation, at least during the early stages of the learning process. While researchers often show a cavalier disdain for issues of syntax, more practically oriented people tend to get confused when presented with a variety of notation. In fact, some industrial organizations cite the absence of a stable language (along with the paucity of tools) as a major reason for their reluctance to embrace formal methods.

The work of the British Standards Institution (BSI) group BSI IST/5/50 has progressed to the point that an outline standard is now available for comment. This presents a timely opportunity to publish a collection of VDM material in a coherent notation which should achieve wide acceptance. There is also evidence that this stability is stimulating tool builders. A second edition of *Systematic Software Development using VDM* [Jon90] has been prepared using the draft BSI standard notation and the current volume adopts the same language.

The case studies illustrate all facets of VDM. Some confine themselves to specifications often providing insight as to why the particular specification was developed. Other examples cover design by data reification[1] or operation decomposition. In many chapters proofs are only sketched but some very detailed proofs are also presented.

Ten authors have contributed a total of twelve case studies (Chapters 2–13). The authors come from backgrounds as varied as their material and – beyond conformity to the specification notation itself – the editors have not tried to force the material into a particular mould. In fact the editors could echo George Bernard Shaw's comment in the preface to *Essays on Socialism* that 'there has been no sacrifice of individuality'. There are several positive reasons for this. Before tackling larger specifications the reader must become aware that there is often no 'right' specification. Furthermore, seeing a range of styles will help the readers focus on what they wish to develop as their own approach.

The size of the chosen case studies is such that they illustrate many of the points made in [Jon90] better than was possible there. This is particularly the case with the exhortation to use more formal approaches in the early stages of design. Another major point which should become clear is the importance of providing a design record. Most readers will probably begin their study of the material with application areas with which

---

[1]The term reification is preferred to the more widely used word 'refinement'. Michael Jackson pointed out to the author that the latter term is hardly appropriate for the step from a clean mathematical abstraction to a messy representation dictated by a particular machine architecture. The *Concise Oxford Dictionary* defines the verb 'reify' as 'convert (person, abstract concept) into thing, materialize'.

they are familiar. This should enable them to perceive the use of formal models in experimenting with alternative architectures.

Apart from the case studies themselves, an appendix covers the notation used. In part, this is just a summary of the language; but it also discusses those aspects which are needed in some case studies but are not covered in [Jon90] (e.g. Lambda expressions). A reader who encounters anything unfamiliar should consult Appendix A. There is also a list of references to the literature (a wider list of references is to be included in the Teacher's Notes associated with [Jon90]; since the material covered here represents only a very small percentage of that published about VDM, the reader is encouraged to follow such references as might be relevant to their own application area). It was decided to confine the material is this book to the major uses of VDM and only Chapter 12 explores extensions to VDM in the area of user interface design. In particular, no attempt has been made to exemplify material which extends VDM to handle concurrency. Work in this area is at the research stage and the interested reader must follow the references to the relevant publications.

Different users of this book will obviously employ it in different ways. It is likely to be background reading for undergraduate courses which use one or the other textbook to teach VDM; while an MSc or industrial course might make detailed analysis of the case studies. A particularly valuable way of doing this is to organize some sort of 'walkthrough' of chosen examples. By their very nature, few of the examples are closed and there is excellent scope for extending a case study as a major project.

The editors are grateful to the long-suffering authors who have provided the bulk of this book, to Prentice Hall and Ruth Freestone for their help and encouragement in its formation and to Peter Luckham for his efforts in obtaining the Linotron output. Cliff Jones wishes to express his thanks for financial support to his research from the Wolfson Foundation and SERC; the latter both from research grants and his Senior Fellowship. He also gratefully acknowledges the stimulus provided by meetings of IFIP WG2.3. Roger Shaw expresses his thanks to Praxis Systems plc for support of his part in editing this book.

Contributors

John S. Fitzgerald
Department of Computer Science
The University
Manchester
United Kingdon M13 9PL

Chris W. George
STC Technology Ltd
London Road
Harlow
Essex
United Kingdon CM17 9NA

Kevin D. Jones
Digital Equipment Corp.
Systems Research Center
130, Lytton Avenue
Palo Alto
Ca 94301, USA

Cliff B. Jones
Department of Computer Science
The University
Manchester
United Kingdon M13 9PL

Lynn S. Marshall
Computing Research Laboratory
Bell-Northern Research Ltd.
P.O. Box 3511, Station C
Ottawa
Ontario
Canada K17 4H7

Richard C. Moore
Department of Computer Science
The University
Manchester
United Kingdon M13 9PL

Roger C. Shaw
Praxis Systems plc
20, Manvers Street
Bath
United Kingdon BA1 1PX

Sunil Vadera
Deptartment of Mathematics and
Computer Science
University of Salford
Salford
United Kingdon M5 4WT

Anne Walshe
18, Brighouse Close
Ormskirk
Lancashire
United Kingdon L39 3NB

Mario I. Wolczko
Department of Computer Science
The University
Manchester
United Kingdon M13 9PL

1

Introduction – Formal Methods and Software Engineering

Roger C. Shaw

In the course of presenting industrial training on formal methods a number of questions relating to the application and relevance of such methods to software engineering have cropped up repeatedly. Some of these questions relate to the scope of such methods as VDM. Others reveal a concern over the use of the term 'method', and suggest that many software engineers have a different understanding of its meaning than do the proponents of formal methods. The intention of this chapter is to explain what is meant by the term 'formal method' and to show how such methods fit naturally into the software development process.

1.1   Introduction

Neither this collection of case studies nor the companion textbook [Jon90] is intended to teach the topic of software engineering: there are many good texts devoted to that subject [Pre87, Rat87, Sho83, Som88] and some of these present a fairly extensive discussion of the role of formal methods [Rat87, Som88] within the software development process. Nonetheless we need to briefly review what is meant by 'software engineering'.

For the purposes of the following discussion software engineering may be viewed as those activities associated with the development of software for computer-based applications. The development activities considered should ensure that the software produced is fit for the purpose, that the development employs the best available practices, and that the development is properly recorded and soundly organized, planned and managed. In other words software engineering encompasses those management, technical and quality related activities that are involved in the professional development of software.

1.2   Process models

In order to manage the software engineering task considerable attention has been focused on the development process itself. Learning from existing engineering disciplines the software community has developed its own process or life cycle models. Essentially these models stress development steps, deliverables, and verification and validation activities.

A number of phases are identified and various tasks associated with these phases. For instance, we usually find a requirements-capture phase, a specification phase, a design phase and so on. Each of these phases is defined in terms of phase inputs, phase related technical and management tasks, and deliverables for input to subsequent phases. Within each phase, methods and tools applicable to the development tasks are used in the specification, design, implementation, testing and acceptance of deliverables. The application of tools, in-phase reviews and audits, end of phase milestone reviews, etc. ensure that verification and validation is carried out. Work produced within a phase is reviewed and placed under change control whence it acts as baselined input to subsequent phases.

Considerable debate surrounds these models, stressing different aspects of the development task, or its management, such as the role of prototyping, how to manage reiteration and rework, the importance of incremental development, transformational development and similar. Figure 1.1 shows a not untypical life cycle model with phases and milestone reviews identified.[1]

---

[1]For completeness such a model should include definitions of the tasks undertaken within each phase, the nature and form of the phase deliverables, guidelines relating to applicable tools, and methods and procedures for configuration management and change control.

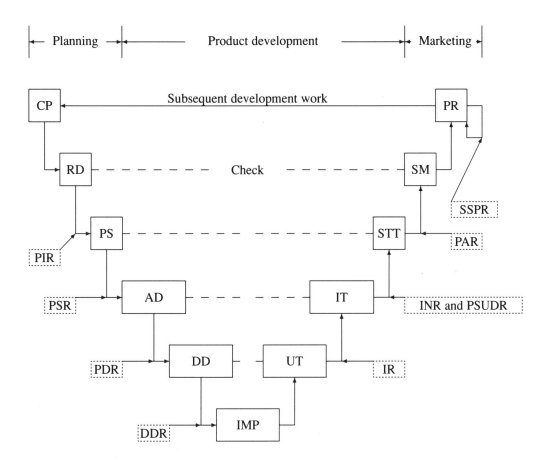

Figure 1.1 A software development life cycle model

PHASES		KEY MILESTONE REVIEWS	
CP	Conceptual planning		
RD	Requirements definition	PIR	Product initiation review
PS	Product specification	PSR	Product specification review
AD	Architectural design	PDR	Product design review
DD	Detailed design	DDR	Detailed design review
IMP	Implementation		
UT	Unit testing	IR	Implementation review
IT	Integration testing	INR	Integration review
		PSUDR	Product support and documentation review
STT	System test and transfer	PAR	Product acceptance review
SM	Sales and marketing		
PR	Product review	SSPR	Sales/Support periodic review

1.3   The contractual model

A particularly useful view of the development process is known as the contractual model [Coh89]. The contractual model views the development process in terms of a number of phases following one from another. Each phase receives as input a statement of requirements and produces a specification which purports to satisfy the requirements. The output of one phase can become the input to a subsequent phase. For instance, a customer produces a statement of requirements which is given to a supplier. The supplier's analyst turns this into a specification which satisfies the requirements. This specification then becomes the requirements statement for the subsequent design phase. A designer then produces a design which satisfies the specification. This process continues until an implementation is forthcoming. If each step in the development process satisfies its statement of requirements then, by an appeal to transitivity, the implementation will satisfy the customer's original requirements.

The idea of a contract arises from the agreement reached, at each stage, between the person producing the specification and the person who has produced the statement of requirements. Perhaps the most important aspect of the contractual model is its stress on the verification and validation activities that take place within each phase step. These are depicted in Figure 1.2. Verification aims to establish the consistency of a specification – essentially 'are we building the system right?' Validation, on the other hand, attempts to establish that a specification satisfies its requirements – 'are we building the right system?' Within the traditional development model verification and validation activities are carried out through the use of tools, formal reviews, audits and walkthroughs.

1.4   The formal methods view of software development

Let us now turn our attention to the formal development paradigm and see how it relates to the conventional phase model view of software development. A formal method has three essential characteristics.

1. **Formal systems.** The use of formal systems, that is, formal languages with well defined syntax, semantics and proof systems. Thus, in the case of VDM, Jones describes, informally, a formal system for the specification of software systems [Jon90]. This includes a logic for partial functions (LPF), set theory, function theory, etc. and their associated proof systems.

2. **Development technique.** The idea of reification, or refinement, whereby an implementation is produced from a specification though the application of a number of development steps each focusing on well understood design decisions.

    This involves capturing the requirements of a system in an abstract specification (SP_0) using a formal specification language. In the case of VDM the abstract spec-

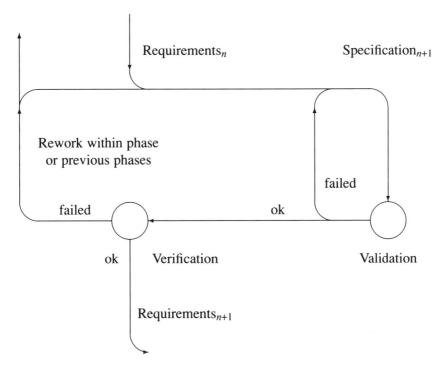

Figure 1.2 Phase verification and validation

ification takes the form of a model of the intended problem that characterizes *what* is required; it eschews, as far as possible, issues to do with *how* the requirements will be implemented. Then, through a series of reification (refinement) steps, the specification is transformed into an implementation which satisfies the specification (SP_1 to IMP_4). The process of reification involves the controlled introduction of detail related to problem space partitioning, abstract algorithm selection, data representation, algorithm decomposition and implementation. Reification is depicted in Figure 1.3.

Figure 1.3 depicts reification in a rather simplistic manner. Firstly, during this process, many considerations have to be analyzed and specification decisions made. Rework is not uncommon and thus the normal iterative and backtracking activities associated with investigating any design are encountered. Secondly, at each step in the development, decisions are taken relating to strategic design objectives. For instance, algorithm or data representation decisions may be made to achieve a minimum store or fastest execution objective. Refinement choices are made depending on whether a prototype implementation or final product imple-

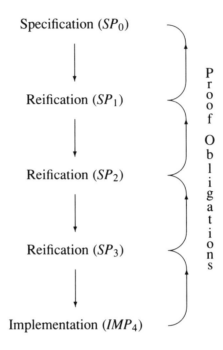

Figure 1.3 Reification development steps

mentation is required. These questions, or similar, will appear at each development step. Secondly, as indicated in Figure 1.4, a development step may result in a single reification or a decomposition into several components which, when composed, satisfy their specification. In this case the composition operator $\odot$ composes specifications SP_{21} and SP_{22} while the $\bullet$ operator composes specifications SP_{31} and SP_{32}. Here we would need to show that $SP_{31} \bullet SP_{32}$ satisfies SP_{21} and that $SP_{21} \odot SP_{22}$ satisfies SP_1. Various composition operators are possible and depend on the particular formal language being used.

Conceptually, reification and decomposition allow us to develop detailed implementation level specifications from our abstract specifications. However, life is not quite so straightforward. While there is considerable agreement on how to specify sequential systems research activity is being expended on finding out how best to specify parallelism. In addition, there is no clear view on how best to specify and decompose problems involving both parallel and sequential components. Should we start with a specification that views parallelism as the natural order and

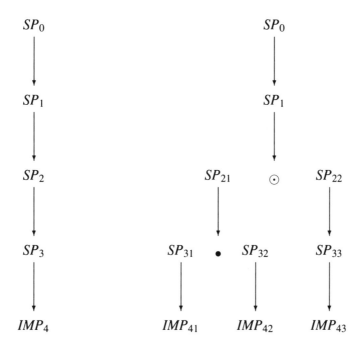

Figure 1.4 Development reification and decomposition

introduce sequentiality within the reification and decomposition process or vice versa? These remain interesting research questions to which answers are eagerly awaited.

3. **Verification technique.** In order to ensure that a series of reification steps preserves correctness, i.e. fulfils the top level specification, there is an obligation to prove that each reification correctly models the previous specification. This is termed a 'proof obligation'. Further, it shows that the implementation satisfies the specification, that is, IMP_4 satisfies SP_3 which in turn satisfies SP_2, which satisfies SP_1 and that, finally, SP_1 satisfies SP_0. In VDM this involves the generation of what are called adequacy and operation modelling proof obligations.[2]

---

[2]Considerable debate has focused on what is meant by the terms 'refinement' and 'reification'. Various applications need different formulations of what is called the refinement proof obligation. Chapter 8 of Jones [Jon90] advocates a specific relationship which is a special case of the more general relations

In addition, proof obligations are generated to show that specifications are implementable, that they satisfy the data type invariant and that initial states exist.
These proof obligations were discussed in Chapters 5 and 8 of [Jon90]. Additionally, when specifications are decomposed into components, compositional proof
obligations are required to show that specifications are satisfied when their components are brought together. Finally, the language itself yields proof obligations
relating to type compatibility and the well formed definition of expressions. Some
of these can be checked by tools (type checkers) while others appear in the form of
proof obligations. For instance, proof obligations arise from the use of data type
invariants and type checking can be said to require theorem proving, that is, the
requirements for a well typed expression can be formulated as proof obligations
or theorems.

1.5   What do we mean by method?

The question we now ask is what is meant by method in the context of the term 'formal
method'? Proprietary methods such as SSADM [NCC86] and JSD [Cam86] are seen as
legitimate exemplars of 'methods'. Where, the question is often asked, is the method
underpinning such formal development approaches as VDM and Z?

What do we mean by method? The purpose of a method is to guide users in undertaking a specific task, to help them get from one point within that task to another;
it is task or process oriented. In order to achieve this objective a method must offer
guidance on how to organize the task and provide rules which guide the undertaking of
those tasks. It is essentially a collection of dependent steps and rules that guide pro-
gression from step to step. Returning to Figure 1.1, a method, depending on its scope,
may suggest what phases are required within the development process and, within those
phases, may suggest how specific tasks such as specification, design and implementation should be organized, approached and undertaken. In these terms, both SSADM and
JSD may be viewed as methods in that they both provide guidance on how to structure
work in terms of dependent steps and how to progress from step to step through the
application of various heuristics or rules. SSADM is much broader in scope than JSD
while JSD provides a far more systematic approach to the design task; nonetheless both
are methods.

How do formal methods bear up under this definition of method? What are the
characteristics of formal methods?

1. Formal methods provide precise notations for capturing functional specification
   decisions be they abstract characterizations of the requirements or implementation
   specific. A specification language is used for this purpose.

---

suggested by other authors [MRG88, HHS87, Nip86]: these should be investigated.

2. The notion of abstraction is essential to the application of a formal method. The first step is to produce an abstract specification characterizing the essential properties of the problem and stating *what* is required rather than *how* it is to be achieved. In VDM implicit specification is the main vehicle for abstraction.

3. The reification process advocates progressive development towards implementation with design- and implementation-specific details being introduced systematically and progressively.

4. Proof obligations provide the substance for verification and validation activities. Discharged rigorously, or formally, they focus attention on critical questions concerning the consistency and correctness of specification and reification steps.

5. Decomposition encourages breaking larger specifications into components which can be reified independently and then, through composition combinators, shown to satisfy the larger specification.

6. Guidelines are provided for assessing specifications – the complexity of data type invariants and proof obligations, the idea of implementation bias [Jon90].

From this discussion it is clear that formal methods have little to say about review procedures, management practices, costing, performance modelling, sizing, reliability modelling, testing [3] and the host of other activities undertaken within the development process. But then most other development methods do not address all of these topics. Procedures, methods and tools appropriate to these activities must be sought elsewhere. In fact, as suggested below, formal methods can quite easily be added to development methods that lack a formal specification language and formal development framework.

The method side of formal methods may be viewed as the use of formal systems, the use of abstraction and reification and the generation and discharging of specific proof obligations. In these terms we have a method, not an all-embracing development method, but nonetheless a method. Formal methods do not proscribe the use of ideas and heuristics drawn from other methods. In fact, formal methods complement existing development approaches such as SSADM by allowing practitioners to formally capture specification and development detail that is only informally captured in these other methods.

Returning to the discussion of the process and contractual models; formal methods provide a framework for recording our specification and designs. The concept of reification provides a formal framework for the phase development steps outlined in the model. Proof obligations formalize the substance of the verification and validation activities and thus underpin reviews. In these terms the formal framework of software development

---

[3]See [Hay85] for an interesting discussion on how formal specifications can assist in the generation of test cases.

may be viewed as an abstract representation of some of the tasks undertaken within the software development process model.

2

NDB: The Formal Specification and Rigorous Design of a Single-user Database System

Ann Walshe

This specification of a general-purpose database system provides a good illustration of the usefulness of model-oriented specification techniques for systems. The chosen system (NDB) also has intrinsic interest. This chapter explains the derivation of the appropriate state; after this is found, writing pre- and post-conditions for the operations is relatively straightforward. The starting point for this specification exercise was an informal description which made heavy use of pictures. It was also couched too much in terms of the implementation to be abstract enough for a concise formal specification. As well as the specification itself, this chapter provides a good example of the development method (particularly data reification).

2.1   Introduction

This chapter illustrates the use of VDM [Jon80, Jon90] in the formal specification and development of a program to implement simple update operations on a binary relational database called NDB [WS79]. It is shown how an initial specification can be formed and then manipulated in a rigorous way through the careful introduction of design detail in the form of data structures and operations until an implementation is reached. The work is described more fully in [Wel82].

The paper has the following structure. Firstly the rigorous method is briefly reviewed. Then NDB, the database to be implemented, is explained before the specification, development and implementation steps are presented.

2.2   VDM – a rigorous method of specification and design

VDM is described in [Jon90]. In the rigorous method, objects are normally specified in terms of a model. The specification of a program takes the form of an *operation* (or operations) on a *state* which defines a class or set of valid states. Well-formedness conditions, known as *data type invariants*, may be used to limit the defined class further. Operations are specified using pre-condition predicates (predicates on a single initial state) and two-state post-condition predicates (predicates over the initial and final state values). This style of specification aims to be implicit, that is it aims to fix the properties required of the program without specifying how they are to be achieved. All operations must preserve any data type invariant which may exist, i.e. they may change the value of the state as long as the new value is a valid state.

The initial specification should aim to capture abstract concepts and avoid implementation detail. Development to a program by gradually including design, algorithmic and implementation detail then proceeds either by data reification or by operation decomposition.

In data reification (refinement), a new state 'closer' to the implementation is defined and the operations are redefined on this state. A *retrieve function* relates the new, more concrete specification to the more abstract specification by showing how, given a state of the representation, the corresponding abstract state can be achieved. At each reification stage, it is important to construct proofs that show why the reification adequately models the previous stage. Some of the relevant proofs that arise in the development of NDB are detailed below as they occur.

In operation decomposition, the state remains unchanged and the operations are redefined in terms of combinations of simpler operations using control constructs such as sequence, selection and iteration. As with the reification process, a number of proof obligations arise; at least one for each of the control constructs used within the decomposition process.

The program development described here uses data reification; four separate states are defined in moving from the most abstract specification to the implementation. Operation decomposition is not used.

2.3 NDB – a binary relational database

A database consists of entities and of relationships linking those entities. One particular database system architecture provides three views of the data in a database. The *internal view* describes the way in which data items are physically stored, the (possibly more than one) *external view* describes an individual's view of the data, and the *conceptual view* provides an abstract view of the whole database. There are three main approaches to designing the conceptual model: the relational approach, the hierarchical approach and the network approach. The relational model organizes data in tables and n-tuples. For further information on databases, see [Dat81].

NDB [WS79] is a database architecture which directly supports the *conceptual view* of data, i.e. the abstract representation of the database. It is based on the *binary relational model,* in which data are organized into tables of pairs as shown in Figure 2.1. In [Wel82], NDB is specified with some small design changes. To avoid confusion, the changed version only is presented here.

In NDB, there are two basic components, *elements* and *connections*, representing entities and named binary relationships respectively. (NDB has only one type of entity, which may or may not have a value.)

The single kind of logical data element used to represent both entities and values is known as a *V-element* and is accessed via a unique identifier. It has two components:

1. An identifier giving access to its connections.

2. A value which is a variable-length string or NULL if the V-element has no value.

Two or more V-elements can have the same value, as they can be distinguished by the V-element identifiers. A V-element can be depicted as in Figure 2.2.

Connections are made between V-elements via *R-elements* and *C-elements*, see Figure 2.3 which represents the relation 'Scotland exports tweed'. Connections represent directed associations where the first component of the R-element is the identifier of the relationship being used (in this case the 'exports' relationship) and the second component of the R-element is the identifier of the C-element, which, in turn, has as its only component the target V-element identifier. This is a one-one relation.

Multiple relations are constructed by means of lists. So to represent a one-many relation the C-element is replaced by a list of C-elements called a *C-list*. Figure 2.4 represents the relation 'China exports silk and satin'. Similarly, to allow a V-element to take part in more than one relation, the R-element can be replaced by a list of R-elements

Country	Currency
Scotland	pound
China	yuan
Australia	dollar

Material	Price per meter
tweed	4.50
wool	6.00
silk	8.00
satin	9.50

Export no.	Country
E1	Scotland
E2	Scotland
E3	China
E4	China
E5	Australia

Export no.	Material
E1	tweed
E2	wool
E3	satin
E4	silk
E5	wool

Export no.	Amount in meters
E1	400
E2	300
E3	200
E4	700
E5	200

Figure 2.1 Conceptual view of a binary relational database

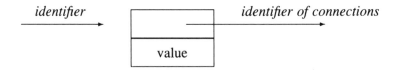

Figure 2.2 A V-element

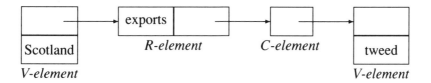

Figure 2.3 A one-one connection

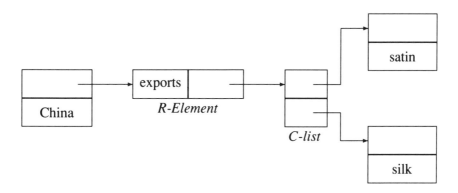

Figure 2.4 A one-many connection

called an *R-list*. Figure 2.5 represents the relations 'Scotland has currency pound' and 'Scotland exports tweed and wool'. Many-one and many-many relations can also be represented by using this structure; Figure 2.6 represents a many-many relation.

The data dictionary of NDB

Operations on the database are controlled by a data dictionary, which is closely integrated with, and uses the same structure as, the database. Entities belong to possibly overlapping sets representing an abstraction of the real world. These sets are metadata as opposed to data, yet are implemented using the elements described above. A single V-element represents each entity set type, its member entities being retrieved via a special membership relation. Similarly, relations are each of a given type, represented by a single V-element. In addition, there are two metasets, namely the set of all entity sets and the set of all relationship types. Sets and relationship types have special attributes. Sets have attributes called 'status', 'picture' and 'width' defined as follows:

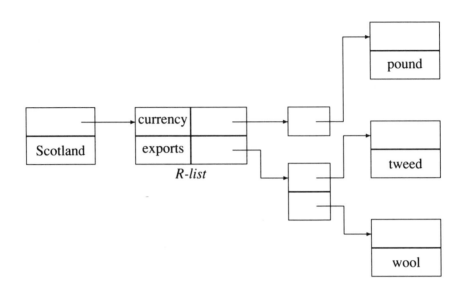

Figure 2.5 A V-element taking part in two relations

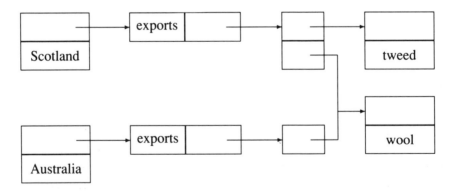

Figure 2.6 A many-many connection

status This states whether or not entities may be added to or deleted from a set.

picture This details the format of the values of member entities.

width This is used in outputting values.

Relationship types have attributes 'fromset', 'name', 'toset' and 'maptype' defined as follows:

fromset This is the type of objects which the relationship may be 'from'.

name This is the name of the relation.

toset This is the type of object which the relation may be 'to'.

maptype This indicates whether the relation may be single- or multi-valued.

These are system-defined relationship types and require system-defined entity sets, such as the set to which every status belongs.

So, although the end user of the database system may see none of the metadata structure, the application programmer will see a set of all sets, containing the system-defined sets, and a set of all relationship types, containing system-defined relations, all accessed via system-given names and enabling him to create further sets and relations.

Context conditions or constraints on the database

There are various constraints to be observed when implementing NDB. These will be expressed in the specification either by an appropriate choice of state or by data type invariants on the state. The following constraints are defined:

1. Every connection has an inverse; there are no facilities for connecting in one direction only. Figure 2.7 shows an inverse connection. The connection 'Scotland exports tweed' has the inverse 'tweed is exported by Scotland'. The first component of the R-element of the backward connection is the first component of the forward connection R-element preceded by a minus sign.

2. Connections are ordered, in that each C-list is ordered by the values of the V-element to which it points. This allows the implementation of the functions 'prior' and 'next' to find the previous or next element in a C-list with respect to a given C-element. (Thus in Figure 2.4, next(satin) is silk.)

3. The first components of the R-elements in an R-list are unique. Unlike the elements in a C-list, they are not ordered.

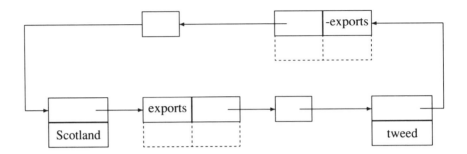

Figure 2.7 An inverse connection

4. The relation from a V-element to a list of V-elements will be known to be a relation from a particular type of object to another particular type of object. Therefore, all V-elements in a C-list are assumed to be of the same entity type, namely the target object type of the relation in which the C-list is involved.

2.4   The specification and design

It may be seen from the above description that although NDB has a simple external structure, the way in which this structure embodies all the information about the database is conceptually quite complicated. In writing the formal specification, it is necessary to understand the structure *exactly*. This means that questions are answered and problems solved long before implementation is begun, ensuring that the final program will capture the essence of NDB.

The specification of NDB, and its operations, and their development through various levels, are now described. The abstraction of NDB, *State-a*, is developed in Section 2.5. The abstraction provides a precise set of criteria by which to judge the correctness of alternative designs, and allows alternative designs to be compared. Section 2.6 describes the reification of *State-a* into a binary relational structure, *State-r*, and Section 2.7 the reification of the binary relations into the NDB model *State-i*. The Pascal level of specification, *State-p*, is presented in Section 2.8.

At each of these levels of reification, two operations are defined and justified. (Further database update operations are defined in [Wel82].) The two operations are:

1. *ADD* – add an entity set.

2. *DELETE* – delete a connection.

To add an entity set, a new V-element must be created, and the parameters of the operation are the set name, its status, picture and width. Recall their definition in Section 2.3. To delete a connection, the parameters given need to identify the connection to be deleted.

At each stage of development a preliminary check needs to be made to ensure that the operations can be defined on the proposed state, but they are not fully specified at that stage until the final state has been formed.

Some proofs are given as examples of the method; in reality all the required proofs should be sketched in enough detail to show that they could be constructed formally if necessary.

Section 2.10 contains a table of abbreviations used in the specification. Additionally it should be noted that not all the auxiliary functions used within the specifications are defined here, as their meaning should be clear enough for the purposes of this paper.

2.5 The abstract state – *State-a*

The first abstract representation of NDB shows the database concepts that have been described. This most abstract level avoids representation details and concentrates on the fundamental characteristics of NDB.

The binary relational database example given in Figure 2.1 above can be represented as in Figure 2.8. Here, members of entity sets have distinct values but in general this will not be the case. It will be remembered that two entities are distinguished by means of their identifiers rather than their values. This must be reflected in the abstract state by giving each entity an (arbitrary but distinct) identifier.

Each table in the database example can be thought of as a relationship type expressed by an optional *name* and the types of the objects between which the relationship can occur. In terms of NDB, wherever the relationship type occurs in an R-list, the type of the V-element to which the R-list belongs is called the *fromset* and the type of the V-elements in the corresponding C-list is called the *toset*. For instance, there is a relationship type with fromset 'country', no name, and toset 'currency'. Associated with each relationship is a set of pairs of entities connected by that relationship.

A step-by-step derivation of *State-a* now follows, to show how a specification will be reworked, either to simplify the state or to simplify the invariant or to make the operations easier to define.

The abstract state comprises two parts:

1. Entity sets with their associated members.

2. Relationship types with their associated connection pairs.

This can be written as:

Entity set	*Members (identifier / value pairs)*
country	(1, Scotland), (2, China), (3, Australia)
currency	(4, pound), (5, yuan), (6, dollar)
material	(7, tweed), (8, wool), (9, satin), (10, silk)
price per meter	(11, 4.50), (12, 6.00), (13, 8.00), (14, 9.50)
amount in meters	(15, 200), (16, 300), (17, 400), (18, 700)
export number	(19, E1), (20, E2), (21, E3), (22, E4), (23, E5)

Relationship type			*Connections*
Fromset	*Name*	*Toset*	
country		currency	(1,4), (2,5), (3,6)
material	cost	price per meter	(7, 11), (8, 12), (10, 13), (9, 14)
export number		country	(19, 1), (20, 1), (21, 2)
			(22, 2), (23, 3)
export number		material	(19, 7), (20, 8), (21, 9)
			(22, 10), (23, 8)
export number		amount in meters	(19, 17), (20, 16), (21, 15)
			(22, 18), (23, 15)

Figure 2.8 Example of a database

$$State\text{-}a_1 \ :: \ esets \ : \ Esetnm \xrightarrow{m} Esetinf$$
$$rels \ \ : \ Reltype \xrightarrow{m} Relinf$$

$$Esetinf \ :: \ membs \ : \ Eid \xrightarrow{m} [Value]$$

$$Reltype \ :: \ fs \ \ : \ Esetnm$$
$$nm \ : \ [Relnm]$$
$$ts \ \ : \ Esetnm$$

$$Relinf \ :: \ conns \ : \ Pair\text{-}set$$

$$Pair \ :: \ fv \ : \ Eid \xrightarrow{m} [Value]$$
$$tv \ : \ Eid \xrightarrow{m} [Value]$$

The structure of *Esetnm, Relnm, Eid* and *Value* are irrelevant to the specification and so they are not defined further. If required, a structure could be given to them later in the development. The NDB NULL value is represented in the abstract state by nil.

Note, the chosen mapping structure ensures that no two entity sets have the same name and no two relationship types have the same fromset, name and toset, fulfilling two of the conditions to be observed when implementing NDB (i.e. entity sets are distinguishable and relationship types are distinguishable).

Note also that since entity identifiers are unique, entity-identifier value pairs are represented as mappings from entity identifiers to values, although in the *fv* or *tv* component of a pair the mapping will contain only a single maplet.

However, in the relation information, a mapping from an entity identifier to a value can be replaced by the entity identifier only, since the value can be retrieved by looking in the relevant entity set information. The abstract state becomes:

$$State\text{-}a_2 \;::\; esets \;:\; Esetnm \xrightarrow{m} Esetinf$$
$$rels \;\;:\; Reltype \xrightarrow{m} Relinf$$

$$Esetinf \;::\; membs \;:\; Eid \xrightarrow{m} [Value]$$

$$Reltype \;::\; fs \;\;:\; Esetnm$$
$$nm \;:\; [Relnm]$$
$$ts \;\;:\; Esetnm$$

$$Relinf \;::\; conns \;:\; Pair\text{-set}$$

$$Pair \;::\; fv \;:\; Eid$$
$$tv \;:\; Eid$$

State-a₂ already represents the fact that all relationship types have a fromset, name and toset. The special attribute 'maptype' can be expressed by adding an extra component to the relation information – a maptype. Similarly, the special attributes of entity sets, namely 'status', 'picture' and 'width', can be added to the information associated with each entity set. The special attributes are system-defined relationship types and require system-defined entity sets, such as the set to which every status belongs. The state now becomes:

$$State\text{-}a_3 \;::\; esets \;:\; Esetnm \xrightarrow{m} Esetinf$$
$$rels \;\;:\; Reltype \xrightarrow{m} Relinf$$

$$Esetinf \;::\; status \;\;\;:\; Status$$
$$picture \;:\; Picture$$
$$width \;\;\;:\; Width$$
$$membs \;\;:\; Eid \xrightarrow{m} [Value]$$

Reltype :: *fs* : *Esetnm*
            nm : [*Relnm*]
            ts : *Esetnm*

Relinf :: *map*   : *Maptype*
            conns : *Pair*-set

Maptype = {1: 1, 1: *M*, *M*: 1, *M*: *M*}

Pair :: *fv* : *Eid*
          tv : *Eid*

Since entities can belong to more than one set, information may be duplicated, i.e. the value associated with an *Eid* is given in every set in which the *Eid* appears. If the mapping *Eid* $\xrightarrow{m}$ [*Value*] is extracted, this information will appear only once; thus inconsistencies will not arise or need to be disallowed by an invariant.

The final version of the abstract state becomes:

State-a :: *esets* : *Esetnm* $\xrightarrow{m}$ *Esetinf*
             rels : *Reltype* $\xrightarrow{m}$ *Relinf*
             ents : *Eid* $\xrightarrow{m}$ [*Value*]

Esetinf :: *status* : *Status*
             picture : *Picture*
             width   : *Width*
             membs : *Eid*-set

Reltype :: *fs* : *Esetnm*
             nm : [*Relnm*]
             ts : *Esetnm*

Relinf :: *map*   : *Maptype*
            conns : *Pair*-set

Maptype = {1: 1, 1: *M*, *M*: 1, *M*: *M*}

Pair :: *fv* : *Eid*
          tv : *Eid*

Status, *Picture*, *Width*, *Eid*, *Esetnm*, *Relnm*, *Value* = NOT YET DEFINED

The invariant on *State-a*

The invariant must state the following:

1. For each set, all values of the members of that set must match the picture of that set, i.e. values have the correct format.

2. The fromset and toset of every relationship type must appear in the set of entity sets.

3. Entities in value pairs must belong to the sets dictated by the relationship type fromset and toset.

4. For each relation information, the value pairs must obey the mapping restriction.

5. All entities in all entity sets must have a value (although this may be NULL).

Following this breakdown the invariant is defined as follows:

$inva : State\text{-}a \rightarrow Bool$
$inva(mk\text{-}State\text{-}a(esm, rm, em)) \quad \triangle$
$\qquad \forall esetnm \in \text{dom } esm \cdot$
$\qquad\qquad inv\text{-}vals(esm(esetnm), em) \wedge inv\text{-}esets(\text{dom } esm, \text{dom } rm) \wedge$
$\qquad\qquad inv\text{-}pairs(esm, rm) \wedge inv\text{-}ents(\text{rng } esm, \text{dom } em)$

$inv\text{-}vals : Esetinf \times Eid \xrightarrow{m} [Value] \rightarrow \mathbb{B}$
$inv\text{-}vals(esetinf, em) \quad \triangle$
$\qquad \forall eid \in membs(esetinf) \cdot picturematch(em(eid), picture(esetinf))$

$inv\text{-}esets : Esetnm\text{-set} \times Reltype\text{-set} \rightarrow \mathbb{B}$
$inv\text{-}esets(esetnms, em) \quad \triangle$
$\qquad \forall reltype \in reltypes \cdot$
$\qquad\qquad fs(reltype) \in esetnms \wedge ts(reltype) \in esetnms$

$inv\text{-}pairs : (Esetnm \xrightarrow{m} Esetinf) \times (Reltype \xrightarrow{m} Relinf) \rightarrow \mathbb{B}$
$inv\text{-}pairs(esm, rm) \quad \triangle$
$\qquad \forall reltype \in \text{dom } rm \cdot$
$\qquad\qquad \text{let } mk\text{-}Reltype(fs, nm, ts) = reltype \text{ in}$
$\qquad\qquad \text{let } prset = conns(rm(reltype)) \text{ in}$
$\qquad\qquad are\text{-}membs(froms(prset), esm(fs)) \wedge$
$\qquad\qquad are\text{-}membs(tos(prset), esm(ts))$

The function *inv-pairs* uses the following auxiliary functions:

$are\text{-}membs : Eid\text{-set} \times Esetinf \rightarrow \mathbb{B}$
$are\text{-}membs(eset, esetinf) \quad \triangleq \quad eset \subset membs(esetinf)$

$froms : Pair\text{-set} \rightarrow Eid\text{-set}$
$froms(prset) \quad \triangleq \quad \{fv(pr) \mid pr \in prset\}$

$tos : Pair\text{-set} \rightarrow Eid\text{-set}$
$tos(prset) \quad \triangleq \quad \{tv(pr) \mid pr \in prset\}$

$inv\text{-}ents : Esetinf\text{-set} \times Eid\text{-set} \rightarrow \mathbb{B}$
$inv\text{-}ents(esetinfs, eids) \quad \triangleq$
      let $ents = \bigcup\{membs(esetinf) \mid esetinf \in esetinfs\}$ in
      $ents = eids$

There is also an invariant on the type *Relinf*, which must be satisfied by any object of that type created in the specification. This is defined as follows:

$inv\text{-}map : Relinf \xrightarrow{m} \mathbb{B}$
$inv\text{-}map(mk\text{-}Relinf(map, prset)) \quad \triangleq$
    cases map of
    $M{:}M \rightarrow true$
    $M{:}1 \;\; \rightarrow \nexists pr1, pr2 \in prset \cdot pr1 \neq pr2 \wedge fv(pr1) = fv(pr2))$
    $1{:}M \;\; \rightarrow \nexists pr1, pr2 \in prset \cdot pr1 \neq pr2 \wedge tv(pr1) = tv(pr2))$
    $1{:}1 \;\; \rightarrow \nexists pr1, pr2 \in prset \cdot$
                $pr1 \neq pr2 \wedge (fv(pr1) = fv(pr2) \vee tv(pr1) = tv(pr2))$
    end

The operations on *State-a*

In designing *State-a*, a check must be made that the database operations can be specified using this data structure, e.g. to add a connection, a value pair would be added to the *conns* field of the relation information corresponding to the relation involved.

Each operation is specified by a pre-condition and a post-condition and a list of the state components (externals) to which it requires read (rd) or read/write (wr) access.

The operation to add an entity set is defined as follows:

$ADDA\ (eset{:}Esetnm, s{:}Status, p{:}Picture, w{:}Width)$
ext wr $esets\ :\ Esetnm \xrightarrow{m} Esetinf$
pre $eset \notin$ dom $esets$

post $esets = \overleftarrow{esets} \cup \{eset \mapsto \textit{mk-Esetinf}(s,p,w,\{\,\})\}$

The parameters to the operation are the new entity set name, and the values which are to be its status, picture and width. The pre-condition states that an entity set of that name must not exist already.

The post-condition states that the state after the operation has been performed (the final state) is the state before the operation is performed (the initial state) with the new entity set added to the *esets* mapping. Note that the specification does not indicate *how* this changed state is to be obtained. It merely specifies a relationship between the initial and final states.

2.6   The first representation state – *State-r*

Having obtained an abstract description of NDB, the aim is to use stepwise reification so as to eventually obtain a programmed implementation. The first attempt employed a representation of *State-a* using structures directly corresponding to the V-, R- and C-elements of NDB (cf. *State-i* below). However, the task of formulating an invariant and of proving that this state was a reification of *State-a* proved to be so great as to warrant an intermediate stage.

Since NDB is based on the binary relational model, it ought to be possible to convert the information contained in *State-a* into a set of binary relations. This becomes the required intermediate stage, *State-r*. To obtain binary relations from the mappings in *State-a*, the records must be split into separate mappings. So the mapping from an entity set name to a record must be split into several mappings, each from the entity set name to one component of the record. The *Reltype* record which identifies a relationship type must also be split, and since this effectively destroys the means of identifying a relationship type, a new means, namely a relationship type identifier (*Rid*), must be introduced. Based on this analysis the new state, *State-r*, becomes:

$$
\begin{array}{llll}
\textit{State-r} :: & \textit{status} & : & \textit{Esetnm} \xrightarrow{m} \textit{Status} \\
& \textit{picture} & : & \textit{Esetnm} \xrightarrow{m} \textit{Picture} \\
& \textit{width} & : & \textit{Esetnm} \xrightarrow{m} \textit{Width} \\
& \textit{membs} & : & \textit{Esetnm} \xrightarrow{m} \textit{Eid}\text{-set} \\
& \textit{fs} & : & \textit{Rid} \xrightarrow{m} \textit{Esetnm} \\
& \textit{nm} & : & \textit{Rid} \xrightarrow{m} [\textit{Relnm}] \\
& \textit{ts} & : & \textit{Rid} \xrightarrow{m} \textit{Esetnm} \\
& \textit{map} & : & \textit{Rid} \xrightarrow{m} \textit{Maptype} \\
& \textit{valof} & : & \textit{Eid} \xrightarrow{m} [\textit{Value}] \\
& \textit{conns} & : & \textit{Triple}\text{-set}
\end{array}
$$

$$Triple :: fv \quad : Eid$$
$$rnm : Rid$$
$$tv \quad : Eid$$

$$Maptype = \{1:1, 1:M, M:1, M:M\}$$

Status, Picture, Width, Eid, Esetnm, Relnm, Value, Rid = NOT YET DEFINED

Note that the *conns* component is a set of triples rather than a mapping,

$$Rid \xrightarrow{m} Pair\text{-set}$$

as would be expected. The decision to represent this component in a different way was made because it contains the actual data rather than the metadata of the database.

The invariant on *State-r*

The conditions which had to be true for *State-a* will also have to be included in the invariant *State-r*. In addition, extra conditions will be required to express conditions which are no longer imposed by the structure of the state, e.g. if lists are used to represent the sets of the previous level, there must be a new condition that ensures values in a list are unique.

In writing the invariant, care must be taken that it is complete and correct. This is likely to become more difficult as the specification develops because at each reification step the invariant may grow longer. To simplify the task of deciding whether the invariant is complete and correct, it is stated as part of *invr* that the state obtained after applying the retrieve function (*retra*) to a state in *State-r* must satisfy *inva*.

The only conditions to be added are those which are new at this level or which are necessary for the validity of the retrieve function. This generalization has the same effect; take, for instance, the condition that values have to have a format matching that (those) of the entity set(s) to which they belong. If the values do not have the correct format in *State-r*, then they will not have the correct format in the retrieved *State-a* ; therefore, for the invariant on *State-a* to be satisfied, this condition must be fulfilled on the *State-r* level and need not be restated in full.

Three additional conditions, related to domains, must be stated:

1. The status, picture and width mappings must all hold information for *every* entity set, i.e. their domains are the same, and the fromset, name, toset and map mappings contain information for every relationship type, i.e. their domains are the same.

2. All elements of type *Rid* appearing in the triples of *conns(State-r)* are valid relationship type identifiers.

3. No two relationship types have the same fromset, name and toset.

The invariant is defined as:

$invr : State\text{-}r \rightarrow \mathbb{B}$
$invr(sr) \quad \triangle$
   $inva(retra(sr)) \land$
   $inv\text{-}domains(sr) \land inv\text{-}rids(conns(sr), \mathsf{dom}\, nm(sr)) \land$
   $inv\text{-}rels(fs(sr), nm(sr), ts(sr))$

$inv\text{-}domains : State\text{-}r \rightarrow \mathbb{B}$
$inv\text{-}domains(sr) \quad \triangle$
   $\mathsf{let}\ statusr = \mathsf{dom}\, status(sr)\ \mathsf{in}$
   $\mathsf{let}\ fsr = \mathsf{dom}\, fs(sr)\ \mathsf{in}$
   $\mathsf{dom}\, width(sr) = statusr \land \mathsf{dom}\, picture(sr) = statusr \land$
   $\mathsf{dom}\, membs(sr) = statusr \land \mathsf{dom}\, nm(sr) = fsr \land$
   $\mathsf{dom}\, ts(sr) = fsr \land \mathsf{dom}\, map(sr) = fsr$

$inv\text{-}rids : Triple\text{-}\mathsf{set} \times Rid\text{-}\mathsf{set} \rightarrow \mathbb{B}$
$inv\text{-}rids(conns, nms) \quad \triangle$
   $\forall t \in conns \cdot rnm(t) \in nms$

$inv\text{-}rels : (Rid \xrightarrow{m} Esetnm) \times (Rid \xrightarrow{m} [Relnm]) \times (Rid \xrightarrow{m} Esetnm) \rightarrow \mathbb{B}$
$inv\text{-}rels(fs, nm, ts) \quad \triangle$
   $\nexists rid1, rid2 \in \mathsf{dom}\, fs \cdot$
     $rid1 \neq rid2 \land fs(rid1) = fs(rid2) \land$
     $nm(rid1) = nm(rid2) \land ts(rid1) = ts(rid2)$

A problem may arise in evaluating $invr(State\text{-}r)$ in that the first term,

  $inva(retra(sr))$

may be undefined if any of the subsequent terms is false, as a valid *State-a* cannot be retrieved from an invalid *State-r*. This situation is cleanly catered for within LPF (Logic for Partial Functions) – see Section 3.3 of [Jon90] – where the conjunction of an undefined value and false is defined to be false.

The retrieve function, *retra*

To show that *State-r* is a valid representation of *State-a*, a function must be written to retrieve *State-a* from *State-r*. This is easily done, e.g. for every entity set name, create its *Esetinf* by collecting status, picture, width and members from the appropriate fields of *State-r*. A pair is extracted from each triple and placed into the correct *Relinf* as designated by the *rnm* component of the triple. *Rids* are discarded, as this means of binding relationship type attributes is not required in the abstract state. The definition of *retra* is:

> *retra* : *State-r* → *State-a*
> *retra*(*sr*)   △
>   let *esets* = {*esetnm* ↦ *esetinfo*(*esetnm*, *sr*) | *esetnm* ∈ dom *status*(*sr*)} in
>   let *rels* = {*reltype*(*rid*, *sr*) ↦ *relinfo*(*rid*, *sr*) | *rid* ∈ dom *fs*(*sr*)} in
>   let *ents* = *valof*(*sr*)) in
>   *mk-State-a*(*esets*, *rels*, *ents*)

> *esetinfo* : *Esetnm* × *State-r* → *Esetinf*
> *esetinfo*(*esetnm*, *sr*)   △
>   let *a_status* = *status*(*sr*)(*esetnm*) in
>   let *a_picture* = *picture*(*sr*)(*esetnm*) in
>   let *a_width* = *width*(*sr*)(*esetnm*) in
>   let *a_membs* = *membs*(*sr*)(*esetnm*) in
>   *mk-Esetinf*(*a_status*, *a_picture*, *a_width*, *a_membs*)

> *reltype* : *Rid* × *State-r* → *Reltype*
> *reltype*(*rid*, *sr*)   △
>   let *a_fs* = *fs*(*sr*)(*rid*) in
>   let *a_nm* = *nm*(*sr*)(*rid*) in
>   let *a_ts* = *ts*(*sr*)(*rid*) in
>   *mk-Reltype*(*a_fs*, *a_nm*, *a_ts*)

> *relinfo* : *Rid* × *State-r* → *Relinf*
> *relinfo*(*rid*, *sr*)   △
>   let *a_map* = *map*(*sr*)(*rid*) in
>   let *a_conns* = {*mk-Pair*(*fv*(*t*), *tv*(*t*)) | *t* ∈ *conns*(*sr*) ∧ *rnm*(*t*) = *rid*} in
>   *mk-Relinf*(*a_map*, *a_conns*)

Now, using this retrieve function, the following adequacy proof obligation must be discharged:

> ∀*a* ∈ *State-a* · ∃*r* ∈ *State-r* · *retra*(*r*) = *a*

The operations on *State-r*

The operations which were defined on *State-a* must now be redefined on *State-r*. The operation to add an entity set is defined by:

from $r \in$ *State-r*, *eset* $\in$ *Esetnm*, $s \in$ *Status*, $p \in$ *Picture*, $w \in$ *Width*
1   from *eset* $\notin$ dom *esets*(*retra*(*r*))
1.1   dom *esets*(*retra*(*r*)) = dom *status*(*r*)   retra
         infer *eset* $\notin$ dom *status*(*r*)   h1, 1.1
2   δ(*eset* $\notin$ dom *esets*(*retra*(*r*)))   h
3   *eset* $\notin$ dom *esets*(*retra*(*r*)) $\Rightarrow$ *eset* $\notin$ dom *status*(*r*) $\Rightarrow$-*I*(2,1)
infer *pre-ADDA*(*eset*, *s*, *p*, *w*, *retra*(*r*)) $\Rightarrow$ *pre-ADDR*(*eset*, *s*, *p*, *w*, *r*)

Figure 2.9 A proof of the domain rule for the *ADDR* operation

ADDR (*eset*: *Esetnm*, *s*: *Status*, *p*: *Picture*, *w*: *Width*)
ext wr *status*   : *Esetnm* $\xrightarrow{m}$ *Status*
    wr *picture* : *Esetnm* $\xrightarrow{m}$ *Picture*
    wr *width*   : *Esetnm* $\xrightarrow{m}$ *Width*
    wr *membs* : *Esetnm* $\xrightarrow{m}$ *Eid*-set
pre *eset* $\notin$ dom *status*
post *status* = $\overleftarrow{status} \cup \{eset \mapsto s\} \wedge$
    picture = $\overleftarrow{picture} \cup \{eset \mapsto p\} \wedge$
    width = $\overleftarrow{width} \cup \{eset \mapsto w\} \wedge$
    membs = $\overleftarrow{membs} \cup \{eset \mapsto \{\}\}$

The parameters are the entity set name, the status, picture and width as before. The pre-condition again states that an entity set of the given name must not exist already; this time the check is made by looking in the *status* mapping although the *picture*, *width* or *membs* mapping could equally well have been used. The post-condition states that the entity set name has been added to the domains of the first four mappings of the state and mapped to the appropriate values.

In order that *ADDR* models *ADDA*, two conditions must be satisfied. They are as follows:

1. *Domain Rule.* If a set of parameters satisfies the pre-condition of *ADDA* (the abstract specification of the *ADD* operation) then it must satisfy the pre-condition of the reified specification of the *ADD* operation, *ADDR*. This proof amounts to showing that the pre-condition of the *ADDR* operation is not too restrictive. The domain rule proof obligation is formalized as follows:

   $\forall r \in$ *State-r* $\cdot$ *pre-ADDA*(*retr*(*r*)) $\Rightarrow$ *pre-ADDR*(*r*)

2. *Result Rule*. Here we are concerned with showing that initial/final state pairs that satisfy the post-condition of *ADDR* must also satisfy the post-condition of *ADDA* when they are viewed through the retrieve function. The proof obligation is stated as follows:

$$\forall r, \overleftarrow{r} \in \textit{State-r} \cdot$$
$$\textit{pre-ADDA}(\textit{retr}(\overleftarrow{r})) \wedge \textit{post-ADDR}(\overleftarrow{r}, r) \Rightarrow$$
$$\textit{post-ADDA}(\textit{retr}(\overleftarrow{r}), \textit{retr}(r))$$

The antecedent of the implication has two conjuncts. The first states that we are only concerned with pre-conditions that satisfy the post-condition of the abstract state (that is, the reified operation may have a wider pre-condition) and the second conjunct restricts consideration to those states that satisfy the post-condition of the reified operation.

Generally, it is not necessary to fully construct a formal proof that these rules are satisfied. The nature of the retrieve function, which directly relates states and state changes on different levels, usually eliminates the need. However, it is important to establish that formal proofs can be constructed if required. Figure 2.9 shows a proof of the domain rule and Figure 2.10 a proof of the range rule.

The operation to delete a connection is defined on *State-r* as follows:

DELCONNR (*eid*1: *Eid*, *rid*: *Rid*, *eid*2: *Eid*)
ext wr *conns* : *Triple*-set
pre *mk-Triple*(*eid*1, *rid*, *eid*2) $\in$ *conns*
post *conns* = $\overleftarrow{conns}$ − {*mk-Triple*(*eid*1, *rid*, *eid*2)}

The parameters are the identifiers of the two connected entities (*eid*1 and *eid*2) and the identifier of the relationship connecting them (*rid*). The pre-condition states that the connection must exist for it to be deleted. The post-condition shows that the triple representing the given connection has been removed from the *conns* component of the state. Note that this operation was not defined on *State-a*. This is because the concept of a *Rid* was not introduced into the specification until *State-r*. An equivalent operation could have been defined, but with different parameters, namely a *Reltype* rather than a *Rid* to define the connection to be deleted.

2.7   The implementation state − *State-i*

The stage has now been reached when the abstract concepts of NDB, stated by *State-a* and formed into binary relations by *State-r*, are modelled in terms of NDB elements by the next reification, *State-i*. The development of the structure of *State-i* is explained step-by-step below.

from $r, \overleftarrow{r} \in State\text{-}r, eset \in Esetnm, s \in Status, p \in Picture, w \in Width$

1	from $pre\text{-}ADDA(eset, s, p, w, retra(\overleftarrow{r})) \wedge post\text{-}ADDR(eset, s, p, w, \overleftarrow{r}, r)$	
1.1	$eset \notin \mathsf{dom}\, esets(retra(\overleftarrow{r}))$	$\wedge\text{-}E(h1), pre\text{-}ADDA$
1.2	$status(r) = status(\overleftarrow{r}) \cup \{eset \mapsto s\} \wedge$	$\wedge\text{-}E(h1), post\text{-}ADDR$
	$picture(r) = picture(\overleftarrow{r}) \cup \{eset \mapsto p\} \wedge$	
	$width(r) = width(\overleftarrow{r}) \cup \{eset \mapsto w\} \wedge$	
	$membs(r) = membs(\overleftarrow{r}) \cup \{eset \mapsto \{\}\}$	
1.3	$eset \notin \mathsf{dom}\, status(\overleftarrow{r})$	$retra, 1.1, 1.2$
1.4	$\mathsf{dom}\, status(r) = \mathsf{dom}\, status(\overleftarrow{r}) \cup \{eset\}$	$\wedge\text{-}E(1.2)$
1.5	$esets(retra(r)) =$	
	$\{esetnm \mapsto mk\text{-}Esetinf(status(r)(esetnm), picture(r)(esetnm),$	
	$width(r)(esetnm), membs(r)(esetnm))$	
	$\mid esetnm \in \mathsf{dom}\, status(r)\}$	$retra$
1.6	$status(r)eset = s \wedge picture(r)eset = p \wedge$	
	$width(r)eset = w \wedge membs(r)eset = \{\}$	$\wedge\text{-}E(1.2)$
1.7	$esets(retra(r)) =$	
	$\{esetnm \mapsto mk\text{-}Esetinf(status(r)(esetnm), picture(r)(esetnm),$	
	$width(r)(esetnm), membs(r)(esetnm))$	
	$\mid esetnm \in \mathsf{dom}\, status(\overleftarrow{r})\} \cup$	
	$\{eset \mapsto mk\text{-}Esetinf(status(r)(eset), picture(r)(eset),$	
	$width(r)(eset), membs(r)(eset))\}$	$1.4, 1.5, 1.6$
1.8	$esets(retra(r)) =$	
	$esets(retra(\overleftarrow{r})) \cup \{eset \mapsto mk\text{-}Esetinf(s, p, w, \{\})\}$	$retra, 1.7$
	infer $post\text{-}ADDA(eset, s, p, w, retra(\overleftarrow{r}), retra(r))$	
2	$\delta(pre\text{-}ADDA(eset, s, p, w, retra(\overleftarrow{r})) \wedge post\text{-}ADDR(eset, s, p, w, \overleftarrow{r}, r))$	h
	infer $pre\text{-}ADDA(eset, s, p, w, retra(\overleftarrow{r})) \wedge post\text{-}ADDR(eset, s, p, w, \overleftarrow{r}, r) \Rightarrow$	$\Rightarrow\text{-}I(1,2)$
	$post\text{-}ADDA(eset, s, p, w, retra(\overleftarrow{r}), retra(r))$	

Figure 2.10 A proof of the range rule for the *ADDR* operation

To understand the reification of *State-r*, the following small example database is used:

Entity set	Members (identifier/value pairs)
country	(1, Scotland), (2, China), (3, Australia)
currency	(4, pound), (5, yuan), (6, dollar)

Relationship type			Connections
Fromset	*Name*	*Toset*	
country		currency	(1, 4), (2, 5), (3, 6)

This is represented in *State-r* by:

mk-State-r(
  {country ↦ s1, currency ↦ s2},
  {country ↦ p1, currency ↦ p2},
  {country ↦ w1, currency ↦ w2},
  {country ↦ {1, 2, 3}, currency ↦ {4, 5, 6}},
  {r1 ↦ country},
  {r1 ↦ nil},
  {r1 ↦ currency},
  {r1 ↦ M: 1},
  {1 ↦ Scotland, 2 ↦ China, 3 ↦ Australia, 4 ↦ pound, 5 ↦ yuan, 6 ↦ dollar},
  {mk-Triple(1, r1, 4), mk-Triple(2, r1, 5), mk-Triple(3, r1, 6)})

where arbitrary identifiers have been introduced.

To see how this is represented in *State-i*, consider first the *conns component*. In *State-r* it is defined as a set of triples of the form:

Triple :: *fv*   : *Eid*
          rnm : *Rid*
          tv   : *Eid*

From this set, a map can be formed as follows. Each entity identifier, *eid1*, which is the first component of a triple in the set is mapped to a list of all pairs (*rid, eid2*) for which the triple (*eid1, rid, eid2*) is in the set, thus:

$$\{1 \mapsto [(r1, 4)], 2 \mapsto [(r1, 5)], 3 \mapsto [(r1, 6)]\}$$

Each sequence in the range of this map can also be transformed into a map as follows. For each sequence, each relation identifier, *rid*, which is the first component of a pair in the sequence is mapped to a list of all the elements *eid2* for which the pair (*rid, eid2*) is in the sequence, thus:

$$\{1 \mapsto \{r1 \mapsto [4]\}, 2 \mapsto \{r1 \mapsto [5]\}, 3 \mapsto \{r1 \mapsto [6]\}\}$$

Now, the values of the entity identifiers in the domain of this map can be incorporated into the range of the map by introducing a composite object as follows:

$$\{1 \mapsto mk\text{-}Vel(\{r1 \mapsto [4]\}, Scotland),$$
$$2 \mapsto mk\text{-}Vel(\{r1 \mapsto [5]\}, China),$$
$$3 \mapsto mk\text{-}Vel(\{r1 \mapsto [6]\}, Australia)\}$$

The reason for calling this object a *Vel* will become apparent below.

State-i contains a map of this form and is written:

$$State\text{-}i_1 \ :: \ vm \ : \ Eid \xrightarrow{m} Vel$$

$$Vel \ :: \ rl \ \ : \ Rid \xrightarrow{m} Eid^*$$
$$val \ : \ [Value]$$

Note that *Eid*s occurring in the domain of *valof*(*State-r*) may not appear as the first component of a triple in *conns*(*State-r*). In such cases, the *Eid* must map to a *Vel* which has as its *rl* component an empty mapping.

Since they can be restated in triple form, all the other components of *State-r* can be incorporated into the above *State-i* structure.

The triples will be formed by the following transformation:

1. Let the component in *State-r* be C and have the following form: $A \xrightarrow{m} B$.

2. For every element *a* in *A*, the domain of C, create for each element *b* to which it maps, a triple (*a, m, b*) where *m* is a special relationship type identifier (metarid) for component C as given in Figure 2.11. So in the above example, since the metarid for STATUS(*State-r*) is 'DBSTATUS', triples of the form (Esetnm, Status) will result, thus, (country, 'DBSTATUS', s1),(currency,'DBSTATUS',s2)

This is not sufficient, since *State-i* requires identifier triples and the triples formed here contain a mixture of identifiers and values. The values must be replaced by identifiers. When the corresponding map is formed, for each value, a new identifier is created and mapped to a *Vel*. This *Vel* has the value as its *val* component and the relationships in which the value is involved as its *rl* component. For example, the resulting map for the *status* component is:

$$\{countryid \mapsto mk\text{-}Vel(\{`DBSTATUS' \mapsto s1id, ...\}, country),$$
$$s1id \mapsto mk\text{-}Vel(\{\ \}, s1),$$
$$currencyid \mapsto mk\text{-}Vel(\{`DBSTATUS' \mapsto s2id, ...\}, currency),$$
$$s2id \mapsto mk\text{-}Vel(\{\ \}, s2)\}$$

Thus all components of *State-r* can be fitted into the *State-i* structure.

State-r component	*Special identifier in State-i*
STATUS	'DBSTATUS'
PICTURE	'DBPICTURE'
WIDTH	'DBWIDTH'
MEMBS	'SMEMBS'
FS	'DBFSET'
NM	'DBREL'
TS	'DBTSET'
MAP	'DBMAP'

Figure 2.11 NDB special relationship type identifiers

vm(*State-i*) will consist not only of mappings from *Eid*s but from other identifiers too, including *Rid*s. All these identifiers (ids) are given the collective name *Vid* (Vel identifier). *State-i* becomes:

$$State\text{-}i \ :: \ vm \ : \ Vid \xrightarrow{m} Vel$$

$$Vel \ :: \ rl \ \ : \ Vid \xrightarrow{m} Vid^*$$
$$val \ : \ [Value]$$

Now some way of indicating which *Vid*s are relationship type ids, entity ids, status ids, etc. is needed. This is done by linking each *Vid* to a *Vel* which describes its type, i.e. which names the set of which the *Vel* to which *Vid* maps is a member, by means of another metarid, the 'is-member' relationship. Another level of special ids (metasets) identifying the sets is created. These identifiers are tabulated in Figure 2.12. All the metasets in Figure 2.12 except 'DBSUSE' and 'DBRUSE' are entity set identifiers (*Esetid*s) so these in turn are mapped via the 'is-member' relationship to 'DB-SUSE'. All the metarids in Figure 2.11 are relationship type identifiers (*Rid*s) so they are mapped to 'DBRUSE'. Therefore, the whole database is linked and can be accessed from 'DBSUSE' and 'DBRUSE'. The metasets and metarids must also have the attributes that ordinary entity sets and relationship types have, namely status etc. These metadata are introduced into the invariant. This is done by including statements that the special identifiers exist, with their own attributes.

The invariant on *State-i*

Having described the structure of *State-i* we can now formally write down the invariant.

Type of element in State-r	Id of set to which it belongs in State-i
Status	'DBSTATUSSET'
Picture	'DBPICTURESET'
Width	'DBWIDTHSET'
Relnm	'RELATIONS'
Maptype	'DBRELMAP'
Esetnm	'DBSUSE'
Rid	'DBRUSE'

Figure 2.12 NDB special entity set identifiers

$inv\text{-}i : State\text{-}i \rightarrow \mathbb{B}$

$inv\text{-}i(si) \quad \triangle$

    $invr(retrr(si)) \wedge$

    let $vm = vm(si)$ in

    $is\text{-}submap(initmap, vm) \wedge$

    $(\forall vid \in \text{dom } vm \cdot$

        $vid = \text{'DBSUSE'} \vee vid = \text{'DBRUSE'}$

            $\vee vid \in getesetids(vm)$

            $\vee vid \in getreltypeids(vm)$

            $\vee vid \in geteids(vm)) \wedge$

    $(\forall esetid \in getesids(vm) \cdot inv\text{-}entset(vm(esetid))) \wedge$

    $(\forall reltypeid \in getreltypeids(vm) \cdot inv\text{-}reltype(vm(reltypeid))) \wedge$

    $inv\text{-}conns(vm) \wedge inv\text{-}order(vm) \wedge inv\text{-}esetnames(vm)$

The following auxiliary functions are used:

$getesetids : Vid \xrightarrow{m} Vel \rightarrow Esetid\text{-set}$

$getesetids(vm) \quad \triangle$

    let $vel = vm(\text{'DBSUSE'})$ in

    rng $rl(vel)(\text{'SSMEMBS'})$

$getreltypeids : Vid \xrightarrow{m} Vel \rightarrow Rid\text{-set}$

$getreltypeids(vm) \quad \triangle$

    let $vel = vm(\text{'DBRUSE'})$ in

    rng $rl(vel)(\text{'RMEMBS'})$

$geteids : Vid \xrightarrow{m} Vel \rightarrow Eid\text{-set}$

$geteids(vm) \quad \triangle \quad \bigcup \{members(esetid, vm) \mid esetid \in getesetids(vm)\}$

$members : Esetid^* \times Vid \xrightarrow{m} Vel \rightarrow Eid\text{-set}$

$members(esetid, vm) \quad \triangle$

    let $rel = rl(vm(esetid))$ in

    if '$SMEMBS$' $\in$ dom rel

    then rng rel('$SMEMBS$')

    else $\{\ \}$

initmap is a mapping representing the information displayed in Figure 2.13.

VID	RID	C-list	VALUE
'DBSUSE'	'SSMEMBS'	'DBSTATUSSET',...(metasets)	NULL
'DBRUSE'	'RMEMBS'	'DBTSET',..(metarels)	NULL

ID	'DBSTATUS'	'DBPICTURE'	'DBWIDTH'
'RELATIONS'	...	...	...
'DBSTATUSSET'	...	...	...
'DBPICTURESET'	...	...	...
'DBWIDTHSET'	...	...	...
'DBRELMAP'	...	...	...

ID	'DBFSET'	'DBTSET'	'DBREL'	'DBMAP'
'DBTSET'	'DBRUSE'	'DBSUSE'	TO	M:1
'DBFSET'	'DBRUSE'	'DBSUSE'	FROM	M:1
'DBREL'	'DBRUSE'	'RELATION'	NAME	M:1
'DBMAP'	'DBRUSE'	'DBRELMAP'	MAP	M:1
'DBSTATUS'	'DBSUSE'	'DBSTATUSSET'	STATUS	M:1
'DBPICTURE'	'DBSUSE'	'DBPICTURESET'	PICTURE	M:1
'DBWIDTH'	'DBSUSE'	'DBWIDTHSET'	WIDTH	M:1
'SSMEMBS'	'DBSUSE'	'DBSUSE'	MEMBS	1:M
'RMEMBS'	'DBRUSE'	'DBRUSE'	MEMBS	1:M
'SMEMBS'	'DBSUSE'	'DBSUSE'	MEMBS	M:M

Figure 2.13 Metamappings

Apart from the prerequisite that a *State-r* retrieved from a *State-i* must satisfy the invariant on *State-r*, the following context conditions apply:

1. The mapping of system-defined entity sets and relationship types to their respective attributes must be part of any database. This is expressed in *invi*(*State-i*) by *is-submap*.

2. The map defined by the table describing *initmap* must be a 'submap' of any valid *State-i*, i.e. all relations in the table must appear in *State-i*. The first part of *initmap* says that the mapping

$$\{\text{`DBSUSE'} \mapsto mk\text{-}Vel(\{\text{`SSMEMBS'} \mapsto metaid\text{-}list\}, nil)\}$$

where *metaid-list* is a list of the metasets, and the mapping

$$\{\text{`DBRUSE'} \mapsto mk\text{-}Vel(\{\text{`RMEMBS'} \mapsto metarid\text{-}list\}, nil)\}$$

where *metarid-list* is a list of all the metarids, must appear in *State-i*.

The second part of the table gives the status, picture and width of each metaset. So *State-i* must include a mapping

$$\{\text{`RELATIONS'} \mapsto$$
$$mk\text{-}Vel(\{\text{`DBSTATUS'} \mapsto [sid],$$
$$\text{`DBPICTURE'} \mapsto [pid], \text{`DBWIDTH'} \mapsto [wid]\}, nil)\}$$

where *sid* (*pid*, *wid*) maps to a Vel which has as its value the status (picture, width) of the entity set mapped to by the identifier 'RELATIONS'. The omitted values in the table (indicated by ellipses) are implementation-dependent and therefore cannot be specified here; the table merely indicates that such values must exist.

The third part of the table gives the fromset, toset, relation name and mapping attribute of each metarelation. The fromset and the toset are the identifiers of the relevant entity sets; the relation name and the mapping are values of entities in the sets identified by 'RELATIONS' and 'DBRELMAP' respectively. So the mapping

$$\{\text{`DBTSET'} \mapsto$$
$$mk\text{-}Vel(\{\text{`DBFSET'} \mapsto [\text{`DBRUSE'}], \text{`DBTSET'} \mapsto [\text{`DBSUSE'}],$$
$$\text{`DBREL'} \mapsto [nameid], \text{`DBMAP'} \mapsto [mapid]\}, nil)\}$$

where the value component of the V-elements identified by *nameid* and *mapid* are 'to' and 'M:1' respectively, must be part of *State-i*.

3. The database must be connected, so that every V-element can be accessed from 'DBRUSE' or 'DBSUSE' via the metadata. This is ensured by the membership relations – all relationship types belong to 'DBRUSE', all entity sets belong to 'DBSUSE' and every entity belongs to at least one entity set.

   Every V-element except 'DBRUSE' and 'DBSUSE' denotes either an entity set or a relationship type or an entity. This coincides with the final version of *State-a*, which also reflects the notion of three types of object, namely entity set, relationship type and entity.

4. All members of 'DBSUSE' are entity sets and therefore have the attributes status, picture and width (expressed by *inv-entset*); all members of 'DBRUSE' are relationship types and therefore have the attributes fromset, name, toset and map (expressed by *inv-reltype*).

5. All connections have an inverse (expressed by *inv-conns*). For each mapping

$$\{eid_1 \mapsto mk\text{-}Vel(\{rid \mapsto eid_2\}, v1)\}$$

representing the triple (eid_1, rid, eid_2), the mapping

$$\{eid_2 \mapsto mk\text{-}Vel(\{rid \mapsto eid_1\}, v2)\}$$

where $v1$ and $v2$ are the values of $eid1$ and $eid2$ respectively, must be included in *State-i*. This allows efficient access of relations in both directions. The inverse of a connection has in the first component of the R-element the first component of the R-element of the forward connection preceded by a minus sign.

6. C-lists are ordered by the values of the V-elements to which they point (expressed by *inv-order*), hence the use of a Vid-list rather than a Vid-set.

7. Entity set names are unique (expressed by *inv-esetnames*). This is an implementation decision, as entity set V-elements are distinguished by their values rather than by their identifiers. This condition is included, because normally, two V-elements can have the same value, e.g. two people can have the same name.

The retrieve function, *retrr*

In retrieving *State-r* from *State-i*, only forward connections are retained. For every entity set which is not a metaset, an entry is made in *status(State-r)*, *picture(State-r)*, *width(State-r)* and *membs(State-r)* (if a set has no 'smembs' relationship then it maps to the empty set in *membs(State-r)*), and similarly for every relationship type which is not a metarelation its attributes are placed in the appropriate fields of *State-r*. Finally, the triples which comprise the actual data connections are retrieved and placed in *conns(State-r)*.

retrr : *State-i* → *State-r*

retrr(mk-State-i(vm)) $\triangleq$

    let *esetids* = *getesetids(vm)-metasets* in

    let *reltypeids* = *getreltypeids(vm)-metarels* in

    let *eids* = *geteids(vm)-metaeids(vm)* in

    let *stam* =

        {*val(vm(esetid))* $\mapsto$ *status(vm(esetid), vm)* | *esetid* ∈ *esetids*} in

    let *picm* =

        {*val(vm(esetid))* $\mapsto$ *picture(vm(esetid), vm)* | *esetid* ∈ *esetids*} in

    let *widm* =

        {*val(vm(esetid))* $\mapsto$ *width(vm(esetid), vm)* | *esetid* ∈ *esetids*} in

    let *membs* =

        {*val(vm(esetid))* $\mapsto$ *members(esetid, vm)* | *esetid* ∈ *esetids*} in

    let *fsm* = {*rid* $\mapsto$ *fromset(vm(rid), vm)* | *rid* ∈ *reltypeids*} in

    let *nm* = {*rid* $\mapsto$ *name(vm(rid), (vm)* | *rid* ∈ *reltypeids*} in

    let *tsm* = {*rid* $\mapsto$ *toset(vm(rid), vm)* | *rid* ∈ *reltypeids*} in

    let *mapm* = {*rid* $\mapsto$ *map(vm(rid), vm)* | *rid* ∈ *reltypeids*} in

    let *valm* = {*eid* $\mapsto$ *val(vm(eid))* | *rid* ∈ *reltypeids*} in

    let *conns* =

      $\bigcup${{*mk-Triple(eid, r, vid)* | *r* ∈ dom *rl(vm(eid))* ∧ *not-minus(r)* ∧

        vid ∈ rng *rl(vm(eid))(r)*} | *eid* ∈ *eids*} in

    mk-Stater(stam, picm, widm, membs, fsm, nm, tsm, mapm, valm, conns)

A number of auxiliary functions are used within *retrr*. Several of these are specified below and in Section 2.7. The specification of the remainder is left as an exercise for the reader. All are specified in [Wel82].

fromset : *Vel* × *Vid* $\xrightarrow{m}$ *Vel* → *Esetnm*

fromset(vel, vm) $\triangleq$

    let *esetid* = *fsetid(vel)* in

    val(vm(esetid))

pre {'-SSMEMBS', 'DBSTATUS', 'DBPICTURE', 'DBWIDTH'} ⊂ dom *rl(vel)*

fsetid : *Vel* → *Esetid*

fsetid(vel) $\triangleq$

    let [*esetid*] = *rl(vel)('DBFSET')* in

    esetid

pre {'-RMEMBS', 'DBFSET', 'DBTSET', 'DBREL', 'DBMAP'} ⊂ dom *rl(vel)*

The operations on *State-i*

The operation to add an entity set is defined as follows:

ADDI (*eset*: *Esetnm*, *s*: *Status*, *p*: *Picture*, *w*: *Width*) *esetid*: *Esetid*

ext wr *vm* : *Vid* $\xrightarrow{m}$ *Vel*

pre $\not\exists vid \in getesetids(vm) \cdot val(vm(vid)) = eset$

post *esetid* $\notin$ dom $\overleftarrow{vm}$ $\wedge$

    dom $\overleftarrow{vm} \cup \{esetid\} \subseteq$ dom *vm* $\wedge$

    esetid $\in getesetids(vm)$ $\wedge$

    val(*vm*(*esetid*)) = *eset* $\wedge$

    let *vel* = *vm*(*esetid*) in

    picture(*vel*, *vm*) = *p* $\wedge$ *status*(*vel*, *vm*) = *s* $\wedge$

      width(*vel*, *vm*) = *w* $\wedge$ *members*(*vel*, *vm*) = { }

The parameters have changed slightly in that a result parameter giving the identifier of the new V-element created is returned. There was no concept of an 'entity set identifier' in the previous two states.

    The operation to delete a connection is defined as:

DELCONNI (*eid1*: *Eid*, *rid*: *Rid*, *eid2*: *Eid*)

ext wr *vm* : *Vid* $\xrightarrow{m}$ *Vel*

pre $\{eid1, eid2\} \subseteq geteids(vm)$ $\wedge$

    let *vel* = *vm*(*eid1*) in

    rid $\in$ dom *rl*(*vel*) $\wedge$ *eid2* $\in$ elems *rl*(*vel*)(*rid*)

post let *vel1* = $\overleftarrow{vm}$(*eid1*) in

    let *rl1* = *rl*(*vel1*) in

    elems *rl1*(*rid*) = elems $\overleftarrow{rl1}$(*rid*) $- \{eid2\}$ $\wedge$

    let *vel2* = $\overleftarrow{vm}$(*eid2*) in

    let *rl2* = *rl*(*vel2*) in

    elems *rl2*(*minus*(*rid*)) = elems $\overleftarrow{rl2}$(*minus*(*rid*)) $- \{eid1\}$ $\wedge$

    ALL OTHER THINGS REMAIN THE SAME

Note the informal use of 'all other things remain the same'. If complete formality were required, this should be expanded.

    Again, although not presented here, proofs should be constructed that *ADDI* and *DELCONNI* respectively model *ADDR* and *DELCONNR*.

2.8 The Pascal version – *State-p*

State-p is designed to resemble the Pascal structure to be used in coding *State-i*. It introduces a design change, which provides some optimization by making use of the observation that the function of a C-element in a connection is to allow many-valued relations. If a relation is known to be single-valued (i.e. it is a many-one or one-one

Figure 2.14 Single-valued relation

relation) the need for a C-element disappears and it can be omitted. The structure shown in Figure 2.14 is sufficient to represent the connection between Scotland and its (only) capital Edinburgh.

So the second component of an R-list is either a C-list identifier or a V-element identifier.

Each V-element has the structure:

$$Velp :: rl \quad : Vid \xrightarrow{m} [Cnlid \mid Vid]$$
$$val : [Value]$$

Note that $[Cnlid \mid Vid]$ allows a nil value as the second R-element component; this occurs when deleting connections – it effectively indicates that there is no connection.

There must also be some mapping from connection list identifiers to connection lists. Connection lists are stored in blocks with pointers between blocks, i.e. a connection list is a list of *Vids* followed by a *next pointer* to a continuation connection list.

The resulting state which expresses this is:

$$State\text{-}p :: vm : Vid \xrightarrow{m} Velp$$
$$cm : Cnlid \xrightarrow{m} Cnl$$

$$Velp :: rl \quad : Vid \xrightarrow{m} [Cnlid \mid Vid]$$
$$val : [Value]$$

$$Cnl :: cl \quad : Vid^*$$
$$np : [Cnlid]$$

The invariant on *State-p*

The new conditions on *State-p* are:

1. R-lists and the *cl* component of *Cnl*s have a fixed maximum length.

2. If a relationship type is many-one or one-one then a *Vid*, otherwise a *Cnlid*, must appear in *rl(rid)*, where *rl* is the *rl* component of a V-element and contains *rid* in its domain, and all *Cnlid*s are in dom *cm(State-p)*.

$invp : State\text{-}p \rightarrow \mathbb{B}$

$invp(sp) \quad \triangle$

   $invi(retri(sp)) \wedge inv\text{-}length(sp) \wedge inv\text{-}optconn(sp) \wedge inv\text{-}clists(sp)$

The retrieve function, *retri*

State-p is similar to *State-i*, so *State-i* can be easily retrieved. The retrieve function shows that *State-p* models *State-i*.

$retri : State\text{-}p \rightarrow State\text{-}i$

$retri(mk\text{-}State\text{-}p(vm, cm)) \quad \triangle$

   $mk\text{-}State\text{-}i(\{vid \mapsto newvel(vm(vid), cm) \mid vid \in \mathsf{dom}\ vm\})$

To retrieve *State-i* from *State-p*, take *vm*(*State-p*) and for each V-element replace the identifiers in the range of *rl* by the lists to which they point. A V-element identifier, *vid*, is replaced by the list [vid]; a C-list identifier *cnlid* is replaced by the list in the *Cnl* to which it maps in *cm* (concatenated to the continuation list(s) if the *np* component of the *Cnl* is not nil).

Note that *State-i* and *State-p* are so similar that they could have been merged into a single refinement step. However, *State-i* resembles NDB more closely than would a state which included the design decisions of *State*-p. Also, one level only would require too great a jump from *State-r*. For these reasons, two separate states are maintained.

The operations on *State-p*

The two operations are defined as follows:

$ADDP\ (eset\!: Esetnm, s\!: Status, p\!: Picture, w\!: Width)\ esetid\!: Esetid$

ext wr $vm\ :\ Vid \xrightarrow{m} Velp$

   rd $cm\ :\ Cnlid \xrightarrow{m} Cnl$

pre $\exists vid \in getesetidsp(vm, cm) \cdot val(vm(vid))) = eset$

post $esetid \notin \mathsf{dom}\ \overleftarrow{vm}\ \wedge$

   $\mathsf{dom}\ \overleftarrow{vm} \cup \{esetid\} \subseteq \mathsf{dom}\ vm\ \wedge$

   $esetid \in getesetidsp(vm, cm)\ \wedge$

   let $velp = vm(esetid)$ in

   $val(velp) = eset\ \wedge$

      $statusp(velp, vm) = s\ \wedge$

      $picturep(velp, vm) = p\ \wedge$

      $widthp(velp, vm) = w\ \wedge$

      $membersp(esetid, vm, cm) = \{\ \}$

$DELCONNP \; (eid1: Eid, rid: Rid, eid2: Eid)$

ext wr $vm \;:\; Vid \xrightarrow{m} Velp$

    wr $cm \;:\; Cnlid \xrightarrow{m} Cnl$

pre $\{eid1, eid2\} \subseteq geteidsp(vm, cm) \;\wedge$

   let $velp = vm(eid1)$ in

   $rid \in \text{dom}\, rl(velp) \wedge$

   $eid2 \in idset(rl(velp)(rid), cm)$

post let $velp1 = \overleftarrow{vm}(eid1)$ in

   let $rl1 = rl(velp1)(rid)$ in

   $idset(rl1, cm) = idset(\overleftarrow{rl1}, \overleftarrow{cm}) - \{eid2\} \;\wedge$

   let $velp2 = \overleftarrow{vm}(eid2)$ in

   let $rl2 = rl(velp2)(minus(rid))$ in

   $idset(rl2, cm) = idset(\overleftarrow{rl2}, \overleftarrow{cm}) - \{eid1\}$

2.9 The implementation

This specification was implemented in Pascal on an Apollo computer. The internal structure of the data is shown in Figure 2.15. The data are stored as an array of V-elements, one for each *Vid*, and an array of connection-list elements, one for each *Cnlid*. Each V-element has a fixed length R-list, which may or may not be filled. The last used R-list position is indicated by a pointer LASTREL. The value of the V-element may vary considerably in length, and so is stored in a long string together with all the other values. It is accessed by a pointer to where it starts, and its length. So the VALUE component of a V-element consists of a starting pointer and a length.

The C-list of a connection-list element is also of fixed length and has a pointer to the last C-element. NP is an identifier as in *State-p* and should be nil if *cl* is not full.

For each array, the free elements (all of them at first) are chained together and accessed via a free chain pointer. So each V-element and connection-list element has a *next pointer*, which is nil if the element is not free.

Once the data structures have been decided, the operations can then be converted to code. Each operation is coded as a procedure.

Finally, to complete the formal specification and development of the program, assertions are included in the procedures to show that the pre- and post-conditions of the operations they implement are satisfied and that the data structure continues to satisfy the invariant.

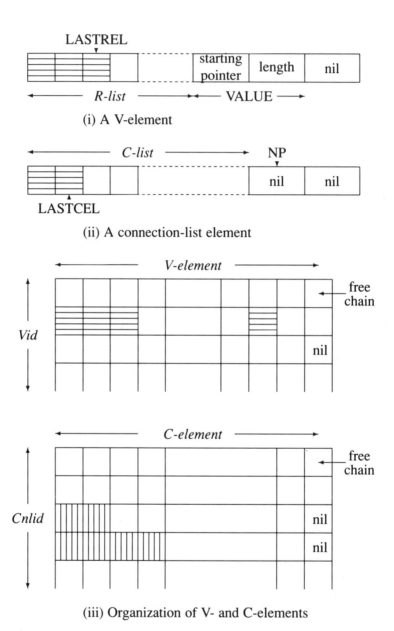

(i) A V-element

(ii) A connection-list element

(iii) Organization of V- and C-elements

Figure 2.15 Internal representation of the database

2.10   Table of abbreviations

Abbreviation	Description
clist	C-list
cnl	connection list
conns	connections
eid	entity identifier
em	entity map
ent	entity
eset	entity set
esetinf	entity set information
esetnm	entity set name
esm	entity set map
fs	fromset
fv	from value
id	identifier
membs	members
nm	name
pr	pair
rel	relationship type
relinf	relation information
relnm	relation name
reltype	relationship type
rid	relationship type identifier
rl	R-list
rm	relation map
ts	toset
tv	to value
val	value
vel	V-element
vid	V-element identifier
vm	V-element map

3

The ISTAR Database

Roger C. Shaw

This chapter discusses the specification of a special-purpose database system. The material therefore complements Chapter 2. The system described is an early version of IST's integrated project support environment known as ISTAR. A link is established – in this chapter – between the task of requirements analysis and the design of the state of a VDM state. The specification goes further into VDM notation by using both the module and exception specification notations.

3.1   Introduction

This chapter presents the design specification of the original ISTAR database management system [Ste86]. Current versions of ISTAR no longer use the binary relationship model described here, rather, a full entity relationship model is now supported.

Section 3.2 describes the informal design requirements that were produced prior to the development of the database system. These requirements have been extracted from the original technical design documents [IST85]. Section 3.3 presents an analysis of the requirements using entity relationship modelling and the various database operations are also identified. From this an outline specification structure is derived in Section 3.4 and presented in Sections 3.5, 3.6 and 3.7.

The problem analysis is rudimentary to the extent that none of the customer/analyst interactions are represented and many of the important steps that would be undertaken when performing the first stages of a data analysis are only hinted at. Nonetheless the material presented here should provide a good indication of how formal specification techniques and traditional data analysis methods blend well together.

3.2   Informal requirements

We start by providing an informal description of the database system.

Organizational model for the database

The database employs the binary relationship model. Data are stored in the database in the form of triples, each of which has the following structure:

[subject , verb , object]

The subject is related to the object through the verb, thus, for example, we may record the following relationship in the database:

['Jennifer' , 'Studies' , 'Computer Science']

Here the verb Studies denotes the relationship between Jennifer and Computer Science.

In the database verbs must be declared before use and each declared verb must be given an inverse. In the above example we may declare the verb and verb-inverse pair as:

'Studies'/ 'Is Studied by'

This leads to relationships of the following form which are said to be synonymous i.e. they represent two alternative ways of saying the same thing:

['Jennifer' , 'Studies' , 'Computer Science']
['Computer Science' , 'Is Studied by' , 'Jennifer']

This single fact can be entered into the database using either of these two forms and can subsequently be returned in either form.

The content of a database consists of a collection of defined verb/verb inverse pairs and a collection of triples of the form described above. For example, the following shows a possible database state in the sense that the indicated verb/verb inverse pair has been entered along with the specific relationships:

Verb and verb inverses
'Studies' 'Is Studied by'

Relationships entered
['Jennifer' , 'Studies' , 'Computer Science']
['Jennifer' , 'Studies' , 'Mathematics']
['Ben' , 'Studies' , 'Mathematics']
['Mathematics' , 'Is Studied by' , 'Ruth']
['Louise' , 'Studies' , 'Physics']

Query of a database

The database is queried by retrieving all those triples in the database that match a given template. A template has three fields corresponding to the subject – verb – object structure of a triple but, as we will see, can also contain some special matching symbols.

In the following discussion we will assume a database set up as shown above. Three forms of query may be identified as follows.

Checking if a specific triple is in the database. A template of the form

['Jennifer' , 'Studies' , 'Computer Science']

would match a triple in our database and thus the query would return **true**. A template of the form

['Mathematics', 'Is Studied by', 'Jennifer']

would likewise return **true** because, for any triple entered into the database, the inverse relation is also considered to be present.

The following query, not being in our database, would return **false**:

['Jennifer' , 'Studies' , 'Physics']

The match anything symbol. The wild card symbol '?' can be used in a template to indicate that any field may be considered as a match for this entry. Thus, in our example database, the query template:

['Jennifer' , 'Studies' , '?']

would yield:

['Jennifer' , 'Studies' , 'Computer Science']
['Jennifer' , 'Studies' , 'Mathematics']

The template:

['?' , 'Studies' 'Mathematics']

would yield:

['Jennifer' , 'Studies' , 'Mathematics']
['Ben' , 'Studies' , 'Mathematics']
['Ruth' , 'Studies' , 'Mathematics']

The template:

['Physics', '?', '?']

would retrieve the triple:

['Physics', 'Is Studied by', 'Louise']

The template:

['?' , '?' , '?']

would yield the entire database, thus:

['Jennifer' , 'Studies' , 'Computer Science']
['Jennifer' , 'Studies' , 'Mathematics']
['Ben' , 'Studies' , 'Mathematics']
['Ruth' , 'Studies' , 'Mathematics']
['Louise' , 'Studies' , 'Physics']
['Computer Science', 'Is Studied by', 'Jennifer']
['Mathematics', 'Is Studied by', 'Jennifer']
['Mathematics', 'Is Studied by', 'Ben']
['Mathematics', 'Is Studied by', 'Ruth']
['Physics', 'Is Studied by', 'Louise']

The don't care symbol. For some queries the value of one or more field is of no interest; in such cases the '*' symbol is used as a don't care indicator. The query template:

['*', 'Studies', '?']

would retrieve the following triples:

['*', 'Studies', 'Computer Science']
['*', 'Studies', 'Mathematics']
['*', 'Studies', 'Physics']

Note that only one triple of the form:

['*', 'Studies', 'Mathematics']

is returned even though there are three entries in the database that would be returned by the query:

['?', 'Studies', 'Mathematics'].

The query:

['?', '*', '*']

would yield each subject and object token used in the database (remember that both the forward and inverse relation is held in the database).

Insertion and deletion of verbs

As stated earlier verbs, and their inverses, must be inserted into the database before they can be used within a triple. Likewise verbs may be deleted from the database. When deleting a verb it is necessary to ensure that no triple within the database uses that verb; if reference is made to the verb then the deletion should not be allowed.

Insertion of triples into the database

Data are inserted into the database simply by inserting specific triples. The subject and object fields must be literal strings and the verb must be a literal string that has already been declared to the database. The insert operation only adds a triple into the database, it does not modify an existing triple in any way. Thus, for instance, if we add the following triple to the database

['Louise' , 'Studies', 'Music']

then 'Louise' will be related to both 'Physics' and 'Music' through the verb 'Studies'. If a course transfer was being registered then we would have to make a deletion removing the triple relating 'Louise' to 'Physics' and then insert the new relationship.

Deletion of triples from the database

Triples can be deleted from the database once again through the provision of a match or query template. All triples matching the template will be deleted from the database. The deletion template is set up in exactly the same way as a query template and may contain both strings and the special character '?'. The don't care symbol '*' may *not* be used as it is too permissive.

Counting triples in a database

An operation is provided to count the number of triples that match a given template. The rules for the template are the same as those that apply when a template is used for a query or deletion. The operation returns a count of the number of distinct triples that match the template – thus it counts the number of triples that would be retrieved if this template were used as a query or the number that would be deleted if this template were used for a deletion. Both the match anything symbol '?' and the don't care symbol '*' can be used.

Database partitions

So far, in discussing the ISTAR database, the impression has been given that we have a single database comprising a collection of triples and a collection of verb/verb-inverse pairs. This is an oversimplification of matters. What we have is zero or more databases, *each* of which comprises a set of *partitions*. Each of these partitions is a logically distinct object having a unique identifier within the system and with a set of declared verbs and a set of triples. Every database consists of one or more partitions.

Thus each partition of a database has all the properties outlined above. A database is a collection of partitions each of which may have verbs declared, triples added to and deleted from it and queries undertaken on its contents. To a considerable degree, then, each partition is a separate logical unit. However, there are logical groupings of partitions, and such a grouping is termed a 'database'. Partitions are important because they can be updated and queried in the manner discussed above. Complete databases are important because of the ideas of a database owner, a database identifier and a database session, as discussed below.

Access control

Every individual database has an owner. Each partition within a database may have a number of users who are authorized readers and writers. Writers are permitted to both read from and write to the partition while readers may only read from the partition. The owner of the database may write to or read from any partition.

At the time that a database is first created the creator is established as the owner of the database. The owner may subsequently create and delete partitions within the database and may modify the authorized readers and writers of any partition as required. Each partition has its own name which is unique within the context of that database.

Database sessions

Databases are accessed during well-defined sessions, where a session can be a read, a write or an owner session. Operations are provided for session initiation and session termination. The owner of a database may initiate any kind of session. A user who is not the owner may initiate a write session only if that user is authorized to write to some partition of the database, or a read session only if authorized to read from some partition. For an individual database there may be many read sessions active at one time; however, there may only be one owner or writer session active at one time although read sessions may be run concurrently.

Partition access

The partitions of a database may be accessed only during a session on that database. Write access to a partition is permitted only during a writer or owner session, and only if the user is the database owner or an authorized writer of the partition. Read access to a partition is permitted during any session by any user who is authorized to access the partition. Subject to the read/write restrictions mentioned above there are no limits to the number of partition sessions that may be initiated on a particular partition.

Creating and destroying database

At the outermost, or user level, facilities are provided for creating and destroying complete individual databases. Every database has a unique identifier, this identifier being specified by the user who creates the database.

Database query operations

The extraction of query results from the database is a two-step process. Firstly a query operation is initiated using a query template. The use of templates has been described in Section 3.2. Such queries result in zero or more triples being detected that satisfy the template. The set of triples that satisfy the query is tagged with a unique reference number, or key, which is then returned to the user. Subsequently the user may wish to extract triples from the query set. This is done by using an extraction operation which, given an appropriate reference number, will yield a triple from the set of triples associated with that particular reference number.

Committing and annulling databases

There are three types of database session – read, write and owner. A read session may be initiated by a user who has authorized read access to at least one partition within a database. There may be any number of concurrent read sessions on a particular database at any one time. Write sessions may similarly be initiated by a user who has authorized write access to at least one partition within the database. Unlike read sessions there can only be one write session on a database at any time; a write session and one or more read sessions on a database are allowed. Owner sessions are like write sessions except that the initiator must be the owner of the database.

Once a write or owner session is initiated, partition changes may be made as already described. On terminating a session the database will become the most recent or committed database and will be used as a basis for all subsequently initiated sessions of any access mode. Alternatively, if a write or owner session wishes to terminate *without* committing the database then an alternative annul session operation is available. During a database session the database may be committed *without* closing the session; in this case the state of the database when committed will become the latest version available for subsequent use. Alternatively, the database may be annulled in which case the session continues but with the last committed database.

3.3   Analysis of the requirements

The purpose of this section is to undertake an analysis of the requirements in order to get a feel for the structure of the problem. The technique known as data analysis will be used for this purpose. Data analysis provides a framework for examining the given requirements and extracting what are known as entities and the relationships that exist between those entities. Having identified entities, their attributes and interrelationships, the operations required are tabulated and the entity relationship model examined to see if it will support the development of the operations. How, then, does this relate to VDM? When producing a VDM specification we are required to design a state model which captures the essential data and data relationships of our problem. Operations are then specified using the state model. Data analysis provides an interesting technique which provides useful insight in the development of the VDM state model. A thorough discussion of data analysis techniques may be found in [How83].

We start by undertaking a simple entity/relationship analysis of the requirements. An **entity** is a concept or object which has independent existence, which can be uniquely identified and about which there is a need to record information. A **relationship** is an association between two or more entities that is significant within the problem space that is being modelled.

The analysis will be undertaken as follows:

1. Identify the important entities arising from the problem description.

2. Identify the list of operations that must be supported.

3. Draw a simple ERA diagram showing how entities are related to one another.

4. For each entity, identify potential attributes and identify any complex relationships that have attributes. If required redraw the ERA diagram.

5. Check that the ERA diagram will support the identified operations.

Entity identification

Based on our reading of the previous section we may identify the following entities.

Database_User
Database
Partition
Triple
Verb
Retrieved Triple

After some consideration a **Database_ Session** and a **Partition_Session** are both considered to be relations that hold between a **Database_User** and a **Database**, and a **Database** and a **Partition** respectively.

Operation list

The next step in our analysis is to examine the various operations that must be supported. These are shown in Figure 3.1.[1] Not all of these operations were explicitly included in the informal requirements. What we have done here is go through the requirements and extract obvious operations such as *INSERT*, *BUILD_TRIPLES*, *GET_TRIPLE*, *COMMIT*, *CREATE_DB*, etc. and introduce others which seem to be useful

---

[1]Abbreviations have been attached to the name of each operation and these will be used in various places within the remaining parts of the chapter. In this case the need for such shortforms arises from page layout problems associated with the use of the longer names.

Entity	*Operation*
Database_User	*REGISTER_USER (RU), DELETE_USER (DU)*
Database	*CREATE_DB (CDB), DELETE_DB (DDB),* *START_SESSION (SS), COMMIT (COM),* *ANNUL (AN), END_SESSION (ES),* *ANNUL_SESSION (ANS)*
Partition	*CREATE_PARTITION (CP),* *DELETE_PARTITION (DP), RENAME (RE),* *COPY_PARTITION (CPYP),* *OPEN_PARTITION (OPP),* *CLOSE_PARTITION (CLP),* *GRANT_ACCESS (GA)*
Verb	*DECLARE_VERB (DV),* *UNDECLARE_VERB (UV),* *VERB_INVERSE (VI), TEST_VERB (TV)*
Triple	*BUILD_TRIPLES (BT), COUNT (CT),* *SHORT_COUNT (SCT),* *DELETE (DLT), INSERT (INS)*
Retrieved_Triple	*GET_TRIPLE (GT)*

Figure 3.1 Operation/entity associations

such as *VERB_INVERSE, RENAME, COUNT*, etc. All these operations will have to be specified and then discussed with the customer.

ERA diagram

We now produce an ERA diagram. An entity relationship diagram shows the relationships that hold between entities. Looking at Figure 3.2, consider the entities **Partition** and **Verb**. An instance of the entity set **Verb** is associated with a single **Partition** instance; this is shown by the single-headed vector running from **Verb** to **Partition**. A **Partition** instance has, optionally, many **Verb** instances associated with it. The one – many relationship is shown by the double-headed arrow and the optional nature of the relationship is shown by the 'O' on the relationship line nearest to the entity which is optional in the relationship. The solid boxes represent the entities indicated above while the dotted boxes represent two relationships that have attributes in their own right. These two relationships have been introduced to remove the many many relationships that exist between **Database_User** and **Database** on the one hand and **Database** and **Partition**

on the other. Howe provides a detailed discussion of this problem [How83]. The relations between the entities should be fairly clear from the discussions in the previous
section. Relationships should all be explicitly named; however, for brevity this has not
been done.

Entity attribute identification

Taking the ERA model shown in Figure 3.2 we now look at each named entity and named
relationship on the diagram and identify attributes which allow us to model them. Firstly
we consider the entities; keys are shown in a typewriter style font.

Database_User. A database user has two attributes, a name and an indication of whether
he or she is an authorized database owner.

Database_User(<code>user_name</code>, can_own)

Database. Recall that databases are owned by users; thus, each database will have an
owner attribute. In addition a database will have a unique name. The rules relating read, write and owner access to a database session suggest that there can
be, at least potentially, several instances of a named database. For example, there
will be the most recently committed version and, depending on session histories,
there may be different historical versions still associated with open read sessions.
In addition a write or owner session will have a copy of the current database
to which updates will be allowed. This analysis suggests an instance indicator
allowing multiple versions of a particular named database. Each instance of a
database represents a repeating group and therefore we need to introduce an instance entity to which partitions associated with that instance can be linked. In
addition database instances are known to be committed or not. For instance, a
write or owner accessed database session will be based on the most recently committed version of a particular named database. While being accessed that database
will not be committed. However, subsequent to the execution of a *COMMIT* or
END_SESSION operation the database instance will become the most recently
committed version. All read access sessions will be based on the most recently
committed version of a particular named database. The introduction of the term
most recently committed suggests that there will be an ordering on the database
instance indicator:

Database(<code>db_name</code>, owner)
Db_instance(<code>db_instance_key</code>, db_name, committed)

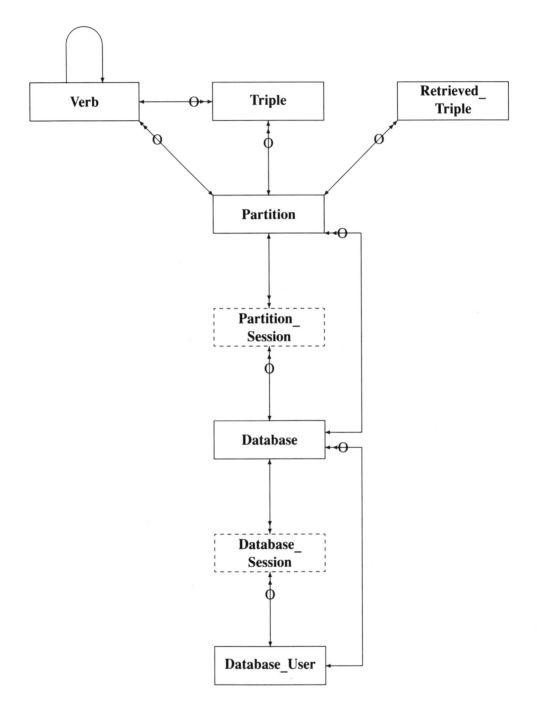

Figure 3.2 ISTAR database – entity relationship model

Partition. Partitions are associated with an instance of a named database. A partition therefore has a name and a reference to the database instance to which it is associated. In addition, partitions have associated authorized readers and writers. We may be tempted to include authorized readers and writers as attributes of a partition. However, note that authorized readers and writers are optionally associated with a partition, that is, a partition may have no such users or a number of them. For this reason we will include them as derived entities. Lastly, for each partition, there is the possibility that several instances may exist associated with different read and write sessions. For example, a write session on a partion creates a new instance of that partition. When the partition is closed it may be reopened by a subsequent read session. That partition instance will remain until the database is closed or the partition is closed. Each write access partition that is closed may be picked up by a read session and thus several instances may coexist:

Partition(p_name, *db_instance_key*)
P_instance(p_instance_key, *p_name*)
Readers(user_name, p_instance_key)
Writers(user_name, p_instance_key)

Verb. A verb is identified by its verbname but is also associated with its inverse. This gives the following structure:

Verb(verb_name, p_instance_key, *verb_name*)

Triple. A triple comprises a subject and object together with a link to the associated verb that makes up the relationship:

Triple(subject, object, p_instance_key, *verb_name*)

Retrieved_Triple. A retrieved triple associates a key with one or more triples resulting from a template query. The associated triples are extracted from the entity set 'triple' but they may be changed to the extent that any of the fields may contain the '*' symbol. We will therefore identify an attribute called r_triple to model this situation:

Retrieved_Triple(key, p_instance_key, *r_triple*)

Two relationships are identified on the ERA diagram which have attributes. These are **Database_Session** and **Partition_Session**. These relationships were put in to resolve the two potential many to many relationships that appear between **Database_User**s and **Databases** and between **Databases** and **Partitions**. These two relationships are modelled as follows.

Database_Session(db_session_key, *db_instance_key, db_mode*)
Partition_Session(p_session_key, *p_instance_key, p_mode*)

In the light of this analysis we can redraw the entity relation diagram showing the newly identified entities and relationships – this is shown in Figure 3.3. In addition we need to reassign operations to entities as shown in Figure 3.4

Relating operations, attributes and relationships

The last stage of our analysis aims to check that the entity/attribute tables identified in the previous section are capable of supporting the operations identified in Section 3.3. To do this we cross-tabulate entity attributes with the operations and, where each operation requires access to an entity, indicate whether the access is a Read (r), Update (u), Store (s) or Delete (d) access. An example of this form of tabulation is given in Figures 3.5. The analysis should be carried out for all attributes and all operations. Some operations contain a number of different access keys representing complex conditions that can arise when that operation is used. For instance, the *COMMIT* operation requires the following accesses:

1. **Database_Session** to check that the mode is write or owner.

2. **Db_Instance, Db_Session, Partition, P_Instance, Partition_Session** to make a copy of the database instance, i.e. create a new instance of the current state for the purposes of continuing the session.

3. **Db_Instance** of the committed instance to change the attribute *committed* to the committed state.

4. **Database_Session, Partition_Session** to close any sessions within the committed instance of the database.

Note that the entity **Database_Session** is now referring to the newly created database instance which is effectively a copy of the state at the time the *COMMIT* operation was issued.

This form of analysis should also be carried out to check that the modelled relations are capable of supporting the operations. Once again refer to Howe [How83] for a full discussion.

3.4   A specification of the ISTAR database system

In Section 3.3 we examined the database requirements using the entity relationship analysis technique. This yielded a number of entities and associated attributes together with

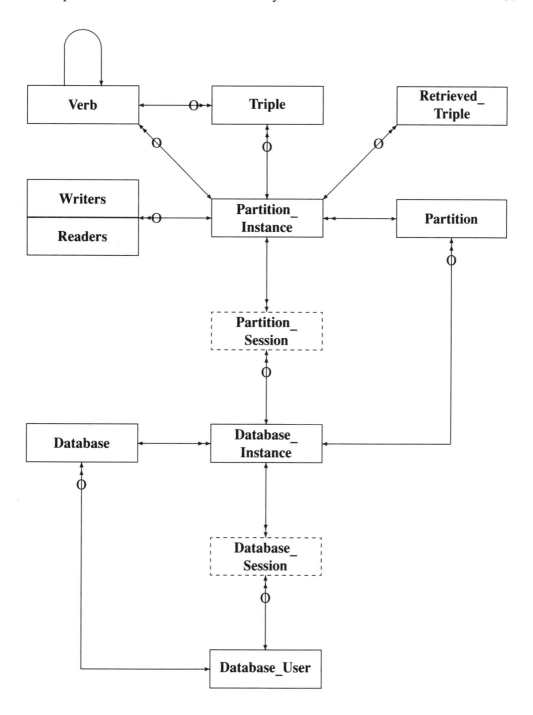

Figure 3.3 ISTAR database – entity relationship model

Entity	Operation
Database_User	*REGISTER_USER (RU), DELETE_USER (DU)*
Database_Instance	*COMMIT (COM), ANNUL (AN),* *END_SESSION (ES),*START_SESSION (SS), ANNUL_SESSION (AS)
Database	*CREATE_DB (CDB), DELETE_DB (DDB),*
Partition_Instance	*OPEN_PARTITION (OPP),* *CLOSE_PARTITION (CLP)*
Partition	*CREATE_PARTITION (CP),* *DELETE_PARTITION (DP), RENAME (RE),* *COPY_PARTITION (CPYP)*
Readers, Writers	*GRANT_ACCESS (GA)*
Verb	*DECLARE_VERB (DV),* *UNDECLARE_VERB (UV),* *VERB_INVERSE (VI), TEST_VERB (TV)*
Triple	*BUILD_TRIPLES (BT), COUNT (CT),* *SHORT_COUNT (SCT),* *DELETE (DLT), INSERT (INS)*
Retrieved_Triple	*GET_TRIPLE (GT)*

Figure 3.4 Revised operation/entity association

a list of operations. We now wish to use that analysis *as a guide* in producing a formal specification of the database problem. Essentially we will examine the set of entities and identify several abstract data types each of which will have a state and associated operations. The states models will be derived from the entity relationship analysis already undertaken and operations will be associated with an appropriate data type. The operations will then be specified using the data type state model. As we will end up with a hierarchy of data types we will have to deal with the problem of migrating the operations associated with basic data types through the specification hierarchy.

If we look at Figure 3.3 we see the need to model the entity sets **Database_User, Database** and the relationship **Database_Session**. This latter relationship captures the concept of a database session where a specific instance of a named database is linked to a session key and mode. A database may be associated with many read mode sessions but only one write or owner session. Thus, a particular named database may have several instances associated with different session keys. Remember a write session may result in several *COMMIT* operations leading to instances of the database which could be picked up by newly initiated read sessions. With this in mind we will produce a specification

Entity	Attribute	Operations						
		CDB	*DDB*	*SS*	*COM*	*AN*	*ES*	*AS*
Database_	*user_nm*	r	r					
User	*can_own*	r	r	r				
Database	*db_name*	r,s	r,d	r	r	d	r	d
	owner	s	r,d	r		d		d
Database_	*db_instance_key*	s	d		s	d		d
Instance	*db_name*	s	d		s	d		d
	committed	s	d		s,u	d	u	d
Database_	*db_session_key*		r	s	r,d	r	r,d	r,d
Session	*db_instance_key*		r	s	r,s,d	u	r,d	r,d
	db_mode		r	s	r,s,d	r	r,d	r,d
Partition	*p_name*		d		s	d		d
	db_instance_key		d		s	d		d
Partition_	*p_instance_key*		d		s	d		d
Instance	*p_name*		d		s	d		d
Partition_	*p_session_key*				s,d	d	d	d
Session	*p_instance_key*				s,d	d	d	d
	p_mode				s,d	d	d	d

Key	Access definition
d	Delete
r	Read
s	Store
u	Update

Figure 3.5 Operation – attribute tabulation

of a data type called *Dbms* which will capture the **User** and **Database_Instance** entity sets as well as the **Database_Session** relationship. The second data type that will be modelled will be called *Database* and will capture the entity set **Partition_Instance** as well as the relationship **Partition_Session**. Lastly, the data type *Partition* will capture the entity sets **Triple, Verb** and **Retrieved_Triple**. These entities and their associated relationships will be modelled using the basic VDM data types of sets, functions and cross-products or records.

We need to consider operations for a moment. As mentioned above we will introduce three data type specifications – *Partition*, *Database* and *Dbms*. The operations associated with these three data types follow more or less from Figure 3.4. However, there are some minor differences. The operations *CREATE_PARTITION*, *DELETE_PARTITION*, *CREATE_DATABASE* and *DELETE_DATABASE* all have the effect of creating or destroying an instance of, respectively, type *Partition* and *Database*. Instances of type *Partition* will be held in a *Database* state and, similarly, instances if type *Database* will be held in the *Dbms* state. Thus, *CREATE_PARTITION* will alter a *Database* state. Considering *CREATE_PARTITION*, we see there are two effects. Firstly an instance of type *Partition* is generated and secondly the instance is associated with a *Database* state. Data type instances are dealt with by an initialization operation or assertion on the initial state of the data type – for this we will use an *INIT* operation. The creation and deletion operations will therefore be associated with the data type whose state is changed as a result of generating an instance of a data type object. To this end *CREATE_PARTITION* will be associated with the data type *Database* and similarly with the remaining operations. The operations *RENAME* and *COPY_PARTITION* offer similar difficulties. *RENAME* requires that the new name is not associated with any partition in a database. Only the *Database* data type has access to partition names within it thus this operation must be a *Database* operation. However, we will require a *CHANGE_NAME* operation on the *Partition* data type. Similarly, *COPY_PARTITION* requires a new instance of type *Partition* to be created and once again has name restrictions associated with it. This operation will also be associated with the *Database* data type.

With these observations in mind we now embark on the specification of the *Partition*, *Database* and *Dbms* data types.

3.5   The *Partition* **data type**

The first task is to address the development of the state model. The heart of the system is the **Partition_instance**. Such an instance may be modelled as follows

p_name. The name of the partition.

verbs_and_inverses. This models the verb/verb inverse pairs that are held in the partition. For each verb entry we record a maplet between the verb and its inverse and the inverse and its verb.

data. Here we model triples within a partition as a set of type *Triple* where a triple is modelled as a cross-product of type (*subject*, *verb*, *object*).

retrieved_triples. The *BUILD_TRIPLE* operation yields a set of triples that match a given template. For each query the resulting set of triples is indexed by a unique query key. The *GET_TRIPLE* operation will access this state component when extracting the results for a particular query key.

readers. Authorized users who may read from the partition.

writers. Authorized users who may write to the partition.

Something should be said about the attribute *p_instance_key* which is clearly not explicitly modelled. The key was used to identify specific partition instances and an ordering was required on that key to determine the latest instance of a partition. Each instance of a *Partition* will be managed in the *Database* specification and as will be seen there is no need to include such a key either to distinguish the latest partition instance or to distinguish one partition from another. For this reason the key is not modelled.

Briefly, some of the type definitions are:

Template. A Template has the same form as a triple but allows any of the fields to contain symbols of type *Match_symbol*.

D_template. A template used by the *DELETE* operation. The type only allows the '?' special symbol and precludes '*'.

R_triple. Partition enquiries can result in triples being returned with the special symbol '*' appearing in some fields. This type allows for results of this form.

Get_triple_result. Used to return information from the *GET_TRIPLE* operation.

Query_key. The *BUILD_TRIPLE* operation constructs query sets which are indexed by instances if this type.

Pr_types. A union type which brings together the types of the results produced by partition operations.

Match_symbol. This type models the special symbols '*' and '?' which are, in turn, represented by members of type *Star* and *Question_mark* respectively.

The full state specification is now presented:

Partition :: *p_name*   : *P_name*
              verbs_and_inverses : *Verbmap*
              data   : *Tripleset*
              retrieved_triples   : *Query_key* $\xrightarrow{m}$ *R_triple*-set
              readers   : *User*-set
              writers   : *User*-set
inv *mk-Partition*(*nm, v-and-i, d, rt, r, w*) $\triangleq$
    $\forall tr \in d \cdot$
        let *mk-Triple*(*subject, verb, object*) = *tr* in
        mk-Triple(*object, v_and_i*(*verb*), *subject*) $\in d \wedge$
        verb $\in$ dom *v_and_i*

Having defined the state careful consideration should be given to identifying any data type invariants applicable to the state as a whole or to any of the types used within the state definition. The invariant on the state asserts that for any (subject, verb, object) relationship within a partition the inverse verb relationship should also be in the partition. The following invariant might be considered to hold:

$$\bigcup \text{rng } rt \subseteq d$$

However, on reflection it seems unreasonable that triples can not be deleted from the database if they exist explicitly in a query set.

Verbmap = *Verbname* $\xrightarrow{m}$ *Verbname*
inv (*vm*) $\triangleq \forall vn \in$ dom *vm* $\cdot vn = vm(vm(vn)) \wedge$
    $vn \neq vm(vn) \wedge$ dom *vm* = rng *vm*

The type *Verbmap* requires an invariant restricting the map to be well formed with respect to verbs and their inverses, that is, the inverse of each verb is the verb itself and the name of the inverse verb should not be the same as the verb itself. The remaining type definitions are given below.

Tripleset = *Triple*-set

Triple :: *subject* : *Text*
            verb   : *Verbname*
            object : *Text*

Template :: *subject* : *Text* | *Match_symbol*
              verb   : *Verbname* | *Match_symbol*
              object : *Text* | *Match_symbol*

R_triple = Template
inv (*mk-R_triple(s, v, o)*) $\triangle$
    {s, o} ⊆ *(Text* ∪ *Star)* ∧ *v* ∈ *(Verbname* ∪ *Star)*

D_template = Template
inv (*mk-D_template(s, v, o)*) $\triangle$
    {s, o} ⊆ *(Text* ∪ *Question_mark)* ∧ *v* ∈ *(Verbname* ∪ *Question_mark)*

Match_symbol = Question_mark ∪ *Star*

Question_mark is not yet defined

Star is not yet defined

*P_access = {*READ, WRITE*}*

Get_triple_result :: *tr*   : *[R-triple]*
                        more : $\mathbb{B}$

*Yes_no = {*OK, FAILED*}*

Verbname = Text

Pr_types = Yes_no | Get_triple_result | Query_key | Verbname | $\mathbb{N}$ *|* $\mathbb{B}$

Query_key, P_name is not yet defined

We now turn to the specification of some auxiliary functions that are used in the specification of other data types. As presented here it appears that these functions are divined before the operations are specified or the other specifications are developed. However, it should be clear that these functions were extracted as the specification was developed and are presented here, together, for convenience.[2]

triplematch : Template × *Tripleset* × *Verbmap* → *R_triple*-set
triplematch(tem, data, v_and_i, res) $\triangle$

---

[2]The definitions given below deliberately employ several different styles, even though this is not really warranted for the present specification, purely for the purposes of illustration.

post let *mk-Template(s, v, o) = tem* in
    $(v \notin$ dom *v_and_i* $\wedge v \notin$ *Match_symbol* $\wedge res = \{\})$
    $\vee$
    $((v \in$ dom *v_and_i* $\vee v \in$ *Match_symbol*$) \wedge$
    res $= \{$*mk-R_triple(sr, vr, or)* | *mk-Triple(su, vb, ob)* $\in$ *data*
    $\wedge$
    $((s \in$ *Question_mark* $\wedge sr = su) \vee (s \in$ *Star* $\wedge sr \in$ *Star*$) \vee$
                                   $(s \in$ *Text* $\wedge sr = su \wedge su = s))$
    $\wedge$
    $((v \in$ *Question_mark* $\wedge vr = vb) \vee (v \in$ *Star* $\wedge vr \in$ *Star*$) \vee$
                                   $(v \in$ *Text* $\wedge vr = vb \wedge vb = v))$
    $\wedge$
    $((o \in$ *Question_mark* $\wedge or = ob) \vee (o \in$ *Star* $\wedge or \in$ *Star*$) \vee$
                                   $(o \in$ *Text* $\wedge or = ob \wedge ob = o))\})$

The *triplematch* function takes a template, a set of triples and the verb inverse map and returns the set of all triples that match the template. This formulation of *triplematch* looks overly complicated and a simplification may be achieved as follows:

simple_match : *Template* $\times$ *Tripleset* $\to$ *Tripleset*
simple_match(tem, data) $\quad \triangle \quad$ let *mk-Template(s, v, o) = tem* in
    $\{$*mk-Triple(su, vb, ob)* | *mk-Triple(su, vb, ob)* $\in$ *data* $\wedge$
    $(su = s \vee s \in$ *Match_symbol*$) \wedge$
    $(vb = v \vee v \in$ *Match_symbol*$) \wedge$
    $(ob = o \vee o \in$ *Match_symbol*$)\}$

star_match : *Template* $\times$ *Tripleset* $\to$ *R_triple*-set
star_match(tem, data) $\quad \triangle \quad$ let *mk-Template(s, v, o) = tem* in
    $\{$*mk-R_triple(su, vb, ob)* | *mk-Triple(subject, verb, object)* $\in$ *data* $\wedge$
    $((su \in$ *Star* $\wedge s \in$ *Star*$) \vee (su = subject \wedge s \notin$ *Star*$)) \wedge$
    $((vb \in$ *Star* $\wedge v \in$ *Star*$) \vee (vb = verb \wedge v \notin$ *Star*$)) \wedge$
    $((ob \in$ *Star* $\wedge o \in$ *Star*$) \vee (ob = object \wedge o \notin$ *Star*$))\}$

With these two subsidiary functions we can now respecify *triplematch* as follows:

triplematch : *Template* $\times$ *Tripleset* $\times$ *Verbmap* $\to$ *R_triple*-set
triplematch(tem, data, v_and_i, res) $\quad \triangle$

post let *mk-Template*(*s*, *v*, *o*) = *tem* in
    (*v* ∉ dom *v_and_i* ∧ *v* ∉ *Match_symbol* ∧ *res* = { })
    ∨
    (*v* ∈ dom *v_and_i* ∨ *v* ∈ *Match_symbol*) ∧
    res = *star_match*(*tem*, *simple_match*(*tem*, *data*))

The following additional functions are required:

p_name_is : *Partition* → *P_name*
p_name_is(*state*) $\triangleq$ *p_name*(*state*)

The *p_name_is* function is used to return the name of the partition.

p_authorized : *Partition* → ((*User* × *P_access*) → $\mathbb{B}$)
p_authorized(*state*) $\triangleq$ λ*user*, *access* ·
        (*access* = READ ∧ *user* ∈ *readers*(*state*)) ∨
        (*access* = WRITE ∧ *user* ∈ *writers*(*state*))

Depending on the setting of the *access* parameter the *p_authorized* function returns true if the indicated user is in the set of authorized readers or writers.

p_change_name : *Partition* → (*P_name* → *Partition*)
p_change_name(*state*)(*name*) $\triangleq$ μ(*state*, *p_name* ↦ *name*)

There is a need to change the name of a partition. This function accepts an argument of type *Partition* and a name and returns the partition state with the name changed.[3]

We can now address the specification of the operations identified earlier in Section 3.3. For this specification exception conditions have been stated in the post condition of each operation. No use has been made of the special syntax available for specifying exceptions. This notation will be employed when we consider the specification of the data type *Database* in Section 3.6. A brief commentry on each operation follows the specification.

BT (*tem*: *Template*) result: *Query_key*
ext wr *retrieved_triples*   : *Query_key* $\xrightarrow{m}$ *R_triple*-set
    rd *data*   : *Tripleset*
    rd *verbs_and_inverses* : *Verbmap*
post let *queryset* = *triplematch*(*tem*, *data*, *verbs_and_inverses*) in
    result ∉ dom $\overleftarrow{retrieved\_triples}$ ∧
    retrieved_triples = $\overleftarrow{retrieved\_triples}$ ∪ {*result* ↦ *queryset*}

---

[3]The functions *p_name_is* and *p_authorized* have been specified using lambda notation; *p_change_name* uses currying. Both of these forms are described in Appendix A.

The *BUILD_TRIPLE* operation takes a template and constructs the set of triples that satisfy the query template. The set of retrieved triples is inserted into the *retrieved_triples* map using a unique key, that is one that has not already been allocated, and the key is returned as an output from the operation.

> *CT* (*tem*: *Template*) *result*: $\mathbb{N}$
> ext rd *data*   : *Tripleset*
>   rd *verbs_and_inverses* : *Verbmap*
> post *result* = card *triplematch*(*tem*, *data*, *verbs_and_inverses*)

This simple operation takes a template as argument and returns a count of the number or triples within the partition that match the template as discussed in Section 3.2.

> *DV* (*fv*: *Verbname*, *iv*: *Verbname*) *result*: *Yes_no*
> ext wr *verbs_and_inverses* : *Verbmap*
> post (*fv* $\notin$ dom $\overleftarrow{verbs\_and\_inverses}$ $\wedge$ *iv* $\notin$ dom $\overleftarrow{verbs\_and\_inverses}$ $\wedge$
>
> $\qquad$ *fv* $\neq$ *iv* $\wedge$ *verbs_and_inverses* = $\overleftarrow{verbs\_and\_inverses}$ $\cup$
>
> $\qquad\qquad\qquad\qquad\qquad\qquad\qquad\qquad$ {*fv* $\mapsto$ *iv*, *iv* $\mapsto$ *fv*} $\wedge$
>
> $\qquad$ *result* = OK)
>
> $\vee$
>
> ((*fv* $\in$ dom $\overleftarrow{verbs\_and\_inverses}$ $\vee$ *iv* $\in$ dom $\overleftarrow{verbs\_and\_inverses}$ $\vee$
>
> $\qquad$ *fv* = *iv*) $\wedge$ *verbs_and_inverses* = $\overleftarrow{verbs\_and\_inverses}$ $\wedge$
>
> $\qquad$ *result* = FAILED)

Verbs and their inverses must be entered into a partition. The *DECLARE_VERB* operation performs that task. Clearly the forward verb and the inverse verb should not have already been defined and they should not be identical to one another. Given this condition the verb/inverse pair will be entered into *verbs_and_inverses* and a satisfactory response returned. If this is not the case then a failed response is returned.

> *DLT* (*tem*: *D_template*) *result*: *Yes_no*
> ext rd *verbs_and_inverses* : *Verbmap*
>   wr *data*   : *Tripleset*

post let $mk\text{-}D\_template(s, v, o) = tem$ in
    let $valid\_verb = v \in$ dom $verbs\_and\_inverses \vee v \in Question\_mark$ in
    let $match\_all = v \in Question\_mark$ in
    cases $valid\_verb$ of
    true $\rightarrow$ ($match\_all \wedge$

        let $fs = triplematch(tem, \overleftarrow{data}, verbs\_and\_inverses)$ in
        let $r\_tem = mk\text{-}Template(s, v, o)$ in
        let $is = triplematch(r\_tem, \overleftarrow{data}, verbs\_and\_inverses)$ in
        $data = \overleftarrow{data} - (fs \cup is) \wedge result = \text{OK})$
        $\vee$
        ($\neg match\_all \wedge$
        let $fs = triplematch(tem, \overleftarrow{data}, verbs\_and\_inverses)$ in
        let $r\_tem = mk\text{-}Template(o, verbs\_and\_inverses(v), s)$ in
        let $is = triplematch(r\_tem, \overleftarrow{data}, verbs\_and\_inverses)$ in
        $data = \overleftarrow{data} - (fs \cup is) \wedge result = \text{OK})$
    others $data = \overleftarrow{data} \wedge result = \text{FAILED}$
    end

How do we remove triples from a partition? The *DELETE* operation is provided to perform this task. Given a template (not containing the star symbol), all those triples which match the template (forward and inverse relations included) are taken out of the partition. An exception is raised when the verb provided within the template is neither of type *Question_mark* nor a verb within *verbs_and_inverses*.

    GT (*key*: *Query_key*) *result*: *Get_triple_result*
    ext wr *retrieved_triples* : *Query_key* $\xrightarrow{m}$ *R_triple*-set

post ($key \in$ dom $\overleftarrow{retrieved\_triples} \wedge$

    ($\overleftarrow{retrieved\_triples}(key) \neq \{\ \}\ \Rightarrow$

       let $triple \in \overleftarrow{retrieved\_triples}(key)$ in

       let $newset = \overleftarrow{retrieved\_triples}(key)\text{-}triple$ in

       let $more = (newset \neq \{\ \})$ in

       $retrieved\_triples = \overleftarrow{retrieved\_triples} \dagger \{key \mapsto newset\} \wedge$

       $result = mk\text{-}Get\_triple\_result(triple, more))$

    $\overset{\wedge}{(\overleftarrow{retrieved\_triples}(key)} = \{\ \}\ \Rightarrow$

       $retrieved\_triples = \{key\} \triangleleft \overleftarrow{retrieved\_triples} \wedge$

       $result = mk\text{-}Get\_triple\_result(\text{NIL}, \text{FALSE}))$

  $\vee$

  ($key \notin$ dom $\overleftarrow{retrieved\_triples} \wedge$

    $retrieved\_triples = \overleftarrow{retrieved\_triples} \wedge$

    $result = mk\text{-}Get\_triple\_result(\text{NIL}, \text{FALSE}))$

Recall the partition query mechanism described in Section 3.2. *BUILD_TRIPLE* is used to create an indexed set of triples satisfying a query template. Extracting elements from this query set is accomplished by the *GET_TRIPLE* operation. Given an argument of type *Query_key* the operation returns a record containing an *arbitrary* element from the query set and a boolean indicator stating whether there are further triples to be retrieved. A final call of the operation when the query set is empty causes the query set to be removed entirely.

  GA (u: *User, access*: P_access)

  ext wr *readers* : *User*-set

    wr *writers* : *User*-set

  post ($access = \text{READ} \wedge$

      $readers = \overleftarrow{readers} \cup \{u\} \wedge writers = \overleftarrow{writers})$

    $\vee$

    ($access = \text{WRITE} \wedge$

      $writers = \overleftarrow{writers} \cup \{u\} \wedge \overleftarrow{readers} = readers)$

This operation *GRANT_ACCESS* alters the read or write access authority as indicated.

  INIT (nm: P_name)

ext wr *p_name*   : *P_name*
   wr *verbs_and_inverses* : *Verbmap*
   wr *data*   : *Tripleset*
   wr *retrieved_triples*   : $Query\_key \xrightarrow{m} R\_triple\text{-set}$
   wr *readers*   : *User*-set
   wr *writers*   : *User*-set
post *p_name* $= nm \wedge$ *verbs_and_inverses* $= \{\ \} \wedge$
     data $= \{\ \} \wedge$ *retrieved_triples* $= \{\ \} \wedge$
     readers $= \{\ \} \wedge$ *writers* $= \{\ \}$

The initialization of a data type is an important specification consideration. When a data type is instantiated, i.e. when a new instance of the type is first created, the initialization operation must be employed. The initialization operation establishes the data type invariant on the initial state of the data type.

INS (*tr*: *Triple*) *result*: *Yes_no*
ext rd *verbs_and_inverses* : *Verbmap*
   wr *data*   : *Tripleset*
post let *mk-Triple*$(s, v, o) = tr$ in
     $(v \in$ dom *verbs_and_inverses* $\wedge$
         $data = \overleftarrow{data} \cup \{tr, mk\text{-}Triple(o, verbs\_and\_inverses(v), s)\} \wedge$
         $result = \text{OK})$
     $\vee$
     $(v \notin$ dom *verbs_and_inverses* $\wedge$
         $data = \overleftarrow{data} \wedge result = \text{FAILED})$

We have already seen the *DELETE* operation that removes triples from a partition. The *INSERT* operation inserts triples into a partition. A triple is provided as input to the operation. If the verb is valid then the triple and its inverse are placed in *data*. Note, if the triple is already present in the database then no indication to this effect is given. If the verb is invalid, that is not in *verbs_and_inverses*, then a failure is signalled.

PCL
ext wr *retrieved_triples* : $Query\_key \xrightarrow{m} R\_triple\text{-set}$
post *retrieved_triples* $= \{\ \}$

The *PARTITION_CLEAR* operation produces a partition without any outstanding triple queries.

SCT (*tem*: *Template*) *result*: $\mathbb{N}$
ext rd *verbs_and_inverses* : *Verbmap*
   rd *data*   : *Tripleset*

post let *count* = card *triplematch*(*tem*, *data*, *verbs_and_inverses*) in
  (*count* <= 1 ⟹ *result* = *count*) ∧
  (*count* > 1 ⟹ *result* > 1)

SHORT_COUNT returns zero or one if there are zero or one template matches. If there is more than one match then an arbitrary natural number, but not zero or one, is returned. Note that the result type constrains the response to being of type natural number; apart from zero or one the specific value is not determined.

TV (*fv*: *Verbname*, *iv*: *Verbname*) *result*: 𝔹
ext rd *verbs_and_inverses* : *Verbmap*
post *result* = (*fv* ∈ dom *verbs_and_inverses* ∧
$$verbs\_and\_inverses(fv) = iv)$$

Given two verbs the *TEST_VERB* operation returns true if the verbs have been declared and are the inverse of one another.

UV (*fv*: *Verbname*, *iv*: *Verbname*) *result*: *Yes_no*
ext wr *verbs_and_inverses* : *Verbmap*
  rd *data*   : *Tripleset*
post let *wf-verb* =
    fv ∈ dom $\overline{verbs\_and\_inverses}$ ∧ $\overline{verbs\_and\_inverses}$(*fv*) = *iv* in
  let *not-in-db* =
    ∀*trip* ∈ *data* · (*verb*(*trip*) ≠ *fv* ∧ *verb*(*trip*) ≠ *iv*) in
  let *undeclare* = *wf-verb* ∧ *not-in-db* in
  (*undeclare* ∧
    verbs_and_inverses = {*fv*, *iv*} ⩤ $\overline{verbs\_and\_inverses}$ ∧
    result = OK)
  ∨
  (¬ *undeclare* ∧
    verbs_and_inverses = $\overline{verbs\_and\_inverses}$ ∧ *result* = FAILED)

The *UNDECLARE_VERB* operation removes a verb and its inverse from the partition. Two conditions must be fulfilled. Firstly, the verb and verb inverse must be well-formed and, secondly, neither the verb nor its inverse should appear in a triple within the partition.

VI (*v*: *Verbname*) *result*: *Verbname* | *Yes_no*
ext rd *verbs_and_inverses* : *Verbmap*
post (*v* ∈ dom *verbs_and_inverses* ∧ *result* = *verbs_and_inverses*(*v*)) ∨
  (*v* ∉ dom *verbs_and_inverses* ∧ *result* = FAILED)

This operation, given a declared verb, will return its inverse.

The bulk of the specification for this data type is now complete. However, there are two further issues that require addressing. The first relates to the use of *Partition* operations on instances of this type and the second concerns the visibility of names outside of the specification.

Recall for a moment how partitions are used. Firstly a user will create a database and then initiate a database session. Subsequently a partition will be created and opened resulting in a partition session. Operations such as *INSERT* and *DECLARE_VERB* will then be available for use within the context of a particular database and partition session. Clearly, we do not want to explicitly specify analogs of these operations in both the *Database* and *Dbms* specifications. Rather we seek to provide an abstract syntax description of these operations which can then be used within these other specifications appropriately linked to partition and session keys. How do we provide such an abstract syntax? Consider the *DECLARE_VERB* operation. This has two arguments representing the forward and inverse verbs. The operation signature can be described as a record type with two fields, thus:

$$Dv :: forward\_verb : Verbname$$
$$\qquad inverse\_verb \ : Verbname$$

The *SCT* operation signature may be described as follows:

$$Sct :: template : Template$$

How these abstract syntax representations will be used is described in Section 3.6. Accepting this mode of description we need to add the following definitions to our collection of types:

$$Partition\_ops = Bt \mid Ct \mid Dv \mid Dlt \mid Gt \mid Ga \mid Ins \mid Sct \mid Tv \mid Uv \mid Vi$$

Abstract syntax representations for all these operations may easily be generated as indicated above.

The final issue remaining is that of name space management. Name visibility is controlled through the use of an interface specification which states what names are to be exported (made visible) outside of the specification and what names are to be imported into the specification i.e. made visible for use within the specification. Import and export clauses are provided within the interface specification to capture this information. Figure 3.6 shows the interface specification for the *Partition* data type.

3.6 The *Database* data type

In this specification we aim to model the type *Database*. Guided by the discussion in Section 3.3, we construct the state as follows:

module *Partition*
exports
  operations
      BT: *Template* $\xrightarrow{o}$ *Query_key*,
      CT: *Template* $\xrightarrow{o}$ $\mathbb{N}$,
      DV: *Verbname* × *Verbname* $\xrightarrow{o}$ *Yes_no*,
      DLT: *D_template* $\xrightarrow{o}$ *Yes_no*,
      GT: *Query_key* $\xrightarrow{o}$ *Get_triple_result*,
      GA: *User* × *P_access* $\xrightarrow{o}$,
      $INIT$: *P_name* $\xrightarrow{o}$,
      INS: *Triple* $\xrightarrow{o}$ *Yes_no*,
      PCL: () $\xrightarrow{o}$,
      SCT: *Template* $\xrightarrow{o}$ $\mathbb{N}$,
      TV: *Verbname* × *Verbname* $\xrightarrow{o}$ $\mathbb{B}$,
      UV: *Verbname* × *Verbname* $\xrightarrow{o}$ *Yes_no*,
      VI: *Verbname* $\xrightarrow{o}$ *Verbname* | *Yes_no*
  functions
      p_name_is: *Partition* → *P_name*,
      p_authorized: *Partition* → ((*User* × *P_access*) → $\mathbb{B}$)
      p_change_name: *Partition* → (*P_name* → *Partition*)
  types
      Pr_types, *Yes_no*, *Get_triple_result*, *Query_key*, *Verbname*,
      P_access, *P_name*, *Template*, *D_template*, *Triple*, *R_triple*,
      Partition_ops, *Bt*, *Ct*, *Dv*, *Dlt*, *Gt*, *Ga*, *Ins*, *Sct*, *Tv*, *Uv*, *Vi*
imports from *Dbms*
  types
      User
end

Figure 3.6 Interface specification for the *Partition* data type

db_name. The name of the database.

owner. The user who owns the database.

partitions. This state element models the set of created partitions. The names of the created partitions should be unique and the set will always contain the most recently commited partition instance.

p_sessions. This map models partition sessions. Associated with each partition is a partition key. The range of this map will feature partitions drawn from *partitions* when the session was initiated by an *OPEN_PARTITION* operation.

p_modes. Once again, associated with each partition session, is a mode indicator which will be either READ or WRITE.

$$
\begin{aligned}
Database \;::\; &name &&: Db\_name \\
&owner &&: User \\
&partitions &&: Partition\text{-set} \\
&p\_sessions &&: P\_key \xrightarrow{m} Partition \\
&p\_modes &&: P\_key \xrightarrow{m} P\_mode
\end{aligned}
$$

inv $(mk\text{-}Database(n, o, p, ps, pm)) \triangleq$
　let *write_sessions* $= \{k \mid k \in \operatorname{dom} pm \land pm(pk) = \text{WRITE}\}$ in
　$\forall i, j \in write\_sessions \cdot$
　　　$i \neq j \implies p\_name\_is(ps(i)) \neq p\_name\_is(ps(j)) \land$
　let *part_names* $= \{p\_name\_is(entry) \mid entry \in p\}$ in
　let *session_p_names* $= \{p\_name\_is(entry) \mid entry \in \operatorname{rng} ps\}$ in
　$session\_p\_names \subseteq part\_names \land$
　$(\forall i, j \in p \cdot p\_name\_is(i) = p\_name\_is(j) \implies i = j) \land$
　$\operatorname{dom} ps = \operatorname{dom} pm$

The data type invariant states that:

1. No partition is associated with more than one WRITE session.

2. The names of partitions associated with sessions are a subset of the names of currently created partitions.

3. The names of created partitions are unique.

4. *p_sessions* and *p_modes* have the same domain set of keys.

The remaining type definitions are:

$P\_mode = \{\text{READ}, \text{WRITE}\}$

Dbr_types = Yes_no | P_key

Db_name, P_key is not yet defined

$close\_partitions : P\_key\text{-set} \times (P\_key \xrightarrow{m} Partition) \times$
$\qquad\qquad\qquad (P\_key \xrightarrow{m} P\_mode) \times Partition\text{-set} \times Partition\text{-set} \to \mathbb{B}$
$close\_partitions(pks, p\_ses, p\_mod, pre\_part, post\_part) \quad \triangle$
$\qquad$ let *updated_partitions* =
$\qquad\qquad \{pt \mid pt \in Partition \land p \in pks \land p\_mod(p) = \text{WRITE} \land$
$\qquad\qquad\qquad\qquad\qquad\qquad\qquad post\text{-}PCL(p\_ses(p), pt)\}$ in
$\qquad$ let *old_partitions* =
$\qquad\qquad \{pt \mid pt \in pre\_part \land p \in pks \land p\_mod(p) = \text{WRITE} \land$
$\qquad\qquad\qquad\qquad\qquad p\_name\_is(pt) = p\_name\_is(p\_ses(p))\}$ in
$\qquad post\_part = (pre\_part - old\_partitions) \cup updated\_partitions$

The function *close_partition* asserts that all write sessions in the paramaterized set of session keys are properly closed and that *partitions* will be updated to contain these latest instances.

$db\_owner : Database \to (User \to \mathbb{B})$
$db\_owner(state) \quad \triangle \quad \lambda user \cdot owner(state) = user$

This function returns true if the user is the owner of the database.

$db\_authorized : Database \to ((User \times P\_mode) \to \mathbb{B})$
$db\_authorized(state) \quad \triangle$
$\qquad \lambda user, mode \cdot$ let $mk\text{-}Database(\text{-}, \text{-}, partitions, \text{-}, \text{-}) = state$ in
$\qquad \exists entry \in partitions \cdot p\_authorized(entry)(user, mode)$

db_authorized returns true if the database allows the user access of the indicated mode. Note the use of VDM's 'don't care' entries in the **let** construct where the record of type *Database* is constructed. The '-' entries indicate that we are not interested in these fields and are therefore willing to accept any value constrained only by type and invariant.

$db\_name\_is : Database \to Db\_name$
$db\_name\_is(state) \quad \triangle \quad name(state)$

We now turn to the specification of the operations. As a contrast to the specification of *Partition*, exceptions will be specified using the notational extensions described in Chapter 9 of [Jon90]. Where exceptions are specified it is assumed that the state is *not* changed and assertions are made only to specify the result conditions. Additionally, exceptions have been specified to return FAILED in all cases; this is clearly unreasonable but suffices for the purpose of this exercise.

CLAP
ext wr *partitions* : *Partition*-set
　　wr *p_sessions* : $P\_key \xrightarrow{m} Partition$
　　wr *p_modes* : $P\_key \xrightarrow{m} P\_mode$
post let *p_keys* = dom *p_sessions* in

　　　close_partitions($\overleftarrow{p\_keys, p\_sessions, p\_modes, partitions}$, *partitions*)
　　　∧
　　　p_sessions = { } ∧ *p_modes* = { }

CLP (*pk*: *P_key*) *result*: *Yes_no*
ext wr *partitions* : *Partition*-set
　　wr *p_sessions* : $P\_key \xrightarrow{m} Partition$
　　wr *p_modes* : $P\_key \xrightarrow{m} P\_mode$
pre *pk* ∈ dom *p_sessions*

post *close_partitions*({*pk*}, $\overleftarrow{p\_sessions, p\_modes, partitions}$, *partitions*) ∧
　　　p_sessions = {*pk*} $\nTriangleleft \overleftarrow{p\_sessions}$ ∧ *p_modes* = {*pk*} $\nTriangleleft \overleftarrow{p\_modes}$ ∧
　　　result = OK
errs *INVALID_SESSION*: *pk* ∉ dom *p_sessions* → *result* = FAILED

The requirements for the *CLOSE_ALL_PARTITIONS* operation arose during the specification of *Dbms*. When a database is committed, for instance, it is required that *all* partitions be properly closed. The second operation is similar but is specific to a single partition. The first operation is not provided to users of the database system while the second is.

CPYP (*from*: *P_name*, *to*: *P_name*) *result*: *Yes_no*
ext wr *partitions* : *Partition*-set
　　rd *p_sessions* : $P\_key \xrightarrow{m} Partition$
pre ∃*entry_from* ∈ *partitions* · *p_name_is*(*entry_from*) = *from* ∧
　　∄*entry_to* ∈ *partitions* · *p_name_is*(*entry_to*) = *to* ∧
　　∄*entry* ∈ rng *p_sessions* · *p_name_is*(*entry*) = *from*

post ∃*entry* ∈ $\overleftarrow{partitions}$ ·
　　　　p_name_is(*entry*) = *from* ∧
　　　　partitions = $\overleftarrow{partitions}$ ∪ {*p_change_name*(*entry*)(*to*)} ∧
　　　　result = OK

errs *NO_SOURCE*: $\not\exists$*entry_from* $\in$ *partitions* ·
$\qquad$ *p_name_is(entry_from) = from* $\rightarrow$ *result* = FAILED
$\quad$ *TO_EXISTS*: $\exists$*entry_to* $\in$ *partitions* ·
$\qquad$ *p_name_is(entry_to) = to* $\rightarrow$ *result* = FAILED
$\quad$ *SESSION*: $\exists$*entry* $\in$ rng *p_sessions* ·
$\qquad$ *p_name_is(entry) = from* $\rightarrow$ *result* = FAILED

This operation duplicates a partition and renames it. The operation requires that the *from* partition exists, that there is no extant session on this partition and that no database exists with the same name as *to*.

CP (*nm*: *P_name*) *result*: *Yes_no*
ext wr *partitions* : *Partition*-set
pre $\not\exists p \in$ *partitions* · *p_name_is(p) = nm*
post $\exists p \in$ *Partition* · *Partition.post-INIT(nm, -, p)* $\wedge$
$\qquad$ *partitions* = $\overleftarrow{partitions}$ $\cup$ {*p*} $\wedge$ *result* = OK
errs *EXISTS*: $\exists p \in$ *partitions* ·
$\qquad$ *p_name_is(p) = nm* $\rightarrow$ *result* = FAILED

DP (*nm*: *P_name*) *result*: *Yes_no*
ext wr *partitions* : *Partition*-set
$\quad$ rd *p_sessions* : *P_key* $\xrightarrow{m}$ *Partition*
pre $\exists entry \in$ $\overleftarrow{partitions}$ · *p_name_is(entry) = nm* $\wedge$
$\quad$ $\not\exists entry \in$ rng *p_sessions* · *p_name_is(entry) = nm*
post $\exists entry \in$ $\overleftarrow{partitions}$ ·
$\qquad$ *p_name_is(entry) = nm* $\wedge$
$\qquad$ *partitions* = $\overleftarrow{partitions}$ $-$ {*entry*} $\wedge$ *result* = OK
errs *NOT_EXIST*: $\not\exists entry \in$ *partitions* ·
$\qquad$ *p_name_is(entry) = nm* $\rightarrow$ *result* = FAILED
$\quad$ *SESSION*: $\exists entry \in$ rng *p_sessions* ·
$\qquad$ *p_name_is(entry) = nm* $\rightarrow$ *result* = FAILED

These two operations create and delete partitions. The specifications should be fairly self-evident. Note the need to distinguish that the *INIT* operation is that operation associated with the type *Partition*.

INIT (*u*: *User*, *nm*: *Db_name*)

ext wr *name*   : *Db_name*

    wr *owner*   : *User*

    wr *partitions*   : *Partition*-set

    wr *p_sessions* : $P\_key \xrightarrow{m} Partition$

    wr *p_modes*   : $P\_key \xrightarrow{m} P\_mode$

post *name* = *nm* $\wedge$ *owner* = *u* $\wedge$ *partitions* = { } $\wedge$

    p_sessions = { } $\wedge$ *p_modes* = { }

INIT establishes the data type invariant for initial instances of the data type.

OPP (*u*: *User*, *nm*: *P_name*,

      mode: *P_mode*) *result*: *P_key* | *Yes_no*

ext rd *owner*   : *User*

    rd *partitions*   : *Partition*-set

    wr *p_sessions* : $P\_key \xrightarrow{m} Partition$

    wr *p_modes*   : $P\_key \xrightarrow{m} P\_mode$

pre $\exists$*entry* $\in$ *partitions* ·

        p_name_is(*entry*) = *nm* $\wedge$

        let *authorized_reader* = *p_authorized*(*entry*)(*u*, READ) in

        let *authorized_writer* = *p_authorized*(*entry*)(*u*, WRITE) in

        let *valid_owner* = (*u* = *owner*) in

        let *no_write_sessions* =

          $\nexists pk \in$ dom *p_sessions* ·

            p_name_is(*p_sessions*(*pk*)) = *nm* $\wedge$

                        p_modes(*pk*) = WRITE

      in

        (*mode* = WRITE $\Rightarrow$

            (*valid_owner* $\vee$ *authorized_writer*) $\wedge$ *no_write_sessions*)

        $\wedge$

        (*mode* = READ $\Rightarrow$

            valid_owner $\vee$ *authorized_reader* $\vee$ *authorized_writer*)

post $\exists$*entry* $\in$ *partitions* · *p_name_is*(*entry*) = *nm* $\wedge$

    let *key* $\notin$ dom $\overleftarrow{p\_sessions}$ in

    p_sessions = $\overleftarrow{p\_sessions}$ † {*key* $\mapsto$ *entry*} $\wedge$

    p_modes = $\overleftarrow{p\_modes}$ † {*key* $\mapsto$ *mode*} $\wedge$ *result* = OK

errs *INVALID_NAME*: $\nexists$ *entry* $\in$ *partitions* ·
        p_name_is(entry) = *nm* → *result* = FAILED
NOT_AUTHORIZED:
let *authorized_reader* = *p_authorized(entry)(u,* READ) in
let *authorized_writer* = *p_authorized(entry)(u,* WRITE) in
let *valid_owner* = (*u* = *owner*) in
(*mode* = WRITE ∧
¬ *authorized_writer* ∧ ¬ *valid_owner*) ∨
(*mode* = READ ∧
(¬ *valid_owner* ∧ ¬ *authorized_reader* ∧ ¬ *authorized_writer*))
                                                                        → *result* = FAILED

SESSION: *mode* = WRITE ∧
∃*pk* ∈ dom *p_sessions* ·
        p_name_is(p_sessions(pk)) = *nm* ∧ *p_modes(pk)* = WRITE
                                                                        → *result* = FAILED

Partition sessions are established by the *OPEN_PARTITION* operation. A session may only be established for a partition if the named partition exists and is owned by the nominated user or the user has access of the appropriate mode. Further, for write sessions, there should be no other write session associated with that partition.

RE (*present_name*: *P_name*, *new_name*: *P_name*) *result*: *Yes_no*
ext wr *partitions*   : *Partition*-set
    rd *p_sessions* : *P_key* $\xrightarrow{m}$ *Partition*
pre ∃*entry* ∈ *partitions* · *p_name_is(entry)* = *present_name* ∧
    $\nexists$ *entry* ∈ rng *p_sessions* · *p_name_is(entry)* = *present_name* ∧
    $\nexists$ *entry* ∈ *partitions* · *p_name_is(entry)* = *new_name*
post ∃*entry* ∈ $\overleftarrow{partitions}$ · *p_name_is(entry)* = *present_name* ∧
    partitions = ($\overleftarrow{partitions}$ − {*entry*}) ∪ {*p_change_name(entry)(new_name)*}
    ∧ *result* = OK
errs *NO_DB*: $\nexists$ *entry* ∈ *partitions* ·
        p_name_is(entry) = *present_name* → *result* = FAILED
    SESSION: ∃*entry* ∈ rng *p_sessions* ·
        p_name_is(entry) = *present_name* → *result* = FAILED
    NAME_EXISTS: ∃*entry* ∈ *partitions* ·
        p_name_is(entry) = *new_name* → *result* = FAILED

The *RENAME* operation renames an existing partition. The partition must not be involved in a session and the new name must be unique.

POPS (*pk*: *P_key*, *op*: *Partition_ops*) *result*: *Pr_types* ext wr *p_sessions* : *P_key* $\xrightarrow{m}$ *Partition*

   rd *p_modes*   : *P_key* $\xrightarrow{m}$ *P_mode*

pre *pk* ∈ dom *p_sessions* ∧ (*op* ∈ *Dv* ∨ *op* ∈ *Dlt* ∨ *op* ∈ *Ins* ∨ *op* ∈ *Uv*)
$$\Rightarrow p\_modes(pk) = \text{WRITE}$$

post let *pre-st* = $\overleftarrow{p\_sessions}(pk)$ in

    ∃*post-st* ∈ *Partition* ·

        cases *op* of

        mk-Bt(t)   → *post-BT(t, pre-st, post-st, result)*,

        mk-Ct(t)   → *post-CT(t, pre-st, post-st, result)*,

        mk-Dv(fv, iv) → *post-DV(fv, iv, pre-st, post-st, result)*,

        mk-Dlt(dt) → *post-DLT(dt, pre-st, post-st, result)*,

        mk-Gt(qk) → *post-GT(qk, pre-st, post-st, result)*,

        mk-Ga(u, a) → *post-GA(u, a, pre-st, post-st, result)*,

        mk-Ins(t)   → *post-INS(t, pre-st, post-st, result)*,

        mk-Sct(t)   → *post-SCT(t, pre-st, post-st, result)*,

        mk-Tv(fv, iv) → *post-TV(fv, iv, pre-st, post-st, result)*,

        mk-Uv(fv, iv) → *post-UV(fv, iv, pre-st, post-st, result)*,

        mk-Vi(v)   → *post-VI(v, pre-st, post-st, result)*,

        end

      ∧ *p_sessions* = $\overleftarrow{p\_sessions}$ † {*pk* ↦ *post-st*}

errs *INVALID_KEY*: *pk* ∉ dom *p_sessions* → *result* = FAILED

   NOT_WRITE: (*op* ∈ *Dv* ∨ *op* ∈ *Dlt* ∨ *op* ∈ *Ins* ∨ *op* ∈ *Uv*) ∧
$$p\_modes(pk) \neq \text{WRITE} \rightarrow result = \text{FAILED}$$

PARTITION_OPERATIONS specifies how partition operations are to be handled by the *Database* data type. Remember that partition operations only have meaning in the presence of a database instance. This operation reveals that all partition operations require a partition key which associates the partition operations with a particular partition instance. In addition, some of the operations can only be used within a write session.

When we specified *Partition*, abstract syntax representations for the various user operations were produced and exported through the interface specification. Those abstract syntax representations are used here. *PARTITION_OPERATIONS* accepts an argument of type *Partition_ops* and one of type *P_key*. All operations of type *Partition_ops* are specific to a particular partition and thus require a partition key as argument. In the post condition the individual operations are identified through their abstract syntax representation and each, individually, results in a specific *Partition* operation being quoted. Quotation is fully described in [Jon90].

Lastly, before defining the interface specification, we need to generate the abstract syntax for the *Database* operations. The types we require are defined as follows:

Database_ops = Clp | Cpyp | Cp | Dp | Opp | Re

Finally, the interface specification is shown in Figure 3.7.

module *Database*
exports
  operations
     CLAP: () $\xrightarrow{o}$,
     CLP: *P_key* $\xrightarrow{o}$ *Yes_no*,
     CPYP: *P_name* × *P_name* $\xrightarrow{o}$ *Yes_no*,
     CP: *P_name* $\xrightarrow{o}$ *Yes_no*,
     DP: *P_name* $\xrightarrow{o}$ *Yes_no*,
     INIT: *User* × *Db_name* $\xrightarrow{o}$,
     OPP: *User* × *P_name* × *P-mode* $\xrightarrow{o}$ *P_key* | *Yes_no*,
     RE: *P_name* × *P_name* $\xrightarrow{o}$ *Yes_no*,
     POPS: *P_key* × *Partition_ops* $\xrightarrow{o}$ *Pr_types*
  functions
     db_name_is: *Database* → *Db_name*,
     db_authorized: *Database* → ((*User* × *P_mode*) → $\mathbb{B}$),
     db_owner: *Database* → (*User* → $\mathbb{B}$)
  types
     Database_ops, Clp, Cpyp, Cp, Dp, Re, Opp,
     Dbr_types, Db_name, P_mode, P_key,
     Partition_ops, Bt, Ct, Dv, Dlv, Gt, Ga, Ins, Sct, Tv, Uv, Vi,
     Pr_types, Yes_no, Get_triple_result, Query_key, Verbname,
     R_triple, P_name, P_access, D_template, Template, Triple
imports from *Partition* all
imports from *Dbms*
types
     User
end

Figure 3.7 Interface specification for the *Database* data type

3.7 The *Dbms* data type

Repeating the specification pattern followed when defining the previous two data types we firstly produce the state model.

db_users. Here we model the entity set **Database_user** and, by using a map, associate each user with a boolean value indicating whether he or she is allowed (**true**) or is not allowed (**false**) to own a database. This is an important distinction. Only owners of databases may create them or write to them.

databases. The set of most recently created and committed databases.

db_sessions. A map from database session key to an associated database instance.

db_modes. Each session key is mapped to the session mode (read, write or owner).

The state outlined above follows almost directly from the entity/relationship analysis carried out in Section 3.3.

$$
\begin{aligned}
Dbms :: \ &db\_users && : \ User \xrightarrow{m} \mathbb{B} \\
&databases && : \ Database\text{-set} \\
&db\_sessions && : \ Sk \xrightarrow{m} Database \\
&db\_modes && : \ Sk \xrightarrow{m} Db\_mode
\end{aligned}
$$

$\text{inv } (mk\text{-}Dbms(du, db, dbs, dbm)) \triangleq$
  $\text{let } write\_sessions = \{k \mid k \in \text{dom } dbm \ \wedge$
$\qquad\qquad\qquad\qquad\qquad (dbm(k) = \text{WRITE} \vee dbm(k) = \text{OWNER})\} \text{ in}$
  $(\forall i, j \in write\_sessions \cdot i \neq j \ \Rightarrow$
$\qquad\qquad\qquad\qquad db\_name\_is(dbs(i)) \neq db\_name\_is(dbs(j))) \ \wedge$
  $\text{let } db\_names = \{db\_name\_is(entry) \mid entry \in db\} \text{ in}$
  $\text{let } session\_db\_names = \{db\_name\_is(entry) \mid entry \in \text{rng } dbs\} \text{ in}$
  $session\_db\_names \subseteq db\_names \ \wedge$
  $(\forall i, j \in db \cdot db\_name\_is(i) = db\_name\_is(j) \ \Rightarrow \ i = j) \ \wedge$
  $\text{dom } dbs = \text{dom } dbm \ \wedge$
  $\forall i \in db \cdot \exists j \in \text{dom } du \cdot db\_owner(i)(j) \wedge du(j)$

The data type invariant follows that developed for the data type *Database* with the addition of the final condition which states that all databases must have an owner who is a legitimate database owner, that is, no database can be owned by an unregistered user.

Associated types are now defined.

$Db\_mode = \{\text{READ}, \text{WRITE}, \text{OWNER}\}$

User, Sk is not yet defined

In the operation specifications that follow no exception conditions are specified. Pre conditions record the assumptions made by each of the operations.

$commit\_db : Sk \times Database\text{-set} \times Database\text{-set} \times (Sk \xrightarrow{m} Database) \rightarrow \mathbb{B}$

$commit\_db(sk, old\_dbs, new\_dbs, db\_sessions) \quad \triangle$

    let $dbname = db\_name\_is(db\_sessions(sk))$ in

    $\exists clean\_db \in Database \cdot$

        $post\text{-}CLAP(db\_sessions(sk), clean\text{-}db) \wedge$

        $\exists entry \in old\_dbs \cdot$

            $db\_name\_is(entry) = dbname \wedge$

            $new\_dbs = (old\_dbs - \{entry\}) \cup \{clean\_db\}$

The *commit_db* function commits the database referenced by the session key. All partitions are closed and the database instance noted as the most recently committed by placing it in *databases*.

$AN\ (sk{:}Sk)$

ext rd *databases*   : $Database\text{-set}$

    wr $db\_sessions$: $Sk \xrightarrow{m} Database$

    rd db_modes : $Sk \xrightarrow{m} Db\_mode$

pre $sk \in$ dom $db\_sessions \wedge$

    $(db\_modes(sk) = \text{WRITE} \vee db\_modes(sk) = \text{OWNER})$

post let $dbname = db\_name\_is(\overleftarrow{db\_sessions}(sk))$ in

    $\exists entry \in databases \cdot$

        $db\_name\_is(entry) = dbname \wedge$

        $db\_sessions = \overleftarrow{db\_sessions} \dagger \{sk \mapsto entry\}$

The *ANNUL* operation causes a database session to be annulled. The session key must be valid and the session must be a write or owner session. Note that the existing session key is unchanged but becomes associated with the most recently committed database. As the database has a current write or owner session associated with it we can safely pick up the last committed version because no other write or owner session will have been allowed.

$ANS\ (sk{:}Sk)$

ext wr $db\_sessions$: $Sk \xrightarrow{m} Database$

    wr db_modes : $Sk \xrightarrow{m} Db\_mode$

pre $sk \in$ dom $db\_sessions \wedge$

    $(db\_modes(sk) = \text{WRITE} \vee db\_modes(sk) = \text{OWNER})$

post $db\_sessions = \{sk\} \triangleleft \overleftarrow{db\_sessions} \wedge$

    $db\_modes = \{sk\} \triangleleft \overleftarrow{db\_modes}$

This operation, *ANNUL_SESSION*, annuls a session removing both the session key and the associated database instance.

COM (*sk*: *Sk*)
ext wr *databases*   : *Database*-set
    rd *db_sessions* : *Sk* $\xrightarrow{m}$ *Database*
    rd *db_modes*   : *Sk* $\xrightarrow{m}$ *Db_mode*
pre *sk* ∈ dom *db_sessions* ∧
    (*db_modes*(*sk*) = WRITE ∨ *db_modes*(*sk*) = OWNER)
post *commit_db*(*sk*, $\overleftarrow{databases}$, *databases*, *db_sessions*)

The *COMMIT* operation causes the current read or owner session database to be committed. A copy of a 'tidy' version of the database is made and is stored as the most recently committed instance of the database. The session then continues.

CDB (*u*: *User*, *nm*: *Db_name*)
ext rd *db_users*   : *User* $\xrightarrow{m}$ $\mathbb{B}$
    wr *databases* : *Database*-set
pre *u* ∈ dom *db_users* ∧ *db_users*(*u*) ∧
    $\nexists$*entry* ∈ *databases* · *db_name_is*(*entry*) = *nm*
post ∃*entry* ∈ *Database* ·
            Database.post-INIT(*u*, *nm*, -, *entry*) ∧ *databases* = $\overleftarrow{databases}$ ∪ {*entry*}

DDB (*u*: *User*, *nm*: *Db_name*)
ext rd *db_users*   : *User* $\xrightarrow{m}$ $\mathbb{B}$
    wr *databases*   : *Database*-set
    rd *db_sessions* : *Sk* $\xrightarrow{m}$ *Database*
pre *u* ∈ dom *db_users* ∧ *db_users*(*u*) ∧
    (∃*entry* ∈ *databases* ·
        db_name_is(*entry*) = *nm* ∧ *db_owner*(*entry*)(*u*)) ∧
    (*∄entry* ∈ rng *db_sessions* · *db_name_is*(*entry*) = *nm*)
post ∃*entry* ∈ $\overleftarrow{databases}$ · *db_name_is*(*entry*) = *nm* ∧
    databases = $\overleftarrow{databases}$-{*entry*}

The two operations specified above create and delete databases. In the first instance no database must exist with the indicated name and in the second case a named instance of the database must exist and no sessions should be associated with an instance of that database. A database may only be created by a user who is authorized to own databases, while a database may only be deleted by its owner.

ES (*sk*: *Sk*)

ext wr *databases*   : *Database*-set
   wr *db_sessions* : $Sk \xrightarrow{m} Database$
   wr *db_modes*   : $Sk \xrightarrow{m} Db\_mode$
pre *sk* ∈ dom *db_sessions*
post $((db\_modes(sk) = \text{WRITE} \vee db\_modes(sk) = \text{OWNER}) \wedge$

$$commit\_db(sk, \overleftarrow{databases}, databases, db\_sessions)$$

$$\vee$$

$$(db\_modes(sk) = \text{READ} \wedge databases = \overleftarrow{databases}))$$

$$\wedge$$

$$db\_sessions = \{sk\} \nleftarrow \overleftarrow{db\_sessions} \wedge db\_modes = \{sk\} \nleftarrow \overleftarrow{db\_modes}$$

The *END_SESSION* operation terminates a read, write or owner session. In the case of owner or write databases the associated database instance is tidied and made the most recently committed version of that database by replacing the previous version.

SS (u: User, nm: Db_name, mode: Db_mode) key: Sk
ext rd *db_users*   : $user \xrightarrow{m} \mathbb{B}$
   rd *databases*   : *Database*-set
   wr *db_sessions* : $Sk \xrightarrow{m} Database$
   wr *db_modes*   : $Sk \xrightarrow{m} Db\_mode$
pre ∃*entry* ∈ *databases* ·
       db_name_is(entry) = *nm* ∧
       let *authorized_reader* = *db_authorized(entry)(u,* READ) in
       let *authorized_writer* = *db_authorized(entry)(u,* WRITE) in
       let *valid_owner* = *db_owner(entry)(u)* in
       let *s_keys* = {*sk* | *sk* ∈ dom *db_sessions* ∧
                        db_name_is(db_sessions(sk)) = *nm*} in
       let *no_write_owner_session* =
        ∄*k* ∈ *s_keys* ·
           db_modes(k) = WRITE ∨ *db_modes(k)* = OWNER   in
       (*mode* = OWNER ⇒ *valid_owner* ∧ *no_write_owner_session*)
       ∧
       (*mode* = WRITE ⇒
          (*authorized_writer* ∨ *valid_owner*) ∧ *no_write_owner_session*)
       ∧
       (*mode* = READ
              ⇒ *authorized_reader* ∨ *authorized_writer* ∨ *valid_owner*)

post let *key* $\notin$ dom *db_sessions* in
    $\exists$*entry* $\in$ *databases* ·
        db_name_is(entry) = *nm* $\wedge$
        db_sessions = $\overleftarrow{db\_sessions}$ † {*key* $\mapsto$ *entry*} $\wedge$
    db_modes = $\overleftarrow{db\_modes}$ † {*key* $\mapsto$ *mode*}

Sessions may be started when the following conditions, asserted in the pre condition, hold:

1. The named database exists.

2. If the session mode indicates an owner session then the database must be owned by the indicated user and there must not be an existing owner or write session on that database.

3. If the session mode is write then the user must be authorized to write to a partition in the database or the user must be the owner and must still be allowed to own a database. Further, no write or owner sessions should be associated with that database.

4. If the session is a read session then the user must be allowed read access to at least one partition in the database or the user must be the owner of the database and still be registered as a database owner.

DBOPS (*sk*: *Sk*, *pk*: [*P_key*],
        op: *Partition_ops* | *Database_ops*) *res*: *Dbr_types* | *Pr_types*
ext rd *db_users*   : *User* $\xrightarrow{m}$ $\mathbb{B}$
    wr *db_sessions* : *Sk* $\xrightarrow{m}$ *Database*
    rd *db_modes*   : *Sk* $\xrightarrow{m}$ *Db_mode*
pre *sk* $\in$ dom (*db_sessions*) $\wedge$
    (*op* $\in$ *Cpyp* $\vee$ *op* $\in$ *Cp* $\vee$ *op* $\in$ *Dp* $\vee$ *op* $\in$ *Re* $\vee$ *op* $\in$ *Ga*) $\Rightarrow$
                                  db_modes(sk) = OWNER $\wedge$
    op $\in$ *Partition_ops* $\Rightarrow$ *pk* $\neq$ NIL $\wedge$
    op $\in$ *Ga* $\Rightarrow$ (let *mk-Ga(u, -)* = *op* in
    u $\in$ dom *db_users*)

post let *pre-st* = $\overleftarrow{db\_sessions}(sk)$ in
      ∃*post-st* ∈ *Partition* ·
           cases *op* of
           mk-Clp(pk)   → *post-CLP(pk, pre-st, post-st, res)*,
           mk-Cpyp(f, t)   → *post-CPYP(f, t, pre-st, post-st, res)*,
           mk-Cp(nm)   → *post-CP(nm, pre-st, post-st, res)*,
           mk-Dp(nm)   → *post-DP(nm, pre-st, post-st, res)*,
           mk-Opp(u, nm, md) → *post-OPP(u, nm, md, pre-st, post-st, res)*,
           mk-Re(on, nn)   → *post-RE(on, nn, pre-st, post-st, res)*,
           others *post-POPS(pk, op, pre-st, post-st, res)*
           end
           ∧ *db_sessions* = $\overleftarrow{db\_sessions}$ † {*sk* ↦ *post-st*}

The interface specification for *Dbms* is given in Figure 3.8

module *Dbms*
exports
   operations
      AN: Sk $\overset{o}{\to}$,
      ANS: Sk $\overset{o}{\to}$,
      COM: Sk $\overset{o}{\to}$,
      CDB: User × Db_name $\overset{o}{\to}$,
      DDB: User × Db_name $\overset{o}{\to}$,
      ES: Sk $\overset{o}{\to}$,
      SS: User × Db_name × Db_mode $\overset{o}{\to}$ *Sk*,
      DBOPS: Sk × [P-key] × Partition_ops | Database_ops $\overset{o}{\to}$

                                            Dbr_types | Pr_types
   types
     Sk, User, Db_mode,
     Database_ops, Clp, Cpp, Cp, Dp, Op, Re,
     Dbr_types, Db_name, P_mode, P_key,
     Partition_ops, Bt, Ct, Dv, Dlt, Gt, Ga, Ins, Sct, Tv, Uv, Vi,
     Pr_types, Yes_no, Get_triple_result, Query_key, Verbname,
     R_triple, P_name, P_access, D_template, Template, Triple
imports from *Database* all
end

Figure 3.8 Interface specification for the *Dbms* data type

4

Muffin: A Proof Assistant

Richard C. Moore

As has already been seen, the use of formal methods introduces the idea of proof obligations, that is, theorems which record desirable properties of our specifications or development steps. How do we go about discharging these proof obligations? What automated support can be provided to help with this task? Richard Moore's chapter discusses these issues. Restricting itself to the propositional calculus, the paper first considers proof style and the various strategies that might be adopted when proving a simple theorem. Having identified how proofs may be performed, the chapter then presents a specification of a proof editor which will support the strategies identified in the earlier discussion. Although only the specification is given here, a development using Smalltalk 80 has been undertaken. Subsequent work by the same group has built a system which handles more general logics.

4.1   Introduction

The prime objective of the formal reasoning work in the Alvey/SERC supported IPSE
2.5 project [JL88, War89] is to design and build a theorem proving assistant which will
provide sufficient support for the task that a user will be encouraged to use it to actually
discover formal proofs rather than just to check the details of proofs already sketched
out on paper. The general consensus amongst the researchers at Manchester University
and Rutherford Appleton Laboratory who are engaged in this part of the project is that
two things in particular could go a long way towards helping achieve this aim. First, the
system should be sufficiently flexible to allow the user to work as 'naturally' as possible;
specifically, it should impose no fixed order of working on the user, and it should allow
the user access to all of its functionality. Second, it should have sufficient 'knowledge'
of the mathematics that it is supporting to allow it both to help the user to decide what
to do next by offering a selection of possible actions consistent with the underlying
mathematics and to advise on the existence of any inconsistencies. The emphasis is,
therefore, on a user-driven, machine-supported theorem prover rather than vice versa.

Very early in the project, an investigation of existing theorem proving systems was
undertaken [Lin88]. Not one of the systems surveyed satisfied all our requirements as
set out above, and it was therefore decided that some experimentation of our own with
user interface issues was required. The resulting system, known as *Muffin* for reasons
which are likely to remain totally obscure here, is the subject of this paper.

Muffin's emphasis as an experiment in the design of a user interface to a theorem
proving assistant meant that it could be restricted to dealing with a single, simple self-
contained branch of mathematics, in fact the propositional calculus. In addition, initial
ideas on the exact form of the surface user interface (i.e. the appearance of the screen)
were somewhat nebulous. The first stage of the development of Muffin therefore consisted of designing and specifying a theorem store for the propositional calculus. This
abstract theorem store could then be 'viewed' in a range of different ways by simply
coding different 'projection functions' on top of it, thus allowing experimentation with
the surface user interface. Having fixed on the surface functionality, the specification
was then extended to cover the whole system.[1] It is interesting to note that this additional
specification exercise led to the discovery of a couple of bugs in the code.

4.2   Proofs in the propositional calculus

Consider the following two statements:

---

[1]Lesser mortals are asked to spare a thought at this point for all true VDM aficionados, who will
undoubtedly have just been sent into paroxysms of foaming at the mouth and demented teeth-gnashing by
this heinous admission.

1. All pink elephants can fly.

2. The only things that can fly are birds, planes and survivors of the wholesale destruction of the planet Krypton.

>From these, together with the two 'obvious' statements

3. An elephant is not a bird.

4. An elephant is not a plane.

most readers should have little difficulty in deducing that

5. All pink elephants are survivors of the wholesale destruction of the planet Krypton.

Let us first rewrite these five statements in terms of six propositions:

(A) X is an elephant.

(B) X is pink.

(C) X can fly.

(D) X is a bird.

(E) X is a plane.

(F) X is a survivor of the wholesale destruction of the planet Krypton.

They turn into:

1'. If X is an elephant <u>and</u> X is pink <u>Then</u> X can fly.

2'. If X can fly <u>Then</u> X is a bird <u>or</u> X is a plane <u>or</u> X is a survivor of the wholesale destruction of the planet Krypton.

3'. If X is an elephant <u>Then</u> X is <u>not</u> a bird.

4'. If X is an elephant <u>Then</u> X is <u>not</u> a plane.

5'. If X is an elephant <u>and</u> X is pink <u>Then</u> X is a survivor of the wholesale destruction of the planet Krypton.

Symbolically,

1''. $A \wedge B \vdash C$

2''. $C \vdash D \vee E \vee F$

3″. $A \vdash \neg\, D$

4″. $A \vdash \neg\, E$

5″. $A \wedge B \vdash F$

The *sequents* express the fact that the proposition on the right of the 'turnstile' ($\vdash$) can be deduced from the proposition(s) on the left, and $\wedge$, $\vee$ and $\neg$ represent <u>and</u>, <u>or</u> and <u>not</u> respectively.

To establish the validity of statement 5, we first assume that both proposition A (X is an elephant) and proposition B (X is pink) are true. Statement 1 then tells us that proposition C is true (X can fly), whence, with the help of statement 2, it follows that either proposition D is true (X is a bird) or proposition E is true (X is a plane) or proposition F is true (X is a survivor of the wholesale destruction of the planet Krypton). Since we know that proposition A is true (X is an elephant), however, statements 4 and 5 allow us to deduce that both proposition D and proposition E are false (X is not a bird; X is not a plane). The only remaining alternative is therefore that proposition F is true (X is a survivor of the wholesale destruction of the planet Krypton). Thus the sequent

5″. $A \wedge B \vdash F$

is established as a valid inference.

The sorts of argument leading to the result above are exactly the same sorts of argument used in proofs in the propositional calculus, the only difference being that the above example employed reasoning about specific propositions whereas the propositional calculus deals with reasoning about propositions in the abstract. Thus, expressions in the propositional calculus are built up from the operators $\neg$ (not), $\wedge$ (and), $\vee$ (or), $\Rightarrow$ (implies) and $\Leftrightarrow$ (equivalence),[2] together with letters to represent the propositions. The fact that one expression follows from another is still represented as a sequent. Note that a sequent with nothing to the left of its turnstile means that whatever is to the right of the turnstile follows from no assumptions: that is, it is itself true. This is exactly what is meant when we write an expression alone, so that a sequent with an empty set of assumptions is equivalent to an expression.

Valid deductions in the propositional calculus are represented by *inference rules*. These have one or more hypotheses and a conclusion, and are often written with the hypotheses and conclusion respectively above and below a horizontal line. An example of such an inference rule is the $\wedge$-E_r (and-elimination-right) rule:

$$\wedge\text{-}E_r \qquad \frac{E_1 \wedge E_2}{E_1}$$

---

[2]The operators are listed in order of decreasing priority.

which effectively corresponds to the statement:

<u>If</u> E_1 <u>and</u> E_2 <u>Then</u> E_1

Note, however, that this represents a valid deduction for *any* propositions E_1, E_2. It can therefore be used to justify results such as:

$(p \lor q) \land (p \lor r) \vdash p \lor q$

Another 'obvious' rule is the $\land$-*I* (and-introduction) rule:

$\land$-*I* $\dfrac{E_1;\ E_2}{E_1 \land E_2}$

which corresponds to the statement:

<u>If both</u> E_1; E_2 <u>Then</u> E_1 <u>and</u> E_2

This could, however, be stated equivalently as either:

<u>If</u> E_1 <u>Then</u> (<u>If</u> E_2 <u>Then</u> E_1 <u>and</u> E_2)

or:

<u>If</u> E_2 <u>Then</u> (<u>If</u> E_1 <u>Then</u> E_1 <u>and</u> E_2)

corresponding respectively to:

$\land$-*I'* $\dfrac{E_1}{E_2 \vdash E_1 \land E_2}$

$\land$-*I''* $\dfrac{E_2}{E_1 \vdash E_1 \land E_2}$

There is thus some duplication inherent in the above description, which is generally removed by insisting that the conclusion of an inference rule should not be a sequent.

A more complicated inference rule, which has sequents among its hypotheses, is the $\lor$-*E* (or-elimination) rule:

$\lor$-*E* $\dfrac{E_1 \lor E_2;\qquad E_1 \vdash E;\qquad E_2 \vdash E}{E}$

This states that if $E_1 \lor E_2$ is known and if some conclusion E has been shown to follow from each of the disjuncts E_1 and E_2, then E can be deduced, or, alternatively:

<u>If all</u> $E_1 \lor E_2$; (<u>If</u> E_1 <u>Then</u> E); (<u>If</u> E_2 <u>Then</u> E) <u>Then</u> E

This rule thus provides a way of reasoning by cases and can be used to justify, for instance, the deduction of $p \vee q \wedge r$ from the three 'knowns' $p \vee q, p \vdash p \vee q \wedge r$ and $q \vdash p \vee q \wedge r$.

Although the individual rules, such as $\wedge$-E_r, might not in themselves appear to be particularly useful, combinations of these rules can be used to build larger proofs and thus establish nontrivial results. One way of presenting such proofs is shown in Figure 4.1.

```
from (p ∨ q) ∧ (p ∨ r)
1      p ∨ q                                              ∧-Eᵣ(h)
2      from p
       infer p ∨ q ∧ r                                   <??>
3      from q
3.1        p ∨ r                                          ∧-Eₗ(h)
3.2        from r
3.2.1          q ∧ r                                      ∧-I(h3,h3.2)
           infer p ∨ q ∧ r                                <??>
       infer p ∨ q ∧ r                                    ∨-E(2,3.1,3.2)
infer p ∨ q ∧ r                                           ∨-E(1,2,3)
```

Figure 4.1 A partial proof

Here, the body of line 1 (i.e. $p \vee q$) has been deduced by applying the rule $\wedge$-E_r to the overall hypothesis $(p \vee q) \wedge (p \vee r)$, referred to in line 1 as h, and the overall conclusion $p \vee q \wedge r$ has been justified by appeal to the instance of the $\vee$-E rule above, applied to line 1 and boxes 2 and 3. Notice how sequent hypotheses in the $\vee$-E rule are justified by appeal to boxes: the hypotheses of the sequent appear on the from line of the box, the conclusion of the sequent on the infer line.

Of course, the fact that the conclusion of the proof is justified does not mean that the proof as a whole is complete – not all of the things used to justify the conclusion are themselves justified. In fact, this example nicely illustrates two aspects of the kind of freedom of action Muffin aims to support. First, there is the ability to reason both 'forwards' and 'backwards'. Forward inferencing corresponds to the creation of lines like line 1 in Figure 4.1 which can be deduced, either directly or indirectly, from the overall hypotheses of the proof. The set of such valid deductions, together with the proof's hypotheses, are called the 'knowns' of the proof. In the example of Figure

4.1 the knowns are thus the two expressions $(p \lor q) \land (p \lor r)$ and $p \lor q$. Backwards inferencing, on the other hand, effectively amounts to filling in the proof from the bottom (the overall conclusion) upwards. Thus, in Figure 4.1 the overall conclusion is justified by appeal to an application of the $\lor$-E rule to the (justified) line 1 and the (unjustified) boxes 2 and 3. The 'goal' of proving $p \lor q \land r$ has therefore been reduced to three 'subgoals', namely to proving $p \lor q$, which has indeed already been established, and the two sequents $p \vdash p \lor q \land r$ and $q \vdash p \lor q \land r$.

Some progress towards establishing the validity of the second of this pair of sequents has indeed already been made. Thus, line 3.1 follows from the overall hypothesis analogously to line 1, this time via the $\land$-E_l (and-elimination-left) rule:

$$\land\text{-}E_l \qquad \frac{E_1 \land E_2}{E_2}$$

and the conclusion of box 3 has again been justified by appeal to the $\lor$-E rule, here applied to the (justified) line 3.1 and the (unjustified) boxes 2 and 3.2. One forward step has also been created in box 3.2, where line 3.2.1 has been deduced by applying the $\land$-I rule to the hypothesis of box 3 and that of box 3.2.

In order to complete the proof of Figure 4.1, the conclusions of both box 2 and box 3.2 need to be correctly justified. It is worth looking at these steps in some detail. The conclusion of box 2 could in principle be correctly justified by appeal to any of the following:

- p – the local hypothesis of box 2.

- $(p \lor q) \land (p \lor r)$ – the overall hypothesis.

- $p \lor q$ – a conclusion which depends only on *outer* hypotheses.

In other words, the knowns of box 2 plus the knowns of all its containing boxes (in this case only the box corresponding to the proof as a whole). Thus, in trying to justify the conclusion of box 2 we are effectively trying to validate the sequent:

$(p \lor q) \land (p \lor r); \ p \lor q; \ p \vdash p \lor q \land r$

This can be done straightforwardly by appeal to the $\lor$-I_r (or-introduction-right) rule:

$$\lor\text{-}I_r \qquad \frac{E_1}{E_1 \lor E_2}$$

which justifies:

$p \vdash p \lor q \land r$

This completes the justification of everything in box 2.

Suppose, however, that the $\vee$-I_r rule had not been shown to be valid. In such a case, a user of Muffin could abandon the proof of Figure 4.1 in the state shown, prove the $\vee$-I_r rule, then return to the current proof some time later and complete the proof of box 2 by appeal to the new $\vee$-I_r rule. This illustrates the second aspect of freedom of action alluded to above that Muffin supports.

Turning attention to box 3.2, its conclusion can similarly be correctly justified by appeal to any of its knowns (in this case both r and $q \wedge r$) or to any of the knowns of its containing boxes. Note that, since box 2 is now completely justified, the sequent $p \vdash p \vee q \wedge r$ which it represents has become a known of the overall proof. Lines and indeed boxes (were there any) inside box 2 are, however, not knowns available within box 3 as they depend on assumptions (namely p) which do not hold there.

The proof of box 3.2 is completed by appeal to the rule $\vee$-I_l (or-introduction-left), analogous to $\vee$-I_r used to justify the conclusion of box 2:

$$\vee\text{-}I_l \qquad \frac{E_2}{E_1 \vee E_2}$$

The proof as a whole is now complete and is shown in Figure 4.2.

from $(p \vee q) \wedge (p \vee r)$
1	$p \vee q$	$\wedge$-E_r(h)
2	from p	
	infer $p \vee q \wedge r$	$\vee$-I_r(h2)
3	from q	
3.1	$p \vee r$	$\wedge$-E_l(h)
3.2	from r	
3.2.1	$q \wedge r$	$\wedge$-I(h3,h3.2)
	infer $p \vee q \wedge r$	$\vee$-I_l(3.2.1)
	infer $p \vee q \wedge r$	$\vee$-E(2,3.1,3.2)
	infer $p \vee q \wedge r$	$\vee$-E(1,2,3)

Figure 4.2 Proof (one direction) that $\vee$ distributes over $\wedge$

One final point, which is important for the understanding of Muffin, is that this complete proof justifies a new *derived* inference rule, namely:

$$\frac{(E_1 \vee E_2) \wedge (E_1 \vee E_3)}{E_1 \vee E_2 \wedge E_3}$$

This rule is then available for use in future proofs in just the same way as the rules mentioned so far.

4.3   The formal specification of Muffin's theorem store

The Muffin theorem store should support all the notions of partial proofs, complete proofs, inference rules, etc. as introduced in the previous section. This section shows how these can be described in VDM. It is important to realize, however, that the specification as developed here is an *abstract* description of the objects introduced above. Thus, for example, the partial proof shown in Figure 4.1 above is one possible 'projection' or 'view' of the underlying abstract object representing an incomplete proof.

Expressions, sequents and problems

The fundamental entities in Muffin are, of course, expressions. As explained above, these are built up from the logical operators $\neg$, $\wedge$, $\vee$, etc.[3] together with letters to represent propositions. In abstract terms, propositions can therefore be represented by some infinite set of structureless tokens. For want of some better name, we shall call them *Atoms*. In the examples of Section 4.2 *Atoms* are being projected as letters.

A composite expression like $p \vee q \wedge r$ can be thought of most simply as some logical operator, here $\vee$, having other expressions as its operands. *Atoms* are therefore to be considered as a kind of expression. The logical operators fall into two distinct classes, unary operators like $\neg$ which have a single operand, and binary operators like $\wedge$ which have two operands.

It is normal in specifications to describe such objects in terms of 'trees', so that, for example, the tree-forms *Tnot* and *Tand* of $\neg$ and $\wedge$ respectively would have the form:

> *Tnot* :: *tn* : *Texp*

> *Tand* :: *tandl* : *Texp*
>   *tandr* : *Texp*

with

> *Texp* = *Atom* | *Tnot* | *Tand* | ...

In such a description, a tree-form unary expression like *Tnot* has a single operand, which is either an *Atom* or some composite tree-form expression, and a tree-form binary ex-

---

[3]A particular set of operators has, in fact, been chosen and is built into Muffin. This is, however, largely for convenience and is by no means crucial. The (fairly simple) modifications that have to be made to the specification developed here in order to accommodate a user-defined set of operators can be found in [Moo87].

pression like *Tand* has both a left and a right operand, each of which is either an *Atom* or a composite tree-form expression. Thus, the expression $p \lor q \land r$ would actually correspond to:

$$mk\text{-}Tor(a_p, mk\text{-}Tand(a_q, a_r))$$

where a_p, a_q and a_r are *Atoms* representing p, q and r respectively.

In these terms, a tree-form sequent (rather inexplicably called *Tsubseq* here) would have a set of tree-form expressions to the left of its turnstile and a single tree-form expression to the right. A *Tsubseq* could then be described in terms of a *left-hand side* and a *right-hand side* as:

$$Tsubseq \; :: \; tlhs \; : \; Texp\text{-set}$$
$$trhs \; : \; Texp$$
$$\text{inv} \; (mk\text{-}Tsubseq(l, r)) \triangleq l \neq \{ \; \}$$

The invariant removes the duplication between expressions and sequents with empty left-hand sides.[4]

Turning attention next to inference rules and proofs, it is clear that some sort of interdependency is needed which is more general than the tree representation described above: a derived inference rule is to have some associated proof(s), the lines of which are justified by appeal to inference rules. The set of inference rules and their proofs thus has a graph-like rather than a tree-like structure, which is normally modelled in formal specifications by associating each object with some sort of structureless reference object.

In fact, it is also possible to treat expressions as graph-like objects, with expressions being associated with some references to expressions (*Exprefs*) via some *expression store* (*Expstore*):

$$Expstore = Expref \xrightarrow{m} Exp$$

where

$$Exp = Atom \mid Not \mid And \mid \dots$$

In such a scheme, expressions have references to expressions rather than expressions themselves as their operands, so that, for example, *Not* and *And* are described by:

$$Not \; :: \; not \; : \; Expref$$

$$And \; :: \; andl \; : \; Expref$$
$$andr \; : \; Expref$$

---

[4]The alternative approach, namely that more complex objects do not contain expressions at all but rather have them represented as sequents with empty left-hand sides, would also have been perfectly feasible.

In order to ensure that this description makes sense, some consistency conditions have to be imposed on the *Expstore*. First, any reference appearing as an operand in some expression in the range of the *Expstore* should be in its domain. This condition ensures that all expressions are completely defined and is itself expressed by the function *is-closed*:

$$is\text{-}closed : Expref \xrightarrow{m} Exp \rightarrow \mathbb{B}$$
$$is\text{-}closed(m) \quad \triangle \quad \forall x \in \mathsf{rng}\, m \cdot args(x) \subseteq \mathsf{dom}\, m$$

This closure condition on the *Expstore* is equivalent to saying that all sub-expressions (*args*) of any expression in the *Expstore* are defined in the *Expstore*. The other consistency condition states that no expression should be a sub-expression of itself:

$$is\text{-}finite : Expref \xrightarrow{m} Exp \rightarrow \mathbb{B}$$
$$is\text{-}finite(m) \quad \triangle \quad \forall y \in \mathsf{dom}\, m \cdot \neg \exists x \in \mathsf{rng}\, trace(\{y\}, m) \cdot y \in args(x)$$

The function *trace* effectively finds the sub-map of *m* having as its domain some set of expressions, in this case the unit set containing *y*, and all their sub-expressions. Full details of the auxiliary functions *args* and *trace*, and indeed the full Muffin specification, can be found in [JM88].

The full invariant on the *Expstore* is therefore:

$$inv\text{-}Expstore : Expstore \rightarrow \mathbb{B}$$
$$inv\text{-}Expstore(es) \quad \triangle \quad is\text{-}closed(es) \wedge is\text{-}finite(es)$$

In this scheme, a *Subseq* has a set of references to expressions as its left-hand side and a single reference to an expression as its right-hand side. The invariant that the left-hand side should not be empty remains:

$$
\begin{aligned}
Subseq :: \quad & lhs \ : \ Expref\text{-set} \\
& rhs \ : \ Expref
\end{aligned}
$$
$$\mathsf{inv}\,(mk\text{-}Subseq(l, r)) \triangle l \neq \{\,\}$$

References are associated with *Subseqs* via the *Subseqstore*:

$$Subseqstore = Subseqref \xrightarrow{m} Subseq$$

For consistency, any *Expref* occurring in the *exps* (that is, the left-hand side plus the right-hand side) of a *Subseq* in the *Subseqstore* should be in the *Expstore*:

$$is\text{-}valid\text{-}subseqstore : Subseqstore \times Expstore \rightarrow \mathbb{B}$$
$$is\text{-}valid\text{-}subseqstore(ss, es) \quad \triangle \quad \forall q \in \mathsf{rng}\, ss \cdot exps(q) \subseteq \mathsf{dom}\, es$$

For convenience, expressions and sequents are collectively referred to as *Nodes*:

$$Tnode = Texp \mid Tsubseq$$

Node = Expref | Subseqref

These form the building blocks for more complex objects in Muffin.

Before proceeding, it is worth reviewing the processes to be supported in Muffin. To begin with, a user will want to define a set of *axioms* for the propositional calculus. These will have the same form as inference rules but will not have associated proofs. The user should then be able to create other objects of the same syntactic form as inference rules (we shall call them *problems*) and try to prove them. Two main classes of problem can therefore be distinguished. On the one hand there are *unsolved problems*, problems which are neither axioms nor have some associated complete proof.[5] On the other hand there are *solved problems*, of which three sub-classes can conveniently be distinguished. First, axioms, which are problems having the special status of being proved but which have no associated proofs.[6] Second, there are derived inference rules, solved problems with at least one associated complete proof and third, there are all the rest of the solved problems, those which are neither axioms nor derived inference rules.[7]

All these classes of problem can be described in terms of a single abstract object, called *Problem*. It has a set of *Nodes* ((references to) expressions and/or sequents) as its hypotheses, and a single (reference to an) expression as its conclusion (cf the ∨-*E* rule).[8]

$$Problem \; :: \; hyp \; : \; Node\text{-set}$$
$$con \; : \; Expref$$

Again, *Problems* are associated with references to *Problems* (*Problemrefs*), this time via the *Problemstore*:

$$Problemstore = Problemref \xleftarrow{\;m\;} Problem$$

The *Problemstore* should be consistent with the *Subseqstore* and the *Expstore* in that the *nodes* (that is, the hypotheses plus the conclusion) of any *Problem* in the *Problemstore* should be in either the *Subseqstore* or the *Expstore*, whichever is appropriate:

$$is\text{-}valid\text{-}problemstore : Problemstore \times Subseqstore \times Expstore \rightarrow \mathbb{B}$$
$$is\text{-}valid\text{-}problemstore(ps, ss, es) \; \triangle \; \forall o \in \mathsf{rng}\, ps \cdot nodes(o) \subseteq \mathsf{dom}\, ss \cup \mathsf{dom}\, es$$

---

[5]They may, of course, have a whole cart-load of incomplete proofs.

[6]That's right, neither complete nor incomplete.

[7]Muffin's inference rules are its axioms plus its derived inference rules, just as you would expect.

[8]Recall the equivalence explained above which allowed the restriction that no sequent should appear as the conclusion of an inference rule.

Proofs

The last primitive object we need to be able to describe is a proof. Let us first consider only complete proofs, in particular the one shown in Figure 4.2. A cursory perusal of this proof reveals a marked similarity between the proof as a whole and any of its boxes (e.g. box 3) – each has a set of hypotheses (the from line) and a conclusion (the infer line) and contains some list of lines and boxes. In fact the only difference between a proof and a box is that the hypotheses of a proof can contain sequent hypotheses whereas those of a box cannot. (Recall that a box is used to justify a sequent hypothesis in some rule, with the hypotheses of the box consisting of the left-hand side of the sequent to be so justified and the conclusion of the box the right-hand side of that sequent. Since the left-hand side of a sequent is a set of expressions, the hypotheses of a box will also be a set of expressions.) This suggests a picture in which a box and a proof are described by the same abstract object.

We have already seen how validating a box corresponds to proving a problem whose conclusion is the expression on the infer line of the box and whose hypotheses are the knowns available inside the box. This is, however, not a good picture to adopt overall as adding lines to containing boxes can change the knowns available inside the box and hence the effective hypotheses of its corresponding problem. The picture can, however, be made unambiguous by noting that it is sufficient to take the effective hypotheses of the problem representing a box to be the hypotheses of the box itself plus the *hypotheses* of all its containing boxes – any nonhypothesis knowns omitted under this scheme can be regenerated inside the box in question via the same set of steps as was used to generate them in their actual positions in the proof, as all the hypotheses on which they depend will be available there. Redrawing the proof of Figure 4.2 in this scheme leads to the alternative projection shown in Figure 4.3. Notice how all the boxes are now disjoint, i.e. all justifications of lines inside a box only refer to things also inside the box.

The last step of the abstraction comes about by rewriting the lines with justifications as sequents. A line like line 1 is effectively recording the fact that its body $p \vee q$ can be deduced by applying the $\wedge\text{-}E_r$ rule to the overall hypothesis $(p \vee q) \wedge (p \vee r)$, or equivalently that $(p \vee q) \wedge (p \vee r) \vdash p \vee q$ is a valid instance of the $\wedge\text{-}E_r$ rule. This results in the alternative projection of Figure 4.3 shown in Figure 4.4.

Here, each line of a proof consists of a problem together with some proof of that problem. That proof can be simply a reference to some inference rule (when the problem is simply an instance of that inference rule) or it can itself be a list of lines. In abstract terms, a proof can therefore be either an *instantiation*, an inference rule together with a mapping recording how atoms in the rule's statement are to be replaced by expressions in order to build the required instance of the rule, or a *composite proof*, a sequence of solved problems. Proofs are also assigned references, this time via the *Proofstore*.

from $(p \vee q) \wedge (p \vee r)$

1	$p \vee q$	$\wedge\text{-}E_r(\text{h})$
2	from p; $(p \vee q) \wedge (p \vee r)$	
	infer $p \vee q \wedge r$	$\vee\text{-}I_r(\text{h}2_1)$
3	from q; $(p \vee q) \wedge (p \vee r)$	
3.1	$p \vee r$	$\wedge\text{-}E_l(\text{h}3_2)$
3.2	from p; q; $(p \vee q) \wedge (p \vee r)$	
	infer $p \vee q \wedge r$	$\vee\text{-}I_r(\text{h}3.2_1)$
3.3	from r; q; $(p \vee q) \wedge (p \vee r)$	
3.3.1	$q \wedge r$	$\wedge\text{-}I(\text{h}3.3_1, \text{h}3.3_2)$
	infer $p \vee q \wedge r$	$\vee\text{-}I_l(3.3.1)$
	infer $p \vee q \wedge r$	$\vee\text{-}E(3.1, 3.2, 3.3)$
	infer $p \vee q \wedge r$	$\vee\text{-}E(1, 2, 3)$

Figure 4.3 Modularized version of Figure 4.2

$$Instantiation :: of : Problemref$$
$$by : Atom \xrightarrow{m} Expref$$
$$\text{inv } (mk\text{-}Instantiation(o, m)) \triangleq m \neq \{ \}$$

$$Composite\text{-}proof = Problemref^*$$

$$Proof = Instantiation \mid Composite\text{-}proof$$

$$Proofstore = Proofref \xrightarrow{m} Proof$$

Note that the invariant on *Instantiation* says that the mapping defining the substitution should not be empty: that is, some substitution should actually be performed. This is to remove the redundancy corresponding to a problem being considered as an instance of itself.

For ease of testing equality, the *Expstore*, *Subseqstore* and *Problemstore* have all been described by 1-1 mappings. Such a restriction turns out to be impractical for proofs, however, because new complete proofs are going to be built by editing (i.e. adding and/or removing steps to/from) incomplete proofs and sometimes different references to essentially the same proof might be needed. (For example, the user might get part way through some proof and then not be able to see exactly how to proceed. Allowing duplication of the current state of the proof at this point would permit the exploration of

<u>from</u> $(p \vee q) \wedge (p \vee r)$
<u>infer</u> $p \vee q \wedge r$
      <u>by</u>

1	$(p \vee q) \wedge (p \vee r) \vdash p \vee q$		$\wedge\text{-}E_r$
2	<u>from</u> $p;\ (p \vee q) \wedge (p \vee r)$		
	<u>infer</u> $p \vee q \wedge r$		
	<u>by</u>		
	2.1 $p \vdash p \vee q \wedge r$		$\vee\text{-}I_r$
3	<u>from</u> $q;\ (p \vee q) \wedge (p \vee r)$		
	<u>infer</u> $p \vee q \wedge r$		
	<u>by</u>		
	3.1 $(p \vee q) \wedge (p \vee r) \vdash p \vee r$		$\wedge\text{-}E_l$
	3.2 <u>from</u> $p;\ q;\ (p \vee q) \wedge (p \vee r)$		
	<u>infer</u> $p \vee q \wedge r$		
	<u>by</u>		
	3.2.1 $p \vdash p \vee q \wedge r$		$\vee\text{-}I_r$
	3.3 <u>from</u> $r;\ q;\ (p \vee q) \wedge (p \vee r)$		
	<u>infer</u> $p \vee q \wedge r$		
	<u>by</u>		
	3.3.1 $q;\ r \vdash q \wedge r$		$\wedge\text{-}I$
	3.3.2 $q \wedge r \vdash p \vee q \wedge r$		$\vee\text{-}I_l$
	3.4 $p \vee r;\ p \rightsquigarrow p \vee q \wedge r;\ r \rightsquigarrow p \vee q \wedge r$		
	$\vdash p \vee q \wedge r$		$\vee\text{-}E$
4	$p \vee r;\ p \rightsquigarrow p \vee q \wedge r;\ q \rightsquigarrow p \vee q \wedge r \vdash p \vee q \wedge r$		$\vee\text{-}E$

Figure 4.4 The proof of Figure 4.2 in Muffin style

different possibilities.) Since there is no concept of editing an *Instantiation*, however, it is possible to restrict the *Proofstore* in such a way that it assigns a unique reference to each *Instantiation*. The following invariant is therefore imposed on the *Proofstore*:

$$inv\text{-}Proofstore : Proofstore \to \mathbb{B}$$
$$inv\text{-}Proofstore(fs) \quad \triangle$$
$$\forall p, q \in \operatorname{dom} fs \cdot fs(p) = fs(q) \wedge is\text{-}instantiation(fs(p)) \implies p = q$$

The exactly opposite position is in fact taken for composite proofs – indeed, parts of the consistency conditions on the *Proofmap* and the *Incomplete-proofmap* (see below) will insist that any *Proofref* referencing a composite proof should not belong to more than one problem. This is actually rather stronger than is absolutely necessary, however, and it would be possible to weaken it such that sharing of *complete* composite proofs was allowed but sharing of *incomplete* ones was not.

In addition, the *Proofstore* has to satisfy the usual consistency condition, namely that all components of each proof in it are in the *Expstore*, the *Subseqstore* or the *Problemstore* as appropriate. For an instantiation this amounts to the conditions that the problem being instantiated (its of field) should be in the *Problemstore*, that the domain of the substitution mapping (its by field) should be a subset of the *Atoms* appearing in that problem, that the expressions in the range of the substitution mapping should all be in the *Expstore*, and that the substitution should not replace some *Atom* with (a reference to) itself. For a composite proof the condition states simply that all elements of the proof should be in the *Problemstore*. The full consistency condition is therefore:

$$is\text{-}valid\text{-}proofstore \ (fs\text{:}\ Proofstore, ps\text{:}\ Problemstore,$$
$$ss\text{:}\ Subseqstore, es\text{:}\ Expstore)\ r\text{:}\ \mathbb{B}$$
pre *is-valid-subseqstore(ss, es)* $\land$ *is-valid-problemstore(ps, ss, es)*
post $r \iff$
$$\forall v \in \mathsf{rng}\, fs \cdot (is\text{-}instantiation(v)$$
$$\Rightarrow\ is\text{-}valid\text{-}instantiation(v, ps, ss, es)) \ \land$$
$$(is\text{-}composite\text{-}proof(v)\ \Rightarrow\ is\text{-}valid\text{-}composite(v, ps))$$

An instantiation is a complete proof of some problem if that problem is obtained as a result of performing the substitution of expressions for atoms defined in its by field on the problem representing the inference rule defined in its of field. A composite proof is a complete proof of some problem if the knowns of the problem with respect to the proof include the conclusion of the problem.

The knowns of a problem p with respect to some composite proof c are obtained as follows:

- If c has no elements, the knowns are just the hypotheses of the problem p.

- If c is not empty, the ith element v of c contributes a new known to the set of knowns k collected from the first $i - 1$ elements of c according to the following rules:

  1. If the hypotheses of v are all in k, the new known is the conclusion of v.

  2. If not, but if there is some sequent s in the *Subseqstore* such that the right-hand side of s is the conclusion of v and the left-hand side of s added to the hypotheses of p gives the hypotheses of v, then the new known is s.

  3. If neither of the above, v contributes no new known to k:

new-known (*p*: *Problemref*, *k*: *Node*-set, *v*: *Problemref*,
        ps: *Problemstore*, *ss*: *Subseqstore*) *r*: *Node*-set
pre $\{p, v\} \subseteq$ dom *ps*
post *r* = if *hyp*(*ps*(*v*)) $\subseteq$ *k*
      then $\{con(ps(v))\}$
      else if $\exists s \in$ dom *ss* ·
                 lhs(*ss*(*s*)) $\cup$ *hyp*(*ps*(*p*)) = *hyp*(*ps*(*v*)) $\wedge$ *rhs*(*ss*(*s*)) = *con*(*ps*(*v*))
        then $\{s\}$
        else $\{\,\}$

Notice how this works in Figure 4.4. Line 1 contributes $p \vee q$ to the knowns, line 2 contributes the sequent $p \vdash p \vee q \wedge r$, line 3 the sequent $q \vdash p \vee q \wedge r$, and line 4 the desired conclusion $p \vee q \wedge r$. Similarly, in box 2, line 2.1 adds its conclusion directly, whilst in box 3 line 3.1 adds $p \vee r$ to its knowns, box 3.2 adds $p \vdash p \vee q \wedge r$, box 3.3 adds $r \vdash p \vee q \wedge r$, and line 3.4 adds its conclusion $p \vee q \wedge r$. Finally, in box 3.2 the conclusion is added directly by line 3.2.1, and in box 3.3 line 3.3.1 adds $q \vee r$ and its conclusion is added by line 3.3.2.

So far only complete proofs like that in Figure 4.2 have been considered. Does this picture work for incomplete proofs like the one in Figure 4.1 too? Let us begin by rewriting that proof in the style of Figure 4.4. The result is shown in Figure 4.5.

At the top level, boxes 2 and 3 remain incomplete, although completing the proofs of boxes 3.2 and 3.3 would be sufficient to complete box 3. The top level proof at this point therefore can contain only lines 1 and 4 – it can not contain boxes 2 and 3 as only solved problems can occur in a proof. The proof at box 2 is empty. Similarly, the proof at box 3 contains just lines 3.1 and 3.4 and that at box 3.2 is empty. Finally, the proof at box 3.3 contains the single line 3.3.1.

As explained earlier, this proof uses examples of both forward and backward inferencing. Thus at the top level line 1 is an example of a forward inferencing step whilst line 4 is an example of backward inferencing – the former adds to the knowns (in this case $p \vee q$) and the latter reduces a goal to subgoals (here, $p \vee q \wedge r$ has been reduced to $p \vee q$, $p \vdash p \vee q \wedge r$ and $q \vdash p \vee q \wedge r$). To progress in the proof, the user can add either forward steps, thereby increasing the knowns, or add backward steps and reduce some goal to subgoals. This amounts to adding new elements to the *middle* of the list constituting an incomplete composite proof. In order to describe incomplete proofs in the above picture we therefore need to know the position in the sequence of elements of an incomplete composite proof marking the division between the forward and the backward steps. This is done by recording the position of the last element of the forward proof in the *Indexmap*:

    Indexmap = *Proofref* $\xrightarrow{m}$ $\mathbb{N}$

<u>from</u> $(p \vee q) \wedge (p \vee r)$
<u>infer</u> $p \vee q \wedge r$
      <u>by</u>
      1          $(p \vee q) \wedge (p \vee r) \vdash p \vee q$ $\wedge\text{-}E_r$
      2   <u>from</u> $p;\ (p \vee q) \wedge (p \vee r)$
                 <u>infer</u> $p \vee q \wedge r$
                       <u>by</u>
                       <??>
      3   <u>from</u> $q;\ (p \vee q) \wedge (p \vee r)$
                 <u>infer</u> $p \vee q \wedge r$
                       <u>by</u>
                       3.1 $(p \vee q) \wedge (p \vee r) \vdash p \vee r$ $\wedge\text{-}E_l$
                       3.2   <u>from</u> $p;\ q;\ (p \vee q) \wedge (p \vee r)$
                                    <u>infer</u> $p \vee q \wedge r$
                                          <u>by</u>
                                          <??>
                       3.3   <u>from</u> $r;\ q;\ (p \vee q) \wedge (p \vee r)$
                                    <u>infer</u> $p \vee q \wedge r$
                                          <u>by</u>
                                          3.3.1 $q;\ r \vdash q \wedge r$ $\wedge\text{-}I$
                                          <??>
                       3.4 $p \vee r;\ p \rightsquigarrow p \vee q \wedge r;\ r \rightsquigarrow p \vee q \wedge r$
                                          $\vdash p \vee q \wedge r$ $\vee\text{-}E$
      4          $p \vee r;\ p \rightsquigarrow p \vee q \wedge r;\ q \rightsquigarrow p \vee q \wedge r \vdash p \vee q \wedge r$ $\vee\text{-}E$

Figure 4.5 The incomplete proof of Figure 4.1 in Muffin style

Next, some record of which proofs, complete and incomplete, are associated with which problems is needed. The *Proofmap* and the *Incomplete-proofmap* store this information

$$Proofmap = Problemref \xrightarrow{m} Proofref\text{-set}$$

$$Incomplete\text{-}proofmap = Problemref \xrightarrow{m} Proofref\text{-set}$$

Note that each maps a *Problemref* to a *set* of *Proofref* – a problem may have many proofs, both complete and incomplete.

There are essentially two different but equivalent ways in which a problem could have no incomplete proofs in this scheme. Either it could map to the empty set under the *Incomplete-proofmap* or it could simply not appear in the domain thereof. In Muffin, the (arbitrary) choice that the latter is the case is made, thus allowing the restriction that the empty set should not occur in the range of the *Incomplete-proofmap*. The restriction that no two problems should have composite proofs in common leads to the second clause of the invariant on the *Incomplete-proofmap*:

$inv\text{-}Incomplete\text{-}proofmap : Incomplete\text{-}proofmap \rightarrow \mathbb{B}$
$inv\text{-}Incomplete\text{-}proofmap(im) \quad \triangle$
$\quad \{\} \notin \mathsf{rng}\,im \wedge \forall k, m \in \mathsf{dom}\,im \cdot im(k) \cap im(m) \neq \{\} \ \Rightarrow \ k = m$

The solved problems are those appearing in the domain of the *Proofmap*. All other problems, that is those in the domain of the *Problemstore* but not in that of the *Proofmap*, are unsolved. The axioms of Muffin are made to conform to this definition by mapping them to the empty set under the *Proofmap*.

Some subset of the solved problems is designated as the rules of inference of Muffin. These problems, which should include all the axioms, are distinguished by giving them names via the *Rulemap*. Again, no two rules may have the same name and the empty string is not a valid name.

$Rulemap = String \xleftarrow{m} Problemref$
$\mathsf{inv}\ rm \triangle [\,] \notin \mathsf{dom}\,rm$

The consistency condition on the *Rulemap* states that all rules should be solved problems, that all axioms should be rules, and that all instantiations should be instances of rules:

$is\text{-}valid\text{-}rulemap : Rulemap \times Proofmap \times Proofstore \rightarrow \mathbb{B}$
$is\text{-}valid\text{-}rulemap(rm, jm, fs) \quad \triangle$
$\quad axioms(jm) \subseteq rules(rm) \wedge rules(rm) \subseteq solved\text{-}problems(jm) \wedge$
$\quad \forall p \in complete\text{-}proofs(jm) \cdot$
$\quad\quad\quad p \in \mathsf{dom}\,fs \ \Rightarrow \ (is\text{-}instantiation(fs(p)) \ \Rightarrow \ of(fs(p)) \in rules(rm))$

The consistency condition on the *Proofmap* is somewhat more complicated. The easy bits state that all solved problems (i.e. everything in the domain of the *Proofmap*) should be in the *Problemstore*, that no two problems share a complete composite proof, and that all proofs attached to a problem via the *Proofmap* are in the *Proofstore*, contain only solved problems in their components, and are actually complete proofs of that problem. The hard bit says that the set of solved problems and their proofs should be logically sound. This bit is further complicated by the fact that a solved problem can in principle have more than one complete proof. This means that circularities can exist in the problem-proof graph – a user might prove a rule *A* directly from the axioms of the system, then construct a proof of a rule *B* in which some line is justified by appeal to the derived rule *A*, and finally construct a second proof of the rule *A* in which some line is justified by appeal to the derived rule *B*, all without destroying the logical soundness of the system (because there is a proof of *A* which does not depend on the rule *B*). The statement of logical soundness for Muffin is therefore that each solved problem should be derivable, at least in principle, directly from the axioms of the system (*is-self-consistent*):

> *is-self-consistent* (*jm*: *Proofmap*, *fs*: *Proofstore*) *r*: $\mathbb{B}$
> pre *complete-proofs*(*jm*) $\subseteq$ dom *fs*
> post *r* $\iff$ *solved-problems*(*jm*) = *derivable-results*(*jm*, *fs*, *axioms*(*jm*))

The full consistency condition on the *Proofmap* then reads:

> *is-valid-proofmap* (*jm*: *Proofmap*, *fs*: *Proofstore*, *ps*: *Problemstore*,
>   *ss*: *Subseqstore*, *es*: *Expstore*) *r*: $\mathbb{B}$
> pre *is-valid-subseqstore*(*ss*, *es*) $\wedge$ *is-valid-problemstore*(*ps*, *ss*, *es*) $\wedge$
>   *is-valid-proofstore*(*fs*, *ps*, *ss*, *es*)
>
> post *r* $\iff$
>   *solved-problems*(*jm*) $\subseteq$ dom *ps* $\wedge$ *complete-proofs*(*jm*) $\subseteq$ dom *fs* $\wedge$
>   *is-self-consistent*(*jm*, *fs*) $\wedge$
> $\forall u \in$ *solved-problems*(*jm*) $\cdot$ $\forall v \in jm(u) \cdot$
>   *problems*(*fs*(*v*)) $\subseteq$ dom *jm* $\wedge$ *is-complete-proof*(*fs*(*v*), *u*, *ps*, *ss*, *es*) $\wedge$
> $\forall k, m \in$ dom *jm* $\cdot$
>   ($\exists v \in jm(k) \cap jm(m) \cdot$ *is-composite-proof*(*fs*(*v*))) $\Rightarrow$ *k* = *m*

The validity condition on the *Incomplete-proofmap* is built up similarly. First, any problem in its domain must be in the *Problemstore* and any incomplete proof attached to that problem in the *Proofstore*. In fact, this condition is extended to state that the *Proofstore* contains only those proofs which are attached to some problem via either the *Proofmap* or the *Incomplete-proofmap*. Here, however, the proof must *not* be a complete proof of the problem, though it must still consist only of solved problems. In addition, no proof should be both an incomplete proof of some problem and a complete proof of some other. Finally, Muffin views the building of an *Instantiation* as an essentially single-step process and provides no operations for editing existing ones. This effectively means that only complete *Instantiations* are considered, thus allowing the restriction that no *Instantiation* should occur in any element in the range of the *Incomplete-proofmap*.

> *is-valid-incomplete-proofmap* (*im*: *Incomplete-proofmap*, *jm*: *Proofmap*,
>   *fs*: *Proofstore*, *ps*: *Problemstore*,
>   *ss*: *Subseqstore*, *es*: *Expstore*) *r*: $\mathbb{B}$
> pre *is-valid-subseqstore*(*ss*, *es*) $\wedge$ *is-valid-problemstore*(*ps*, *ss*, *es*) $\wedge$
>   *is-valid-proofstore*(*fs*, *ps*, *ss*, *es*) $\wedge$ *is-valid-proofmap*(*jm*, *fs*, *ps*, *ss*, *es*)

post r ⇔ dom im ⊆ dom ps ∧ $axioms(jm)$ ∩ dom im = { } ∧
   $complete\text{-}proofs(jm)$ ∪ $incomplete\text{-}proofs(im)$ = dom fs ∧
   $complete\text{-}proofs(jm)$ ∩ $incomplete\text{-}proofs(im)$ = { } ∧
   $∀u ∈$ dom $im · ∀v ∈ im(u) · problems(fs(v))$ ⊆ $solved\text{-}problems(jm)$ ∧
   $is\text{-}composite\text{-}proof(fs(v))$ ∧ ¬ $is\text{-}complete\text{-}proof(fs(v), u, ps, ss, es)$

As we have already seen, incomplete proofs consist effectively of two parts, the *forward proof* and the *backward proof*, with the proof as a whole being the concatenation of the backward proof onto the forward proof. When attempting to convert an incomplete proof of some problem into a complete proof thereof, new elements can be added either to the tail of the forward proof or to the head of the backward proof, corresponding respectively to forward inferencing and backward inferencing. The index of the last element of the forward proof is stored in the *Indexmap*.

The elements of the forward proof give rise to all the knowns, with part of the validity condition on the *Indexmap* being that each element of the forward proof should actually contribute to the knowns. The elements of the backward proof, on the other hand, provide a proof of the conclusion of the relevant problem from some set of subgoals. Proving all these subgoals would be sufficient to complete the proof. In this case, a new element can be added to the head of the backward proof if the conclusion of that element is amongst the current subgoals. This condition also forms part of the validity constraint.

Another part of the validity condition on the *Indexmap* states that the backward proof should contain no element all of whose hypotheses are among the current knowns – such an element would correctly contribute its conclusion to the knowns and should therefore be positioned at the tail of the forward proof. Finally, the *Indexmap* should record an index for each incomplete proof but for no complete proof, with the value of that index lying somewhere between zero and the number of elements in the proof.

$is\text{-}valid\text{-}indexmap$ (xm: *Indexmap*, im: *Incomplete-proofmap*, jm: *Proofmap*,
         fs: *Proofstore*, ps: *Problemstore*,
         ss: *Subseqstore*, es: *Expstore*) r: $\mathbb{B}$
pre $is\text{-}valid\text{-}subseqstore(ss, es)$ ∧ $is\text{-}valid\text{-}problemstore(ps, ss, es)$ ∧
   $is\text{-}valid\text{-}proofstore(fs, ps, ss, es)$ ∧ $is\text{-}valid\text{-}proofmap(jm, fs, ps, ss, es)$ ∧
   $is\text{-}valid\text{-}incomplete\text{-}proofmap(im, jm, fs, ps, ss, es)$

post dom $xm = incomplete\text{-}proofs(im) \land \forall u \in \text{dom } im \cdot \forall v \in im(u) \cdot$
   let $fp = forward\text{-}proof(v, fs, xm),$
       $bp = backward\text{-}proof(v, fs, xm),$
       $gp = reverse(bp)$ in
   $0 \leq xm(v) \leq \text{len } fs(v) \land$
   $\neg \exists z \in \text{rng } bp \cdot hyp(ps(z)) \subseteq knowns(u, hyp(ps(u)), fp, ps, ss) \land$
   $\forall g \in \text{dom } gp \cdot$
       $con(ps(gp(g))) \in goals(\{con(ps(u))\}, \{g, \dots, \text{len } gp\} \triangleleft gp, ps) \land$
   $\forall b \in \text{dom } fp \cdot$
       $adds\text{-}known(u, knowns(u, hyp(ps(u)), \{b, \dots, \text{len } fp\} \triangleleft fp, ps, ss),$
                                                                        $fp(b), ps, ss)$

Finally, each of the primitive objects introduced above can be given a name in Muffin so that a user can more easily identify those objects of particular interest. The names are stored in a name store, mapping strings to the appropriate class of reference object, for each of the basic types of object. There is a restriction that no two objects of the same type can have the same name, and another that the empty string is not a valid name. The *ProofNames* map is typical of the class:

$ProofNames = String \xleftarrow{\; m \;} Proofref$
inv $fn \triangleq [\,] \notin \text{dom } fn$

$String = Character^*$

The consistency condition for each name store ensures that only objects in the relevant object store are assigned names, for example:

$is\text{-}valid\text{-}proofnames : ProofNames \times Proofstore \rightarrow \mathbb{B}$
$is\text{-}valid\text{-}proofnames(fn, fs) \quad \triangleq \quad \text{rng } fn \subseteq \text{dom } fs$

Putting all this together leads to the following description of the full Muffin state:

Muffin :: *es* : *Expstore*
     ss : *Subseqstore*
     ps : *Problemstore*
     fs : *Proofstore*
     en : *ExpNames*
     sn : *SubseqNames*
     pn : *ProblemNames*
     fn : *ProofNames*
     jm : *Proofmap*
     rm : *Rulemap*
     im : *Incomplete-proofmap*
     xm : *Indexmap*

inv $(mk\text{-}Muffin(es, ss, ps, fs, en, sn, pn, fn, jm, rm, im, xm)) \triangleq$
  is-valid-subseqstore(ss, es) $\wedge$ *is-valid-problemstore(ps, ss, es)* $\wedge$
  is-valid-proofstore(fs, ps, ss, es) $\wedge$ *is-valid-expnames(en, es)* $\wedge$
  is-valid-subseqnames(sn, ss) $\wedge$ *is-valid-problemnames(pn, ps)* $\wedge$
  is-valid-proofnames(fn, fs) $\wedge$ *is-valid-proofmap(jm, fs, ps, ss, es)* $\wedge$
  is-valid-rulemap(rm, jm, fs) $\wedge$
  is-valid-incomplete-proofmap(im, jm, fs, ps, ss, es) $\wedge$
  is-valid-indexmap(xm, im, jm, fs, ps, ss, es)

4.4 Operations on the Muffin state

This section explores some of the exciting things one might want to do to the Muffin state in the process of building up a theory of the propositional calculus. The reader is referred to the full specification [JM88] for the complete story.

First of all, it is almost certainly going to be useful to be able to build new expressions, sequents and problems. There are two methods provided for this. The first of them allows a new object to be built provided all the objects needed to make up its fields already exist, the second builds an instance of some existing object by replacing *Atoms* occurring within it with existing expressions. Thus you can add a new expression to the *Expstore* if the immediate sub-expressions of that expression are already in the *Expstore*:

add-exp $(x: Exp)$ $y: Expref$
ext wr *es* : *Expstore*
pre $args(x) \subseteq$ dom *es*
post $x \in$ rng $\overleftarrow{es} \wedge y \in$ dom $\overleftarrow{es} \wedge \overleftarrow{es}(y) = x \wedge es = \overleftarrow{es}$ $\vee$
   $x \notin$ rng $\overleftarrow{es} \wedge y \notin$ dom $\overleftarrow{es} \wedge es = \overleftarrow{es} \cup \{y \mapsto x\}$

and you can add a new sequent to the *Subseqstore* if all the expressions you want it to consist of are already in the *Expstore*:

add-subseq (z: *Expref*-set, y: *Expref*) g: *Subseqref*
ext rd *es* : *Expstore*
   wr *ss* : *Subseqstore*
pre $z \cup \{y\} \subseteq$ dom *es* $\wedge z \neq \{\,\}$
post let $t = mk\text{-}Subseq(z, y)$ in
$$t \in \text{rng } \overleftarrow{ss} \wedge g \in \text{dom } \overleftarrow{ss} \wedge \overleftarrow{ss}(g) = t \wedge ss = \overleftarrow{ss} \vee$$
$$t \notin \text{rng } \overleftarrow{ss} \wedge g \notin \text{dom } \overleftarrow{ss} \wedge ss = \overleftarrow{ss} \cup \{g \mapsto t\}$$

Finally, you can add a new problem to the *Problemstore* if all the sequents and expressions you want to make it out of are in the *Subseqstore* and the *Expstore* respectively.[9]

add-problem (n: *Node*-set, y: *Expref*) u: *Problemref*
ext rd *es* : *Expstore*
   rd *ss* : *Subseqstore*
   wr *ps* : *Problemstore*
pre $y \in$ dom *es* $\wedge n \subseteq$ dom *es* $\cup$ dom *ss*
post let $t = mk\text{-}Problem(n, y)$ in
$$t \in \text{rng } \overleftarrow{ps} \wedge u \in \text{dom } \overleftarrow{ps} \wedge \overleftarrow{ps}(u) = t \wedge ps = \overleftarrow{ps} \vee$$
$$t \notin \text{rng } \overleftarrow{ps} \wedge u \notin \text{dom } \overleftarrow{ps} \wedge ps = \overleftarrow{ps} \cup \{u \mapsto t\}$$

Alternatively, you can add new expressions to the *Expstore* by building instances of old ones. The function *is-substitution* appearing in the pre-condition essentially ensures that *Atoms* are only replaced with existing expressions. The invariant on the *Expstore* is maintained by adding not only the new instantiated expression but also any sub-expressions (*descendents*) which are not already in the *Expstore*.

instantiate-exp (y: *Expref*, m: *Atom* $\xrightarrow{m}$ *Expref*) r: *Expref*
ext wr *es* : *Expstore*
pre $y \in$ dom *es* $\wedge$ *is-substitution*($\{y\}, m, \{\,\}, es$)
post $\overleftarrow{es} \subseteq es \wedge r \in$ dom *es* $\wedge$ *is-exp-match*(y, r, m, es) $\wedge$
$$\text{dom } es = \text{dom } \overleftarrow{es} \cup descendents(\{r\}, es)$$

New sequents and problems can also be added by this method, but the operations for doing this are even more unspeakable than the above. They are all in the full specification, of course.

    Flushed with success at having created a new problem, you will no doubt be eager to call it 'fred', in which case the operation *name-problem* is just the thing you will need.

---

[9]The functions *add-subseq* and *add-problem*, although depressingly similar to *add-exp*, are included here because their pre-conditions are incorrect in [JM88].

Its pre-condition means, however, that you can only name some problem 'fred' if the problem exists and if no other problem is called 'fred', though it rather magnanimously allows you to call a problem 'fred' if it is already called 'fred'. Not only that, but if the problem is actually called 'gladys' it gets renamed 'fred'. And that's not all. Naming something with the empty string actually unnames it.

name-problem (*n*: *String*, *p*: *Problemref*)
ext wr *pn* : *ProblemNames*
  rd *ps* : *Problemstore*
pre *p* ∈ dom *ps* ∧ (*n* ∈ dom *pn* ⟹ *pn*(*n*) = *p*)
post *n* ∈ dom $\overleftarrow{pn}$ ∧ *pn* = $\overleftarrow{pn}$ ∨ *n* = [ ] ∧ *pn* = $\overleftarrow{pn}$ ▷ {*p*} ∨
  n ∉ dom $\overleftarrow{pn}$ ∧ *n* ≠ [ ] ∧ *pn* = ($\overleftarrow{pn}$ ▷ {*p*}) ∪ {*n* ↦ *p*}

The operations for naming expressions, sequents and proofs are entirely analogous.

So you have a new problem called 'fred'. What can you do with it? One thing you might want to do is throw it away. There is a catch here, though. You can only throw away unsolved problems (on the grounds that throwing away a solved problem is dangerous – it might have been used to justify some step in a proof of some other problem[10]). Not only that, but it is not just a case of removing it from the *Problemstore* and the *ProblemNames* either – it might have a whole slew of incomplete proofs. In that case, it also has to be removed from the domain of the *Incomplete-proofmap* and any proofs which were attached to it there have to be removed from the *Proofstore*, their names from the *ProofNames*, and their indices from the *Indexmap*:

remove-problem (*p*: *Problemref*)
ext wr *ps* : *Problemstore*
  wr *fs* : *Proofstore*
  wr *im* : *Incomplete-proofmap*
  wr *xm* : *Indexmap*
  wr *pn* : *ProblemNames*
  wr *fn* : *ProofNames*
  rd *jm* : *Proofmap*
pre *p* ∈ dom *ps* ∧ *p* ∉ dom *jm*

---

[10]Of course, it would be possible to get around this and write an operation for throwing away solved problems. The only snag would be that proofs using it would become invalid, so that some problems would have to revert from being solved problems to being unsolved problems, then any proofs using those would become invalid, so more problems would go back to being unsolved, etc. Such an operation is, thankfully, outside Muffin's scope.

$$\text{post } ps = \{p\} \vartriangleleft \overleftarrow{ps} \wedge pn = \overleftarrow{pn} \vartriangleright \{p\} \wedge$$
$$(p \in \text{dom } \overleftarrow{im} \wedge im = \{p\} \mathbin{\overline{\vartriangleleft}} \overleftarrow{im} \wedge fs = \overleftarrow{im}(p) \mathbin{\overline{\vartriangleleft}} \overleftarrow{fs} \wedge$$
$$xm = \overleftarrow{im}(p) \mathbin{\overline{\vartriangleleft}} \overleftarrow{xm} \wedge fn = \overleftarrow{fn} \vartriangleright \overleftarrow{im}(p)$$
$$\vee\; p \notin \text{dom } \overleftarrow{im} \wedge im = \overleftarrow{im} \wedge fs = \overleftarrow{fs} \wedge xm = \overleftarrow{xm} \wedge fn = \overleftarrow{fn})$$

Another thing you might want to do to your wonderful new problem is make it an axiom of your system. To do this you have to give it a name (some non-empty string) in the *Rulemap*. If the problem in question is already an axiom, the effect of the operation *make-axiom* is simply to rename it, though unnaming it by renaming it with the empty string (which amounts to removing it from the set of axioms) is not allowed as this might destroy the logical soundness of the system. In addition, the pre-condition will not let you convert a derived rule to an axiom – after all, if you have already proved something from your existing axioms, turning it into an axiom gains you nothing. Converting an unsolved problem to an axiom is thus the only case of any interest. Here, any incomplete proofs of the problem are removed from the *Proofstore* and their names and indices from the *ProofNames* and the *Indexmap* respectively. The problem itself is removed from the *Incomplete-proofmap* and an association mapping it to the empty set is added to the *Proofmap*.

make-axiom (*p*: *Problemref, n*: *String*)
ext wr *im* : *Incomplete-proofmap*
    wr *jm* : *Proofmap*
    wr *rm* : *Rulemap*
    wr *xm* : *Indexmap*
    wr *fs* : *Proofstore*
    wr *fn* : *ProofNames*
pre $n \neq [\,] \wedge [p \in axioms(jm) \wedge (n \in \text{dom } rm \Rightarrow rm(n) = p) \vee p \notin \text{dom } jm]$
post $p \notin \text{dom } \overleftarrow{jm} \wedge jm = \overleftarrow{jm} \cup \{p \mapsto \{\}\} \wedge rm = \overleftarrow{rm} \cup \{n \mapsto p\} \wedge im = \{p\} \mathbin{\overline{\vartriangleleft}} \overleftarrow{im} \wedge$
$$(p \in \text{dom } \overleftarrow{im} \wedge xm = \overleftarrow{im}(p) \mathbin{\overline{\vartriangleleft}} \overleftarrow{xm} \wedge fs = \overleftarrow{im}(p) \mathbin{\overline{\vartriangleleft}} \overleftarrow{fs} \wedge fn = \overleftarrow{im}(p) \mathbin{\overline{\vartriangleleft}} \overleftarrow{fn} \vee$$
$$p \notin \text{dom } \overleftarrow{im} \wedge xm = \overleftarrow{xm} \wedge fs = \overleftarrow{fs} \wedge fn = \overleftarrow{fn}) \vee$$
$$p \in \text{dom } \overleftarrow{jm} \wedge im = \overleftarrow{im} \wedge xm = \overleftarrow{xm} \wedge jm = \overleftarrow{jm} \wedge rm = (\overleftarrow{rm} \vartriangleright \{p\}) \cup \{n \mapsto p\} \wedge$$
$$fs = \overleftarrow{fs} \wedge fn = \overleftarrow{fn}$$

A third possibility is that the problem named 'fred' is justifiable by some *Instantiation*, in which case the operation *add-instantiation* should prove useful. In order that the invariants on *Instantiation* and *Proofmap* be respected, the problem *p* being instantiated should be a rule and the instantiation mapping *m* should not be empty, should have a domain which is a subset of the *Atoms* occurring in *p* and should have a range containing only expressions existing in the *Expstore*. Building the instance of the problem *p* with the instantiation mapping m should result in the problem q (i.e. the problem called 'fred'). The whole process is, however, forbidden if the problem named 'fred' is an axiom – adding proofs to an axiom would convert it to a derived rule, possibly destroying the logical soundness of the system into the bargain.

If the *Instantiation i* (i.e. *mk-Instantiation*(p, m)) is in the range of the *Proofstore*, the *Proofref f* referencing it is added as a new complete proof of the problem q by adding f to the set to which q is mapped under the *Proofmap*. Otherwise, some new association $f \mapsto i$ is added to the *Proofstore* first, where f is now some new *Proofref* not previously existing in the domain of the *Proofstore*, then the *Proofmap* is updated as above. These contortions ensure that the invariant on the *Proofstore*, in particular the part insisting that *Instantiations* are assigned unique references therein, is maintained.

add-instantiation $(p: Problemref, m: Atom \xrightarrow{m} Expref, q: Problemref)$

ext wr *fs* : *Proofstore*
   wr *jm* : *Proofmap*
   rd *rm* : *Rulemap*
   rd *ps* : *Problemstore*
   rd *ss* : *Subseqstore*
   rd *es* : *Expstore*

pre $p \in \text{rng } rm \wedge m \neq \{\} \wedge \text{dom } m \subseteq vars(nodes(ps(p)), ss, es) \wedge$
   $is\text{-}substitution(nodes(ps(p)), m, ss, es) \wedge is\text{-}problem\text{-}match(p, q, m, ps, ss, es) \wedge$
   $q \notin axioms(jm)$

post let $i = mk\text{-}Instantiation(p, m)$ in
   $[i \in \text{rng } \overleftarrow{fs} \wedge f \in \text{dom } \overleftarrow{fs} \wedge \overleftarrow{fs}(f) = i \wedge \overleftarrow{fs} = fs \vee$
   $\qquad\qquad\qquad\qquad i \notin \text{rng } \overleftarrow{fs} \wedge f \notin \text{dom } \overleftarrow{fs} \wedge fs = \overleftarrow{fs} \cup \{f \mapsto i\}] \wedge$
   $[q \in \text{dom } \overleftarrow{jm} \wedge s = \overleftarrow{jm}(q) \cup \{f\} \vee q \notin \text{dom } \overleftarrow{jm} \wedge s = \{f\}] \wedge$
   $jm = \overleftarrow{jm} \dagger \{q \mapsto s\}$

If the conclusion of some problem is amongst its hypotheses, it already automatically satisfies the condition by which a composite proof of it is complete (the conclusion of the problem is in its knowns with respect to the proof). It can therefore be proved by an empty composite proof (not an empty set of proofs as this would mean it was an axiom). The operation *add-assumption* thus adds an empty composite proof to the set of complete proofs of such a problem. Of course, the problem should not be an axiom for exactly the same reasons as given above.

add-assumption $(p: Problemref)$

ext wr *fs* : *Proofstore*
   wr *jm* : *Proofmap*
   rd *ps* : *Problemstore*

pre $p \in \text{dom } ps \wedge p \notin axioms(jm) \wedge con(ps(p)) \in hyp(ps(p))$

post $f \notin$ dom $\overleftarrow{fs} \wedge fs = \overleftarrow{fs} \cup \{f \mapsto [\,]\} \wedge$
$$(p \in \text{dom } \overleftarrow{jm} \wedge jm = \overleftarrow{jm} \dagger \{p \mapsto \overleftarrow{jm}(p) \cup \{f\}\} \vee$$
$$p \notin \text{dom } \overleftarrow{jm} \wedge jm = \overleftarrow{jm} \cup \{p \mapsto \{f\}\})$$

If none of the above appeals, you might like to try to construct a non-trivial composite proof of your new problem. The first step in this process is to add a new empty composite proof to the incomplete proofs of the problem. Again, the problem should not be an axiom. It should, however, be an existing problem (in the *Problemstore*). In addition, its hypotheses should not include its conclusion – if they did the empty composite proof would actually be a complete proof of the problem, in which case it should not be attached to it via the *Incomplete-proofmap*. The operation *add-empty-proof* therefore adds a new empty composite proof to the *Proofstore*, assigns it the index 0 in the *Indexmap* (corresponding to it having no forward proof), and adds this new proof to the set of incomplete proofs of the problem as recorded in the *Incomplete-proofmap*.

add-empty-proof (*p*: *Problemref*)
ext wr *im*   : *Incomplete-proofmap*
    wr *xm* : *Indexmap*
    wr *fs*   : *Proofstore*
    rd *jm* : *Proofmap*
    rd *ps* : *Problemstore*
pre $p \notin$ *axioms*(*jm*) $\wedge p \in$ dom *ps* $\wedge con(ps(p)) \notin hyp(ps(p))$
post $f \notin$ dom $\overleftarrow{fs} \wedge fs = \overleftarrow{fs} \cup \{f \mapsto [\,]\} \wedge xm = \overleftarrow{xm} \cup \{f \mapsto 0\} \wedge$
$$(p \in \text{dom } \overleftarrow{im} \wedge im = \overleftarrow{im} \dagger \{p \mapsto \overleftarrow{im}(p) \cup \{f\}\} \vee$$
$$p \notin \text{dom } \overleftarrow{im} \wedge im = \overleftarrow{im} \cup \{p \mapsto \{f\}\})$$

There are operations for naming and removing proofs similar to those given above for doing likewise to problems. The restriction here is that only incomplete proofs can be thrown away – throwing away a complete proof might cause the problem of which it was a proof to revert to being unsolved, thus leading to the selfsame set of undesirable consequences as arise when throwing away a solved problem. See the complete specification for the full details of these operations.

Having created a new empty composite proof, you will want to add steps to it, either forward (via *add-fwd-step*) or backward (via *add-bwd-step*). You can add a new *Problemref s* to the tail of the forward proof of some incomplete proof if *s* is a solved problem and if it satisfies the condition for adding some new known to the proof. The new step is inserted immediately after the element whose position is defined by the index of the proof. As a result of the insertion, however, that part of the invariant saying that the backward proof contains no element whose hypotheses are amongst the current knowns might have been violated – addition of the new forward step will have increased the knowns. Thus, any step in the backward proof whose hypotheses are indeed amongst the new knowns must be transferred to the tail of the forward proof, this process being repeated until the backward proof contains no more such elements. In turn, shifting elements out of the backward proof may have destroyed the part of the invariant that insists that the steps of the backward proof taken in reverse order progressively reduce goals to subgoals. Those elements remaining in the backward proof after the transference of elements to the forward proof which do not satisfy this condition should therefore be discarded.

If the new forward proof is a complete proof of the problem in question, the whole of the backward proof is discarded and the new forward proof is added as a complete proof of the problem, reference to the proof being removed from the *Incomplete-proofmap* and the *Indexmap* into the bargain. Otherwise, the proof as a whole (still incomplete) becomes the new forward proof concatenated with the new backward proof, with its new index being the number of elements in the new forward proof.

add-fwd-step $(p: Problemref, f: Proofref, s: Problemref)$

ext wr *fs* : *Proofstore*
 wr *im* : *Incomplete-proofmap*
 wr *xm* : *Indexmap*
 wr *jm* : *Proofmap*
 rd *ps* : *Problemstore*
 rd *ss* : *Subseqstore*
 rd *es* : *Expstore*

pre let $k = knowns(p, hyp(ps(p)), forward\text{-}proof(f, fs, xm), ps, ss)$ in
$$p \in \text{dom } im \wedge f \in im(p) \wedge s \in \text{dom } jm \wedge adds\text{-}known(p, k, s, ps, ss)$$

post let $y = forward\text{-}proof(f, \overleftarrow{fs}, \overleftarrow{xm})\,\widehat{}\,[s],$

$z = backward\text{-}proof(f, \overleftarrow{fs}, \overleftarrow{xm}),$
$k = knowns(p, hyp(ps(p)), y, ps, ss),$
$l = new\text{-}fwd\text{-}steps(k, z, ps),$
$bwd = new\text{-}bwd\text{-}steps(\{con(ps(p))\}, reverse(z \triangleright \text{rng } l), ps),$
$fwd = y\,\widehat{}\,l,$
$new\text{-}proof = fwd\,\widehat{}\,bwd$

in

$\neg\, is\text{-}complete\text{-}proof(fwd, p, ps, ss, es) \wedge fs = \overleftarrow{fs}\,\dagger\,\{f \mapsto new\text{-}proof\} \wedge$
$jm = \overleftarrow{jm} \wedge im = \overleftarrow{im} \wedge xm = \overleftarrow{xm}\,\dagger\,\{f \mapsto \overleftarrow{xm}(f) + \text{len } l + 1\} \vee$
$is\text{-}complete\text{-}proof(fwd, p, ps, ss, es) \wedge xm = \{f\} \triangleleft \overleftarrow{xm} \wedge$
$(\overleftarrow{im}(p) = \{f\} \wedge im = \{p\} \triangleleft \overleftarrow{im} \vee \overleftarrow{im}(p) \neq \{f\} \wedge im = \overleftarrow{im}\,\dagger\,\{p \mapsto \overleftarrow{im}(p) - \{f\}\})$

Adding a backward step is somewhat easier as no reorganization of the proof is required – the pre-condition ensures that the new step being added to the head of the backward proof is not a valid forward step and none of the existing backward steps can be because they would have been transferred previously if they were. The rest of the pre-condition just checks that the new step is a solved problem and that its conclusion is one of the current goals. The proof becomes the old forward proof, the new element and the old backward proof in that order. Its index does not change as its forward proof has not altered.

> *add-bwd-step* (*p*: *Problemref*, *f*: *Proofref*, *s*: *Problemref*)
> ext wr *fs*   : *Proofstore*
>   rd *im*   : *Incomplete-proofmap*
>   rd *xm*   : *Indexmap*
>   rd *jm*   : *Proofmap*
>   rd *ps*   : *Problemstore*
>   rd *ss*   : *Subseqstore*
> pre let *k* = *knowns*(*p*, *hyp*(*ps*(*p*)), *forward-proof*(*f*, *fs*, *xm*), *ps*, *ss*),
>   *g* = *goals*({*con*(*ps*(*p*))}, *reverse*(*backward-proof*(*f*, *fs*, *xm*)), *ps*)
>   in
> $p \in$ dom *im*$\wedge f \in im(p) \wedge s \in$ dom *jm*$\wedge \neg (hyp(ps(s)) \subseteq k) \wedge con(ps(s)) \in g-k$
>
> post let *new-proof* = *forward-proof*(*f*, $\overleftarrow{fs}$, *xm*) $^\frown$
>
> $\qquad\qquad\qquad\qquad\qquad$ [*s*] $^\frown$ *backward-proof*(*f*, $\overleftarrow{fs}$, *xm*) in
>
> $fs = \overleftarrow{fs} \dagger \{f \mapsto new\text{-}proof\}$

If you have completely messed things up as a result of the above, you can always remedy the situation with the help of the 'undo' functions *undo-fwd-step* and *undo-bwd-step*. The former removes the tail of the forward proof (provided there is a forward proof), the latter the head of the backward proof under a similar condition. There is a surprise in store here for the unwary, though – *undo-fwd-step* is not necessarily the inverse of *add-fwd-step* as some steps might have been transferred from the backward proof to the forward proof as part of the *add-fwd-step* action. The corresponding operations on the backward proof are mutually inverse, however, as no reorganization of the proof occurs. Both operations are fairly predictable, simply removing the relevant element from the proof. In addition, *undo-fwd-proof* decrements the proof's index by one. You can only apply them to incomplete proofs, of course.

> *undo-fwd-step* (*p*: *Problemref*, *f*: *Proofref*)
> ext wr *fs*   : *Proofstore*
>   wr *xm* : *Indexmap*
>   rd *im*   : *Incomplete-proofmap*
> pre $p \in$ dom *im* $\wedge f \in im(p) \wedge xm(f) \neq 0$
>
> post $xm = \overleftarrow{xm} \dagger \{f \mapsto \overleftarrow{xm}(f) - 1\} \wedge fs = \overleftarrow{fs} \dagger \{f \mapsto \overleftarrow{xm}(f) \triangleleft \overleftarrow{fs}(f)\}$

undo-bwd-step (*p*: *Problemref*, *f*: *Proofref*)
ext wr *fs* : *Proofstore*
    wr *xm* : *Indexmap*
    rd *im* : *Incomplete-proofmap*
pre *p* ∈ dom *im* ∧ *f* ∈ *im*(*p*) ∧ *xm*(*f*) ≠ len *fs*(*f*)
post *xm* = $\overleftarrow{xm}$ ∧ *fs* = $\overleftarrow{fs}$ † {*f* ↦ (*xm*(*f*) + 1) ◁ $\overleftarrow{fs}$ (*f*)}

If you get stuck in some proof and want to try out different strategies from that point you can copy the current state of your proof with the *spawn-proof* operation. Your problem then acquires a new incomplete proof which looks just like the one you got stuck in. The new proof is added to the *Proofstore* and its index to the *Indexmap* as part of the process.

spawn-proof (*p*: *Problemref*, *f*: *Proofref*)
ext wr *im* : *Incomplete-proofmap*
    wr *xm* : *Indexmap*
    wr *fs* : *Proofstore*
pre *p* ∈ dom *im* ∧ *f* ∈ *im*(*p*)
post *g* ∉ dom $\overleftarrow{fs}$ ∧ *fs* = $\overleftarrow{fs}$ ∪ {*g* ↦ $\overleftarrow{fs}$ (*f*)} ∧ *xm* = $\overleftarrow{xm}$ ∪ {*g* ↦ $\overleftarrow{xm}$(*f*)} ∧
                        im = $\overleftarrow{im}$ † {*p* ↦ $\overleftarrow{im}$(*p*) ∪ {*g*}}

Finally, when you have completed your proof you can make the problem it was a proof of into a derived rule with the help of the operation *name-rule*. This just associates a name (non-empty string) with the problem via the *Rulemap*. Note that the operation can also be used for renaming existing rules.

name-rule (*n*: *String*, *p*: *Problemref*)
ext wr *rm* : *Rulemap*
    rd *jm* : *Proofmap*
pre *n* ≠ [ ] ∧ *p* ∈ dom *jm* ∧ (*n* ∈ dom *rm* ⇒ *rm*(*n*) = *p*)
post *rm* = ($\overleftarrow{rm}$ ▷ {*p*}) ∪ {*n* ↦ *p*}

4.5 Muffin

This final section gives some details of the actual implementation of Muffin in Smalltalk 80 which was based on the specification described in the two preceding sections.[11]

The various components of the system can conveniently be divided into three categories, the *browser*, the *builder* and the *prover*.

---

[11]The system is an 'Alvey deliverable' and copies of the code are available via M.K.Tordoff, STL NW, Copthall House, Nelson Place, Newcastle-under-Lyme, Staffs ST5 1EZ.

Muffin's browser essentially allows the user to inspect the current state of Muffin. The user can select the type of object of interest from the list *axioms*, *proofs*, *rules*, *problems*, *subsequents* (i.e. sequents) and *expressions*. The browser will then show all objects of the selected type. Where the particular type selected has multiple subtypes, e.g. *complete* and *incomplete* for proofs, *and*, *or*, etc. for expressions, the user can additionally select one of these subtypes and the browser will then show only those objects of the selected subtype. Objects can be accessed via their names or some textual representation of the objects themselves. When the object selected is a problem, the browser shows additionally either the status of any existing proofs of that problem or that the selected problem is an axiom. In the latter case, the axiom name is also shown. Figure 4.6 shows the browser where the selection is the unsolved problem named *or-and-dist* and its incomplete proof of the same name, the completed version of which is shown in Figure 4.2.

In addition, the browser allows a few simple changes to be made to the state of Muffin, such as naming and renaming of objects, conversion of an unsolved problem to an axiom, conversion of a solved problem to a (derived) rule, and addition of a new empty composite proof to the set of incomplete proofs of some problem.

Finally, the browser acts as a controller for the other components of Muffin. Thus, for instance, it allows the user to start up either a builder or a prover, to inspect the current status of some existing proof, to remove incomplete proofs and unsolved problems from Muffin's store, and to restart some abandoned proof at the point at which it was abandoned.

The *builder*, of which there are several different forms, allows the user to create new expressions, (sub)sequents and problems and add them to the relevant object stores.

Lastly, the *prover* allows the user to edit an incomplete proof with a view to converting it into a complete proof. It uses a display based on the ideas of the knowns and the goals of the problem in question with respect to the proof. Figure 4.7 shows a prover at that point during the construction of the proof of Figure 4.2 at which the proof is complete apart from the subproof at box 3.

The top pane of the prover shows the problem which is to be solved, the middle pane the knowns of the problem with respect to the proof, and the bottom pane the current subgoals. Subproofs of the proof, for example the one at box 3 in Figure 4.2, each appear in a separate prover, where the problem to be solved has as its conclusion the conclusion of the relevant box and as its hypotheses the hypotheses of the box itself plus all the hypotheses of each of its containing boxes. If the amount of information becomes too great, the user can chose to reduce it by making use of the facility of *elision* of knowns. Thus, for instance, if a user decides that some particular known is not going to be useful in the remainder of the proof it can be designated as *hidden* and it is then removed from the display. When a prover has hidden knowns, Muffin reminds the user of this by displaying ellipsis points at the foot of the list of displayed knowns. Any

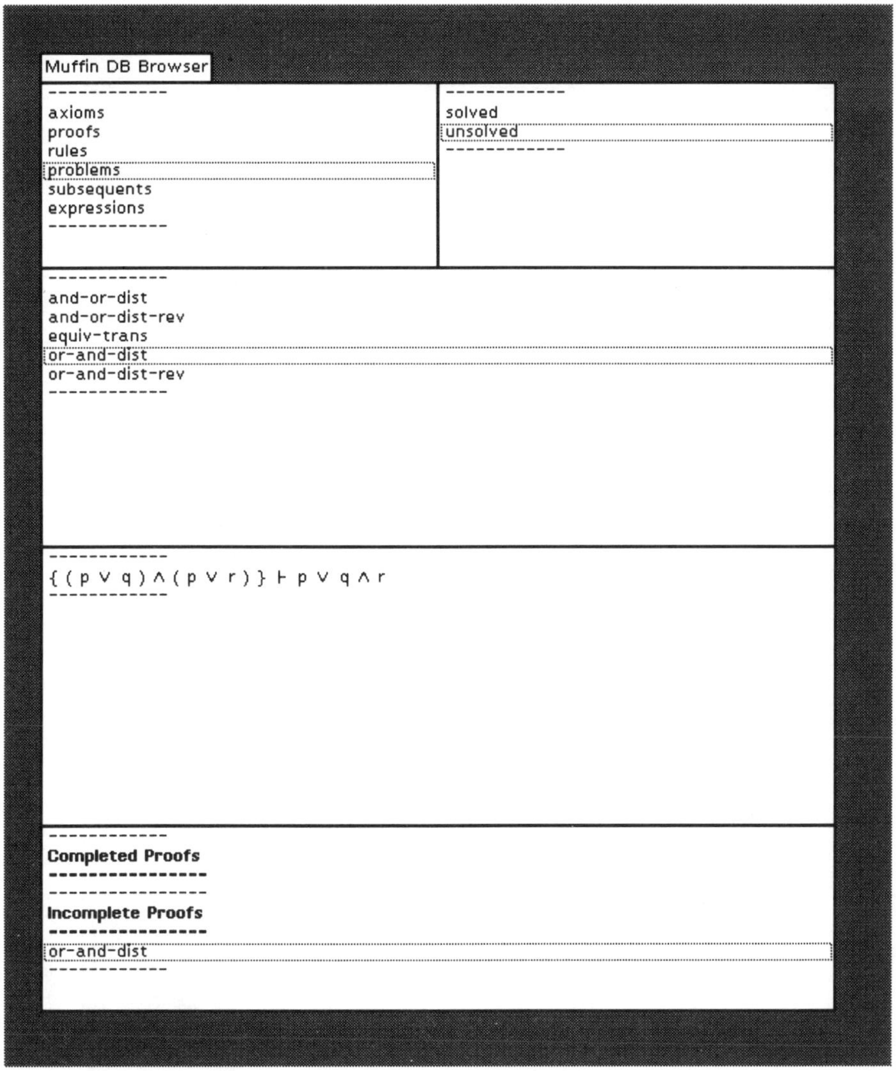

Figure 4.6 Muffin's browser

Figure 4.7 Muffin's prover

hidden known remains a known of the proof, of course, and the reverse operation of redisplaying hidden knowns is available at any time.

Muffin offers some assistance with the process of proof creation, largely through its 'matching' facilities. Thus, the user can select an expression from either the knowns or the goals and ask Muffin for a list of all rules matching that expression, that is any rules which might be applicable. In the case where the selection is a known, Muffin provides a list of all the rules so far proved which contain some expression amongst their hypotheses which could be instantiated to the selected expression. When the selection is a goal, the list provided is of those rules whose conclusion can be instantiated to the selected expression. Selecting a rule from the list returned then causes Muffin to try to build the appropriate instance of the selected rule and add this as a new step to the proof.

The variable substitution deduced from the matching process is not always complete, however. For instance, more than one element of the hypotheses of the selected rule might match the selected expression, or the rule might contain more *Atoms* than the expression which was used in the matching procedure. In such circumstances, Muffin prompts the user to complete the parts of the instantiation mapping it was unable to deduce for itself. When this has been completed satisfactorily, it adds the new step to the proof.

The other way in which Muffin offers assistance with the proof is in the case where one of the subgoals is a sequent (as in Figure 4.7). We have already seen that, in order to make a sequent a known of a proof it is necessary to add to the tail of the forward proof a (solved) problem, the conclusion of which is the right-hand side of the sequent and the hypotheses of which are the hypotheses of the sequent plus those of its containing problem (the containing problem is the problem appearing in the top pane of the prover). The user can therefore select a sequent in the goals pane of the prover and ask Muffin to search through all its solved problems to see whether the appropriate problem is amongst them. If it is, Muffin adds it to the tail of the forward proof, and the sequent becomes a known of the proof. Otherwise, Muffin offers the user the opportunity to open a new prover in order to attempt to solve that problem.

The user may have as many provers, browsers and builders as desired active and displayed on the screen at once and can switch the focus of attention between them at will. In particular, there may be provers in which different problems are being proved as well as provers showing different attempted proofs of the same problem. Thus, for example, if, while working on some proof, the user decides that the proof would be more straightforward if some new derived rule were proved first, the current proof can be abandoned and the problem stating that derived rule can be built in a builder, proved in some other prover, then designated as a derived rule, maybe in a browser. On returning to the original proof, the new rule will now be available and it can be used there as desired.

The surface user interface as described here thus offers the user several different 'views' of the underlying Muffin state, together with ways of altering that state. Each component of the user interface thus essentially filters out that part of the total information held in the Muffin state as a whole which is relevant to the particular task in hand and presents it to the user, hopefully in a way which makes assimilation of that information straightforward and which allows the user to carry out the desired actions as 'naturally' (whatever that might mean) as possible. Of course, the abstract state defined above places only a single restriction on the surface user interface, namely that only information actually stored in the state can be projected. Thus, a user interface of radically different appearance to the one described here would be an equally valid way of interacting with the Muffin state as specified. Indeed, the experimentation with user interface issues carried out in the Muffin project indicates that different users will prefer different interaction styles (in tests, some expressed a preference for the 'knowns-goals' style described above, others would prefer to interact with a display based on the layout of a proof shown in Figure 4.1.). The conclusion is therefore that a whole range of (preferably user-tailorable) user interface components offering a variety of ways of performing essentially the same set of tasks should be provided in order to really support the process of interactive theorem proving.

5

Unification: Specification and Development

John S. Fitzgerald

This and the next chapter apply VDM to a problem of considerable practical importance in computing. Proofs in propositional calculus, discussed in Chapter 3, require simple pattern matching to determine how inference rules can be used. For the full predicate calculus, unification is required. The realization that unification is a fundamental process in many applications has led to much study aimed at producing algorithms of satisfactory time/space complexity. This chapter sets the scene by showing how certain 'obvious algorithms' do not work and uses these to construct a simple unification algorithm *informally*. By constrast, a *formal* specification is constructed and one particular algorithm developed from it. This illustrates the use of operation decomposition rules and proofs in guiding the development of code.

5.1   Introduction

This case study concerns the specification of a practically important problem and the
rigorous development of an algorithm from the specification.

The idea of unification of first order terms in an empty equational theory is introduced; its importance as the basis of many practical applications and the wide range
of extant algorithms are noted. It is argued that a formal specification of unification is
required as a basis for the rigorous development of such algorithms. An algorithm is
developed entirely informally. A formal specification of first order unification is developed and the necessary supporting proofs are outlined. The obligation to prove implementability of the specification is discharged by means of a constructive proof using
operation decomposition rules to guide design of an algorithm similar to the one developed informally, but this time with some assurance of correctness because of the rigor
of the development.

Some comments on the specification and development processes conclude the case
study.

The idea of unification

Unification is a process of pattern matching. This case study concerns pattern matching
between *first order terms*. A first order term is either a *variable* symbol (e.g. x, y, z)
or a function name followed by a (possibly empty) list of arguments (usually shown in
parentheses). The arguments are themselves terms. So

$$g(f(x), h(x, y))$$

is a first order term with function symbol g and arguments $f(x)$ and $h(x, y)$.

A *substitution* is a mapping from variables to terms. When a substitution is *applied*
to a term the variables in the term are replaced by their images under the substitution
mapping. Thus the substitution σ:

$$\sigma = \{x \mapsto g(y), z \mapsto y\}$$

when applied to the term t_1:

$$t_1 = f(x, z)$$

yields the term

$$f(g(y), y)$$

by replacing each occurrence of x in t_1 by $g(y)$ and each occurrence of z by y. Applying
σ to t_2:

$$t_2 = f(g(y), z)$$

yields the same result, namely $f(g(y), y)$. σ is said to *unify* t_1 and t_2 and is called a *unifier* of those terms. This study is restricted to unifiers which make terms *exactly equal*, not merely equal modulo properties of the functions denoted by the function names (such as associativity or commutativity).

Notice that $\sigma' = \{x \mapsto g(y)\}$ is also a unifier of t_1 and t_2. σ' is said to be *more general* than σ, because σ can be derived from σ' (by adding the maplet $\{z \mapsto y\}$ to it). Not all sets of first order terms have unifiers, but those which do always have a *most general unifier*, i.e. a unifier from which all the other unifiers of the terms can be derived. These ideas will be expressed more rigorously in Section 5.2.

This study concerns procedures for finding the most general unifier of sets of first order terms in the absence of equational properties of the functionals. Such procedures are called *unification algorithms*.

Developing a naïve unification algorithm

A unification algorithm will be regarded as a procedure which, given some terms as input, returns a most general unifier if one exists and a failure flag otherwise. Consider the terms t_1 and t_2 as input. A unifying substitution u is to be returned if they are unifiable. A failure flag is to be set if they are not. The unifier must reconcile all disagreements between t_1 and t_2. It seems a good idea to look for a disagreement between t_1 and t_2 and to try to resolve it by applying a suitable substitution. This could be repeated until all the disagreements are resolved and the terms unified.

Suppose disagreeing subterms of t_1 and t_2 will be reconciled from left to right. Consider the example:

$$t_1 = f(x, h(a))$$
$$t_2 = f(a, y)$$

where x and y are variables and f, h and a are function symbols (a takes no arguments – it is a constant). Here the first disagreement is between x and a. The first *disagreement pair* for t_1 and t_2 is $\langle x, a \rangle$.

Algorithm 1 below works in the way suggested above, generating the disagreement pair (one component of which must be a variable), recording the assignment needed to resolve the disagreement in u and updating t_1 and t_2. The process is repeated until all disagreements are resolved:

Algorithm 1
Input: t_1, t_2
Output: substitution u, failure flag
$u := \{\}$;
while $t_1 \neq t_2$
      Generate disagreement pair $\langle d1, d2 \rangle$;

let $d1$ be the variable in the pair in
    Record $\{d1 \mapsto d2\}$ in u;
    Apply u to t_1 and t_2
endwhile

The means of recording pairs in substitutions will be more fully discussed in Section 5.2. Applying Algorithm 1 to the above example yields:

1. Initialize u: $u = \{\}$.
2. Generate disagreement pair $\langle x, a \rangle$.
3. Reconcile disagreement: $u = \{x \mapsto a\}$.
4. Apply u to t_1 and t_2:

$$t_1 \; = \; f(a, h(a))$$
$$t_2 \; = \; f(a, y)$$

5. Generate disagreement pair $\langle h(a), y \rangle$.
6. Reconcile disagreement: $u = \{x \mapsto a, y \mapsto h(a)\}$.
7. Apply u to t_1 and t_2:

$$t_1 \; = \; f(a, h(a))$$
$$t_2 \; = \; f(a, h(a))$$

8. $t_1 = t_2$ – **Stop.**

So the algorithm works for some pairs of terms but not for all. For example, in trying to unify:

$$t_1 \; = \; f(g(x))$$
$$t_2 \; = \; f(h(x))$$

the first disagreement pair is $\langle g(x), h(x) \rangle$. This disagreement cannot be reconciled since no substitution will make the functionals g and h the same. Clearly t_1 and t_2 are not unifiable. The algorithm should test for this kind of failure (called a *clash* because it is due to clashing function symbols). A clash occurs when there is no variable in the disagreement pair, so a check for the variable's presence should be incorporated into the algorithm. This yields Algorithm 2:

Algorithm 2
Input: t_1, t_2
Output: substitution u, failure flag
$u := \{\}$;
while $t_1 \neq t_2$ *and not failed*
    Generate disagreement pair $\langle d1, d2 \rangle$;

> if neither $d1$ nor $d2$ a variable then *FAIL(Clash)*
> else let $d1$ be the variable in the pair in
> > begin
> > Record $\{d1 \mapsto d2\}$ in u;
> > Apply u to t_1 and t_2
> > end
> endwhile
> End Algorithm 2

Algorithm 2 still fails on some inputs. Consider:

$$
\begin{aligned}
t_1 &= f(x) \\
t_2 &= f(h(x))
\end{aligned}
$$

The first disagreement pair is $\langle x, h(x) \rangle$. According to Algorithm 2:

$$u = \{x \mapsto h(x)\}$$

but applying u to t_1 and t_2 yields

$$
\begin{aligned}
t_1 &= f(h(x)) \\
t_2 &= f(h(h(x)))
\end{aligned}
$$

The algorithm goes on generating the same disagreement and never making the terms equal. It will not terminate because the substitutions generated do not eliminate x. The substitution is called *cyclic* and t_1 and t_2 are *not finitely unifiable*. This study – and the majority of practical applications – deal only in finitely unifiable terms, so a check (the 'Occurs' check) is included to look for a variable in the disagreement occurring in another term of the disagreement. Termination can then be forced when such a disagreement is detected. This gives Algorithm 3:

> Algorithm 3
> Input: t_1, t_2
> Output: substitution u, failure flag
> $u := \{\ \}$;
> while $t_1 \neq t_2$ *and not failed*
> > Generate disagreement pair $\langle d1, d2 \rangle$;
> > if neither $d1$ nor $d2$ a variable then *FAIL(Clash)*
> > else let $d1$ be the variable in the pair in
> > > if $d1$ occurs in $d2$ then *FAIL(Cycle)*
> > > else begin
> > > Record $\{d1 \mapsto d2\}$ in u;
> > > Apply u to t_1 and t_2

```
                end
        endwhile
        End Algorithm 3
```

Algorithm 3 is similar to Robinson's well-known unification algorithm [Rob65]. It is also related to the algorithm developed rigorously in Section 5.4.

Exponential time complexity is the main vice of Robinson's algorithm, countering its virtue of intuitive simplicity. This exponentiality, according to Corbin and Bidoit [CB83], derives from the choice of data structure used to represent terms. The next example illustrates this.

Consider terms represented as ordered trees (we assume ordering of arguments left to right in the diagrams below). Consider unifying:

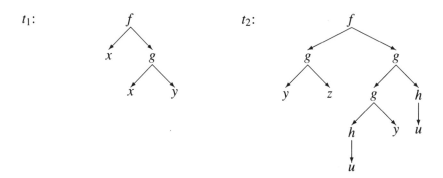

The unifier is $\{x \mapsto g(h(u), h(u)), y \mapsto h(u), z \mapsto h(u)\}$. The resultant unified term has five copies of the subterm $h(u)$ if represented as a tree:

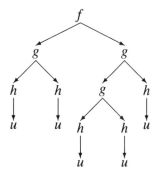

The $h(u)$ subterm is copied eight times during the execution of Algorithm 3 on this problem. The unification computation done in this way on tree structures can lead to exponential growth. To take an extreme example, consider unifying the following terms by Robinson's algorithm (or Algorithm 3):

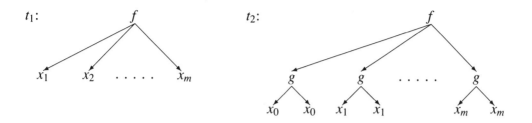

The first disagreement pair is $\langle x_1, g(x_0, x_0) \rangle$. Applying the resultant substitution to t_1 and t_2 yields:

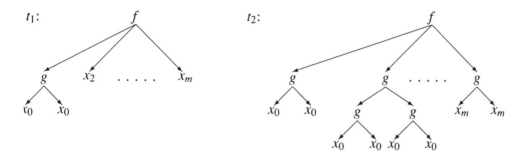

In general the kth disagreement results in adding a component of the form $\{x \mapsto a\ term$
$of\ 2^{k+1} nodes\}$ to the substitution. This is the source of the exponential complexity in
Robinson's algorithm. Corbin and Bidoit [CB83] proposed the use of directed acyclic
graphs to represent terms to allow sharing of subterms and thus minimize copying. Thus
the term

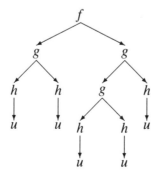

could be represented with one $h(u)$ subterm and one $g(h(u), h(u))$ subterm:

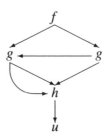

The use of this term representation is claimed to bring about a dramatic improvement in the algorithm's performance.

The process of deriving a unification algorithm appears to be nontrivial. Apart from the need to handle all kinds of disagreement, the algorithm's efficiency is greatly influenced by such issues as the choice of data structure. Is it worth the effort? How useful is unification?

Why unification is important

Unification algorithms are fundamental to a wide range of practical applications, for instance:

Automated theorem proving. The first unification algorithm proper appeared in the 1930s in Herbrand's thesis [Her67] but the subject did not receive popular attention until the development of automated theorem proving in the 1960s, Robinson [Rob65] employed it in his resolution rule, which involves the unification of literals in antecedent clauses to obtain a consequent clause.

Prolog. The invocation of a Prolog procedure is like a resolution step. It is pattern-directed and involves the unification of a goal with a clause-head. A unification algorithm is thus at the heart of a Prolog system. The occurs check is an expensive overhead in many Prolog systems since it may involve search of deep trees. This, coupled with the frequency of its execution, causes it to have a serious effect on the algorithm's performance. Most Prolog systems omit the occurs check, but these have to handle the potential generation of infinitely large terms. Some systems terminate in error when very large terms are generated. Other systems use finite (cyclic) internal representations for infinite terms [Fil84].

Computer algebra. Consider symbolic integration, for example. The integrand might be matched against certain patterns to determine the class of problems to which it belongs. The appropriate integration method can then be invoked.

Type checking. Type checking in an environment with polymorphic functions involves substitution of type expressions for type variables. In checking the compatibility of two type expressions, they must be unified [ASU86].

Other applications. Examples include string handling, information retrieval, computer vision (unification of graphs) and knowledge representation in expert systems.

The variety of algorithms

The unification operation is as fundamental to many of its applications as arithmetic operations are to numerical computing, so choice of algorithm has a significant effect on the performance of any application of which it is a part. Siekmann [Sie84] considers 'The Next 700 Unification Algorithms' – and he has a point: the importance of unification to practical applications has motivated the development of a large corpus of algorithms differing widely on a number of counts:

Method. Some algorithms, like that of Corbin and Bidoit [CB83] are based on Robinson. Others, like Paterson and Wegman's [PW78] or Martelli and Montanari's [MM82] are based on the idea of equivalence classes of terms.

Complexity. One major aim in the development of novel unification algorithms has been the relief of inefficiencies inherent in Robinson's original. Improvements have been suggested which lower the original algorithm's exponential space complexity [Rob71, BM72]. Corbin and Bidoit [CB83] suggest the different term representation described above and claim that it brings improved complexity in both time and space, their algorithm being quadratic in the number of symbols in the input terms. Paterson and Wegman [PW78] mention the existence of nonrecursive $\mathcal{O}(AE + V)$-time algorithms (where V is the number of vertices and E the number of edges in the directed acyclic graph representation of the input terms and A is the functional inverse of Ackerman's function). Vitter and Simons [VS86] present an algorithm which satisfies this. They also give an $\mathcal{O}(E + V)$ sequential algorithm and a parallel version for an exclusive read/write parallel random access machine which is $\mathcal{O}(E/P + V \log P)$-time where P is the number of processors.

Data structures. Corbin and Bidoit's improvements are based on the use of directed acyclic graphs as an alternative to the more conventional tree-structures used to represent terms. It is shown below how this can bring about an improvement in unification algorithm complexity. Martinelli and Montanari [MM82] use multiterms and multisets of terms.

Reaction to environment. One cannot simply state than one algorithm is 'better' than another. Algorithms behave differently in different environments. Unification algorithm performance can depend on a number of environmental factors, such as the 'shape' (depth of nesting and number of arguments) of the input terms and the probability that they are not unifiable.

The development of a correct and efficient unification algorithm is, then, an activity of considerable practical value. In this section a simple (and probably highly inefficient) unification algorithm has been developed in an *ad hoc* way. The design methodology was crude: think of a possible algorithm and find bugs; correct the bugs and check the algorithm again; repeat the process until convinced of the algorithm's 'correctness'. The reader with any practical experience in algorithm design will wonder if the development has gone far enough at Algorithm 3. Does it *really* find a unifier for all unifiable input terms and stop with failure on all nonunifiable inputs ... and is that unifier the *most general*? This question of gaining conviction of correctness is at the center of this case study, where a rigorous approach to the specification of unification gives a basis for judging the correctness of proposed algorithms. It also provides a starting point for the analysis of the variety of algorithms described above in a controlled and rigorous manner. Different algorithms can be viewed as alternative developments of the same specification.

The rest of this case study illustrates part of this approach. First, unification is defined by means of a formal specification. Then the rigorous development of an algorithm similar to Algorithm 3 is considered. The methods used should ensure the correctness of the result.

5.2   Building a specification of unification

Section 5.1 considers the motivation for a rigorous approach to the specification, development and verification of unification algorithms. Such a specification is now presented piece by piece.

Two types of data object are involved in unification: terms and substitutions. Specifications for each of these types and primitive operations on them are developed, working towards an implicit specification for most general unification.

Terms

Functional terms consist of a function name and a list of arguments which are themselves terms. The name has an associated 'arity' – a natural number giving the correct number of arguments in any well-formed term containing the function name. Let *FT* be the type of functional terms and *GT* the type of general terms (defined below). Functional terms may then be specified thus:

FT :: fn : $F\text{-}Id$
       $args$: GT^*

The arity is taken to be part of the function name fn. Informally, the arity will be shown as a superscript in the function name. Thus $f^2(x, y)$ and $f^3(x, y, z)$ are valid terms with different function names. Note that *FT*s with no arguments are individual constants.

Let the type of variables be *V-Id*. A term is either a variable or a functional term, so the type *GT* of terms is defined as the union of *V-Id* and *FT*:

$GT = V\text{-}Id \cup FT$

Note that *V-Id* and *F-Id* are considered atomic types. It is assumed that equality on them is defined. Equality is also assumed to be defined on *FT* and *GT* in the obvious structural way.

This specification does not admit infinite terms involving cycles, like:

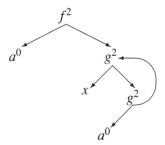

The reason is that, in VDM, recursively-defined objects are required to be finite. This is essential for the well-foundedness of structural induction rules. Such a rule can be written for *GT*. It allows the proof of assertions about 'all t in *GT*'. The rule is called *GT-Ind*:

$$\boxed{GT\text{-}Ind} \; \frac{t \in V\text{-}Id \vdash p(t); \quad f \in F\text{-}Id, l \in GT^*, \forall a \in \mathsf{rng}\, l \cdot p(a) \vdash p(mk\text{-}FT(f, l))}{t \in GT \vdash p(t)}$$

Informally, this rule says that if $p(v)$ can be shown to hold for any variable v and $p(mk\text{-}FT(f, l))$ can be shown to hold if $p(a)$ holds on each argument a in l, then $p(t)$ holds whenever t is a *GT*.

Now that variables and terms are dealt with, the occurs check mentioned above can be specified. *Occurs* is a function which takes a variable and a term and returns the boolean value true if and only if the variable occurs somewhere in the term.

A variable 'occurs' inside itself. Thus:

   Occurs (x, x) = true

$$Occurs\,(x, f^2(a^0, y)) = \text{false}$$

$$Occurs\,(y, f^2(a^0, y)) = \text{true}$$

Occurs is specified as follows:

$Occurs\ : V\text{-}Id \times GT \to \mathbb{B}$
$Occurs\,(v, t) \ \triangleq \ \text{if } t \in V\text{-}Id$
$\qquad\qquad\qquad \text{then } v = t$
$\qquad\qquad\qquad \text{else } \exists a \in \text{rng}\,args(t) \cdot Occurs\,(v, a)$

If the term t is a variable, the check reduces to $v = t$. Otherwise t must be a functional term and for the variable to occur in t it must occur in some argument of t. Since *Occurs* is a defined function, we can derive inference rules describing its behavior:

$$\boxed{Occurs\,\text{-}Def}\ \ \frac{v \in V\text{-}Id;\, t \in GT \cap V\text{-}Id}{Occurs\,(v, t) \ \Leftrightarrow \ v = t}$$

$$\boxed{Occurs\,\text{-}Def}\ \ \frac{v \in V\text{-}Id;\, t \in GT - V\text{-}Id}{Occurs\,(v, t) \ \Leftrightarrow \ \exists a \in \text{rng}\,args(t) \cdot Occurs\,(v, a)}$$

Such rules can be derived for all the defined functions in the specification, and this is left as an exercise for the reader.

It is now possible to write a function which returns the disagreement set of a set of terms. This will be used in the algorithm developed in Section 5.4 below.

$Dis\ : GT\text{-set} \to GT\text{-set}$
$Dis\,(s) \ \triangleq \ \text{if card } s \leq 1$
$\qquad\qquad\quad \text{then } \{\,\}$
$\qquad\qquad\quad \text{else if } V\text{-}Id \cap s \neq \{\,\}$
$\qquad\qquad\qquad\qquad \vee\, \exists t_1, t_2 \in s \cdot fn(t_1) \neq fn(t_2) \vee \text{len}\,args(t_1) \neq \text{len}\,args(t_2)$
$\qquad\qquad\quad \text{then } s$
$\qquad\qquad\quad \text{else } SeqDis\,(\{args(t) \mid t \in s\})$

where

$SeqDis\ : GT^{*}\text{-set} \to GT\text{-set}$
$SeqDis\,(q) \ \triangleq \ \text{if } q = \{[\,]\}$
$\qquad\qquad\qquad \text{then } \{\,\}$
$\qquad\qquad\qquad \text{else if } Dis\,(\{\text{hd}\,l \mid l \in q\}) = \{\,\}$
$\qquad\qquad\qquad\qquad \text{then } SeqDis\,(\{\text{tl}\,l \mid l \in q\})$
$\qquad\qquad\qquad\qquad \text{else } Dis\,(\{\text{hd}\,l \mid l \in q\})$

Dis returns $\{\,\}$ if the supplied set is empty or singleton. If the set contains a variable, then *all* the other terms must disagree with that variable, so *Dis* returns the whole set.

If the set contains a clash, then *all* the terms are in disagreement, so again *Dis* returns the whole set. Otherwise, *SeqDis* works through the arguments of the terms 'from left to right' and returns the leftmost set of disagreeing subterms. Of course, a different function could be chosen which works 'right to left' or even in no particular order at all. Indeed, an implicit specification of *SeqDis* would not suggest an order. However, this function is really for use in the development of an algorithm later on, so the deterministic definition above will suffice.

Substitutions

A substitution may be viewed as a mapping from *V-Id* to *GT*:

$$Subst = V\text{-}Id \xrightarrow{\ m\ } GT$$

When a substitution is applied to a term, all occurrences of variables which appear in both the term and the domain of the substitution are replaced by their images under the substitution. For example, under the substitution $\{x \mapsto g^1(z), y \mapsto a^0\}$, the term $f^3(x, g^1(y), z)$ becomes $f^3(g^1(z), g^1(a^0), z)$. As in this example, the mapping can be partial (i.e. need not apply to all variables in *V-Id*).

It has been shown how *cyclic* substitutions might arise in the unification process. Such substitutions can be characterized and excluded from the type *Subst* by means of an invariant, the derivation of which follows.

Consider the directed graph of a substitution. Variables and functionals are represented by nodes. Variable nodes each occur only once in the graph. When a variable is in the domain of a substitution it has one outgoing arc pointing to its image. If a variable is in the range of the substitution, it will have at least one incoming arc. Functional terms are represented in the usual way, with a functional node and arcs pointing to arguments. Thus the substitution $\{x \mapsto g^2(a^0, y), z \mapsto u\}$ has graph:

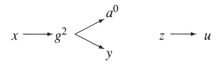

This graph is acyclic, and so is the substitution.

The substitution $\{x \mapsto f^2(x, y)\}$ is cyclic (x on both sides of the same component) and so is its graph:

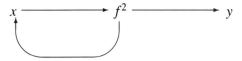

This kind of substitution in which a domain variable occurs in its own image is called *directly* or *immediately cyclic*. A more pernicious kind of substitution is the *indirectly cyclic* type. Here the cycle may not be clear until one examines the graph:

$$\{x \mapsto f^1(y), y \mapsto g^2(u,z), u \mapsto f^1(z), z \mapsto g^2(v,x)\}$$

An invariant on *Subst* is used to characterize and eliminate cyclic substitutions. This is done in the spirit of Jones [Jon90] so that subsequent searches for representation data types can capitalize on this invariant property, though it is quite possible to develop algorithms which do not *rely* on acyclicity as an invariant on substitutions, and this is just what is done in the development below. A cyclicity testing function could be derived which would search the substitution graph to see if any variable can be reached from itself ([Vad86, Nil84]). The definition of such a function is avoided by using a property of substitutions pointed out by Manna and Waldinger [MW81] and Eder [Ede85].

If a substitution is cyclic then there is a variable in its graph which can be reached from itself. The variable's node must have both an incoming and an outgoing arc (the incoming arc shows that the variable is in some term of the substitution's range, while the outgoing arc shows that the variable occurs in the domain of the substitution). If the domain and set of variables in the range are disjoint then there will be no variable nodes with both incoming and outgoing arcs. Hence the substitution represented by the graph will be acyclic. A substitution with this disjointness property will be called *var-disjoint*.

Var-disjoint substitutions are always acyclic, but not all acyclic substitutions are var-disjoint. This is why Vadera [Vad86] argues that his specification of substitutions is more general than that presented here. This is indeed so, but for the purposes of this application, we do not 'lose out' by insisting on var-disjoint substitutions. This point is considered with substitution reduction below.

Now for a function describing var-disjointedness:

$$VarDisj : V\text{-}Id \xrightarrow{m} GT \to \mathbb{B}$$
$$VarDisj(\sigma) \triangleq \forall x, y \in \mathsf{dom}\ \sigma \cdot \neg Occurs(x, \sigma(y))$$

$VarDisj(\sigma)$ is true if and only if no variable in the domain of σ occurs in a term in the range of σ. One rule derived from this function definition is used in the proof in Figure 5.1 below.

$$\text{VarDisj-Def} \quad \frac{\sigma \in \textit{V-Id} \xrightarrow{\ m\ } \textit{GT}, \quad \forall x, y \in \text{dom } \sigma \cdot \neg \textit{Occurs}\,(x, \sigma(y))}{\textit{VarDisj}(\sigma)}$$

There are some acyclic substitutions which are not var-disjoint. These substitutions have graphs containing paths through one or more domain variables. For example:

$$\sigma = \{y \mapsto g^1(x), x \mapsto a^0, z \mapsto a^0\}$$

$$y \longrightarrow g^1 \longrightarrow x \longrightarrow a^0$$

$$z \longrightarrow a^0$$

Here the variable x occurs in the domain of σ and in a term of the range, yet the substitution is acyclic. Is *inv-Subst* too strong in excluding this type of substitution? In fact, non-var-disjoint acyclic substitutions can be reduced to var-disjoint ones. For example, σ can be reduced to σ':

$$\sigma' = \{y \mapsto g^1(a^0), x \mapsto a^0, z \mapsto a^0\}$$

$$y \longrightarrow g^1 \longrightarrow a^0$$

$$x \longrightarrow a^0$$

$$z \longrightarrow a^0$$

A reduction function which, given a non-var-disjoint acyclic substitution, returns its var-disjoint equivalent can be defined. (Two substitutions are *equivalent* if, when applied to any term, they yield the same resultant term.) Thus it is possible to show that any non-var-disjoint acyclic substitution has a var-disjoint equivalent. For this reason, the *VarDisj* invariant on *Subst* will be used. This may appear to give a simpler specification for substitutions, but there is no such thing as a free lunch. In fact, the gain in the simplicity of substitution application (all of the substitution can be applied at once) may be countered by the complexity of substitution composition, which must preserve var-disjointedness. At this stage in the specification, one can see that var-disjointedness may bring gains in the speed of substitution application, but at the price of maintaining the invariant. This will be a favourable trade-off in applications where substitution application is more important than fast substitution construction or modification.

Application of a substitution to a term is simply specified. If the term is a variable in the domain of the substitution then the variable is replaced by its image under the substitution. Var-disjointedness of substitutions ensures that this does not have to be done recursively. If the term is a variable not in the domain of the substitution, then it is unaffected by application of the substitution. If the term is functional, then the function name is unaffected by the substitution, and the arguments all have the substitution applied to them. Hence we specify the application operator ($\overset{t}{\leadsto}$) thus:

$$\overset{t}{\leadsto} : Subst \times GT \to GT$$
$$\overset{t}{\leadsto}(\sigma, t) \quad \triangle \quad \text{if } t \in V\text{-}Id$$
$$\qquad \text{then if } t \in \text{dom } \sigma$$
$$\qquad\qquad \text{then } \sigma(t)$$
$$\qquad\qquad \text{else } t$$
$$\qquad \text{else } \mu(t, args \mapsto \{i \mapsto \overset{t}{\leadsto}(\sigma, args(t)(i)) \mid i \in \text{dom } args(t)\})$$

Infix notation will be used for this function, so for $\overset{t}{\leadsto}(\sigma, t)$, $\sigma \overset{t}{\leadsto} t$ is preferred.

Application has been explicitly defined, so the definition can be followed through on an example.

Let $t = mk\text{-}FT(f^3, [x, y, z])$ and $\sigma = \{x \mapsto mk\text{-}FT(g^1, [z])\}$. Then:

$$
\begin{aligned}
\sigma \overset{t}{\leadsto} t &= \mu(t, args \mapsto \{1 \mapsto \sigma \overset{t}{\leadsto} x, 2 \mapsto \sigma \overset{t}{\leadsto} y, 3 \mapsto \sigma \overset{t}{\leadsto} z\}) \\
&= \mu(t, args \mapsto [\sigma(x), y, z]) \\
&= \mu(t, args \mapsto [mk\text{-}FT(g^1, [z]), y, z]) \\
&= mk\text{-}FT(f, [mk\text{-}FT(g^1, [z]), y, z])
\end{aligned}
$$

The operator $\overset{s}{\leadsto}$ extends $\overset{t}{\leadsto}$ to cope with the application of a substitution to a set of terms:

$$\overset{s}{\leadsto} : Subst \times GT\text{-set} \to GT\text{-set}$$
$$\overset{s}{\leadsto}(\sigma, s) \quad \triangle \quad \{\sigma \overset{t}{\leadsto} t \mid t \in s\}$$

This will also be used in infix form: $\sigma \overset{s}{\leadsto} s$.

In the informal development of a simple unification algorithm, it was necessary to combine substitutions in some way. Indeed, this is the case for all unification algorithms which accumulate a unifier component by component.

An infix composition operator, $\circ$, can be specified so that for substitutions σ_1, σ_2, $(\sigma_1 \circ \sigma_2)$ is a substitution which has the same effect on any term as applying σ_1 to the term and then applying σ_2 to the result. So, the composition $\sigma_1 \circ \sigma_2$ is a (var-disjoint) substitution r such that for any term t in GT, $r \overset{t}{\leadsto} t = \sigma_2 \overset{t}{\leadsto} (\sigma_1 \overset{t}{\leadsto} t)$. This gives an obvious post-condition for an implicit specification of $\circ$. The pre-condition is rather more complex. First, the full function specification is given, and then the derivation of the pre-condition is considered:

$$\_ \circ \_ (\sigma_1, \sigma_2 : Subst) \; r : Subst$$
$$\text{pre } \forall x, y \in \text{dom } \sigma_1 \cup \text{dom } \sigma_2 \cdot$$
$$\qquad Occurs\,(x, \sigma_2 \overset{t}{\leadsto} (\sigma_1 \overset{t}{\leadsto} y)) \;\Rightarrow\; x = \sigma_2 \overset{t}{\leadsto} (\sigma_1 \overset{t}{\leadsto} x)$$

post $\forall t \in GT \cdot r \overset{t}{\leadsto} t = \sigma_2 \overset{t}{\leadsto} (\sigma_1 \overset{t}{\leadsto} t)$

The pre-condition on an operation or function specification delimits the domain of states and input values over which the operation or function must be defined. When specifying ○, it must be ensured that there are no input values for which it is impossible to give an output satisfying the post-condition. This is the essence of the *implementability* proof obligation in Jones [Jon90]. The pre-condition in the specification of ○ above is there to exclude pairs of substitutions which have no var-disjoint composed form. For example:

$$\sigma_1 = \{x \mapsto u, y \mapsto z\}$$
$$\sigma_2 = \{u \mapsto w, z \mapsto f^1(x)\}$$

A composed substitution should map x to w and y to $f^1(x)$, but such a substitution would not be var-disjoint. *pre-* ○ excludes cases like this by requiring that no variables in the input substitutions can participate in a cycle in the result (unless the cycle is a trivial one like $\{x \mapsto x\}$ in which case the component can be eliminated).

Var-disjoint substitutions have an interesting property, namely idempotence under substitution composition. In general, x is *idempotent* under a binary operation ◇ if and only if $x \diamond x = x$. Var-disjoint substitutions are idempotent under substitution composition (defined below).The reader is invited to formulate and prove this property.

It is claimed that *pre-* ○ is sufficiently weak, i.e. no σ_1, σ_2 excluded by *pre-* ○ could have a var-disjoint composed form. See Section 5.6 for a consideration of the proof of this assertion. The claim that all σ_1, σ_2 permitted by *pre-* ○ have var-disjoint composed forms satisfying *post-* ○ is the implementability proof obligation (see Section 5.3).

Unification

It is now possible to specify unification of a set of terms. A substitution unifies a set of terms if and only if applying it to all terms in the set yields the same result. The function *unifies* defines just this:

unifies $: Subst \times GT\text{-set} \to \mathbb{B}$

unifies $(\sigma, s) \overset{\triangle}{=} \forall t_1, t_2 \in s \cdot \sigma \overset{t}{\leadsto} t_1 = \sigma \overset{t}{\leadsto} t_2$

Again, infix form will be preferred: σ *unifies* s. Following this definition, any substitution *unifies* the empty set of terms.

The most general unifier for a set of terms is that unifier from which any other unifier of the set may be constructed by composing it with a suitable substitution. The function *MGen* , given a set of terms and a substitution, checks that the substitution is indeed the most general unifier of the set.

$MGen : Subst \times GT\text{-set} \to \mathbb{B}$

$MGen\,(\sigma, s) \quad \triangle$

$\quad \sigma \ unifies \ s \wedge (\forall \theta \in Subst \cdot \theta \ unifies \ s \ \Rightarrow \ \exists \lambda \in Subst \cdot \theta = \sigma \circ \lambda)$

A set of terms is unifiable if and only if it has a unifier:

$Unifiable : GT\text{-set} \to \mathbb{B}$

$Unifiable\,(s) \quad \triangle \quad \exists \sigma \in Subst \cdot \sigma \ unifies \ s$

The operation *MGU* operates over a set of terms, a unifier and a boolean flag. If a set of terms s is not unifiable, *MGU* must leave the flag $b =$ false. In that case the value of the unifying substitution u is irrelevant and may be arbitrary. If s is unifiable, *MGU* must leave $b =$ true and u set to the most general unifier of the set.

MGU

ext rd s : GT-set

    wr b : $\mathbb{B}$

    wr u : $Subst$

post $b \wedge MGen\,(u, s)$

    $\vee \neg b \wedge \neg Unifiable\,(s)$

It is not necessary to write to s to find a unifier and so the operation has read access only (this might be different if the unified term had to be returned). Since a unifier is to be constructed in u and the flag b must be set, read and write access is given to them.

5.3 Proofs supporting the specification

At each stage in the design of a piece of software, claims are made about the consistency of design decisions with preceding work. In the approach employed here such claims become *proof obligations*.

Obviously, specifications which cannot be met should not be used as the basis for further development. Implementability must therefore be proved for each specified function/operation which we intend to implement. In this section such proofs are considered, with examples.

The implementability proof obligation given by Jones [Jon90] requires that there should be an output satisfying the post-condition of the specification for every input over which it is defined (i.e. every input satisfying the pre-condition). For functions, the obligation is:

$$\forall d \in D \cdot pre\text{-}f(d) \ \Rightarrow \ \exists r \in R \cdot post\text{-}f(d, r)$$

where D is the domain space of f and R its result space. For operations the obligation is:

$$\forall \overleftarrow{\sigma} \in \Sigma \cdot pre\text{-}OP(\overleftarrow{\sigma}) \;\Rightarrow\; \exists \sigma \in \Sigma \cdot post\text{-}OP(\overleftarrow{\sigma}, \sigma)$$

where Σ is the state space (including the operation parameters). The extension of this rule to operations with input and result parameters is obvious.

When the implementability obligation is discharged, one must show that a result of the appropriate type exists for a given input. This existential proof is often constructive and is thus not very different from the process of building an implementation at the same level of abstraction as the specification. In such situations, the implementation often proceeds given the (strong) feeling that the obligation can be discharged.

An example proof: implementability of substitution composition

In this case the obligation reduces to proving:

$$\forall \sigma_1, \sigma_2 \in Subst \cdot pre\text{-}\circ(\sigma_1, \sigma_2) \;\Rightarrow\; \exists \phi \in Subst \cdot post\text{-}\circ(\sigma_1, \sigma_2, \phi)$$

i.e. that for any pair of substitutions satisfying $pre\text{-}\circ$ it is possible to construct a substitution ϕ which is their composition and so satisfies $post\text{-}\circ$. The proof is constructive, i.e. for any σ_1, σ_2, a suitable ϕ is constructed. To do this, a function R is defined. It is to be proved that $R(\sigma_1, \sigma_2)$ is a substitution satisfying $inv\text{-}Subst$ and, furthermore, $post\text{-}\circ(\sigma_1, \sigma_2, R(\sigma_1, \sigma_2))$ holds. First, however, the definition of R:

$R : Subst \times Subst \rightarrow Subst$

$R(\sigma_1, \sigma_2) \;\triangleq\; \{v \mapsto \sigma_2 \overset{t}{\leadsto} (\sigma_1 \overset{t}{\leadsto} v) \mid v \in \mathrm{dom}\, \sigma_1 \cup \mathrm{dom}\, \sigma_2 \wedge v \neq \sigma_2 \overset{t}{\leadsto} (\sigma_1 \overset{t}{\leadsto} v)\}$

$R(\sigma_1, \sigma_2)$ maps each variable v in the domains of σ_1 and σ_2 to $\sigma_2 \overset{t}{\leadsto} (\sigma_1 \overset{t}{\leadsto} v)$, unless this would introduce an identity cycle such as $\{x \mapsto x\}$, in which case the guilty variable is ignored. Consider an example:

$$
\begin{aligned}
\sigma_1 &= \{x \mapsto f^2(u, v), w \mapsto y\} \\
\sigma_2 &= \{u \mapsto a^0, y \mapsto w\} \\
R(\sigma_1, \sigma_2) &= \{x \mapsto f^2(a^0, v), u \mapsto a^0\}
\end{aligned}
$$

The main proof (Figure 5.3) has two parts. Firstly, the invariant preservation proof, that for any $\sigma_1, \sigma_2 \in Subst$, $R(\sigma_1, \sigma_2)$ is still a well-formed substitution:

$$\boxed{InvPres\text{-}R} \; \frac{\sigma_1, \sigma_2 \in Subst; pre\text{-}\circ(\sigma_1, \sigma_2)}{inv\text{-}Subst(R(\sigma_1, \sigma_2))}$$

This is dealt with separately in Figure 5.1 and is used at line 1.1 in the main proof. Secondly, the proof that $R(\sigma_1, \sigma_2)$ satisfies $post\text{-}\circ$: $post\text{-}\circ$ is a predicate quantified over *all* $t \in GT$, so the structural induction rule *GT-Ind* introduced above is used. The base case:

from $\sigma_1, \sigma_2 \in \textit{Subst}, \textit{pre-}\circ(\sigma_1, \sigma_2)$

1     $\forall v \in \text{dom } \sigma_1 \cup \text{dom } \sigma_2 \cdot \sigma_2 \overset{t}{\rightsquigarrow} (\sigma_1 \overset{t}{\rightsquigarrow} v) \in GT$ $h, \overset{t}{\rightsquigarrow}, \textit{Subst}$

2     $R(\sigma_1, \sigma_2) \in \textit{V-Id} \xrightarrow{m} GT$ 1, h

3   from $x, y \in \text{dom } R(\sigma_1, \sigma_2)$

3.1 $x, y \in \text{dom } \sigma_1 \cup \text{dom } \sigma_2$ h3, R

3.2 $x \neq \sigma_2 \overset{t}{\rightsquigarrow} (\sigma_1 \overset{t}{\rightsquigarrow} x)$ h3, R

3.3 $R(\sigma_1, \sigma_2)(x) = \sigma_2 \overset{t}{\rightsquigarrow} (\sigma_1 \overset{t}{\rightsquigarrow} x)$ h3, R

3.4 $R(\sigma_1, \sigma_2)(y) = \sigma_2 \overset{t}{\rightsquigarrow} (\sigma_1 \overset{t}{\rightsquigarrow} y)$ h3, R

3.5 $\textit{Occurs}(x, \sigma_2 \overset{t}{\rightsquigarrow} (\sigma_1 \overset{t}{\rightsquigarrow} y)) \Rightarrow x = \sigma_2 \overset{t}{\rightsquigarrow} (\sigma_1 \overset{t}{\rightsquigarrow} x)$ $\textit{pre-}\circ, \forall\text{-E}(\text{h},3.1)$

3.6 $\textit{Occurs}(x, R(\sigma_1, \sigma_2)(y)) \Rightarrow x = R(\sigma_1, \sigma_2)(x)$

                                               =-subs (3.3, =-subs (3.4, 3.5))

3.7 $x \neq R(\sigma_1, \sigma_2)(x)$ =-subs (3.3, 3.2)

      infer $\neg \textit{Occurs}(x, R(\sigma_1, \sigma_2)(y))$ vac$\Rightarrow$-E (3.6, 3.7)

4     $\forall x, y \in \text{dom } R(\sigma_1, \sigma_2) \cdot \neg \textit{Occurs}(x, R(\sigma_1, \sigma_2)(y))$ $\forall\text{-I } (3)$

5     $\textit{VarDisj}(R(\sigma_1, \sigma_2))$ $\textit{VarDisj-Def } (2, 4)$

infer $\textit{inv-Subst}(R(\sigma_1, \sigma_2))$ $\textit{inv-Subst}, 2, 5$

Figure 5.1 *InvPres R* – invariant preservation by *R*

$$\boxed{\textit{Base}} \quad \frac{\sigma_1, \sigma_2 \in \textit{Subst}; \textit{pre-}\circ(\sigma_1, \sigma_2)}{\forall t \in \textit{V-Id} \cdot R(\sigma_1, \sigma_2) \overset{t}{\rightsquigarrow} t = \sigma_2 \overset{t}{\rightsquigarrow} (\sigma_1 \overset{t}{\rightsquigarrow} t)}$$

is shown in Figure 5.2 which contributes line 1.2 to the main proof. The induction step itself is shown in the main proof at 1.4.

Implementability of MGU

At this point it is worth considering the implementability proof for *MGU*. As *MGU* is an operation capable of modifying the state on which it operates, the obligation amounts to showing that:

$$\forall \overleftarrow{\sigma} \in \Sigma \cdot \text{true} \Rightarrow \exists \sigma \in \Sigma \cdot \textit{post-OP}(\overleftarrow{\sigma}, \sigma)$$

A brief examination of this obligation (as expanded by substituting the full post-condition) and an outline of its proof (left as an exercise for the reader) shows that discharging the obligation depends on the proposition that for any unifiable set of terms there is a *most general* unifier. The truth of this proposition can be proved by designing a correct algorithm which generates such a most general unifier for any unifiable set of

from $\sigma_1, \sigma_2 \in \textit{Subst}, \textit{pre-} \circ (\sigma_1, \sigma_2)$

1	$R(\sigma_1, \sigma_2) \in \textit{Subst}$		Lemma 1
2	from $t \in \textit{V-Id}$		
2.1	from $t \in \mathrm{dom}\, R(\sigma_1, \sigma_2)$		
2.1.1	$R(\sigma_1, \sigma_2) \overset{t}{\leadsto} t = R(\sigma_1, \sigma_2)(t)$		h2, h2.1, 1, $\overset{t}{\leadsto}$
	infer $R(\sigma_1, \sigma_2) \overset{t}{\leadsto} t = \sigma_2 \overset{t}{\leadsto} (\sigma_1 \overset{t}{\leadsto} t)$		$\triangle$-inst (h2.1, 2.1.1)

2.2   from $t \notin \mathrm{dom}\, R(\sigma_1, \sigma_2)$

2.2.1	$t \notin \mathrm{dom}\, \sigma_1 \wedge t \notin \mathrm{dom}\, \sigma_2 \vee t = \sigma_2 \overset{t}{\leadsto} (\sigma_1 \overset{t}{\leadsto} t)$		h2.2, R, $\cup$
2.2.2	from $t \notin \mathrm{dom}\, \sigma_1 \wedge t \notin \mathrm{dom}\, \sigma_2$		
2.2.2.1	$\sigma_1 \overset{t}{\leadsto} t = t$		h2, $\wedge$-E (h2.2.2), $\overset{t}{\leadsto}$
2.2.2.2	$\sigma_2 \overset{t}{\leadsto} (\sigma_1 \overset{t}{\leadsto} t) = \sigma_2 \overset{t}{\leadsto} (t)$		2.2.2.1, $\overset{t}{\leadsto}$
2.2.2.3	$\sigma_2 \overset{t}{\leadsto} t = t$		h2, $\wedge$-E (h2.2.2), $\overset{t}{\leadsto}$
	infer $t = \sigma_2 \overset{t}{\leadsto} (\sigma_1 \overset{t}{\leadsto} t)$		=-trans (2.2.2.2, 2.2.2.3)
2.2.3	$t = \sigma_2 \overset{t}{\leadsto} (\sigma_1 \overset{t}{\leadsto} t)$		2.2.1, 2.2.2
2.2.4	$R(\sigma_1, \sigma_2) \overset{t}{\leadsto} t = t$		h2.2, $\overset{t}{\leadsto}$
	infer $R(\sigma_1, \sigma_2) \overset{t}{\leadsto} t = \sigma_2 \overset{t}{\leadsto} (\sigma_1 \overset{t}{\leadsto} t)$		2.2.3, 2.2.4
2.3	$t \in \mathrm{dom}\, R(\sigma_1, \sigma_2) \vee t \notin \mathrm{dom}\, R(\sigma_1, \sigma_2)$		h2, 1, $\in$
	infer $R(\sigma_1, \sigma_2) \overset{t}{\leadsto} t = \sigma_2 \overset{t}{\leadsto} (\sigma_1 \overset{t}{\leadsto} t)$		$\vee$-E(2.3, 2.1, 2.2)

infer $\forall t \in \textit{V-Id} \cdot R(\sigma_1, \sigma_2) \overset{t}{\leadsto} t = \sigma_2 \overset{t}{\leadsto} (\sigma_1 \overset{t}{\leadsto} t)$ $\forall$-I(2)

Figure 5.2 *Base* – base case property for main implementability proof

terms. This is the subject of Section 5.4.

5.4 Developing a correct algorithm

In Section 5.2 a specification for most general unification of a set of terms was given. In this section, a unification algorithm based on Robinson's (operating on the data types defined in the specification) is developed using operation decomposition techniques to assure correctness.

The algorithm

In Section 5.1 a simple unification algorithm (Algorithm 3) was developed in an *ad hoc* manner. Now a development can be presented more rigorously, working on the data

from $\sigma_1, \sigma_2 \in Subst$
1 from $pre\text{-}\circ(\sigma_1, \sigma_2)$
1.1 $inv\text{-}Subst(R(\sigma_1, \sigma_2))$ h, *InvPres R*
1.2 $\forall t \in V\text{-}Id \cdot R(\sigma_1, \sigma_2) \overset{t}{\leadsto} t = \sigma_2 \overset{t}{\leadsto} (\sigma_1 \overset{t}{\leadsto} t)$ h, *Base*
1.3   from $t \in V\text{-}Id$
     infer $R(\sigma_1, \sigma_2) \overset{t}{\leadsto} t = \sigma_2 \overset{t}{\leadsto} (\sigma_1 \overset{t}{\leadsto} t)$ $\forall$-E(h1.3, 1.2)
1.4   from $f \in F\text{-}Id, l \in GT^*, inv\text{-}FT(mk\text{-}FT(f, l)),$
       $\forall a \in \operatorname{rng} l \cdot R(\sigma_1, \sigma_2) \overset{t}{\leadsto} a = \sigma_2 \overset{t}{\leadsto} (\sigma_1 \overset{t}{\leadsto} a)$
1.4.1 $R(\sigma_1, \sigma_2) \overset{t}{\leadsto} mk\text{-}FT(f, l) =$
     $mk\text{-}FT(f, \{i \mapsto R(\sigma_1, \sigma_2) \overset{t}{\leadsto} l(i) \mid i \in \operatorname{dom} l\})$ $\overset{t}{\leadsto}$, h1.4
1.4.2   from $i \in \operatorname{dom} l$
1.4.2.1 $l(i) \in \operatorname{rng} l$ h1.4, h1.4.2
      infer $R(\sigma_1, \sigma_2) \overset{t}{\leadsto} l(i) = \sigma_2 \overset{t}{\leadsto} (\sigma_1 \overset{t}{\leadsto} l(i))$ $\forall$-E (1.4.2.1, h1.4)
1.4.3 $\forall i \in \operatorname{dom} l \cdot R(\sigma_1, \sigma_2) \overset{t}{\leadsto} l(i) = \sigma_2 \overset{t}{\leadsto} (\sigma_1 \overset{t}{\leadsto} l(i))$ $\forall$-I (1.4.2)
1.4.4 $R(\sigma_1, \sigma_2) \overset{t}{\leadsto} mk\text{-}FT(f, l) =$
     $mk\text{-}FT(f, \{i \mapsto \sigma_2 \overset{t}{\leadsto} (\sigma_1 \overset{t}{\leadsto} l(i)) \mid i \in \operatorname{dom} l\})$ 1.4.1, 1.4.3
1.4.5 $\sigma_1 \overset{t}{\leadsto} mk\text{-}FT(f, l) =$
     $mk\text{-}FT(f, \{i \mapsto \sigma_1 \overset{t}{\leadsto} l(i) \mid i \in \operatorname{dom} l\})$ h, h1.4, $\overset{t}{\leadsto}$
1.4.6 $\sigma_2 \overset{t}{\leadsto} (\sigma_1 \overset{t}{\leadsto} mk\text{-}FT(f, l)) =$
     $mk\text{-}FT(f, \{i \mapsto \sigma_2 \overset{t}{\leadsto} (\sigma_1 \overset{t}{\leadsto} l(i)) \mid i \in \operatorname{dom} \{i \mapsto \sigma_1 \overset{t}{\leadsto} l(i) \mid i \in \operatorname{dom} l\}\})$
                     h, 1.4.5, h1.4, $\overset{t}{\leadsto}$
1.4.7 $\sigma_2 \overset{t}{\leadsto} (\sigma_1 \overset{t}{\leadsto} mk\text{-}FT(f, l)) =$
     $mk\text{-}FT(f, \{i \mapsto \sigma_2 \overset{t}{\leadsto} (\sigma_1 \overset{t}{\leadsto} l(i)) \mid i \in \operatorname{dom} l\})$ 1.4.6, $\overset{t}{\leadsto}$, μ
    infer $R(\sigma_1, \sigma_2) \overset{t}{\leadsto} mk\text{-}FT(f, l) = \sigma_2 \overset{t}{\leadsto} (\sigma_1 \overset{t}{\leadsto} mk\text{-}FT(f, l))$ 1.4.7, 1.4.4
1.5 $\forall t \in GT \cdot R(\sigma_1, \sigma_2) \overset{t}{\leadsto} t = \sigma_2 \overset{t}{\leadsto} (\sigma_1 \overset{t}{\leadsto} t)$ $\forall$-I (*GT-Ind* (1.3, 1.4))
1.6 $post\text{-}\circ(\sigma_1, \sigma_2, R(\sigma_1, \sigma_2))$ 1.5, $\circ$
1.7 $R(\sigma_1, \sigma_2) \in Subst$ 1.1
  infer $\exists \phi \in Subst \cdot post\text{-}\circ(\sigma_1, \sigma_2, \phi)$ $\exists$-I (1.7, 1.6)
2 $\delta(pre\text{-}\circ(\sigma_1, \sigma_2))$ $\overset{t}{\leadsto}$, $\in$
infer $pre\text{-}\circ(\sigma_1, \sigma_2) \Rightarrow \exists \phi \in Subst \cdot post\text{-}\circ(\sigma_1, \sigma_2, \phi)$ $\Rightarrow$ -I (1,2)

Figure 5.3 Main proof of implementability of substitution composition

types introduced in the specification via the operators also introduced there.

As in Algorithm 3, the procedure will be iterative, generating and resolving disagreement sets until either the set of terms reduces to a singleton under application of the constructed substitution or a clash or cycle is found and the set is deemed nonunifiable.

Algorithm development

Technique

Now that a specification of unification has been given, we can consider the design of an algorithm which meets the specification. In Section 5.1, Algorithm 3 was developed informally, but here the design will proceed in a controlled manner, starting from the specification. We begin with the specification of the operation we wish to implement (in this case *MGU*) and break it down into structured code in some suitable implementation language. The development proceeds in stages. For example, if we are developing an algorithm similar to Algorithm 3 above, we can break *MGU* into two operations which are sequentially composed:

Initialization; MainPhase

Initialization will itself be broken down into sequentially composed assignments while MainPhase employs a while-loop whose body breaks down into nested conditionals and so on. This process of breaking an operation down into component operations linked by combinators is called *operation decomposition*. The combinators are usually based on constructs of an implementation language, but need not be so concrete. Successive decompositions can be used to eliminate the more abstract combinators so that the fully decomposed operation specification is a program in the implementation language.

At each step in a decomposition, the code designer chooses to introduce a new construct from a range of alternatives. The step involves a design decision – and in a rigorous development such design decisions must be shown to preserve the properties of the specification which forms the input to the decomposition step. Thus each step generates a proof obligation. The behaviour of each construct in the combinator/implementation language is described by rules which are used to justify the decomposition step.

What do the operation decomposition rules look like? It is possible to 'comment' a program with assertions over the state variables. Operation decomposition rules allow the manipulation of these assertions. The set of rules used in a development clearly depend on the particular implementation language chosen. For the purposes of this case study, the rules needed are as follows.

Assignment. $\dfrac{:=\text{-}I}{\{WD(e) \wedge E\}\ x\colon= e\ \{x = \overleftarrow{e}\ \wedge E(\overleftarrow{x}\,/x)\}}$

where $E(\overleftarrow{x}/x)$ is E with all free xs replaced by $\overleftarrow{x}$. Thus if E is asserted before an assignment, it can, properly qualified, be asserted afterwards. $WD(e)$ indicates that e should denote a proper value (i.e. it should not be undefined). Strictly, there is a class of such assignment rules, one for each possible type. Thus if T is the class of all types, then for each $T\colon T$.

$$\boxed{:= \text{-}I}\frac{}{\{e \in T \wedge E\}\ x\colon= e\ \{x = \overleftarrow{e} \wedge E(\overleftarrow{x}/x)\}}$$

Conditional. $\boxed{\text{if-}I}\dfrac{\{pre \wedge test\}\ TH\ \{post\};\ \{pre \wedge \neg test\}\ EL\ \{post\}}{\{pre\}\ (\text{if } test \text{ then } TH \text{ else } EL)\ \{post\}}$

In order to introduce a conditional given *pre*, show that the *post*-assertion holds in both limbs separately.

Iteration. $\boxed{\text{while-}I}\dfrac{\{inv \wedge test\}\ S\ \{inv \wedge rel\}}{\{inv\}\ \text{while } test \text{ do } S \text{ end } \{inv \wedge rel^* \wedge \neg test\}}$

inv is an invariant predicate which is true before and after each iteration of the loop. The predicate *rel* denotes a well-founded and transitive relation on states before and after execution on the loop body. rel^* is its reflexive closure.

Sequential composition. $\boxed{;\text{-}I}\dfrac{\{pre_1\}\ S_1\ \{post_1 \wedge pre_2\};\ \{pre_2\}\ S_2\ \{post_2\}}{\{pre_1\}\ (S_1;S_2)\ \{post_1 \mid post_2\}}$

where

$$post_1 \mid post_2(\overleftarrow{\sigma}, \sigma) \quad \triangleq \quad \exists \sigma_i \in \Sigma \cdot post_1(\overleftarrow{\sigma}, \sigma_i) \wedge post_2(\sigma_i, \sigma)$$

The hypotheses ensure that the two operations S_1 and S_2 *can* be connected sequentially, i.e. that S_1 sets up a state in which S_2 is defined. The conclusion states that there is then an intermediate state linking the state before $S_1;S_2$ to that after. Note that if $post_1$ and $post_2$ are single-state predicates, so that they refer only to σ and not to $\overleftarrow{\sigma}$, this rule simplifies to

$$\boxed{;\text{-}I'}\frac{\{pre_1\}\ S_1\ \{post_1\};\ \{post_1\}\ S_2\ \{post_2\}}{\{pre_1\}\ (S_1;S_2)\ \{post_2\}}$$

Consequence. $\boxed{weaken}\dfrac{pre_s \Rightarrow pre;\ \{pre\}\ S\ \{post\};\ post \Rightarrow post_w}{\{pre_s\}\ S\ \{post_w\}}$

If S satisfies a specification then it satisfies a weaker specification.

Nondeterministic choice. $\boxed{\text{let-}I}\ \dfrac{s \neq \{\ \};\ \{pre \wedge v \in s\}\ S\ \{post\}}{\{pre\}\ \text{let } v \in\ s \text{ in } S\ \{post\}}$

This rule does not appear in [Jon90]. It allows the introduction of a nondeterministic choice construct provided the set over which selection is made is nonempty.

Inheritance. $\boxed{pre}\ \dfrac{\{pre\}\ S\ \{post\}}{\{pre\}\ S\ \{\overleftarrow{pre} \wedge post\}}$

This allows the strengthening of a *post*-assertion by addition of the *pre*-assertion with all the free variables hooked. Note that for any variable v to which the S operation has only rd or no access, $\overleftarrow{v} = v$. We will tend to use this fact implicitly below.

The development

As has been indicated above, the development process involves the manipulation of assertions about the state and program variables. We kick this process off by using the pre- and post-conditions of the operation we wish to implement. MGUAlg will be *correct* with respect to the specification of *MGU* if, for all starting states satisfying *pre-MGU*, the algorithm terminates and does so with a state satisfying *post-MGU*. Note that *post-MGU* is a single-state predicate so we may write *post-MGU* (s, b, u) instead of *post-MGU* $(\overleftarrow{s}, \overleftarrow{b}, \overleftarrow{u}, s, b, u)$. Note that since s is a rd-only component of the state, we can use the fact that $s = \overleftarrow{s}$ when appropriate.

Thus the following should hold:

$$\{\text{true}\}\ \text{MGUAlg}\ \{post\text{-}MGU\ (s, b, u)\}$$

We must construct a proof which concludes this from definitions.

The first development step breaks MGUAlg into an initialization phase and a main processing phase (the loop which will construct the unifier). Then:

$$\{\text{true}\}\ \text{Initialization; MainPhase}\ \{post\text{-}MGU\ (s, b, u)\}$$

This decomposition has to be justified by the ;-*I* rule. Our proof is then of the form shown in Figure 5.4. The lemmas[1] used in Figure 5.4 are:

$$\{\text{true}\}\ \text{Initialization}\ \{u = \{\ \} \wedge b\} \tag{5.1}$$

$$\{u = \{\ \} \wedge b\}\ \text{MainPhase}\ \{post\text{-}MGU\ (s, b, u)\} \tag{5.2}$$

---

[1]In the sequel, lemmas are shown as numbered formulae.

from *Definitions*

1   {true} Initialization; MainPhase $\{\overleftarrow{u} = \{\} \wedge b \wedge post\text{-}MGU\,(s,b,u)\}$

                                              ;-*I'*(Lemma 5.1, Lemma 5.2)

2    $\overleftarrow{u} = \{\} \wedge \overleftarrow{b} \wedge post\text{-}MGU\,(s,b,u) \implies post\text{-}MGU\,(s,b,u)$

                                                $\implies$, $\mathbb{B}$, *Set*

infer {true} MGUAlg $\{post\text{-}MGU\,(s,b,u)\}$ *weaken*(1,2)

Figure 5.4 Form of main developmental proof for MGUAlg

from *Definitions*

1    $WD(\{\})$ *WD*
2    $WD(\text{true})$ *WD*
3   true $\implies WD(\{\}) \wedge$ true   1, $\implies$
4    $u = \{\} \wedge$ true $\implies WD(\text{true}) \wedge u = \{\}$ 2, $\implies$, $\wedge$
5    $\{WD(\{\}) \wedge$ true$\}$ $u := \{\}$ $\{u = \{\} \wedge$ true$\}$:= -*I*
6    $\{$true$\}$ $u := \{\}$ $\{WD(\text{true}) \wedge u = \{\}\}$ *weaken*(3,5,4)
7    $\{WD(\text{true}) \wedge u = \{\}\}$ $b := $ true $\{b = $ true $\wedge u = \{\}\}$:= -*I*
infer $\{$true$\}$ $u := \{\}$; $b := $ true $\{u = \{\} \wedge b = $ true$\}$;-*I'*(6,7)

Figure 5.5 Developmental proof for Initialization

   Lemma 5.1's proof justifies the development of Initialization and Lemma 5.2's that of MainPhase. First consider Initialization. It can be decomposed into:

$$\{\text{true}\}\ u := \{\};\ b := \text{true}\ \{u = \{\} \wedge b\}$$

The proof of Lemma 5.1 in Figure 5.5 is one possible justification for this decomposition. In the rest of this study, arguments relating to the 'definedness' of assigned expressions will be suppressed to avoid obscuring the substance of the development.

   Now for the (more complex) decomposition of MainPhase. It is intended that, as in Algorithm 3, MainPhase be a loop which generates disagreements and tries to resolve them, adding a new component to u each time (unless a clash or cycle is detected). So

from *Definitions*

1    $\{inv\}$ MainPhase $\{inv \land \neg test \land rel^*\}$ while-*I* (Lemma 5.3)

infer $\{u = \{\,\} \land b\}$ MainPhase $\{post\text{-}MGU\,(s,b,u)\}$

weaken (Lemma 5.4, 1, Lemma 5.5)

Figure 5.6 Justifying the while loop introduction

one possible decomposition of MainPhase is as follows:

$$\{u = \{\,\} \land b\}$$
$$\text{while card}\, u \stackrel{s}{\rightsquigarrow} s > 1 \land b$$
$$\quad \text{Body}$$
$$\text{endwhile}$$
$$\{post\text{-}MGU\,(s,b,u)\}$$

We would like to use while-*I* to justify this decomposition via a proof of Lemma 5.2 of the form shown in Figure 5.6 (where *test* stands for card $u \stackrel{s}{\rightsquigarrow} s > 1 \land b$) and the lemmas used are:

$$\{inv \land test\}\ \text{Body}\ \{inv \land rel\} \tag{5.3}$$

$$u = \{\,\} \land b \ \Rightarrow\ inv \tag{5.4}$$

$$inv \land \neg test \land rel^* \ \Rightarrow\ post\text{-}MGU\,(s,b,u) \tag{5.5}$$

Now *inv* and *rel* must be chosen so that Lemmas 5.4 and 5.5 are satisfied and Body must be developed so that Lemma 5.3 holds.

The relation *rel* should be well-founded, relating states at the beginning of each execution of the loop body to the corresponding states at the end of the loop body. It describes the possible state transitions caused by the loop body. It should refer to a decreasing quantity in the system and should not have an infinitely descending chain of values of that quantity, so that termination of the loop can be proved. In the case of Body, two possible kinds of state transitions have to be described: *either* the terms are found to be nonunifiable (clash or cycle discovered) and *b* is set false to force termination *or* a disagreement is resolved and the number of variables in $u \stackrel{s}{\rightsquigarrow} s$ is reduced (since the new substitution component replaces the variable in the disagreement with a term which introduces no new variables). The number of variables in $u \stackrel{s}{\rightsquigarrow} s$ has to be at least zero, so the following well-founded transitive *rel* is suggested:[2]

---

[2]The interested reader may care to prove the well-foundedness and transitivity of this relation.

$$rel \quad \triangleq \quad \overleftarrow{b} \wedge \neg b$$
$$\vee \; \overleftarrow{b} \wedge b \wedge NV(\overleftarrow{u} \overset{s}{\leadsto} s) > NV(u \overset{s}{\leadsto} s)$$

What factors need to be invariant over all iterations of MainPhase? These form *inv*. As the loop executes, disagreements are resolved and each resolution brings *u* closer to being a most general unifier for *s* and if *b* is ever set false then *s* is not unifiable.

$$inv \quad \triangleq \quad (\forall \theta \in Subst \cdot \theta \; unifies \; s \; \Rightarrow \; \exists \lambda \in Subst \cdot \theta = u \circ \lambda)$$
$$\wedge \neg b \; \Rightarrow \; \neg Unifiable \, (s)$$

Does this choice of *inv* and *rel* satisfy the criteria imposed by Lemmas 5.4 and 5.5?

Lemma 5.4 holds because if $u = \{\,\}$ then θ itself is a suitable λ in *inv* since $\theta = \{\,\} \circ \lambda$. The second conjunct of *inv* is vacuously true because *b* is true.

Lemma 5.5 holds because if $inv \wedge \neg (card \, u \overset{s}{\leadsto} s > 1 \wedge b) \wedge rel^*$ then:

Case: if *b* then $card \, u \overset{s}{\leadsto} s \leq 1$, in which case *u unifies s* and (by *inv*) $MGen \, (u, s)$.

Case: if $\neg b$ then (by *inv*) $\neg Unifiable \, (s)$.

These two cases construct *post-MGU* (s, b, u).

So now we have an *inv* and *rel* which can serve for the development of the loop body. Body is to be filled out so that the following holds where $test = card \, u \overset{s}{\leadsto} s > 1 \wedge b$:

$$\{inv \wedge test\} \; \mathsf{Body} \; \{inv \wedge rel\}$$

The body must check the disagreement set for clashes of function symbols and cycles. If none are found, a new component must be added to *u*. Let the cycle and clash checks be done by nested if-statements. Firstly the clash check:

$$\{inv \wedge test\}$$
if $V\text{-}Id \cap Dis \, (u \overset{s}{\leadsto} s) = \{\,\}$ then $b := \mathsf{false}$
else CycleCheck
$$\{inv \wedge rel\}$$

This decomposition can be proved valid (using if-*I*) if Lemmas 5.6 and 5.7 hold:

$$\{inv \wedge test \wedge V\text{-}Id \cap Dis \, (u \overset{s}{\leadsto} s) = \{\,\}\} \; b := \mathsf{false} \; \{inv \wedge rel\} \tag{5.6}$$

$$\{inv \wedge test \wedge V\text{-}Id \cap Dis \, (u \overset{s}{\leadsto} s) \neq \{\,\}\}$$
CycleCheck
$$\{inv \wedge rel\} \tag{5.7}$$

One proof of Lemma 5.6 using $:= \text{-}I$, *weaken* and *pre* is shown in Figure 5.7.

from *Definitions*

1   *WD*(false)   WD

2    $\{WD(\text{false}) \land \neg\, Unifiable\,(s)\}$ $b := \text{false}$ $\{\neg\, Unifiable\,(s) \land \neg b\}$ $:= \text{-}I$

3    $\neg\, Unifiable\,(s) \;\Rightarrow\; WD(\text{false}) \land \neg\, Unifiable\,(s)$ $1, \Rightarrow, \land$

4    $\{\neg\, Unifiable\,(s)\}$ $b := \text{false}$ $\{\neg\, Unifiable\,(s) \land \neg b\}$ *weaken*(3,2)

5    $\{inv \land test \land V\text{-}Id \cap Dis\,(u \overset{s}{\leadsto} s) = \{\,\}\}$

     $b := \text{false}$

     $\{\neg\, Unifiable\,(s) \land \neg b\}$ *weaken* (Lemma 5.8, 4)

6    $\{inv \land test \land V\text{-}Id \cap Dis\,(u \overset{s}{\leadsto} s) = \{\,\}\}$

     $b := \text{false}$

     $\{\overleftarrow{inv} \land \overleftarrow{test} \land V\text{-}Id \cap Dis\,(\overleftarrow{u} \overset{s}{\leadsto} s) = \{\,\} \land \neg\, Unifiable\,(s) \land \neg b\}$ *pre* (5)

infer $\{inv \land test \land V\text{-}Id \cap Dis\,(u \overset{s}{\leadsto} s) = \{\,\}\}$ $b := \text{false}$ $\{inv \land rel\}$

                                                      weaken (6, Lemma 5.9)

Figure 5.7 Proving the first conditional limb

Note that the lemmas required by this proof are really facts about the data types and operations in the specification. They can be proved separately, independent of the algorithm development and operation decomposition rules. Since at this point we can stop using the operation decomposition rules and appeal to the theory associated with the original specification, we call these 'terminal lemmas'. They are:

$$(inv \land test \land V\text{-}Id \cap Dis\,(u \overset{s}{\leadsto} s) = \{\,\}) \;\Rightarrow\; \neg\, Unifiable\,(s) \tag{5.8}$$

$$\overleftarrow{inv} \land \overleftarrow{test} \land V\text{-}Id \cap Dis\,(\overleftarrow{u} \overset{s}{\leadsto} s) = \{\,\} \land \neg\, Unifiable\,(s) \land \neg b \;\Rightarrow\; inv \land rel \tag{5.9}$$

The proof of Lemma 5.8 depends on the fact that if there are no variables in $Dis\,(u \overset{s}{\leadsto} s)$ then s is not unifiable because a clash has been detected. For Lemma 5.9, since s is not unifiable, *inv* holds. *rel* holds after the assignment because b has been changed from true to false.

Proving Lemma 5.7 guides the development of CycleCheck. The idea is to select a variable from the disagreement set (using nondeterministic choice) and then check for a term containing it in the disagreement set. The presence of such a term means the original set of terms was un-unifiable. First, the introduction of the let statement:

$$\{inv \land test \land V\text{-}Id \cap Dis\,(u \overset{s}{\leadsto} s) \neq \{\,\}\}$$

let $v \in V\text{-}Id \cap Dis\,(u \overset{s}{\leadsto} s)$ in

CycleCheck′

$$\{inv \land rel\}$$

For this to be a correct decomposition (by let-*I*) we require that:

$$\{inv \wedge test \wedge V\text{-}Id \cap Dis(u \overset{s}{\leadsto} s) \neq \{\} \wedge v \in V\text{-}Id \cap Dis(u \overset{s}{\leadsto} s)\}$$
CycleCheck′
$$\{inv \wedge rel\}$$

Now let CycleCheck′ be a conditional which looks for a potential cycle. If none is found, resolve a disagreement. So we will have:

$$\{inv \wedge test \wedge V\text{-}Id \cap Dis(u \overset{s}{\leadsto} s) \neq \{\} \wedge v \in V\text{-}Id \cap Dis(u \overset{s}{\leadsto} s)\}$$
if $\exists t \in Dis(u \overset{s}{\leadsto} s) - \{v\} \cdot Occurs(v, t)$ then $b := \mathsf{false}$
else Resolve
$$\{inv \wedge rel\}$$

If this is to be a valid decomposition (by if-*I*), the following two lemmas must hold:

$$
\begin{array}{l}
\{inv \wedge test \wedge V\text{-}Id \cap Dis(u \overset{s}{\leadsto} s) \neq \{\} \wedge v \in V\text{-}Id \cap Dis(u \overset{s}{\leadsto} s) \\
\wedge \exists t \in Dis(u \overset{s}{\leadsto} s) - \{v\} \cdot Occurs(v, t)\} \\
b := \mathsf{false} \\
\{inv \wedge rel\}
\end{array}
\tag{5.10}
$$

$$
\begin{array}{l}
\{inv \wedge test \wedge V\text{-}Id \cap Dis(u \overset{s}{\leadsto} s) \neq \{\} \wedge v \in V\text{-}Id \cap Dis(u \overset{s}{\leadsto} s) \\
\wedge \not\exists t \in Dis(u \overset{s}{\leadsto} s) - \{v\} \cdot Occurs(v, t)\} \\
\mathsf{Resolve} \\
\{inv \wedge rel\}
\end{array}
\tag{5.11}
$$

Discharging 5.10 proceeds in a similar way to 5.6, and the terminal lemmas are:

$$
\begin{array}{l}
(inv \wedge test \wedge V\text{-}Id \cap Dis(u \overset{s}{\leadsto} s) \neq \{\} \wedge v \in V\text{-}Id \cap Dis(u \overset{s}{\leadsto} s) \\
\wedge \exists t \in Dis(u \overset{s}{\leadsto} s) - \{v\} \cdot Occurs(v, t)) \\
\Rightarrow \neg Unifiable(s)
\end{array}
\tag{5.12}
$$

$$
\begin{array}{l}
(\overleftarrow{inv} \wedge \overleftarrow{test} \wedge V\text{-}Id \cap Dis(\overleftarrow{u} \overset{s}{\leadsto} s) \neq \{\} \wedge v \in V\text{-}Id \cap Dis(\overleftarrow{u} \overset{s}{\leadsto} s) \\
\wedge \exists t \in Dis(\overleftarrow{u} \overset{s}{\leadsto} s) - \{v\} \cdot Occurs(v, t)) \\
\wedge (\neg Unifiable(s) \wedge \neg b) \\
\Rightarrow inv \wedge rel
\end{array}
\tag{5.13}
$$

The proof of Lemma 5.12 depends on the fact that if there is a term t in $Dis(u \overset{s}{\leadsto} s) - \{v\}$ containing v then the original set s is not unifiable.[3] Given this we can show Lemma 5.13. *inv* holds because s has no unifiers and *rel* holds because b has been set to false.

---

[3] Again, this property can be proved separately.

The proof of Lemma 5.11 governs the decomposition of Resolve. Resolve will (non-deterministically) select a term t' from $Dis\,(u \overset{s}{\leadsto} s) - \{v\}$ and compose $\{v \mapsto t'\}$ into u. Lemma 5.11 would then be:

$$\begin{aligned}
&\{inv \wedge test \wedge V\text{-}Id \cap Dis\,(u \overset{s}{\leadsto} s) \neq \{\,\} \wedge v \in V\text{-}Id \cap Dis\,(u \overset{s}{\leadsto} s) \\
&\wedge \not\exists t \in Dis\,(u \overset{s}{\leadsto} s) - \{v\} \cdot Occurs\,(v,t)\} \\
&\text{let } t' \in \{t \in Dis\,(u \overset{s}{\leadsto} s) - \{v\} \mid \neg Occurs\,(v,t)\} \text{ in} \\
&u := R(u, \{v \mapsto t'\}) \\
&\{inv \wedge rel\}
\end{aligned}$$

For this to be a valid decomposition (by *let-I*) the following must hold:

$$\begin{aligned}
&\{inv \wedge test \wedge V\text{-}Id \cap Dis\,(u \overset{s}{\leadsto} s) \neq \{\,\} \wedge v \in V\text{-}Id \cap Dis\,(u \overset{s}{\leadsto} s) \\
&\wedge \not\exists t \in Dis\,(u \overset{s}{\leadsto} s) - \{v\} \cdot Occurs\,(v,t) \\
&\wedge t' \in \{t \in Dis\,(u \overset{s}{\leadsto} s) - \{v\} \mid \neg Occurs\,(v,t)\}\} \\
&u := R(u, \{v \mapsto t'\}) \\
&\{inv \wedge rel\}
\end{aligned} \qquad (5.14)$$

Let the pre-assignment assertion be called X for brevity. To show the validity of this decomposition, use $:= \text{-}I$, *weaken* and *pre* in the usual way, the terminal lemmas being:

$$X \Rightarrow {}^{\textbf{.}} WD(R(\overset{\leftarrow}{u}, \{v \mapsto t'\})) \qquad (5.15)$$

$$X(\overset{\leftarrow}{u}/u) \wedge u = R(\overset{\leftarrow}{u}, \{v \mapsto t'\}) \Rightarrow inv \wedge rel \qquad (5.16)$$

Discharging Lemma 5.15 involves showing that $\overset{\leftarrow}{u}$ and $\{v \mapsto t'\}$ are indeed well-formed substitutions. Discharging Lemma 5.16 amounts to showing that, for any substitution θ unifying s which could be constructed from u, θ can still be constructed from u. This construction is, in fact, unchanged. It is also necessary (for *rel*) to show a reduction in the number of variables in $u \overset{s}{\leadsto} s$. Since v and t' are drawn from terms in $\overset{\leftarrow}{u} \overset{s}{\leadsto} s$, v occurs in a term in $\overset{\leftarrow}{u} \overset{s}{\leadsto} s$. v does not occur in t' so replacing all occurrences of v in $\overset{\leftarrow}{u} \overset{s}{\leadsto} s$ by t' will not introduce any variables into $\overset{\leftarrow}{u} \overset{s}{\leadsto} s$ which were not there already and will eliminate v altogether. Hence $NV(\overset{\leftarrow}{u} \overset{s}{\leadsto} s) > NV(u \overset{s}{\leadsto} s)$.

We have now shown

$$\{inv \wedge test\} \text{ Body } \{inv \wedge rel\}$$

and so by *while-I*:

$$\{inv\} \text{ MainPhase } \{inv \wedge \neg test \wedge rel^*\}$$

as required, and the development is completed as per the proof outlined at the beginning of the decomposition. The final algorithm is:

Algorithm MGUAlg
  ext rd s: GT-set
    wr b: $\mathbb{B}$
    wr u: *Subst*
    u: = { };
    b: = true;
    while card $u \overset{s}{\leadsto} s > 1 \wedge b$
      if $V\text{-}Id \cap Dis\,(u \overset{s}{\leadsto} s) = \{\,\}$ then b: = false
      else let $v \in V\text{-}Id \cap Dis\,(u \overset{s}{\leadsto} s)$ in
        if $\exists t \in Dis\,(u \overset{s}{\leadsto} s) \cdot Occurs\,(v, t)$ then b: = false
        else let $t' \in \{t \in Dis\,(u \overset{s}{\leadsto} s) \mid \neg\,Occurs\,(v, t)\}$ in
        u: = $R(u, \{v \mapsto t'\})$
    endwhile
End MGUAlg

It is worth standing back from the minutiae of the development illustrated above to look at the process of development itself. Each program construct introduced represented a *design decision*. Each design decision generated a *proof obligation* to justify the introduction by the operation decomposition rules. The chain of design decisions involved in the development of the algorithm terminated when the obligation could be proved by appealing to properties of the data types and operations on which the algorithm was based. These properties are then proved separately (perhaps using a natural deduction format). Examples of such terminal obligations are 5.8, 5.12 and 5.15. The use of the operation decomposition rules restricts the freedom of the algorithm designer at the point of each design decision to only those possible design options which preserve the truth of the required assertions. This 'chains back' all the way through the development, so that the only justifiable designs are those which respect the original assertions imposed at the start of the development, namely the pre- and post-conditions on the specification of the implemented operation.

5.5   Conclusions

About specification

It is worth considering the process by which the specification was derived, as it illustrates a few interesting points. The brevity of the specification itself is in stark contrast to the amount of time taken over its construction. A first attempt at the specification yielded a simple, but faulty, product. Subsequently it grew more complex, including features like a cyclicity testing function for substitutions. After a certain level of complexity had been reached, it became more apparent that a simpler specification (which still dealt with acyclic substitutions) would result from using ideas like the idempotence property.

Introducing the idempotence invariant on substitutions did have a complicating effect on the specification's explanation, necessitating the introduction of ideas such as var-disjointedness and substitution reduction. It is often the case that devoting a little extra time to the specification phase in a rigorous development produces a more considered, and possibly much simplified, result for delivery to the developer.

It is noted (Section 5.2) that the idempotence (var-disjointedness) requirement on substitutions is a restriction on this theory of unification. Idempotence is documented as an invariant primarily for the benefit of further development. The algorithm developed does not use the property, but other algorithms might use results from a theory of unification which does exploit idempotence. However, the aim of this case study is not to develop such a theory, but rather to develop a specification for practical use. *inv-Subst* may reduce the generality of substitutions permitted, but the excluded substitutions can be reduced to an acceptable form.

Only some simple proofs of properties about the specification have been shown, and those not in great depth. It is worth noting that the level of detail required in proofs should be decided with an awareness of the consequences of opting for low-level detailed proofs in terms of the effort required. These proofs are often long and routine, requiring relatively little mathematical insight, a characteristic which makes their development susceptible to automated assistance [JL88].

Implementability proofs play an important role in this study. In the case of substitution composition, an implementation (the function R) is developed in the proof. This method is related to the *constructive mathematics* approach illustrated in [MW80, MW81, C+86]. Development can be viewed as the constructive discharging of the implementability proof, but there are major pragmatic differences discharge the implementability obligation at an abstratct level and actually going about the development of executable code. For example, R may not be directly executable in the language or on the machine of our choice. It merely shows the existence of an implementation defined on the data types of the specification. The algorithm MGUAlg, based round more classical imperative programming constructs, may be nearer executable code for a particular application. Operation decomposition would not be an appropriate technique for constructing the abstract proof of *MGU* implementability. Certainly the development of an implementation does discharge the implementability obligation, but failure to *attempt* the implementability proof at the abstract level of a specification can result in a huge amount of wasted development time if it transpires that no implementation exists.

About development

This intimate connection between development and proof has other consequences. The author freely confesses great difficulty experienced in choosing how to present the development of Section 5.4. Should one begin with the terminal lemmas and provide a bottom-up construction, building the necessary program constructs? No, for who would begin a development by producing Lemma 5.15 out of thin air? The development process itself is not purely bottom-up. Nor is it purely top-down: the designer does not groundlessly choose to introduce a conditional construct here and a while-loop there. In this study an attempt has been made to steer a middle course. The overall development is top-down in that it decomposes the specification of *MGU* , but individual steps have been bottom-up, introducing constructs derived from the informally developed algorithm of Section 5.1. It is important to note, however, that a formal development is more than just a pretty way of documenting the design.

It is suggested in Section 5.1 that the 'hack it until you think it's right' approach to algorithm design may benefit from some formalism. Controlled development from a formal specification allows real conviction of the algorithm's correctness to be gained. But how does one gain conviction of the *specification's* correctness? Has the 'hack it' approach only been shifted out of the implementation phase and put into the specification phase of development? The interface between intuitive ideas and formalism must come somewhere. The advantage of the approach described here is that there are obligations to be met by the specification. The proofs of obligations provide an environment in which the details of the specification can be opened to systematic scrutiny in a way in which raw code cannot. Faults discovered at this stage can be corrected before they reach code. This method results in a top-down approach to proving lemmas about the data objects and operations in the specification. Only those properties required for the main obligation-discharging proof are proved.

About further work

One motivating factor for this case study is the need to provide a formal basis for the development and analysis of a *range* of unification algorithms. How far has the work presented gone towards meeting that need? Success in this respect depends on the degree of abstraction inherent in the specification. One might ask what changes are needed to the specification to allow development of another algorithm and whether those changes just amount to reifications. MGUAlg is a derivative of Robinson's original, so other algorithms sharing this approach should be relatively easy to develop in a manner similar to that used above. Operation decomposition techniques might also be used to develop other types of algorithm (e.g. [PW78]) and this is one area for future work. The level of abstraction at which the specification is set means that reification steps can be taken to develop algorithms working on more concrete data structures, such as the directed acyclic graph structure for terms discussed in Section 5.1.

There are several other areas into which the approach described here on model-oriented specifications of unification might extend. For example:

- The extension of the specification to allow equational theories on first order terms:

particular properties (such as associativity) can be built into a unification algorithm [Bun83].

- A universal unification algorithm is one which, given a set of terms and a theory, returns a complete set of unifiers for the terms within the theory [Sie84]. One approach to specifying this might be the representation of equational axioms as sets of rewrite rules.

- The semidecidable problem of unification of second order terms: Bundy [Bun83] presents an algorithm due to Huet which incorporates the α-,β- and η- rules of λ-calculus. The specification of this sort of problem might require not only the specification of a data type for second order terms, but the incorporation of equational axioms as well.

5.6 Additional material

Weakness of pre-condition on substitution composition

It is to be shown that no pairs of substitutions excluded by *pre-* $\circ$ have a var-disjoint composed form satisfying *post-* $\circ$, i.e.:

$$\forall \sigma_1, \sigma_2 \in Subst \cdot \neg pre\text{-} \circ (\sigma_1, \sigma_2) \;\Rightarrow\; \nexists r \in Subst \cdot post\text{-} \circ (\sigma_1, \sigma_2, r)$$

Consider any $\sigma_1, \sigma_2 \in Subst$ such that $\neg pre\text{-} \circ (\sigma_1, \sigma_2)$. Then:

$$\neg \forall x, y \in \mathrm{dom}\,\sigma_1 \cup \mathrm{dom}\,\sigma_2 \cdot Occurs\,(x, \sigma_2 \overset{t}{\leadsto} (\sigma_1 \overset{t}{\leadsto} y)) \;\Rightarrow\; x = \sigma_2 \overset{t}{\leadsto} (\sigma_1 \overset{t}{\leadsto} x)$$

by definition of *pre-* $\circ$.

So now consider $x, y \in \mathrm{dom}\,\sigma_1 \cup \mathrm{dom}\,\sigma_2$ under the assumption:

$$Occurs\,(x, \sigma_2 \overset{t}{\leadsto} (\sigma_1 \overset{t}{\leadsto} y)) \wedge x \neq \sigma_2 \overset{t}{\leadsto} (\sigma_1 \overset{t}{\leadsto} x)$$

and consider any substitution r:

Case $x \in \mathrm{dom}\,r$ and $y \in \mathrm{dom}\,r$.

   1.1 $r \in Subst$, so $Var\text{-}Disj(r)$

   1.2   So $\neg \exists x', y' \in \mathrm{dom}\,r \cdot Occurs\,(x', r(y'))$

   1.3   In particular $\neg Occurs\,(x, r(y))$

   1.4   and $\neg Occurs\,(x, r \overset{t}{\leadsto} y)$ since $r \overset{t}{\leadsto} y = r(y)$ by definition of $\overset{t}{\leadsto}$.

So $r \overset{t}{\leadsto} y \neq \sigma_2 \overset{t}{\leadsto} (\sigma_1 \overset{t}{\leadsto} y)$ because otherwise (by assumption) $Occurs\,(x, \sigma_2 \overset{t}{\leadsto} (\sigma_1 \overset{t}{\leadsto} y))$; hence $Occurs\,(x, r \overset{t}{\leadsto} y)$, which would contradict line 1.4 above.

Case $x \in \mathrm{dom}\,r$ and $y \notin \mathrm{dom}\,r$.

   2.1 $r \overset{t}{\leadsto} y = y$ by definition of $\overset{t}{\leadsto}$

  2.2 $x \neq y$, by the case assumption

  2.3 $\neg\, Occurs\,(x, y)$ by definition of *Occurs*

  2.4 $\neg\, Occurs\,(x, r \overset{t}{\leadsto} y)$ by line 2.1 above

So $r \overset{t}{\leadsto} y \neq \sigma_2 \overset{t}{\leadsto} (\sigma_1 \overset{t}{\leadsto} y)$ because otherwise (by assumption) $Occurs\,(x, \sigma_2 \overset{t}{\leadsto} (\sigma_1 \overset{t}{\leadsto} y))$; hence $Occurs\,(x, r \overset{t}{\leadsto} y)$, which would contradict line 2.4 above.

Case $x \notin \operatorname{dom} r$

  3.1 $r \overset{t}{\leadsto} x = x$ by definition of $\overset{t}{\leadsto}$

  3.2   So $r \overset{t}{\leadsto} x \neq \sigma_2 \overset{t}{\leadsto} (\sigma_1 \overset{t}{\leadsto} x)$ by assumptions.

Thus, in this case, x is a term for which r does not generate the same result as applying σ_1 and then σ_2. So when $x \in \operatorname{dom} r$, *post-* ∘ does not hold. This exhausts the possible cases. Thus under the current assumption, there is a term (x or y) for which r does not generate the same result as applying σ_1 and then σ_2.

    By case distinction, for any r, *post-* ∘ does not hold. It is, therefore, not possible to generate a suitable r when the assumption $\neg\, pre\text{-} \circ (\sigma_1, \sigma_2)$ holds. Hence

$$\forall \sigma_1, \sigma_2 \in Subst \cdot \neg\, pre\text{-} \circ (\sigma_1, \sigma_2) \;\Rightarrow\; \nexists\, r \in Subst \cdot post\text{-} \circ (\sigma_1, \sigma_2, r)$$

Acknowledgements

The work described here was begun as an undergraduate project in the Computing & Information Systems degree course at Manchester University. The author owes a debt of gratitude to Ursula Martin and Cliff Jones for their careful supervision. Thanks are also due to Tim Clement, Peter Lindsay, Steve Palmer and Ralf Kneuper for their helpful comments. This work has been financed by the Department of Education for Northern Ireland.

6

Building a Theory of Unification

Sunil Vadera

The same application is addressed here as in the previous chapter. The emphasis in Sunil Vadera's work is on building a theory of the basic concepts which are discussed in the specification and development. Sunil Vadera's work was done independently of John Fitzgerald's and a comparison of the two chapters well illustrates the point that there is no single 'right' approach to a specification. The chapters can be read independently but a careful comparison pinpoints interesting differences like the precise invariant on substitution mappings. The algorithm developed in this chapter is quite space efficient.

6.1   Introduction

Unification is an important concept. It is used in Prolog, resolution, term rewriting, and natural language understanding. As the use of formal methods increase, unification will be part of formally developed systems. Hence a theory of unification is desirable.

We use VDM to formalize unification. We define substitution application recursively, develop a theory of noncircular substitutions, and write an implicit specification of unification. Some example proofs are presented in the theory.

The correctness of a particular unification algorithm is proved with respect to the specification. The algorithm proved is more space efficient than the one proved by Manna and Waldinger. We also compare the theory developed with that of Manna and Waldinger and present some advantages of using VDM.

The unification algorithm is used in many systems. It is used in resolution [Rob65] and term rewriting [HO80] approaches to theorem proving. It is a key feature of the programming language Prolog [CM84]. It is used in natural language understanding [SA77]. Siekmann [Sie84] describes the uses of unification, and Fitzgerald (see Chapter 5 of this book) lists the applications.

The systems that use unification obviously rely on its correctness, and on specific properties of unification. Further, as the use of formal methods of software development increase, unification will be part of systems which are developed formally (e.g. [Nil84]). Hence, we develop a theory of unification.

Section 6.1 summarizes some conventions, and the induction rule that we use. It also introduces the main ideas of unification. These ideas are then formalized in sections 6.2 to 6.6. Section 6.7 uses this formalization to prove a particular unification algorithm correct. Section 6.8 compares the theory developed with that of Manna and Waldinger [MW81].

In formalizing our notion of unification, we also present the proofs of some lemmas. For conciseness, we omit a number of proofs. These can be found in Vadera [Vad86].

Some conventions

Proof obligation

To show that a function, f with domain Tp and range Tr satisfies a specification, we have to prove:

$$\forall p \in Tp \cdot \textit{pre-f}(p) \;\Rightarrow\; \textit{post-f}(p, f(p)) \wedge f(p) \in Tr$$

When the pre-condition is true, and the result is clearly of the right type, we will write this in the more compact form: $\textit{post-f}(p)f(p)$.

Induction

Mathematical induction is a technique of proving that a property P holds for the set of natural numbers. To show that $P(n)$ is true for all $n \in \mathbb{N}$, we first show that $P(0)$ is true. Then, we show that $P(j)$ is true under the assumption that $P(k)$ is true for all $k < j$, where $j > 0$.

To use induction on a set other than $\mathbb{N}$, say D, we define a total function which maps the elements of D onto $\mathbb{N}$. We also use induction on $\mathbb{N}_1$, and on $\mathbb{N} \times \mathbb{N}_1$.

Proof presentation

We present proofs as in [Jon86a]. However, when referencing a line in a justification we adopt the convention that *.n* refers to a line *m.n* where *m* refers to the enclosing from/infer box. This helps to reduce references like '2.2.3.2.3.2' in a deep proof.

Introduction to unification

A number of problem solving tasks can be posed as finding a proof for a theorem in predicate calculus. When proving theorems, it is often necessary to unify certain expressions. For example, given

good-student(jim)

and

good-student(X) $\Rightarrow$ *pass(X)*

we want to show that *pass(jim)* is true.

We first have to unify *good-student(X)* with *good-student(jim)*. We can do this by setting the variable X to *jim*. We can record this fact in a *substitution*: $\{X \mapsto jim\}$. We call such a substitution a *unifier* of the two terms. We can now *apply* the substitution to *good-student(X)* $\Rightarrow$ *pass(X)*, and eliminate the implication to prove *pass(jim)*.

In general, both the terms to be unified may contain variables. For example, the terms *line(X, 1)* and *line(2, Y)* have a unifier $\{X \mapsto 2, Y \mapsto 1\}$.

Of course, it is not always possible to unify two terms. Thus *line(X, X)* and *line(1, 2)* cannot be unified. Further, the unification process must find the most general unifier. For example, although the terms *line(X)* and *line(Y)* can be unified by an infinite set of unifiers:

$$\{\{X \mapsto 1, Y \mapsto 1\}, \{X \mapsto 2, Y \mapsto 2\}...\}$$

the unification algorithm must return one of the following unifiers:

$$\{X \mapsto Y\} \text{ or } \{Y \mapsto X\}$$

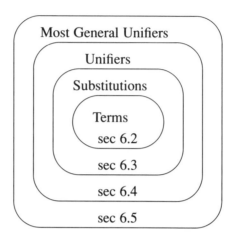

Figure 6.1 Layer by layer formalization

When formalizing unification, we must also decide whether our theory will cater for *circular* substitutions like $\{X \mapsto f(X)\}$.

We formalize these ideas in a layer by layer manner as shown in Figure 6.1. We begin by developing a theory of terms. The theory of substitutions formalizes the notions of substitution application, circular substitutions, substitution equality, substitution composition, and idempotent substitutions. The concepts of a substitution being a unifier and a most general unifier are then formalized.

6.2   Terms

Abstract syntax

Terms are the basic objects that are unified. A term may be a compound term, or a variable. A compound term is one which has a function name followed by a sequence of terms. We specify terms by:

Term = Cmpterm ∪ Var

Cmpterm :: Fid
         Terms

Terms = Term*

Var, Fid = Ident

We denote terms by $t_1, t_2, \ldots, t_n$, and lists of terms by $tl, tl_1, tl_2, \ldots, tl_n$. Variables are denoted by $v, v_1, \ldots, v_n$, or by capital letters. For readability, we prefer to write a well-formed term:

mk-Cmpterm(person, mk-Cmpterm(age, X))

in the concrete syntax:

person(age(X))

Properties of terms

There are a number of properties of terms that we may believe to be true. Thus, the property *the variables in the head of a list of terms is a subset of the variables in the list of terms* is intuitively true. To formalize such properties, we define the functions:

vars-Term : *Term* → *Var*-set
vars-Term(t) △
    cases *t* of
    mk-Cmpterm(fid, tl) → *vars-Terms(tl)*,
    v   → {*v*}
    end

vars-Terms : *Terms* → *Var*-set
vars-Terms(tl) △ ⋃{*vars-Term(tl(i))* | $i \in$ inds *tl*}

vars-Term and *vars-Terms* are abbreviated to *vars* when it is obvious which is meant. Thus,

vars([X, f(Y, g(Z))]) = {*X, Y, Z*}

We can now write the above property as:

len *tl* > 0 ⇒ *vars(hd tl)* ⊆ *vars(tl)*

Notice that we make use of the logic of partial functions. Since, when *tl* is the empty list, hd *tl* is undefined and we have a situation false ⇒ *. Which, by the logic of partial functions, is true.

To carry out the proofs by induction, we will need to order the terms. This is achieved by mapping the terms to natural numbers by the functions:

tm 1 $\text{len}\, tl > 0 \;\Rightarrow\; (vars(\text{hd}\, tl) \subseteq vars(tl))$

tm 2 $\text{len}\, tl > 0 \;\Rightarrow\; (vars(\text{tl}\, tl) \subseteq vars(tl))$

tm 3 $\text{len}\, tl > 0 \;\Rightarrow\; (no\text{-}Term(\text{hd}\, tl) \leq no\text{-}Terms(tl))$

tm 4 $\text{len}\, tl > 0 \;\Rightarrow\; (no\text{-}Terms(\text{tl}\, tl) < no\text{-}Terms(tl))$

tm 5 $no\text{-}Term(mk\text{-}Cmpterm(id,tl)) = no\text{-}Terms(tl) + 1$

tm 6 $vars(mk\text{-}Cmpterm(id,tl)) = vars(tl)$

tm 7 $v \in vars(tl) \;\Leftrightarrow\; (\exists i \in \text{inds}\, tl \cdot v \in vars(tl(i)))$

Figure 6.2 Lemmas about terms

$$
\begin{array}{l}
no\text{-}Term : Terms \to \mathbb{N}_1 \\
no\text{-}Term(t) \;\triangleq\; \text{cases } t \text{ of} \\
\qquad mk\text{-}Cmpterm(fid, tl) \to no\text{-}Terms(tl) + 1, \\
\qquad v \to 1 \\
\qquad \text{end}
\end{array}
$$

$$
\begin{array}{l}
no\text{-}Terms : Terms \to \mathbb{N} \\
no\text{-}Terms(tl) \;\triangleq\; \text{if } tl = [\,] \\
\qquad \text{then } 0 \\
\qquad \text{else } no\text{-}Terms(\text{tl}\, tl) + no\text{-}Term(\text{hd}\, tl)
\end{array}
$$

Thus, $no\text{-}Term(f(Y, g(Z)) = 4$.

Lemmas about terms are straightforward and are listed in Figure 6.2.

6.3 Substitutions

Abstract syntax

A substitution records the bindings of a variable to a term. Hence, a natural VDM specification for substitutions uses maps:

$$Subst = Var \xrightarrow{m} Term$$

VDM's dom operator can be used to obtain the variables in the domain of the substitution. The variables in the range of a substitution can be obtained by applying the function:

$range : Subst \rightarrow Var\text{-set}$
$range(s) \quad \triangleq \quad \bigcup \{vars(s(v)) \mid v \in \mathsf{dom}\, s\}$

Thus $range(s) = \{X, Y, Z\}$ for the substitution:

$s = \{X \mapsto f(Z, Y), Y \mapsto f(X, Y)\}$

For the union of two maps to be defined, their domains must be disjoint. Hence we define:

$dom\text{-}disjoint : Subst \times Subst \rightarrow \mathbb{B}$
$dom\text{-}disjoint(s_1, s_2) \quad \triangleq \quad \mathsf{dom}\, s_1 \cap \mathsf{dom}\, s_2 = \{\,\}$

We will also encounter situations where we discuss a substitution whose domain is disjoint from the range of another. Hence we define:

$dom\text{-}range\text{-}disjoint : Subst \times Subst \rightarrow \mathbb{B}$
$dom\text{-}range\text{-}disjoint(s_1, s_2) \quad \triangleq \quad \mathsf{dom}\, s_1 \cap range(s_2) = \{\,\}$

Thus, given $s_1 = \{X \mapsto f(Z), Z \mapsto f(Y)\}$, and $s_2 = \{Q \mapsto f(X)\}$, then $dom\text{-}disjoint(s_1, s_2)$ is true but $dom\text{-}range\text{-}disjoint(s_1, s_2)$ is false.

Substitution application

Applying the substitution:

$s = \{X \mapsto f(Y), Z \mapsto g\}$

to a term has the effect of replacing any Xs by $f(Y)$, and any Zs by g. Thus applying s to $t(X, f(Z, g))$ results in the term $t(f(Y), f(g, g))$. However, what is the result of applying

$\{X \mapsto f(Z), Z \mapsto g\}$ to $t(X, f(Z, g))$

If we simply replace the variables with their associated term in the range, we obtain $t(f(Z), f(g, g))$. Do we now replace the Z in this term by g? Some authors [Ede85, MW81] define substitution application so that this further replacement is not done. As we shall see, this constrains their specification to the extent that the unification algorithm we prove does not satisfy their specification. Hence, we define substitution application recursively:

ap 1 $mk\text{-}Cmpterm(fid, [\,])s = mk\text{-}Cmpterm(fid, [\,])$

ap 2 $ts \in Var \implies t \in Var$

ap 3 $(\text{dom } s \cap vars(t) = \{\,\}) \implies (ts = t)$

ap 4 $v \notin \text{dom } s \wedge v \in vars(t) \implies v \in vars(ts)$

ap 5 $vars(ts) = \bigcup \{vars(vs) \mid v \in vars(t)\}$

ap 6 $vars(ts) \subseteq vars(t) \cup range(s)$

Figure 6.3 Lemmas about substitution application

$apply\text{-}sub : Term \times Subst \rightarrow Term$
$apply\text{-}sub(t, s) \quad \underline{\triangle}$
       cases t **of**
       $mk\text{-}Cmpterm(fid, tl_1) \rightarrow$ **let** $tl_2 = [apply\text{-}sub(tl(i), s) \mid i \in \text{inds } tl]$
                                     in
                                     $mk\text{-}Cmpterm(fid, tl_2),$
       v $\rightarrow$ **if** $v \in \text{dom } s$ **then** $apply\text{-}sub(s(v), \{v\} \vartriangleleft s)$ **else** t
       end

We abbreviate $apply\text{-}sub(t, s)$ to ts. We also write tls for

    $[apply\text{-}sub(tl(i), s) \mid i \in \text{inds } tl]$

Thus, $t(X, f(Z, g)) \{X \mapsto f(Z), Z \mapsto g\} = t(f(g), f(g, g))$.

    Lemmas about substitutions are listed in Figure 6.3. For example, Lemma ap4 states that substitution application does not remove those variables which are not in the domain of the substitution.

    A proof of ap4 is given in Figure 6.4. The proof proceeds by induction on *no-Term(t)*. The base case is proved by line 1, and the induction step is proved by line 2.

    The base case distinguishes between two cases. First, when t is a variable, line 1.2.2 proves the consequence of ap4 from the antecedent of ap4. It achieves this by the fact that t must be v, and that applying s does not remove v. Line 1.2 then introduces the implication to obtain ap4 from line 1.2.2. Second, when t is a compound term, line 1.3 proves ap4 by showing that the antecedent of ap4 is false since there are no variables in t.

    The induction step is carried out by first showing that the induction hypothesis can

from true
1	from *no-Term(t)* = 1	
1.1	$t \in Var \lor t \in Cmpterm$	(h1,*no-Term*)
1.2	from $t \in Var$	
1.2.1	$vars(t) = \{t\}$	(*vars*, h1.2)
1.2.2	from $v \notin dom\ s \land v \in vars(t)$	
1.2.2.1	$t = v$	(1.2.1, h1.2.2, $\in$)
1.2.2.2	$dom\ s \cap vars(t) = \{\ \}$	(1.2.1, .1, h1.2.2,$\cap$)
1.2.2.3	$ts = v$	(.2, ap3, $\Rightarrow$-E, .1)
	infer $v \in vars(ts)$	(*vars*, .3, $\in$)
	infer *ap4*	($\Rightarrow$-*I*, δ(h1.2.2),1.2.2)
1.3	from $t \in Cmpterm$	
1.3.1	$t = Cmpterm(fid, [\ ])$	(h1.3, h1, *no-Term*)
1.3.2	$vars(t) = \{\ \}$	(1.3.1, *vars*)
	infer *ap4*	(*vars*, $\Rightarrow$*vac-I*)
	infer *ap4*	(1.1,1.2,1.3,$\lor$-*E*)
2	from ap4 true for all *no-Term(t)* $< n, n > 1, no\text{-}Term(t) = n$	
2.1	*no-Term(t)* > 1	(h2)
2.2	let $t = mk\text{-}Cmpterm(fid, tl)$ in	(2.1, *no-Term*)
2.3	$\forall i \in inds\ tl \cdot no\text{-}Term(tl(i)) < n$	
		(2.2,tm5,tm3,tm4, *no-Terms*, h2)
2.4	$vars(t) = vars(tl)$	(2.2, tm6)
2.5	from $v \in vars(t) \land v \notin dom\ s$	
2.5.1	$v \in vars(tl)$	(h2.5, 2.4)
2.5.2	$\exists i \in inds\ tl \cdot v \in vars(tl(i))$	(2.5.1, tm7)
2.5.3	$\exists i \in inds\ tl \cdot v \in vars(tl(i)s)$	(h2.5,2.3,2.5.2,h2)
2.5.4	$v \in vars(tls)$	(2.5.3,tm7)
	infer $v \in vars(ts)$	(2.2,2.5.4,tm6)
	infer ap4 for *no-Term(t)* $= n$	(2.5,$\Rightarrow$-*I*)
infer *ap4*		(1,2, induction)

Figure 6.4 Proof of ap4

be applied to all subterms of t (line 2.3) and then proving the consequence of ap4 from he antecedent of ap4 (line 2.5). This is done by applying the induction hypothesis to a subterm of t to obtain the consequence for the subterm (line 2.5.3). Lemmas tm7 and m6 are then used to convert this into the consequence of ap4 for t.

Circularity

Notice that the above definition of *apply-sub* removes the possibility of nontermination in cases like:

$s = \{X \mapsto f(Y), Y \mapsto g(X)\}$ and Xs produces $f(g(X))$

Substitutions like s are known as *circular* since their graph is circular.

Circular substitutions can arise when we attempt to unify terms. For example, consider an attempt to unify the terms:

$t_1 = t(X, Y), t_2 = t(f(Y), g(X))$

The first components of t can be unified by $\{X \mapsto f(Y)\}$. Now the second components of t could be unified by $\{Y \mapsto g(X)\}$. However, when these two substitutions are combined by taking their union, we obtain a circular substitution $\{X \mapsto f(Y), Y \mapsto g(X)\}$. To formalize our notions of circularity we introduce a function:

$reach : Var \times Var \times Subst \to \mathbb{B}$
$reach(v_1, v_2, s)$ $\triangleq$
    if $v_1 \notin$ dom s
    then false
    else let $vset = vars(s(v_1))$ in
        if $v_2 \in vset$
        then true
        else $\exists v_3 \in vset \cdot reach(v_3, v_2, \{v_1\} \triangleleft s))$

Figure 6.5 lists some properties of reach. We examine the first lemma below, but leave the others as exercises for the reader (see [Vad86] if your theorem prover fails).

Lemma re1 relates the ideas of reachability and substitution application. It states that the variables left after applying a substitution to v_1 are reachable from v_1 provided that v_1 is in the domain of the substitution. Thus, since $X \in vars(X\{X \mapsto f(Y), Y \mapsto g(X)\})$, we may conclude that $reach(X, X, \{X \mapsto f(Y), Y \mapsto g(X)\})$.

We present a proof of Lemma re1 in Figure 6.6. The proof proceeds by induction on card s. The base case is straightforward since an empty substitution means that the antecedent of re1 is false.

The inductive step is carried out by proving the consequent of re1 from its antecedent (line 2.1). To use the induction hypothesis we must reduce the size of the substitution. We do this by unfolding *apply-sub* to obtain line 2.1.1. However, this is still not in the form required by the second conjunct of the induction hypothesis since $s(v_1)$ may be a term. Fortunately, by Lemma ap5, there must be a variable in $s(v_1)$ such that applying the substitution $\{v_1\} \triangleleft s$ to it results in a term which contains v_2. We consider two cases for such a variable. First, when it is v_2, line 2.1.3.2 obtains $reach(v_1, v_2, s)$ by folding

re 1 $v_1 \in \text{dom } s \wedge v_2 \in vars(v_1 s) \implies reach(v_1, v_2, s)$

re 2 $reach(v_1, v_2, s) \wedge reach(v_2, v_3, s) \implies reach(v_1, v_3, s)$

re 3 $dom\text{-}disjoint(s_1, s_2) \wedge reach(v_1, v_2, s_1) \implies reach(v_1, v_2, s_1 \cup s_2)$

re 4 $v_1 \in \text{dom } s_1 \wedge v_2 \notin \text{dom } s_2 \wedge dom\text{-}disjoint(s_1, s_2) \wedge$
$(\exists v_3 \in \text{dom } s_2 \cdot reach(v_1, v_3, s_1 \cup s_2) \wedge reach(v_3, v_2, s_1 \cup s_2)) \wedge$
$reach(v_1, v_2, s_1 \cup s_2) \implies reach(v_1, v_2, s_1)$

re 5 $dom\text{-}disjoint(s_1, s_2) \wedge v_1 \in \text{dom } s_1 \wedge v_2 \notin \text{dom } s_1 \wedge reach(v_1, v_2, s_1 \cup s_2) \wedge$
$v_2 \notin vars(v_1 s_1) \implies (\exists v_3 \in vars(v_1 s_1) \cdot reach(v_3, v_2, s_1 \cup s_2))$

re 6 $v_1 \in \text{dom } s_2 \wedge v_2 \notin \text{dom } s_1 \wedge dom\text{-}disjoint(s_1, s_2) \wedge reach(v_1, v_2, s_1 \cup s_2)$
$\implies reach(v_1, v_2, s_1 \cup reduce(s_2, s_1))$

Figure 6.5 Lemmas about reachability

the definition of *reach*. Second, when it is not v_2, lines 2.1.3.3.1 and 2.1.3.3.2 show that this variable must be in the domain of $\{v_1\} \triangleleft s$. Line 2.1.3.3.3 can then use the induction hypothesis and the $\implies$-*E* rule to deduce that v_2 is reachable from this variable in $\{v_1\} \triangleleft s$. We then use the definition of *reach* to obtain $reach(v_1, v_2, s)$.

We now return to use *reach* to define circularity:

$circular : Subst \to \mathbb{B}$
$circular(s) \quad \triangle \quad \exists v \in \text{dom } s \cdot reach(v, v, s)$

For conciseness, we will denote noncircular substitutions by θ, θ_1, $\dots \theta_n$. We are now in a position to examine some properties of noncircular substitutions.

Given a noncircular substitution, we can partition the substitution into two noncircular substitutions using the lemma:

cr 1 $dom\text{-}disjoint(s_1, s_2) \wedge \neg circular(s_1 \cup s_2)$
$\implies \neg circular(s_1) \wedge \neg circular(s_2)$

As the example at the start of this section illustrated, the union of two noncircular substitutions is not necessarily noncircular. However, if their domains are disjoint, and the domain of one of the substitutions is disjoint from the range of the other substitution, then their union will also be noncircular:

cr 2 $dom\text{-}disjoint(\theta_1, \theta_2) \wedge dom\text{-}range\text{-}disjoint(\theta_1, \theta_2) \implies \neg circular(\theta_1 \cup \theta_2)$

from true
1   from card $s = 0$
    infer re1
2   from re1 is true for all card $s < n, n > 0$, card $s = n$
2.1   from $v_1 \in$ dom $s \wedge v_2 \in vars(v_1 s)$
2.1.1 $v_2 \in vars(s(v_1)(\{v_1\} \blacktriangleleft s))$ (*apply-sub*, h2.1)
2.1.2 $v_2 \in \bigcup \{vars(v_3(\{v_1\} \blacktriangleleft s)) \mid v_3 \in vars(s(v_1))\}$ (2.1.1, ap5)
2.1.3   from $v_2 \in vars(v_3\{v_1\} \blacktriangleleft s), v_3 \in vars(s(v_1))$
2.1.3.1 $v_3 = v_2 \vee v_3 \neq v_2$
2.1.3.2   from $v_3 = v_2$
2.1.3.2.1 $v_2 \in vars(s(v_1))$ (h2.1.3.2, h2.1.3)
           infer $reach(v_1, v_2, s)$ (2.1.3.2.1, *reach*)
2.1.3.3   from $v_3 \neq v_2$
2.1.3.3.1   from $v_3 \notin$ dom $(\{v_1\} \blacktriangleleft s)$
2.1.3.3.1.1 $v_3(\{v_1\} \blacktriangleleft s) = v_3$ (h2.1.3.3.1, ap3)
            infer $v_2 \notin vars(v_3(\{v_1\} \blacktriangleleft s))$ (.1, *vars*, h2.1.3.3)
2.1.3.3.2 $v_3 \in$ dom $(\{v_1\} \blacktriangleleft s)$ (.1, h2.1.3, contra)
2.1.3.3.3 $reach(v_3, v_2, \{v_1\} \blacktriangleleft s)$ (.2, h2.1.3, h2)
          infer $reach(v_1, v_2, s)$ (h2.1.3, .3, *reach*)
        infer $reach(v_1, v_2, s)$ (.1, .2, .3, $\vee$-*E*)
      infer $reach(v_1, v_2, s)$ (2.1.2, 2.1.3)
    infer re1 true for card $s = n$ (2.1, δ(h2.1) $\Rightarrow$-*I*)
infer *re*1   (induction, 1, 2)

Figure 6.6 Proof of Lemma re1

Thus, given that

$$\{X \mapsto f(Y)\}, \text{ and } \{Y \mapsto g(Z), W \mapsto Y, Z \mapsto g(V)\}$$

are noncircular substitutions, whose domains are disjoint, and the variables in the second substitution's range do not occur in the domain of the first substitution, we can conclude that their union:

$$\{X \mapsto f(Y), Y \mapsto g(Z), W \mapsto Y, Z \mapsto g(V)\}$$

is noncircular.

    Lemmas cr1 and cr2 do not allow us to conclude that the union of the substitutions $\{X \mapsto f(Y)\}$ and $\{Y \mapsto Z, P \mapsto X\}$ is noncircular. But it clearly would be (why?). We can reach this conclusion by:

cr 3 $dom\text{-}disjoint(\theta_1, \theta_2) \wedge \neg\, circular(\theta_1 \cup reduce(\theta_2, \theta_1)) \;\Rightarrow\; \neg\, circular(\theta_1 \cup \theta_2)$

where

$reduce : Subst \times Subst \rightarrow Subst$

$reduce(s_1, s_2) \;\;\triangleq\;\; \{v \mapsto s_1(v)s_2 \mid v \in \text{dom}\, s_1\}$

We restrict ourselves to noncircular substitutions although algorithms for producing circular substitutions do exist (see [Fil84]).

An elegant property, which is true for noncircular substitutions, but does not hold for circular substitutions is:

ap8 $v \in \text{dom}\, \theta \;\Rightarrow\; v \notin vars(t\theta)$

Thus, this does not hold for the circular substitution

$\{X \mapsto f(X)\}$

since $X \in vars(X\{X \mapsto f(X)\})$.

Equality

We define two substitutions to be equivalent if substitution application has the same effect on any term:

$equal\text{-}sub : Subst \times Subst \rightarrow \mathbb{B}$

$equal\text{-}sub(s_1, s_1) \;\;\triangleq\;\; \forall t \cdot ts_1 = ts_2$

We write $equal\text{-}sub(s_1, s_2)$ in the infix notation $s_1 \cong s_2$. Thus, for example,

$\{X \mapsto Y, Y \mapsto a\} \cong \{X \mapsto a, Y \mapsto a\}$

but

$\neg(\{X \mapsto Y\} \cong \{Y \mapsto X\})$

Instead of using the definition to show that two substitutions are equal, we can use the result:

eq 1 $s_1 \cong s_2 \;\Leftrightarrow\; \forall v \in Var \cdot vs_1 = vs_2$

Thus, with

$s_1 = \{X \mapsto Y, Y \mapsto a\}$ and $s_2 = \{X \mapsto a, Y \mapsto a\}$

$s_1 \cong s_2$

since

$$Xs_1 = Xs_2 = a, Ys_1 = Ys_2 = a, \text{ and } Vs_1 = Vs_2 = V \text{ for any other variable } V$$

Composition

Consider how we could proceed to unify the terms: $t_1 = f(X, g(X))$ and $t_2 = f(a, Y)$. We can unify the first components by $\{X \mapsto a\}$. In the context of this substitution, we can unify the second components by $\{Y \mapsto g(a)\}$. Now applying these two substitutions in sequence unifies the two terms: $t_1\{X \mapsto a\}\{Y \mapsto g(a)\} = t_2\{X \mapsto a\}\{Y \mapsto g(a)\} = f(a, g(a))$.

Now since we seek one substitution to unify t_1 and t_2, we would like a substitution which has the same effect as applying the two substitutions in sequence. In our example, the obvious choice is $\{X \mapsto a, Y \mapsto g(a)\}$. However, $\{X \mapsto a, Y \mapsto g(X)\}$ also has the same effect.

Hence, we say that a substitution s_3 is a *composition* of two substitutions s_1 and s_2, written $s_1 \circ s_2$, if:

$$\forall t \cdot ts_1 s_2 = ts_3$$

In the above example, we obtained the composition of the substitutions $\{X \mapsto a\}$ and $\{Y \mapsto f(a)\}$ by simply taking their union. However, if we do this for the substitutions:

$$\{X \mapsto f(Y)\} \text{ and } \{Z \mapsto X\}$$

we obtain

$$\{X \mapsto f(Y), Z \mapsto X\}$$

This, however, is not equivalent to applying them in sequence since

$$Z\{X \mapsto f(Y), Z \mapsto X\} = f(Y)$$

but

$$Z\{X \mapsto f(Y)\}\{Z \mapsto X\} = X$$

We therefore develop the lemmas given in Figure 6.7 to guide us when composing substitutions. In particular, Lemma cp4 allows us to deduce that:

$$\{X \mapsto a\} \circ \{Y \mapsto f(a)\} \cong \{X \mapsto a, Y \mapsto f(X)\}$$

and Lemma cp5 allows us to conclude:

$$\{X \mapsto a, Y \mapsto f(X)\} \cong \{X \mapsto a, Y \mapsto f(a)\}$$

cp 1 $\theta \cong \theta \circ \theta$

cp 2 $reduce(\theta_1, \theta_2 \circ \theta_3) = reduce(reduce(\theta_1, \theta_2), \theta_3)$

cp 3 $v \notin \mathrm{dom}\ \theta \wedge v \notin vars(t\theta) \implies t\theta = treduce(\theta, \{v \mapsto x\})$

cp 4 $dom\text{-}disjoint(\theta_1, \theta_2) \wedge \neg\, circular(\theta_1 \cup \theta_2)$
$$\implies (\theta_1 \cup \theta_2 \cong \theta_1 \circ reduce(\theta_2, \theta_1))$$

cp 5 $dom\text{-}disjoint(\theta_1, \theta_2) \wedge \neg\, circular(\theta_1 \cup \theta_2) \implies$
$$(\theta_1 \cup \theta_2) \cong (\theta_1 \circ (\theta_1 \cup \theta_2)) \cong (\theta_1 \cup reduce(\theta_2, \theta_1)).$$

Figure 6.7 Lemmas to guide substitution composition

id 1 $idempotent(s) \implies \neg\, circular(s)$

id 2 $dom\text{-}range\text{-}disjoint(s, s) \implies idempotent(s)$

id 3 $(\theta_2 = reduce(\theta_1, \theta_1)) \implies (idempotent(\theta_2) \wedge \theta_2 \cong \theta_1)$

Figure 6.8 Lemmas about idempotence

Idempotence

Idempotence does not play a significant role in our theory. However, we include it to relate to the work of Manna and Waldinger [MW81].

We define a substitution s to be idempotent if $reduce(s, s) = s$. Manna and Waldinger define a substitution, s to be *idempotent* if $s \cong s \circ s$. With our recursive definition of *apply-sub*, all noncircular substitutions would be idempotent if we adopted their definition (by Lemma cp1), and idempotent substitutions in our theory would not be idempotent in Manna and Waldinger's theory. Lemmas about idempotence are given in Figure 6.8.

6.4 Unifiers

A substitution θ, is a unifier of two terms, t_1 and t_2 if:

$unifier : Term \times Term \times Subst \rightarrow \mathbb{B}$
$unifier(t_1, t_2, \theta) \triangleq t_1\theta = t_2\theta$

un 1 *unifier*$(v, t, \theta) \;\Rightarrow\; \theta \cong \{v \mapsto t\} \circ \theta$

un 2 $t \in Cmpterm \wedge v \in vars(t) \;\Rightarrow\; \exists \theta \cdot unifier(v, t, \theta)$

Figure 6.9 Lemmas about unifiers

Thus, the substitutions:

$$\{X \mapsto Y, Y \mapsto g\}, \{X \mapsto g\}$$

are both unifiers of the terms: g, and X. Two useful lemmas about unifiers are given in Figure 6.9.

As mentioned in the introduction, a unification algorithm must produce a most general unifier (when one exists). We therefore need to formalize the notions of generality. We say that a substitution θ_1 is *more general* than another substitution θ_2 if:

more-general : $Subst \times Subst \rightarrow \mathbb{B}$
more-general$(\theta_1, \theta_2) \;\triangleq\; \exists \theta \cdot \theta_2 \cong \theta_1 \circ \theta$

We write $\theta_1 \succeq \theta_2$, or $\theta_2 \preceq \theta_1$ for *more-general*(θ_1, θ_2). For example:

$$\{X \mapsto f\} \succeq \{X \mapsto f, Y \mapsto X\}$$

since

$$\{X \mapsto f, Y \mapsto X\} \cong \{X \mapsto f\} \circ \{Y \Rightarrow f\} \text{ (by Lemma cp4)}$$

Substitution generality is transitive:

gn 1 $\theta_1 \preceq \theta_2 \wedge \theta_2 \preceq \theta_3 \;\Rightarrow\; \theta_1 \preceq \theta_3$

Given a unifier, θ_1, of two terms t_1, and t_2, any substitution which is less general than θ_1 is also a unifier of t_1 and t_2. More formally:

gn 2 $\theta_2 \preceq \theta_1 \wedge unifier(t_1, t_2, \theta_1) \;\Rightarrow\; unifier(t_1, t_2, \theta_2)$

Thus, since $\{X \mapsto f\}$ is a unifier of X and f, $\{X \mapsto f, Y \mapsto X\}$ is also a unifier of X and f.

6.5   Most general unifiers

We can define a substitution θ to be a most general unifier of two terms if it unifies the terms, and any other unifier is less general than θ. In practice, unification is often performed in the context of an existing substitution ([Nil84, SA77] for example). Hence, we also include a context substitution in our specification.

A substitution θ_2 is a most general unifier of two terms t_1 and t_2 in the context of an existing substitution θ_1 if:

$$mgu : Term \times Term \times Subst \times Subst \to \mathbb{B}$$
$$mgu(t_1, t_2, \theta_1, \theta_2) \quad \triangleq$$
$$\qquad \theta_2 \preceq \theta_1 \wedge unifier(t_1, t_2, \theta_2) \wedge$$
$$\qquad \forall \theta \cdot \theta \preceq \theta_1 \wedge unifier(t_1, t_2, \theta) \;\Rightarrow\; \theta \preceq \theta_2$$

When *mgu* has list arguments, the above definition is applied to the corresponding elements of the two lists. The arguments will make it obvious which definition is meant.

To construct a most general unifier of two terms t_1 and t_2 in the context of a substitution θ_1 consider two situations. First when one of the terms is a variable and the other is a compound term, and second when both terms are compound.

When t_1 is a variable but t_2 is a compound term in the context of θ_1, the following lemma can be used to construct a most general unifier.

mg 1 $t_1\theta_1 \in Var \wedge t_1\theta_1 \notin vars(t_2\theta_1) \;\Rightarrow\; mgu(t_1, t_2, \theta_1, \theta_1 \cup \{t_1\theta_1 \mapsto t_2\})$

Thus, X and Y have a most general unifier

$$\{X \mapsto Z, Y \mapsto f(a), Z \mapsto Y\} \text{ in the context of } \{X \mapsto Z, Y \mapsto f(a)\}$$

The conjunct $t_1\theta_1 \in Var \wedge t_1\theta_1 \notin vars(t_2\theta_1)$ in Lemma mg1 ensures that the constructed substitution is not circular. If the constructed substitution is circular, then the following lemma tells us that there is no most general unifier:

mg 2 $t_2\theta_1 \in Cmpterm \wedge t_1\theta_1 \in vars(t_2\theta_1) \;\Rightarrow\; \exists\theta_2 \cdot mgu(t_1, t_2, \theta_1, \theta_2)$

Now consider how we could proceed to unify the compound terms:

$$t_1 = t(X, f(b, Y)), t_2 = t(Y, f(X, a)) \text{ in the context } \{\,\}$$

The first components have a most general unifier:

$$\{X \mapsto Y\} \text{ or } \{Y \mapsto X\}$$

Suppose we choose $\{X \mapsto Y\}$ to proceed to unify the second components. However, in the context of this substitution, the second components: $f(b, Y)$ and $f(Y, a)$, cannot be unified. At this stage, should we backtrack to the first components and choose the alternative most general unifier $\{Y \mapsto X\}$ before again attempting to unify the second components? Fortunately, the following lemma allows us to conclude that there is no unifier without the need to backtrack:

mg 3 $mgu(t_1, t_2, \theta_1, \theta_2) \wedge \exists \theta_3 \cdot mgu(tl_1, tl_2, \theta_2, \theta_3) \Rightarrow$

$$\exists \theta_4 \cdot mgu([t_1] \frown tl_1, [t_2] \frown tl_2, \theta_1, \theta_4)$$

Of course, if the first components can not be unified, then we can conclude that there is no most general unifier without attempting to unify the remaining components:

mg 4 $\exists \theta_2 \cdot mgu(t_1, t_2, \theta_1, \theta_2) \Rightarrow \exists \theta_3 \cdot mgu([t_1] \frown tl_1, [t_2] \frown tl_2, \theta_1, \theta_3)$

If a most general unifier does exist, we can find it in a sequential manner:

mg 5 $mgu(t_1, t_2, \theta_1, \theta_2) \wedge mgu(tl_1, tl_2, \theta_2, \theta_3)$

$$\Rightarrow mgu([t_1] \frown tl_1, [t_2] \frown tl_2, \theta_1, \theta_3)$$

Thus, given that $\{V \mapsto g(X, X)\}$ is a most general unifier of $g(X, X)$ and V in the context $\{\ \}$, and $\{V \mapsto g(X, X), W \mapsto g(Y, Y), X \mapsto Y\}$ is a most general unifier of $[W, W]$ and $[g(Y, Y), V]$ in the context $\{V \mapsto g(X, X)\}$, we may use Lemma mg5 to conclude that $\{V \mapsto g(X, X), W \mapsto g(Y, Y), X \mapsto Y\}$ is a most general unifier of $[g(X, X), W, W)]$ and $[V, g(Y, Y), V]$ in the context $\{\ \}$.

Note that if θ_2 is a most general unifier of the terms t_1 and t_2 in the context θ_1, then θ_2 must not have any variables which are not in $t_1 \theta_1$ and $t_2 \theta_1$. We state this as a proposition rather than complicate the definition:

mg 6 $mgu(t_1, t_2, \theta_1, \theta_2) \Rightarrow$

$\quad (\exists \theta_3 \cdot \theta_2 \cong \theta_1 \circ \theta_3 \wedge$

$\quad\quad (\text{dom } \theta_3 \subseteq vars\text{-}term(t_1 \theta_1) \cup vars\text{-}term(t_2 \theta_1)) \wedge$

$\quad\quad (range(\theta_3) \subseteq vars\text{-}term(t_1 \theta_1) \cup vars\text{-}term(t_2 \theta_1)))$

The proof of the mg lemmas can be based on the earlier lemmas and do not require induction. As an example, Figure 6.10 presents the proof of Lemma mg2. The proof proceeds by establishing each requirement for the substitution to be a most general unifier.

6.6   Specification of unification

We now write an implicit specification of the unification algorithm:

$\quad unify\ (t_1, t_2 \colon Term, \theta_1 \colon Subst)\ b \colon \mathbb{B},\ \theta_2 \colon Subst$

$\quad$ pre true

$\quad$ post $(b \wedge mgu(t_1, t_2, \theta_1, \theta_2)) \vee (\neg b \wedge \exists \theta \cdot mgu(t_1, t_2, \theta_1, \theta))$

The specification of *unifylist* is similar.

from $(t_1\theta_1 \in Vars) \wedge t_1\theta \notin vars(t_2\theta_1)$

1	let $v = t_1\theta_1$ in	(h)
2	$v \notin dom\ \theta_1$	(1, ap8)
3	$vars(t_2\theta_1) \cap dom\ \theta_1 = \{\ \}$	(ap8)
4	$\neg circular(\{v \mapsto t_2\theta_1\})$	(h, 1, *reach*, *circular*)
5	$\neg circular(\theta_1 \cup \{v \mapsto t_2\theta_1\})$	(2, 3, 4, cr2)
6	$\neg circular(\theta_1 \cup \{v \mapsto t_2\})$	(2, 5, cr3)
7	$\theta_1 \cup \{v \mapsto t_2\} \cong \theta_1 \circ \{v \mapsto t_2\theta_1\}$	(2, 6, cp4)
8	$t_1\theta_1 \circ \{v \mapsto t_2\theta_1\} = t_2\theta_1$	(1, $\circ$, *apply-sub*)
9	$t_2\theta_1 \circ \{v \mapsto t_2\theta_1\} = t_2\theta_1$	(h, ap3)
10	$unifier(t_1, t_2, \theta_1 \cup \{v \mapsto t_2\})$	(6, 7, 8, 9, *unifier*, $\cong$)
11	$\theta_1 \cup \{v \mapsto t_2\} \preceq \theta_1$	(7, $\preceq$)
12	from $\theta \preceq \theta_1 \wedge t_1\theta = t_2\theta$	
12.1	$\exists\theta_3 \cdot \theta \cong \theta_1 \circ \theta_3 \wedge t_1\theta_1\theta_3 = t_2\theta_1\theta_3$	(h12, $\preceq$, $\cong$)
12.2	$\exists\theta_3 \cdot \theta \cong \theta_1 \circ \theta_3 \wedge \theta_3 \cong \{v \mapsto t_2\theta_1\} \circ \theta_3$	(1, 12.1, h, un1)
12.3	$\exists\theta_3 \cdot \theta \cong \theta_1 \circ \{v \mapsto t_2\theta_1\} \circ \theta_3$	(12.2, $\cong$)
12.4	$\exists\theta_3 \cdot \theta \cong (\theta_1 \cup \{v \mapsto t_2\}) \circ \theta_3$	(7, 12.3, $\cong$, $\circ$)
	infer $\theta \preceq (\theta_1 \cup \{v \mapsto t_2\})$	(12.4, $\preceq$)
13	$\forall\theta \cdot \theta \preceq \theta_1 \wedge unifier(t_1, t_2, \theta) \implies \theta \preceq (\theta_1 \cup \{v \mapsto t\})$	
		(12, *unifier*, $\implies$-*I*, $\forall$-*I*)

infer $mgu(t_1, t_2, \theta_1, \theta_1 \cup \{t_1\theta_1 \mapsto t_2\})$ (6, 10, 11, 13, *mgu*)

Figure 6.10 Proof of mg2

6.7 Proof of a unification algorithm

A common unification algorithm takes the form [BM72, Nil84]:

$unify : Term \times Term \times Subst \rightarrow Subst$

$unify(term_1, term_2, \theta_1)$ $\triangleq$

    let $t_1 = coerce(term_1, \theta_1), t_2 = coerce(term_2, \theta_1)$ in

    cases (t_1, t_2) of

    $(mk\text{-}Cmpterm(id_1, tl_1), mk\text{-}Cmpterm(id_2, tl_2)) \rightarrow$

        if $id_1 = id_2$ then $unifylist(tl_1, tl_2, \theta_1)$ else (false, { })

    $(mk\text{-}Cmpterm(id_1, tl_1), v_2)$ $\rightarrow$

        if $v_2 \notin vars(t_1\theta_1)$ then (true, $\theta_1 \cup \{v_2 \mapsto term_1\}$) else (false, { })

    $(v_1, mk\text{-}Cmpterm(id_2, tl_2))$ $\rightarrow$

        if $v_1 \notin vars(t_2\theta_1)$ then (true, $\theta_1 \cup \{v_1 \mapsto term_2\}$) else (false, { })

    (v_1, v_2) $\rightarrow$

        if $v_1 = v_2$ then (true, θ_1) else (true, $\theta_1 \cup \{v_2 \mapsto term_1\}$)

    end

where

$coerce : Term \times Subst \rightarrow Subst$

$coerce(t, \theta)$ $\triangleq$

    cases t of

    $mk\text{-}Cmpterm(,) \rightarrow t,$

    v $\rightarrow$ if $v \in$ dom θ then $coerce(\theta(v), \{v\} \triangleleft \theta)$ else t

    end

and *unifylist* takes the form:

$unifylist : Terms \times Terms \times Subst \rightarrow \mathbb{B} \times Subst$

$unifylist(tl_1, tl_2, \theta_1)$ $\triangleq$

    if $tl_1 = [\,]$ or $tl_2 = [\,]$

    then $(tl_1 = tl_2, \theta_1)$

    else let $(succ, \theta_4) = unify(\text{hd } tl_1, \text{hd } tl_2, \theta_1)$ in

        if $succ$

        then $unifylist(\text{tl } tl_1, \text{tl } tl_2, \theta_4)$

        else (false, θ_1))

The use of *coerce* avoids the need to apply the context substitution to the terms, and therefore reduces the overheads. Thus to unify Y and $g(X, X)$ in the context:

$$\{X \mapsto g(Z, Z), Z \mapsto g(V, V)\}$$

Y is unified with $g(X, X)$ to produce a substitution:

$$\{X \mapsto g(Z, Z), Z \mapsto g(V, V), Y \mapsto g(X, X)\}$$

instead of the substitution:

$$\{X \mapsto g(Z,Z),$$
$$Z \mapsto g(V,V),$$
$$Y \mapsto g(g(g(V,V),g(V,V)),g(g(V,V),g(V,V)))\}$$

The following two lemmas relate coerce to substitution application:

co 1 $coerce(t, \theta)\theta = t\theta$

co 2 $coerce(t_1, \theta_1) = v \iff (t_1\theta_1 = v)$

For example, with

$$\theta = \{X \mapsto Y, Y \mapsto Z, Z \mapsto g(V), V \mapsto U, U \mapsto W\}$$

we have:

$$coerce(X, \theta)\theta = X\theta = g(W), \text{ and } coerce(V, \theta) = V\theta = W$$

We can show an analogous result to Lemma mg1:

co 3 $v_2 \notin vars(t_1\theta_1) \land t_1 = coerce(term_1, \theta_1) \land$
$$v_2 = coerce(term_2, \theta_1) \implies mgu(t_1, v_2, \theta_1, \theta_1 \cup \{v_2 \mapsto term_1\})$$

Further, the most general unifier of coerced terms is the same as the most general unifier of the terms (under the context):

co 4 $t_1 = coerce(term_1, \theta_1) \land t_2 = coerce(term_2, \theta_1) \implies$
$$(mgu(t_1, t_2, \theta_1, \theta_2) \iff mgu(term_1, term_2, \theta_1, \theta_2))$$

In examining the above algorithm, we notice that the length of the terms (*no-Term*) may increase on a subsequent recursive call to *unify*. Hence, we can not prove the algorithm by simply using induction on the length of the terms. However, we can use the fact that the number of variables decreases (after application of the context) when the length of the terms does not decrease. We therefore use the following ordering:

$$\chi : Terms \times Terms \times Subst \to \mathbb{N} \times \mathbb{N}$$
$$\chi(tl_1, tl_2, \theta) \triangleq$$
$$\mathsf{card}\,(vars(tl_1\theta) \cup vars(tl_2\theta)), no\text{-}Terms(tl_1\theta) + no\text{-}Terms(tl_2\theta))$$

A similar definition holds for term arguments.

We will need the following properties of this ordering when proving the above algorithm correct.

or 1 $\mathsf{len}\,tl_1 > 0 \land \mathsf{len}\,tl_2 > 0 \implies \chi(\mathsf{hd}\,tl_1, \mathsf{hd}\,tl_2, \theta) \leq \chi(tl_1, tl_2, \theta)$

or 2 $\chi(tl_1, tl_2, \theta) < \chi(mk\text{-}Cmpterm(id_1, tl_1), mk\text{-}Cmpterm(id_2, tl_2), \theta)$

or 3 $\text{len } tl_1 > 0 \wedge \text{len } tl_2 > 0 \wedge mgu(\text{hd } tl_1, \text{hd } tl_2, \theta_1, \theta_2) \Rightarrow$
$$\chi(tl_1, tl_2, \theta_2) \leq \chi(tl_1, tl_2, \theta_1)$$

As an example of Lemma or3 in operation, consider the following situation:

$$\theta_1 = \{X \mapsto g(Z, Z), Z \mapsto g(V, V)\}$$
$$\theta_2 = \{X \mapsto g(Z, Z), Z \mapsto g(V, V), Y \mapsto g(X, X)\}$$
$$tl_1 = [Y, P], tl_2 = [g(X, X), Z]$$

where θ_2 is a most general unifier of $\text{hd } tl_1$ and $\text{hd } tl_2$ in the context of θ_1,

$$tl_1\theta_1 = [Y, P]\theta_1 = [Y, P]$$
$$tl_2\theta_1 = [g(X, X), Z]\theta_1$$
$$= [g(g(g(V, V), g(V, V)), g(g(V, V), g(V, V))), g(V, V)]$$
$$tl_1\theta_2 = [Y, P]\theta_2$$
$$= [g(g(g(V, V), g(V, V)), g(g(V, V), g(V, V))), P]$$
$$tl_2\theta_2 = [g(X, X), Z]\theta_2$$
$$= [g(g(V, V), g(V, V)), g(g(V, V), g(V, V))), g(V, V)]$$

Thus, although the total number of terms after application of θ_2 is larger than the total number of terms after application of θ_1, the number of variables in the terms after application of θ_2 is less than the number of variables after application of θ_1. The number of variables reduces because the domain of θ_2 has an additional variable Y, which is removed from the terms by the application of θ_2 (Lemma ap8) without introducing any new variables.

A proof of Lemma or3 is presented in Figure 6.11. It has two cases. When θ_3 is empty, the result clearly holds (line 2.3). When θ_3 is not empty, line 2.4 obtains or3 by showing that the number of variables in $t_1\theta_2 \cup t_2\theta_2$ reduces .

We approach the proof that *unify* is correct in two stages. We first prove that *unifylist* is relatively correct. That is, we prove:

rc $(\chi(t_1, t_2, \theta_1) < (n, k) \Rightarrow post\text{-}unify(t_1, t_2, \theta_1) unify(t_1, t_2, \theta_1))$
$$\Rightarrow$$
$$(\chi(tl_1, tl_2, \theta_2) < (n, k) \Rightarrow post\text{-}unifylist(tl_1, tl_2, \theta_2) unifylist(tl_1, tl_2, \theta_2))$$

Before we present the proof of this lemma it is worth outlining the key ideas upon which the proof is based. Each recursive call to *unifylist* reduces the length of tl_1. Hence the proof is by induction on the length of tl_1. The proof relies on the fact that if the initial arguments satisfy $\chi(tl_1, tl_2, \theta_2) < (n, k)$ then any subsequent call to *unifylist*, say with arguments tl_4, tl_5, θ_5, will also maintain the relationship $\chi(tl_4, tl_5, \theta_5) < (n, k)$. This is shown with the aid of Lemmas or1 and or3. When *unifylist* produces a most general unifier, Lemma mg5 informs us that it satisfies our specification. When *unifylist* from len $tl_1 > 0 \wedge$ len $tl_2 > 0 \wedge mgu($hd $tl_1,$ hd $tl_2, \theta_1, \theta_2)$

1	$\exists\theta_3 \cdot \theta_2 \cong \theta_1 \circ \theta_3 \wedge$ dom $\theta_3 \subseteq vars(tl_1\theta_1) \cup vars(tl_2\theta_1)\wedge$	
	$range(\theta_3) \subseteq vars(tl_1\theta_1) \cup vars(tl_2\theta_1)$	(h, mg6, tm1)
2	from $\theta_2 \cong \theta_1 \circ \theta_3 \wedge$ dom $\theta_3 \subseteq vars(tl_1\theta_1) \cup vars(tl_2\theta_1)\wedge$	
	$range(\theta_3) \subseteq vars(tl_1\theta_1) \cup vars(tl_2\theta_1)$	
2.1	$\theta_2 \cong \theta_1 \circ \theta_3$	(h2, $\wedge$-E)
2.2	$\theta_3 = \{\,\} \vee \theta_3 \neq \{\,\}$	
2.3	from $\theta_3 = \{\,\}$	
2.3.1	$\theta_1 \cong \theta_2$	(h2.3, 2.1, $\circ$)
	infer $\chi(tl_1, tl_2, \theta_2) \leq \chi(tl_1, tl_2, \theta_1)$	(2.3.1, $\cong$, χ)
2.4	from $\theta_3 \neq \{\,\}$	
2.4.1	$vars(tl_1\theta_1\theta_3) \subseteq vars(tl_1\theta_1) \cup range(\theta_3)$	(ap6)
2.4.2	$vars(tl_2\theta_1\theta_3) \subseteq vars(tl_2\theta_1) \cup range(\theta_3)$	(ap6)
2.4.3	$vars(tl_1\theta_2) \cup vars(tl_2\theta_2) \subseteq$	
	$vars(tl_1\theta_1) \cup vars(tl_2\theta_1) \cup range(\theta_3)$	
		(2.4.1, 2.4.2, $\cup$, 2.1, $\cong$)
2.4.4	$vars(tl_1\theta_2) \cup vars(tl_2\theta_2) \subseteq vars(tl_1\theta_1) \cup vars(tl_2\theta_1)$	
		(2.4.3, h2, $\subseteq$)
2.4.5	dom $\theta_3 \subseteq vars(tl_1\theta_1) \cup vars(tl_2\theta_1)$	(h2, $\wedge$-E)
2.4.6	$\exists v \in vars(tl_1\theta_1) \cup vars(tl_2\theta_1) \cdot v \notin vars(tl_1\theta_2) \cup vars(tl_2\theta_2)$	
		(h2.4, 2.4.5, 2.1 ap8)
2.4.7	$vars(tl_1\theta_2) \cup vars(tl_2\theta_2) \subset vars(tl_1\theta_1) \cup vars(tl_2\theta_1)$	
		(2.4.4, 2.4.6)
	infer $\chi(tl_1, tl_2, \theta_2) \leq \chi(tl_1, tl_2, \theta_1)$	(2.4.7, χ)
	infer $\chi(tl_1, tl_2, \theta_2) \leq \chi(tl_1, tl_2, \theta_1)$	(2.2, 2.3, 2.4,$\vee$-E)
infer $\chi(tl_1, tl_2, \theta_2) \leq \chi(tl_1, tl_2, \theta_1)$		(1,2,$\exists$-E)

Figure 6.11 Proof of Lemma or3

from true
1   rc is true for len $tl_1 = 0$ (*unifylist, post-unifylist,* $\Rightarrow$ *vac-I*)
2   from rc is true for all len $tl_1 < m, m > 0$, len $tl_1 = m$
2.1   from $\chi(t_1, t_2, \theta_1) < (n, k)$ $\Rightarrow$
                 post-unify(t_1, t_2, θ_1) *unify*(t_1, t_2, θ_1)
2.1.1   from $\chi(tl_1, tl_2, \theta_2) < (n, k)$
2.1.1.1 $tl_2 = [\,] \vee tl_2 \neq [\,]$
2.1.1.2   from $tl_2 = [\,]$
                            infer *post-unifylist*(tl_1, tl_2, θ_1)
                            unifylist(tl_1, tl_2, θ_1) (**see Figure 6.13**)
2.1.1.3   from $tl_2 \neq [\,]$
                            infer *post-unifylist*(tl_1, tl_2, θ_2)
                            unifylist(tl_1, tl_2, θ_2) (**see Figure 6.14**)
                       infer *post-unifylist*(tl_1, tl_2, θ_2) *unifylist*(tl_1, tl_2, θ_2)
                                                                 (2.1.1.1, 2.1.1.2, 2.1.1.3, $\vee$-E)
                  infer $\chi(tl_1, tl_2, \theta_2) < (n, k)$ $\Rightarrow$ *post-unifylist*(tl_1, tl_2, θ_2)
                  unifylist(tl_1, tl_2, θ_2) (2.1.1, δ(h2.1.1), $\Rightarrow$-I))
            infer rc is true for len $tl_1 = m$ (2.1, ,δ(h2.1), $\Rightarrow$-I)
infer *rc*   (1, 2, induction)

Figure 6.12 Top level proof of relative correctness

2.1.1.2   from $tl_2 = [\,]$
2.1.1.2.1 $tl_1 \neq [\,]$ (h2)
2.1.1.2.2 $\not\exists\theta \cdot tl_1 \theta = tl_2\theta$ (.1, *apply-sub*, =)
             infer *post-unifylist*(tl_1, tl_2, θ_1) *unifylist*(tl_1, tl_2, θ_1)
                                          (.2, *post-unifylist*, h2.1.1.2, *unifylist*)

Figure 6.13 Proof when *tl* is empty

fails to find a unifier, Lemmas mg3 and mg4 inform us that there is no most general
unifier. Figure 6.12 presents the top level of the proof. Figure 6.13 presents the the
proof when tl is empty, whilst Figure 6.14 presents the proof when tl is not empty.
     To show that *unify* satisfies our specification, we prove:

2.1.1.3	from $tl_2 \neq [\ ]$	
2.1.1.3.1	$\chi(\text{hd } tl_1, \text{hd } tl_2, \theta_2) < (n, k)$	(h2.1.1, h2.1.1.3, h2, or1)
2.1.1.3.2	let $(succ, \theta_3) = unify(\text{hd } tl_1, \text{hd } tl_2, \theta_2)$ in	
2.1.1.3.3	$post\text{-}unify(\text{hd } tl_1, \text{hd } tl_2, \theta_2) succ, \theta_3$	(.1, .2, h2.1)
2.1.1.3.4	$succ \vee \neg succ$	
2.1.1.3.5	from $succ$	
2.1.1.3.5.1	$mgu(\text{hd } tl_1, \text{hd } tl_2, \theta_2, \theta_3)$	
		(h2.1.1.3.5, 2.1.1.3.3, $post\text{-}unify$)
2.1.1.3.5.2	$\chi(tl_1, tl_2, \theta_3) < (n, k)$	(h2.1.1.3, h2, .1, or3, h2.1.1)
2.1.1.3.5.3	$\chi(\text{tl } tl_1, \text{tl } tl_2, \theta_3) < (n, k)$	(.2, h2.1.1.3, h2, tl, χ)
2.1.1.3.5.4	len tl $tl_1 < m$	(h2, tl, len)
2.1.1.3.5.5	let $(b, \theta_4) = unifylist(\text{tl } tl_1, \text{tl } tl_2, \theta_3)$ in	
2.1.1.3.5.6	$post\text{-}unifylist(\text{tl } tl_1, \text{tl } tl_2, \theta_3) b, \theta_4$	(h2.1, .3, .4, .5, h2)
2.1.1.3.5.7	$b \vee \neg b$	
2.1.1.3.5.8	from b	
	infer $post\text{-}unifylist(tl_1, tl_2, \theta_2) b, \theta_4$	(**See Figure 6.15**)
2.1.1.3.5.9	from $\neg b$	
	infer $post\text{-}unifylist(tl_1, tl_2, \theta_2) b, \theta_4$	(**See Figure 6.15**)
2.1.1.3.5.10	$post\text{-}unifylist(tl_1, tl_2, \theta_2) unifylist(\text{tl } tl_1, \text{tl } tl_2, \theta_3)$	
		(.7, .8, .9, $\vee$-E, .5)
	infer $post\text{-}unifylist(tl_1, tl_2, \theta_2) unifylist(tl_1, tl_2, \theta_2)$	
		(.10, h2.1.1.3.5, 2.1.1.3.2, h2.1.1.3, h2, $unifylist$)
2.1.1.3.6	from $\neg succ$	
2.1.1.3.6.1	$\nexists \theta_3 \cdot mgu(\text{hd } tl_1, \text{hd } tl_2, \theta_2, \theta_3)$	
		(h2.1.1.3.6, 2.1.1.3.3, $post\text{-}unify$)
2.1.1.3.6.2	$post\text{-}unifylist(tl_1, tl_2, \theta_2) succ, \theta_2$	
		(.1, h2.1.1.3.6, mg4, $post\text{-}unifylist$)
	infer $post\text{-}unifylist(tl_1, tl_2, \theta_2) unifylist(tl_1, tl_2, \theta_2)$	
		(.2, h2.1.1.3.6, 2.1.1.3.2, h2.1.1.3, h2, $unifylist$)
	infer $post\text{-}unifylist(tl_1, tl_2, \theta_2) unifylist(tl_1, tl_2, \theta_2)$	
		(.4, .5, .6, $\vee$-E)

Figure 6.14 Proof when *tl* is not empty

2.1.1.3.5.8   from b

2.1.1.3.5.8.1 $mgu(\text{tl } tl_1, \text{tl } tl_2, \theta_3, \theta_4)$

(2.1.1.3.5.6,*post-unifylist*, h2.1.1.3.5.8)

2.1.1.3.5.8.2 $mgu(\text{hd } tl_1, \text{hd } tl_1, \theta_2, \theta_3)$

(2.1.1.3.3, h2.1.1.3.5, *post-unify*)

2.1.1.3.5.8.3 $mgu(tl_1, tl_2, \theta_2, \theta_4)$ (.1,.2, mg5)

infer *post-unifylist*$(tl_1, tl_2, \theta_2)\, b, \theta_4$

(.3, h2.1.1.3.5.8, *post-unifylist*)

2.1.1.3.5.9   from $\neg b$

2.1.1.3.5.9.1 $\exists \theta_4 \cdot mgu(\text{tl } tl_1, \text{tl } tl_2, \theta_3, \theta_4)$

(2.1.1.3.5.6, *post-unifylist*, h2.1.1.3.5.9)

2.1.1.3.5.9.2 $mgu(\text{hd } tl_1, \text{hd } tl_2, \theta_2, \theta_3)$

(2.1.1.3.3, h2.1.1.3.5, *post-unify*)

2.1.1.3.5.9.3 $\exists \theta_4 \cdot mgu(tl_1, tl_2, \theta_2, \theta_4)$ (.1,.2, mg3)

infer *post-unifylist*$(tl_1, tl_2, \theta_2)\, b, \theta_4$

(.3, h2.1.1.3.5.9, *post-unifylist*)

Figure 6.15 Proof cases of b

post-unify$(term_1, term_2, \theta_1)\, unify(term_1, term_2, \theta_1)$

As mentioned above, the proof is by induction on $\chi(term_1, term_2, \theta_1)$. Letting $t_1 = coerce(term_1, \theta_1)$, and $t_2 = coerce(term_2, \theta_1)$, there are four cases that may occur. In each case we first deduce:

cl *post-unify*$(t_1, t_2, \theta_1)\, unify(term_1, term_2, \theta_1)$.

Then we use Lemma co4 to obtain

post-unify$(term_1, term_2, \theta_1)\, unify(term_1, term_2, \theta_1)$

The first case, when both t_1 and t_2 are compound terms, leads to Lemma c1 with the aid of Lemma rc and Lemma or2. The second and third cases, when one of t_1 and t_2 is a variable but the other is a compound term, leads to Lemma c1 by Lemma co3 (when there is a unifier), and Lemma mg2 (when there is no unifier). In the fourth case, when both t_1 and t_2 are variables, Lemma c1 is proved with the aid of Lemmas co2 and co3.

We present the detailed proof in two stages. Figure 6.16 shows how the four cases are combined, whilst Figures 6.17 to 6.19 prove each case. The third case is anologous to the second case and is therefore omitted.

from $term_1, term_2 \in Term, \theta_1 \in Subst$
1   from $\chi(term_1, term_2, \theta_1) = (0, 2)$
      infer $post\text{-}unify(term_1, term_2, \theta_1)$ $unify(term_1, term_2, \theta_1)$

                                                                     $(\chi, post\text{-}unify, unify)$

2   from $post\text{-}unify(term_1, term_2, \theta_1)$ $unify(term_1, term_2, \theta_1)$ is true
           for $\chi(term_1, term_2, \theta_1) < (n, k), (n, k) > (0, 2),$
           $\chi(term_1, term_2, \theta_1) = (n, k)$
2.2   let $t_1 = coerce(term_1, \theta_1), t_2 = coerce(term_2, \theta_1)$ in
2.3   first case   **see Figure 6.17**
2.4   second and third cases   **see Figure 6.18**
2.5   fourth case   **see Figure 6.19**
2.6 $(t_1, t_2) = (mk\text{-}Cmpterm(id_1, tl_1), mk\text{-}Cmpterm(id_2, tl_2)) \vee$
           $(t_1, t_2) = (mk\text{-}Cmpterm(id_1, tl_1), v_2) \vee$
           $(t_1, t_2) = (v_1, mk\text{-}Cmpterm(id_2, tl_2)) \vee$
           $(t_1, t_2) = (v_1, v_2)$ *(Term)*
2.7 $post\text{-}unify(t_1, t_2, \theta_1)$
      cases (t_1, t_2) of
      $(mk\text{-}Cmpterm(id_1, tl_1), mk\text{-}Cmpterm(id_2, tl_2)) \rightarrow \ldots,$
      $(mk\text{-}Cmpterm(id_1, tl_1), v_2)$ $\rightarrow \ldots,$
      $(v_1, mk\text{-}Cmpterm(id_2, tl_2))$ $\rightarrow \ldots,$
      (v_1, v_2) $\rightarrow \ldots$
      end

                                        (2.3, 2.4, 2.5, 2.6, Cases-I)
2.8 $post\text{-}unify(t_1, t_2, \theta_1)$ $unify(term_1, term_2, \theta_1)$ (2.2, 2.7, *unify*)
      infer $post\text{-}unify(term_1, term_2, \theta_1)$ $unify(term_1, term_2, \theta_1)$

                                          (2.8, 2.2, co4, *post-unify*)
infer $post\text{-}unify(term_1, term_2, \theta_1)$ $unify(term_1, term_2, \theta_1)$

                                                         (1,2, induction)

Figure 6.16 Proof of correctness

2.3   from $(t_1, t_2) = (mk\text{-}Cmpterm(id_1, tl_1), mk\text{-}Cmpterm(id_2, tl_2))$
2.3.1 $id_1 = id_2 \lor id_1 \neq id_2$
2.3.2   from $id_1 = id_2$
2.3.2.1 $\chi(t_1, t_2, \theta_1) = \chi(term_1, term_2, \theta_1)$ (2.2, col, χ)
2.3.2.2 $\chi(tl_1, tl_2, \theta_1) < \chi(t_1, t_2, \theta_1)$ (h2.3, or2)
2.3.2.3 $\chi(tl_1, tl_2, \theta_1) < (n, k)$ (.1, .2, h2)
2.3.2.4   let $(b, \theta) = unifylist(tl_1, tl_2, \theta_1)$ in
2.3.2.5 $post\text{-}unifylist(tl_1, tl_2, \theta_1)\, b, \theta$ (h2, .3, .4, rc)
2.3.2.6 $post\text{-}unify(t_1, t_2, \theta_1)\, b, \theta$
                                              (.5, h2.3, h2.3.2, =, $post\text{-}unifylist$, $post\text{-}unify$)
               infer $post\text{-}unify(t_1, t_2, \theta_1)$
                 (if $id_1 = id_2$ then $unifylist(tl_1, tl_2, \theta_1)$ else (false, $\{\,\}$))
                                                                        (.6, .4, h2.3.2, $ifth\text{-}subs$)
2.3.3   from $id_1 \neq id_2$
2.3.3.1 $\nexists \theta \cdot mgu(t_1, t_2, \theta_1, \theta)$ (h2.3.3, h2.3, =, mgu)
               infer $post\text{-}unify(t_1, t_2, \theta_1)$
                 (if $id_1 = id_2$ then $unifylist(tl_1, tl_2, \theta_1)$ else (false, $\{\,\}$))
                                                                        (.1, $post\text{-}unify$, h2.3.3, $ifel\text{-}subs$)
           infer $post\text{-}unify(t_1, t_2, \theta_1)$
             (if $id_1 = id_2$ then $unifylist(tl_1, tl_2, \theta_1)$ else (false, $\{\,\}$))
                                                                        (2.3.1, 2.3.2, 2.3.3, $\lor\text{-}E$)

Figure 6.17 Proof of first case

6.8   Discussion

In this section we compare the above theory with those of Manna and Waldinger
[MW81], and Paulson [Pau85].

   First, we must bear in mind that our objectives are different. Manna and Waldinger
use unification as a nontrivial example of the 'constructive proof' approach to derive
programs. Paulson automates the proof in LCF to increase our understanding of the
automatic proof and development of programs. In pursuing these objectives, they restrict
their attention to a theory of idempotent substitutions. Our aim has been to develop a
more general theory and to use it to prove a more space efficient algorithm. Manna and
Waldinger use an algebraic approach to specification. As a result they need to develop
a theory of maps. Paulson also needs to do this because maps are not 'in-built' in LCF.
VDM includes maps as a data type; thus we have avoided defining maps. We have used

2.4   from $(t_1, t_2) = (mk\text{-}Cmpterm(id_1, tl_1), v_2)$

2.4.1 $v_2 \notin vars(t_1\theta_1) \vee v_2 \in vars(t_1\theta_1)$

2.4.2   from $v_2 \notin vars(t_1\theta_1)$

2.4.2.1 $mgu(t_1, t_2, \theta_1, \theta_1 \cup \{v_2 \mapsto term_1\})$

                                                (h2.4.2, 2.2, h2.4, =, co3)

        infer *post-unify*(t_1, t_2, θ_1)

           (if $v_2 \notin vars(t_1\theta_1)$ then $(true, \theta_1 \cup \{v_2 \mapsto term_1\})$ else $(false, \{\ \}))$

                            (2.4.2.1, *post-unify*, h2.4.2, *ifth-subs*)

2.4.3   from $v_2 \in vars(t_1\theta_1)$

2.4.3.1 $t_2\theta_1 = v_2$ (2.2, h2.4, co2)

2.4.3.2 $\nexists \theta \cdot mgu(t_1, t_2, \theta_1, \theta)$ (.1, h2.4.3, h2.4, mg2, *mgu*)

        infer *post-unify*(t_1, t_2, θ_1)

           (if $v_2 \notin vars(t_1\theta_1)$ then $(true, \theta_1 \cup \{v_2 \mapsto term_1\})$ else $(false, \{\ \}))$

                                 (.2, *post-unify*, h2.4.3, *ifel-subs*)

    infer *post-unify*(t_1, t_2, θ_1)

       (if $v_2 \notin vars(t_1\theta_1)$ then $(true, \theta_1 \cup \{v_2 \mapsto term_1\})$ else $(false, \{\ \}))$

                                   (2.4.1, 2.4.2, 2.4.3, $\vee$-E)

Figure 6.18 Proof of second case

the logic of partial functions [BCJ83]. Hence, we did not require our definitions to be total. The logic of partial functions has been particularly useful in expressing lemmas of the form:

$$dom\text{-}disjoint(\theta_1, \theta_2) \;\Rightarrow\; P(\theta_1 \cup \theta_2)$$

A theory of noncircular substitutions is developed. To do this, we have had to formalize the notion of circularity. Since idempotent substitutions are noncircular, this theory is more general. Substitution application is defined recursively, whereas Manna and Waldinger define it as parallel application. For example, if in parallel substitution application:

$$\theta = \{X \mapsto Y, Y \mapsto Z\}$$
$$X\theta = Y$$

but in recursive substitution application:

$$X\theta = Z$$

The specification of a most general unifier differs from Manna and Waldinger's in

2.5   from $(t_1, t_2) = (v_1, v_2)$
2.5.1 $v_1 = v_2 \lor v_1 \neq v_2$
2.5.2   from $v_1 \neq v_2$
2.5.2.1 $mgu(t_1, t_2, \theta_1, \theta_1 \cup \{v_2 \mapsto term_1\})$

(2.2, h2.5, *vars*,co2, h2.5.2, co3)

infer *post-unify*(t_1, t_2, θ_1)
(if $v_1 = v_2$ then (true, θ_1) else (true, $\theta_1 \cup \{v_2 \mapsto term_1\}$))

(.1, *post-unify*, h2.5.2, *ifel-subs*)

2.5.3   from $v_1 = v_2$
infer *post-unify*(t_1, t_2, θ_1)
(if $v_1 = v_2$ then (true, θ_1) else (true, $\theta_1 \cup \{v_2 \mapsto term_1\}$))

(h2.5.3, h2.5, *post-unify*, *ifth-subs*)

infer *post-unify*(t_1, t_2, θ_1)
(if $v_1 = v_2$ then (true, θ_1) else (true, $\theta_1 \cup \{v_2 \mapsto term_1\}$))

(2.5.1, 2.5.2, 2.5.3, $\lor$-*E*)

Figure 6.19 Proof of fourth case

two respects. First, we allow the unification of terms in an existing context substitution. We can, of course, remove this context substitution by setting it to the empty map. As a result of a theory of noncircular substitutions, substitutions which may be most general unifiers in our work, may not be most general unifiers in Manna and Waldinger's definition. For example, with

$$\theta = \{X \mapsto Y, Y \mapsto Z\}$$

although:

$$f(X, X)\theta = f(Y, Z)\theta = f(Z, Z)$$

in our definition; in Manna and Waldinger's theory this substitution is not a unifier:

$$f(X, X)\theta = f(Y, Y) \text{ but } f(Y, Z)\theta = f(Z, Z)$$

The algorithm we have proved is more space efficient than the one 'proved' by Manna and Waldinger provided that the check for circularity (the occurs check) is ignored (or implemented using the definition of reach). For example, to unify the terms (from [CB83, p. 910]):

$t_1 = f(X_1, X_2, ..., X_m)$, and
$t_2 = f(g(X_0, X_0), g(X_1, X_1), ..., g(X_{m-1}, X_{m-1}))$

The algorithm in Manna and Waldinger gives:

$\{X_1 \mapsto g(X_0, X_0),$
$X_2 \mapsto g(g(X_0, X_0), g(X_0, X_0))$
$X_3 \mapsto g(g(g(X_0, X_0), g(X_0, X_0)),$
$\qquad\qquad g(g(X_0, X_0), g(X_0, X_0)))$
$\vdots$
$X_m \mapsto ...\}$

Thus the space complexity of the algorithm they prove is exponential with respect to the length of the terms to be unified. The algorithm we prove gives:

$\{X_1 \mapsto g(X_0, X_0), X_2 \mapsto g(X_1, X_1), ..., X_m \mapsto g(X_{m-1}, X_{m-1})\}$

In general, the use of coerce in the above algorithm ensures that any pair $\{v \mapsto t\}$ that is accumulated in the substitution is such that the length of t is less than or equal to the larger of the terms to be unified (assuming that the initial context is empty). Thus the space complexity is of order $m * n$ where m is the length of the larger of the terms to be unified, and n is the number of variables occurring in the terms. However, the above algorithm does not improve upon the exponential time complexity of the algorithm proved by Manna and Waldinger.

The major benefit of our more general theory has been that we have captured the behavior of a wider class of unification algorithms. The example above illustrates the fact that the algorithm we prove does not satisfy Manna and Waldinger's definition of the most general unifier, that is, the algorithm we prove does not satisfy their specification of unification.

6.9 Conclusion

We have developed a theory of noncircular substitutions. Since idempotent substitutions are a proper subset of noncircular substitutions, and when restricted to idempotent substitutions, our definition of substitution application is equivalent to Manna and Waldinger's, a theory of noncircular substitutions is more general than a theory of idempotent substitutions.

We have presented a proof of an algorithm which does not satisfy Manna and Waldinger's specification and is more space efficient than the one they prove. More efficient unification algorithms than the one we prove do exist [CB83]). These tend to represent substituitions as graphs [CB83, PW78]). To prove these in VDM, we would have to use the ideas of reification [Jon86a]. There are also a number of extensions to unification that we have not discussed [Hue75, SR88]. Specifying and proving these algorithms correct would require further research. For example, we would have to tackle the problem of 'variable capture' if we attempt to extend our work to cater for quantified terms [SR88].

Acknowledgements

I am grateful to Professor Cliff Jones for his help throughout this work. Professor Howard Barringer provided the reference to Corbin and Bidoit's paper [CB83] and enlightenment about the use of unification in rewrite rules.

7

Heap Storage

Chris W. George

The specification describes the *NEW* and *DISPOSE* operations of the heap storage in Pascal. It contains several levels of specification, each intended to implement the previous one. It shows how an efficient implementation may be gradually created from an abstract specification by successive commitments to data structures and algorithms: VDM is used to capture design decisions one at a time. The example was originally created as an exercise for a VDM course. It has the advantage of being a problem many programmers are aware of while not being trivial.

7.1   The heap as a set of locations

The first specification, level 0, is an attempt to be as abstract as possible. The free space is simply a set of locations; disposal is then simply a matter of set union. Allocating free space with *NEW0* involves finding a sufficiently long sequence.

$Loc = \mathbb{N}$

NEW0 (*req*: $\mathbb{N}$) *res*: *Loc*-set
ext wr *FREE* : *Loc*-set
pre $\exists s \in Loc^* \cdot has\_seq(s, req, free)$
post $\exists s \in Loc^* \cdot$

$\qquad (has\_seq(s, req, \overleftarrow{free}) \wedge$
$\qquad res = \text{elems } s \wedge$
$\qquad free = \overleftarrow{free} - res)$

DISPOSE0 (*ret*: *Loc*-set)
ext wr *FREE* : *Loc*-set
pre $ret \cap free = \{ \}$
post $free = \overleftarrow{free} \cup ret$

$has\_seq : Loc^* \times \mathbb{N} \times Loc\text{-set} \to Bool$
$has\_seq(s, n, free) \quad \triangle \quad is\_sequential(s) \wedge$
$\qquad \text{elems } s \subseteq free \wedge$
$\qquad \text{len } s = n$

$is\_sequential : \mathbb{N}^* \to Bool$
$is\_sequential(s) \quad \triangle \quad \exists i, j \in \mathbb{N} \cdot s = \{i, \dots, j\}$

7.2   The heap as a set of pieces

Level 1 tries to tackle the inefficiency of *NEW*, which in level 0 consisted of a search for a suitable set. The free space is now held as a set of nonoverlapping, nonabutting pieces. *NEW* is now a matter of finding a suitable piece. It was originally intended that it would be undecided at this stage whether the pieces were nonabutting, but it was realized that if they were allowed to abut then either the pre-condition of *NEW1* would need changing to show that there existed a set of pieces that could be assembled to form the requirement, or there would be cases where *NEW0* would satisfy its pre-condition and *NEW1* would not. Hence the level 1 invariant now insists on nonabutting pieces.

The retrieve function is:

$retr1\_0 = locs$

Note that the normal refinement rules, as for example in [Jon90], will not work for *NEW*1 and *DISPOSE*1 since their signatures have changed. (A careful examination will also show that in level 1 we have also added the restriction that the argument to *DISPOSE* must be a single piece, i.e. a sequential set of locations. This was not true at level 0.)

$Free1 = Piece$-set
inv $(ps) \triangleq \forall p1, p2 \in ps \cdot$
$\qquad (p1 = p2 \vee locs\_of(p1) \cap locs\_of(p2) = \{ \} \wedge$
$\qquad LOC(p1) + SIZE(p1) \neq LOC(p2))$

/* pieces must be disjoint and nonabutting */

$Piece :: LOC : Loc$
$\qquad\quad SIZE : \mathbb{N}$

$Loc = \mathbb{N}$

$NEW1$ $(req:\mathbb{N})$ $res:Piece$
ext wr $FREE$: $Free1$
pre $\exists p \in free \cdot SIZE(p) \geq req$
post $locs(free) = locs(\overleftarrow{free}) - locs\_of(res) \wedge$
$\qquad locs\_of(res) \subseteq locs(\overleftarrow{free}) \wedge$
$\qquad SIZE(res) = req$

$DISPOSE1$ $(ret:Piece)$
ext wr $FREE$: $Free1$
pre $locs\_of(ret) \cap locs(free) = \{ \}$
post $locs(free) = locs(\overleftarrow{free}) \cup locs\_of(ret)$

$locs : Free1 \rightarrow Loc$-set
$locs(ps) \quad \triangleq \quad \bigcup \{locs\_of(p) \mid p \in ps\}$

$locs\_of : Piece \rightarrow Loc$-set
$locs\_of(p) \quad \triangleq \quad \{LOC(p), \dots, LOC(p) + SIZE(p) - 1\}$

7.3   Ordering the pieces

Having tried to deal with the problem of *NEW* in level 1, it still seems that *DISPOSE* has a problem of checking for abutment of the pieces it tries to add to the free space with those already there – apparently checking each of the free set of pieces. The level 2 state now holds the pieces in a recursive and ordered structure allowing for a simple search. The retrieve function to level 1 is:

$retr2\_1 : [Fp] \rightarrow Piece\text{-set}$
$retr2\_1(free) \quad \triangleq$
$\qquad \{mk\text{-}Piece(FPLOC(fp), FPSIZE(fp)) \mid$
$\qquad\qquad fp \in Fp \wedge is\_reachable(fp, free)\}$

but it is perhaps easier to give that back to level 0 as:

$retr2\_0 = locs2$

since the post-conditions of *NEW2* and *DISPOSE2* use *locs2*. Note that it would be more convenient to represent the level 2 state by:

$Free2 = Piece^{*}$

when the type *Fp* and the function *is_reachable* are no longer necessary – the quantification in the pre-condition of *NEW2* can be done over the 'elems' of the state. This example was written without using the list data type of VDM, but effectively modelling it, to show how recursive structures may be defined, and to show the use of predicates like *is_reachable* with such structures.

$Free2 = [Fp]$
$\text{inv } (x) \triangleq is\_ok2(x)$

$Fp :: FPLOC \quad : Loc$
$\qquad FPSIZE \quad : \mathbb{N}$
$\qquad FPNEXT \ : [Fp]$

$Piece :: LOC \ : Loc$
$\qquad\quad SIZE \ : \mathbb{N}$

$Loc = \mathbb{N}$

$is\_ok2 : Free2 \rightarrow Bool$
$is\_ok2(fp) \quad \triangle$
    if $fp = $ nil
    then true
    else if $FPNEXT(fp) = $ nil
        then true
        else $FPLOC(fp) + FPSIZE(fp) < FPLOC(FPNEXT(fp)) \land$
            $is\_ok2(FPNEXT(fp))$

/* Note that the pieces are in ascending order. Note also that the use of '<' rather than '≤' forces the pieces not to abut. */

$NEW2 \; (req\text{:}\mathbb{N}) \; res\text{:}Piece$
ext wr $FREE \; : \; Free2$
pre $\exists fp \in Fp \cdot$
        $(FPSIZE(fp) \geq req \land$
        $is\_reachable(fp, free))$
post $locs2(free) = locs2(\overleftarrow{free}) - locs\_of(res) \land$
    $locs\_of(res) \subseteq locs2(\overleftarrow{free}) \land$
    $SIZE(res) = req$

$DISPOSE2 \; (ret\text{:}Piece)$
ext wr $FREE \; : \; Free2$
pre $locs\_of(ret) \cap locs2(free) = \{\,\}$
post $locs2(free) = locs2(\overleftarrow{free}) \cup locs\_of(ret)$

$locs2 : Free2 \rightarrow Loc\text{-set}$
$locs2(fp) \quad \triangle$
    if $fp = $ nil
    then $\{\,\}$
    else $\{FPLOC(fp), \dots, FPLOC(fp) + FPSIZE(fp) - 1\} \cup$
        $locs2(FPNEXT(fp))$

$is\_reachable : Fp \times Free2 \rightarrow Bool$
$is\_reachable(fp, start) \quad \triangle$
    if $start = $ nil
    then false
    else if $fp = start$
        then true
        else $is\_reachable(fp, FPNEXT(start))$

7.4   Proof of a refinement step

So far we have defined retrieve functions for each level but not given any proofs. We will now give an example proof of the refinement from level 1 to level 2.

Adequacy

The retrieve function from level 2 to level 1 is:

$retr2\_1 : Free2 \rightarrow Free1$
$retr2\_1(free) \quad \triangleq$
$\qquad \{mk\text{-}Piece(FPLOC(fp), FPSIZE(fp)) \mid$
$\qquad\qquad fp \in Fp \wedge is\_reachable(fp, free)\}$

This is clearly a total function, being given a well defined explicit definition. The next thing we have to do is to prove adequacy, i.e. that:

$$\forall ps \in Free1 \cdot \exists fp \in Free2 \cdot retr2\_1(fp) = ps$$

Frequently, the easiest way to prove such an adequacy requirement is to invent a function that is an inverse of the retrieve function. The existence of an appropriate *fp* is then shown by applying this inverse function to the *ps* value. In this case the algorithm for the inverse function is clear. If *ps* is empty the result is nil. Otherwise, since by its invariant all the pieces in *ps* are disjoint we can select the first as the one with the lowest initial location and construct a record of type *Fp*. The *FPNEXT* field will be the result of applying the same function to the rest of *ps*. More formally, we define a function *split* that splits a (nonempty) set of pieces into the first piece and the rest, and the inverse retrieve in terms of *split*.

$split \ (ps: Free1) \ r: Piece \times Free1$
pre $ps \neq \{\ \}$
post let $(p, s) = r$ in
$\qquad p \in ps \ \wedge$
$\qquad s = ps - \{p\} \ \wedge$
$\qquad \forall q \in s \cdot LOC(p) < LOC(q)$

$inv\_retr2\_1 : Free1 \rightarrow Free2$
$inv\_retr2\_1(ps) \quad \triangleq \quad$ if $ps = \{\ \}$
$\qquad\qquad\qquad\qquad$ then nil
$\qquad\qquad\qquad\qquad$ else let $(p, s) = split(ps)$ in
$\qquad\qquad\qquad\qquad\qquad mk\text{-}Fp(LOC(p), SIZE(p), inv\_retr2\_1(s))$

It is worth noting that the result of *inv_retr2_1* is in the type *Free2*, not just [*Fp*], and so the invariant on *Free2* is claimed to hold for it. This is easily proved from the invariant on *Free1* that holds on its input.

If we now assume that *split* is a well defined function with a unique result (which could also be proved formally) we can give the following proof that *inv_retr2_1* is a right inverse of *retr2_1* and hence of the required adequacy result:

from $ps \in Free1$
1   from $ps = \{\}$
1.1 $inv\_retr2\_1(ps) = \text{nil}$ *inv_retr2_1*
1.2 $retr2\_1(inv\_retr2\_1(ps)) = \{\}$ *retr2_1*
       infer $retr2\_1(inv\_retr2\_1(ps)) = ps$ =-trans(h1,1.2)
2   from $p \in Piece, s \in Piece\text{-set},$
            $(p, s) = split(ps), retr2\_1(inv\_retr2\_1(s)) = s$
2.1 $inv\_retr2\_1(ps) =$
            $mk\text{-}Fp(LOC(p), SIZE(p), inv\_retr2\_1(s))$ *inv_retr2_1*
2.2 $retr2\_1(inv\_retr2\_1(ps)) =$
            $p \cup retr2\_1(inv\_retr2\_1(s))$ *retr2_1*
2.3 $retr2\_1(inv\_retr2\_1(ps)) = \{p\} \cup s$ h2
       infer $retr2\_1(inv\_retr2\_1(ps)) = ps$ *split*
3    $retr2\_1(inv\_retr2\_1(ps)) = ps$ set-ind(1,2)
infer $\exists fp \in Free2 \cdot retr2\_1(fp) = ps$ ∃-I

Refined operations

We now have to prove the domain and result proof obligations for the refinement. For *DISPOSE* the domain rule is:

$\forall fp \in Free2, ret \in Piece \cdot$
$\quad locs\_of(ret) \cap locs(retr2\_1(fp)) = locs\_of(ret) \cap locs2(fp)$

which suggests that we might start by proving the lemma:

$\forall fp \in Free2 \cdot locs(retr2\_1(fp)) = locs2(fp)$

The proof of the lemma is as follows, using structural induction on the type *Free2*:

from $fp \in Free2$
1 from $fp = $ nil
1.1 $retr2\_1(fp) = \{\,\}$ $retr2\_1$
1.2 $locs(retr2\_1(fp)) = \{\,\}$ $locs$
1.3 $locs2(fp) = \{\,\}$ $locs2,\text{h1}$
   infer $locs(retr2\_1(fp)) = locs2(fp)$ $\text{=-trans}(1.2,1.3)$
2 from $l \in Loc, n \in \mathbb{N}, f \in Free2,$
     $fp = mk\text{-}Fp(l,n,f), locs(retr2\_1(f)) = locs2(f)$
2.1 $retr2\_1(fp) = \{mk\text{-}Piece(l,n)\} \cup retr2\_1(f)$ $retr2\_1$
2.2 $locs(retr2\_1(fp)) =$
     $\{l, \ldots, l+n-1\} \cup locs(retr2\_1(f))$ $locs$
2.3 $locs(retr2\_1(fp)) =$
     $\{l, \ldots, l+n-1\} \cup locs2(f)$ h2
2.4 $locs2(fp) = \{l, \ldots, l+n-1\} \cup locs2(f)$ $locs2,\text{h2}$
   infer $locs(retr2\_1(fp)) = locs2(fp)$ $\text{=-trans}(2.3,2.4)$
infer $locs(retr2\_1(fp)) = locs2(fp)$ $Free2\text{-ind}$

The domain rule for *DISPOSE* is now proved immediately from the lemma. The
result rule, which also follows immediately from the lemma, is:

$$\forall \overleftarrow{fp}, fp \in Free2, ret \in Piece \cdot$$
$$pre\text{-}DISPOSE(ret, \overleftarrow{fp}) \wedge$$
$$locs2(fp) = locs2(\overleftarrow{fp}) \cup locs\_of(ret) \Rightarrow$$
$$locs(retr2\_1(fp)) = locs(retr2\_1(\overleftarrow{fp})) \cup locs\_of(ret)$$

For *NEW* the domain rule is:

$$\forall fp \in Free2, req \in \mathbb{N} \cdot$$
$$\exists p \in retr2\_1(fp) \cdot SIZE(p) \geq req \Rightarrow$$
$$\exists f \in Fp \cdot FPSIZE(f) \geq req \wedge is\_reachable(f, fp)$$

A proof of this is:

from $fp \in Free2, req \in \mathbb{N}$

1     $\forall f \in Fp \cdot \neg is\_reachable(f, fp) \lor FPSIZE(f) < req \Rightarrow$
      $\forall p \in retr2\_1(fp) \cdot SIZE(p) < req$ *retr2_1*

2     $\neg \forall p \in retr2\_1(fp) \cdot SIZE(p) < req \Rightarrow$
      $\neg \forall f \in Fp \cdot \neg is\_reachable(f, fp) \lor FPSIZE(f) < req$ $\Rightarrow$-contrp

infer $\exists p \in retr2\_1(fp) \cdot SIZE(p) \geq req \Rightarrow$
    $\exists f \in Fp \cdot FPSIZE(f) \geq req \land is\_reachable(f, fp)$ $\forall$-defn,$\neg\neg$,deM

The result rule for *NEW* is:

$$\forall \overleftarrow{fp}, fp \in Free2, req \in Nat, res \in Piece \cdot$$

$$pre\text{-}NEW(req, retr2\_1(\overleftarrow{fp})) \land$$

$$locs(retr2\_1(fp)) = locs(retr2\_1(\overleftarrow{fp})) - locs\_of(res) \land$$

$$locs\_of(res) \subseteq locs(retr2\_1(\overleftarrow{fp})) \land$$

$$SIZE(res) = req \Rightarrow$$

$$locs2(fp) = locs2(\overleftarrow{fp}) - locs\_of(res) \land$$

$$locs\_of(res) \subseteq locs2(\overleftarrow{fp}) \land$$

$$SIZE(res) = req$$

which follows immediately from the lemma proved earlier.

    Since there are no initial states specified we have completed the data reification proof for the development step from level 1 to level 2.

7.5   Using the heap to record its structure

Having achieved a state structure that will allow reasonably efficient procedures for *NEW* and *DISPOSE* (or at least procedures that are an improvement on searching sets), there is still the problem that in implementing this structure much storage will be used. We wish instead to use the free storage as the space in which the information about its structure is held. Hence in level 3 we model storage as a map from location to value, where a value may also represent a location. Since each piece of free space must now store its length and a pointer to the next, a new requirement is added that *NEW* and *DISPOSE* will not work on pieces of length 1.

    The retrieve function is:

$retr3\_2 : Free3 \rightarrow Free2$
$retr3\_2(start, store) \quad \triangleq$
     if $start = $ nil
     then nil
     else $mk\text{-}Fp(start, store(start), retr3\_2(store(start + 1), store))$
   pre $is\_ok3(start, store)$

but as with level 2 it might be easier to use:

$retr3\_0 = locs3$

Neither of these retrieve functions will be adequate, of course, because of the ban on pieces of length 1.

It should also be noted that this is the first level at which a location is anything other than a natural number. In order to allow the heap to hold information about its structure we have introduced the notion of storage. Now its presence in the state would allow *NEW* and *DISPOSE* to change it arbitrarily, so we have added to the post-conditions of *NEW*3 and *DISPOSE*3 extra conjuncts to prevent them altering nonfree locations, i.e. locations 'in use' by some program. The conjunct for *NEW*3 says that any location that was in use before *NEW*3 was invoked must remain in use with the same contents; the conjunct for *DISPOSE*3 says that any location that was in before *DISPOSE*3 was invoked, and has not just been disposed, must remain in use with the same contents. These constraints might well be regarded as part of the requirements of the specification, but can only be expressed once we have actually modelled storage. Such an inability to capture all requirements at the most abstract level of specification is quite common.

$Free3 = [Loc] \times Store$
inv $(start, store) \triangleq is\_ok3(start, store)$

$Store = Loc \xrightarrow{m} [\mathbb{N}]$

$Piece :: LOC : Loc$
$ SIZE : \mathbb{N}$

$Loc = \mathbb{N}$

$is\_ok3 : [Loc] \times Store \rightarrow Bool$

$is\_ok3(a, store) \quad \triangle$

    if a = nil

    then true

    else $\{a, a + 1\} \subseteq$ dom $store \wedge$

        $store(a) \neq$ nil $\wedge$

        $store(a) > 1 \wedge$

        $store(a + 1) \neq$ nil $\Rightarrow$

        $(a + store(a) < store(a + 1) \wedge is\_ok3(store(a + 1), store))$

/* Note the new restriction, carried into *NEW3* and *DISPOSE3*, that the size of a piece must be at least 2 */

NEW3 (*req*: $\mathbb{N}$) *res*: *Piece*

ext wr *FREE* : *Free3*

pre $req > 1 \wedge$

    let $(start, store) = free$ in

    $\exists a \in$ dom $store \cdot$

        $store(a) \neq$ nil $\wedge$

        $(store(a) = req \vee store(a){-}req > 1) \wedge$

        $is\_reachable3(a, start, store)$

post $locs3(free) = locs3(\overleftarrow{free}) - locs\_of(res) \wedge$

    $locs\_of(res) \subseteq locs3(\overleftarrow{free}) \wedge$

    $SIZE(res) = req \wedge$

    let $(start, store) = free$ in

    $\forall loc \in$ dom $\overleftarrow{store} - locs3(\overleftarrow{start}, \overleftarrow{store}) \cdot$

        $(loc \in$ dom $store \wedge store(loc) = \overleftarrow{store}(loc))$

DISPOSE3 (*ret*: *Piece*)

ext wr *FREE* : *Free3*

pre $SIZE(ret) > 1 \wedge$

    $locs\_of(ret) \cap locs3(free) = \{ \}$

post $locs3(free) = locs3(\overleftarrow{free}) \cup locs\_of(ret) \wedge$

    let $(start, store) = free$ in

    $\forall loc \in$ dom $\overleftarrow{store} - locs3(start, store) \cdot$

        $(loc \in$ dom $store \wedge store(loc) = \overleftarrow{store}(loc))$

is_reachable3 : $Loc \times [Loc] \times Store \rightarrow Bool$
is_reachable3($a, start, store$) $\triangleq$
    if *start* = nil
    then false
    else if $a = start$
        then true
        else *is_reachable3*($a, store(start + 1), store$)
pre *is_ok3*($start, store$)

locs3 : $[Loc] \times Store \rightarrow Loc$-set
locs3($start, store$) $\triangleq$
    if *start* = nil
    then $\{\,\}$
    else $\{start, \ldots, start + store(start)-1\} \cup$
        locs3($store(start + 1), store$)
pre *is_ok3*($start, store$)

7.6   Providing explicit algorithms

*NEW*4 and *DISPOSE*4 are new versions of *NEW* and *DISPOSE* working on the level 3 state, but supplying explicit instead of implicit specifications. There is no algorithm for any of the previous definitions of *NEW* and *DISPOSE* – the specifications are in terms of the sets of locations represented and the state invariants. It is an interesting question whether it would have been better to try to introduce these algorithms at level 2. In the opinion of the author the algorithms are difficult to introduce, but would have been no easier at level 2.

*NEW*4 (*req*: $\mathbb{N}$) *res*: *Piece*
ext wr *FREE* : *Free3*
pre *req* > 1 $\wedge$
    let ($start, store$) = *free* in
    $\exists a \in$ dom *store* ·
        ($store(a) \neq$ nil $\wedge$
        ($store(a) = req \vee store(a)-req > 1$) $\wedge$
        is_reachable3($a, start, store$))

post let $(start, store) = free$ in

     $start =$ if $store(\overleftarrow{start}) = req$

         then $store(\overleftarrow{start} + 1)$

         else $\overleftarrow{start}$

    $\wedge$

    $(store, res) = remove4(\text{nil}, \overleftarrow{start}, \overleftarrow{store}, req)$

$remove4 : [Loc] \times [Loc] \times Store \times \mathbb{N}_1 \to (Store \times Piece)$

$remove4(prev, current, store, n)$ $\triangle$

    if $(store(current) < n) \vee (store(current) = n + 1)$

    then $remove4(current, store(current + 1), store, n)$

    else let $store1 =$ if $store(current) = n$

                  then if $prev = $ nil

                       then $store$

                       else $store \dagger \{prev + 1 \mapsto store(current + 1)\}$

                  else $store \dagger \{current \mapsto store(current) - n\}$

         in

       $(store1, mk\text{-}Piece(current + store(current) - n, n))$

pre $n > 1 \wedge$

    $\exists a \in$ dom $store \cdot$

       $(store(a) \neq$ nil $\wedge$

       $(store(a) = n \vee store(a) - n > 1) \wedge$

       $is\_reachable3(a, current, store))$

    $\wedge$

    $(prev = $ nil $\vee current = $ nil $\vee prev < current) \wedge$

    $is\_ok3(prev, store) \wedge$

    $is\_ok3(current, store)$

$DISPOSE4 (ret: Piece)$

ext wr $FREE$: $Free3$

pre $SIZE(ret) > 1 \wedge$

    $locs\_of(ret) \cap locs3(free) = \{\}$

post let $mk\text{-}Piece(a, s) = ret$ in

    let $(start, store) = free$ in

    $start =$ if $\overleftarrow{start} = $ nil

          then a

          else $\min\{\overleftarrow{start}, a\}$

    $\wedge$

    $store = insert(\text{nil}, \overleftarrow{start}, \overleftarrow{store}, a, s)$

$insert : [Loc] \times [Loc] \times Store \times Loc \times \mathbb{N}_1 \to Store$
$insert(prev, current, store, a, s) \quad \triangle$
  if $current \neq$ nil $\land a > current$
  then $insert(current, store(current + 1), store, a, s)$
  else let $store1 = store \dagger \{a \mapsto s, a + 1 \mapsto current\}$ in
    let $store2 =$ if $prev =$ nil
       then $store1$
       else $store1 \dagger \{prev + 1 \mapsto a\}$
    in
    let $store3 =$ if $current =$ nil $\lor a + s < current$
       then $store2$
       else $(\{current, current + 1\} \triangleleft store2) \dagger$
         $\{a \mapsto s + store2(current),$
         $a + 1 \mapsto store2(current + 1)\}$
    in
    let $store4 =$ if $prev =$ nil $\lor prev + store(prev) < a$
       then $store3$
       else $(\{a, a + 1\} \triangleleft store3) \dagger$
         $\{prev \mapsto store3(prev) + store3(a),$
         $prev + 1 \mapsto store3(a + 1)\}$
    in
    $store4$
 pre $s > 1 \land$
  $(prev =$ nil $\lor current =$ nil $\lor prev < current) \land$
  $is\_ok3(prev, store) \land$
  $is\_ok3(current, store)$

In this specification:

- $store1$ has new piece hooked up to next.

- $store2$ has new piece hooked up to previous one.

- $store3$ has new piece merged with next if possible.

- $store4$ has new piece merged with previous if possible.

- *DISPOSE4* is an implementation of *DISPOSE3*.

7.7 Further refinements

The removal of domain elements from the store map in *DISPOSE4* is difficult to model, and should be deleted on the basis that the presence of unreachable elements in the domain of the the map is irrelevant.

The pre-conditions for *DISPOSE*4 and *NEW*4 should be replaced by exception conditions, and the exceptions raised at appropriate points in the algorithms. Note that this is more than encapsulation in some operation whose body (for *NEW*, say) is effectively:

if *pre-NEW*(*req*)
then *NEW*(*req*)
else *RAISE exception*

since an implementation of this implies in general two searches for a suitable piece.

The type *Loc* should then be replaced by some range of values representing possible heap locations. (This introduction of bounds is, of course, an inadequate refinement.) An extra exception for exhaustion of heap space should also be added.

The operations could then be implemented in some suitable programming language, though of course we would only be modelling heap space by some (presumably large) array.

A development along these lines into Pascal has in fact been completed and is documented in [Eva86].

7.8 More interesting data structures

It could be argued that the data structures used are still fairly trivial. A more interesting level 2 structure would use a B-tree instead of the linear recursive structure, and a further refinement to the operations would be to keep the tree balanced. This involves a further restriction on the minimum size of pieces to 3.

An even more interesting structure can be obtained by noting that the balanced B-tree gives an $O(\log(n))$ algorithm for *DISPOSE* but still leaves *NEW* as $O(n)$, where n is the number of pieces. If most *NEW* and *DISPOSE* operations are of the same size, or from a small range of sizes, this should not be too much of a problem. If *NEW* is also required to be $O(\log(n))$ then some other structure might be used.

Acknowledgements

This study was originally intended to provide an example of development for use in courses on VDM, and has benefited from the comments of course participants. A version of this paper was published in [BJMN87]. Several colleagues have also provided suggestions and pointed out errors, particularly J. Bicarregui, A. J. Evans, P. Goldsack and C. B. Jones.

This work was partially funded by the Commission of the European Communities (CEC) under the ESPRIT program in the field of software technology, project number

315 'Rigorous Approach to Industrial Software Engineering (RAISE)'

8

Garbage Collection

Mario I. Wolczko

Like the preceding chapter, this specification is concerned with storage management. In this case, the topic of garbage collection algorithms is discussed. Standard algorithms such as reference counting and mark-sweep are related to an abstract VDM specification. These specifications show how to record a body of knowledge about algorithms: VDM can be used to describe algorithms at a level of abstraction which makes their reimplementation in various languages straightforward.

8.1   Introduction

A milestone was achieved in the history of the development of programming languages with the introduction of automatic storage reclamation. In contrast to many lower-level languages such as C and Pascal, languages like LISP and Smalltalk-80[1] relieve the programmer from the burden of storage management. In these languages the programmer is free to create data structures at will, and the resources used by these data structures will be reclaimed automatically by the run-time system when it can prove that they are no longer required. Unusable data structures are known as *garbage*, and the task of reclaiming garbage is more commonly known as *garbage collection*.[2]

It is of paramount concern that any implementation of a garbage collector be correct. An incorrect garbage collector can fill memory with unreclaimable garbage, or, more seriously, can reclaim data structures that are still in use. Clearly, the implications for a system using such a collector are severe: data will be modified in ways which seem to bear no relation to the program activity at the time. Indeed, a malfunctioning garbage collector can render a system as unusable as malfunctioning hardware.

In principle, the task of a garbage collector is simple: it must detect garbage, and reclaim the resources it uses it for future use. In practice, however, this is a nontrivial task, especially when one considers efficiency. The aim of this chapter is to introduce a VDM specification for the abstract problem of garbage collection, divorced from any implementation details, and then present several different reifications which lead to garbage collection algorithms with different properties. By concentrating on the essence of each algorithm using a formal notation, the reader can gain insight into the operation of the algorithm, and its potential gains and drawbacks.

8.2   An abstract characterization of garbage collection

A garbage collector operates on a collection of *objects*, where each object may contain references to other objects. Therefore, the entire collection of objects can be considered as a directed graph, with each object as a node and each reference as an arc. Some of the objects are distinguished by being *roots*: they can never become inaccessible, and their storage cannot be reclaimed. The task of the garbage collector is to find all the nodes in the graph which cannot be reached by traversing arcs from the root nodes, and reclaiming their resources for future use.

In a real system, objects may contain all sorts of data in addition to references to other objects: characters and numbers, for example. For the purposes of garbage collection

---

[1] Smalltalk-80 is a trademark of ParcPlace Systems, Inc.

[2] Early texts on automatic storage reclamation [Knu79] used the term 'garbage collection' to denote a specific class of storage reclamation algorithms. Nowadays it is often used for all such algorithms, and in this chapter the terms garbage collection and automatic storage reclamation are used interchangeably.

these items are of no consequence. To model object references we introduce the data type *Oop* (ordinary object pointer). Every object has its own unique *Oop*, and can contain within itself other *Oops* referring to other objects. The particular set of *Oops* is of no consequence at this stage in the specification; for the moment we will simply assume that the set contains enough distinct values to assign one to each object in the largest memory structure that we might be interested in. At the implementation level it may be a subrange of the integers representing the available address space of a machine.

In addition to being identified by an *Oop*, the data within an object will most likely be ordered, so that each datum can be accessed by position. However, the ordering of references is of no consequence to the garbage collector; it is only concerned with *what* is referenced. Hence, our initial model of an object might be a set of references to other objects:

Object = *Oop*-set

However, this model is in some sense 'too abstract.' When one considers the operations that take place on objects in a real system, one finds that it is important to know *how many times* one object refers to another. In other words, the graph of objects should be allowed to contain multiple arcs from one object to another. We shall say more about this later.

Hence, our abstract model for an object is as a *bag* of references to other objects:

Object = *Bag*(*Oop*)

There is no ordering defined on the references, but if a reference is added to a bag more than once, it can be removed more than once. For a more complete exposition of bags, see [Jon90]. We shall use several operations involving bags: *add* to add an element to a bag, *remove* to remove an element from a bag, *count* to count the number of occurrences of an element in a bag, + to add bags together, and *set* to obtain the set of elements in a bag. These are defined in the appendix.

At this stage we shall also define a number of auxiliary functions that operate on objects. As the definition of an object is reified, the definitions of these functions will be altered, but the interface will remain the same. Hence the set of functions can be thought of as a small 'object language.'

The first function simply tests whether one object refers to another:

refers_to : *Oop* × *Object* → $\mathbb{B}$
refers_to(*p*, *obj*) $\triangleq$ *count*(*p*, *obj*) > 0

The next two add and remove a reference to an object, respectively:

add_to_obj : *Oop* × *Object* → *Object*
add_to_obj(*p*, *obj*) $\triangleq$ *add*(*p*, *obj*)

$remove\_from\_obj : Oop \times Object \rightarrow Object$
$remove\_from\_obj(p, obj) \quad \triangleq \quad remove(p, obj)$

Finally, we shall need to know which objects an object refers to:

$all\_refs : Object \rightarrow Oop\text{-set}$
$all\_refs(obj) \quad \triangleq \quad set(obj)$

In addition to the object manipulation functions, we shall also define what the initial state of a newly created object is:

$init\_object = init\text{-}Bag$

The memory system will contain a collection of these objects, and distinguish some of them as roots:

$State_A \quad :: \quad mem \quad : \quad Oop \xrightarrow{\ m\ } Object$
$\qquad\qquad\quad roots \ : \ Oop\text{-set}$

(The subscript *A* indicates that this is our abstract state. As it is reified in later sections, the subscript will be altered.)

For example, given a state $s \in State_A$, and an *Oop* p, we can discover which objects p references by looking up p in the memory of s: $all\_refs(mem(s)(p))$ (p must be in the domain of $mem(s)$, of course).

Operations on the abstract state

Having defined the abstract state (the invariant follows at the end of this section), we now come to the operations on that state. We need to be able to create a new object and to modify an object. Collectively, these are known as the *mutator* operations:

- *create*(*f*) creates a new object in the memory, installs a reference to it in the object referred to by the *Oop* f, and returns the *Oop* of the new object.

- *add_ref*(*f, t*) adds a reference from f to t.

- *remove_ref*(*f, t*) removes a reference to t from f. It is here that the distinction between objects as bags and sets is made: had the model for an object been a set of *Oops*, a single *remove_ref* application would have removed all references to t from f. In reality, pointer manipulation operations do not have this property, and references are added and removed one at a time.

Operations could also be provided to modify the set of roots. As these are not important in this chapter, they will be omitted.

It should be obvious that garbage can only come into being as the result of a *remove_ref* operation. Hence, we could state in the post-condition for *remove_ref* that all garbage be removed immediately. However, by placing in the invariant the restriction that no garbage is ever in the state, we will make later development steps easier.

Here are the operations:

create (*from*: *Oop*) *to*: *Oop*
ext wr *mem* : *Oop* $\xrightarrow{m}$ *Object*
pre *from* ∈ dom *mem*
post *to* ∉ dom $\overleftarrow{mem}$
$\qquad$ ∧ *mem* = $\overleftarrow{mem}$ † {*from* ↦ *add_to_obj*(*to*, $\overleftarrow{mem}$(*from*)), *to* ↦ *init_object*}

The post-condition of *create* chooses *to* from the set of *Oops* that are not in use; this allows an implementor as much freedom as possible in *Oop* allocation.

add_ref (*from*, *to*: *Oop*)
ext wr *mem* : *Oop* $\xrightarrow{m}$ *Object*
pre {*from*, *to*} ⊆ dom *mem*
post *mem* = $\overleftarrow{mem}$ † {*from* ↦ *add_to_obj*(*to*, $\overleftarrow{mem}$(*from*))}

In the post-condition of *remove_ref* we need only state that all objects remaining in the state (except the one being altered) are unchanged; the invariant will take care of garbage for us:

remove_ref (*from*, *to*: *Oop*)
ext wr *mem* : *Oop* $\xrightarrow{m}$ *Object*
pre {*from*, *to*} ⊆ dom *mem* ∧ *refers_to*(*to*, *mem*(*from*))
post *mem*(*from*) = *remove_from_obj*(*to*, $\overleftarrow{mem}$(*from*))
$\qquad$ ∧ ∀*p* ∈ dom *mem* · *p* ≠ *from* ⇒ *mem*(*p*) = $\overleftarrow{mem}$(*p*)

The invariant is now defined to ensure that no garbage appears in the state.

inv-State$_A$(*mk-State$_A$*(*mem*, *roots*)) $\quad \triangleq$
$\qquad$ *roots* ⊆ dom *mem* ∧ *no_garbage*(*roots*, *mem*)

The test for absence of garbage states that the set of objects in the memory is precisely the set that is reachable from the roots:

no_garbage(*roots*, *mem*) $\quad \triangleq \quad$ *reachable_from*(*roots*, *mem*) = dom *mem*

Reachability is determined by following all references from the roots recursively until no new objects are encountered. The set of objects encountered and recorded as reachable is known as the *visited* set; those objects referenced from the visited objects but not in the visited set are known as *unvisited* objects, and are visited in the next step of the recursion. When the unvisited set becomes empty, all accessible objects have been traced, and are in the visited set.

$reachable\_from : Oop\text{-set} \times (Oop \xrightarrow{m} Object) \to Oop\text{-set}$
$reachable\_from(roots, mem) \quad \triangle \quad visit(\{\,\}, roots, mem)$

$visit : Oop\text{-set} \times Oop\text{-set} \times (Oop \xrightarrow{m} Object) \to Oop\text{-set}$
$visit(visited, unvisited, mem) \quad \triangle$
      if $unvisited = \{\,\}$
      then $visited$
      else let $visited' = visited \cup unvisited$ in
           $visit(visited', \bigcup\{all\_refs(mem(p)) \mid p \in unvisited\} - visited', mem)$

The state, invariant and operations describe an ideal system in which garbage is reclaimed immediately it is created. This is an example of a specification for which there is no known efficient implementation. All known garbage collection algorithms either do not guarantee that all garbage is reclaimed or take time proportional to the number of objects in the system to reclaim garbage. Clearly, having such behavior for each *remove_ref* operation will be unacceptable.

We need therefore to relax our constraint that no garbage ever appears in the state. A 'safe' garbage collector is one that never reclaims active objects, and we can specify safety properties by relaxing the invariant:

$inv\text{-}State(mk\text{-}State(mem, roots)) \quad \triangle$
    $roots \subseteq \text{dom } mem \wedge no\_dangling\_refs(mem)$

In our new, less abstract state (the *A* subscript has disappeared), any number of garbage objects may appear, but there must be no references to nonexistent objects.

$no\_dangling\_refs : (Oop \xrightarrow{m} Object) \to \mathbb{B}$
$no\_dangling\_refs(mem) \quad \triangle \quad \forall p \in \text{dom } mem \cdot all\_refs(mem(p)) \subseteq \text{dom } mem$

We can relate this new state to the abstract one by means of a retrieve function that discards all garbage:

$retr : State \to State_A$
$retr(mk\text{-}State(mem, roots)) \quad \triangle$
    $mk\text{-}State_A(reachable\_from(roots, mem) \triangleleft mem, roots)$

Now that garbage may appear in the state, we need a separate operation to reclaim it.

GC
ext wr mem : $Oop \xrightarrow{m} Object$
post $\text{dom } mem \subseteq \text{dom } \overleftarrow{mem} \wedge \forall p \in \text{dom } mem \cdot mem(p) = \overleftarrow{mem}(p)$

This specification states that the garbage collector may not introduce new objects, and that all objects present after garbage collection must be unchanged. The post-condition, taken in conjunction with the invariant, ensures that only garbage has been removed from the state.

Note that the garbage collector can be very simple: it need not collect any garbage at all! We have to be this lax because some garbage collectors do not guarantee that all garbage is reclaimed.

The *create*, *add_ref* and *remove_ref* operations require stricter pre-conditions stating that their arguments must not refer to garbage objects; these modifications are left as an exercise for the reader.

8.3   The mark-sweep garbage collector

The principle behind a mark-sweep garbage collector is simple: in one phase all the objects accessible from the root set are traced and marked (leaving inaccessible objects unmarked); in a second phase, all unmarked objects are reclaimed. Several different algorithms satisfy this specification (see [Knu79], pp. 413–420, and [Coh81]), differing in how they trade time for space.

The definition of an object is altered to incorporate the mark bit:

Object :: *body* : *Bag(Oop)*
             marked : $\mathbb{B}$

The object manipulation functions are suitably modified:

refers_to : *Oop* × *Object* → $\mathbb{B}$
refers_to(p, obj) $\triangleq$ *count(p, body(obj))* > 0

add_to_obj : *Oop* × *Object* → *Object*
add_to_obj(p, obj) $\triangleq$ μ(*obj, body* ↦ *add(p, body(obj))*)

remove_from_obj : *Oop* × *Object* → *Object*
remove_from_obj(p, obj) $\triangleq$ μ(*obj, body* ↦ *remove(p, body(obj))*)

all_refs : *Object* → *Oop*-set
all_refs(obj) $\triangleq$ *set(body(obj))*

init_object = *mk-Object(init-Bag,* false)

Given these definitions, the *create* and *add_ref* specifications for the previous state, *State*, can be used unchanged. The *remove_ref* operation is defined so that it does not attempt to reclaim any garbage:

remove_ref (*from, to*: *Oop*)

ext wr *mem* : *Oop* $\xrightarrow{m}$ *Object*

    rd *roots* : *Oop*-set

pre {*from, to*} ⊆ *reachable_from*(*roots, mem*) ∧ *refers_to*(*to, mem*(*from*))

post *mem* = $\overleftarrow{mem}$ † {*from* ↦ *remove_from_obj*(*to,* $\overleftarrow{mem}$(*from*))}

The *mark* and *sweep* operations are combined into a single *GC* operation by quoting their individual post-conditions and using an intermediate state:

GC

ext wr *mem* : *Oop* $\xrightarrow{m}$ *Object*

    rd *roots* : *Oop*-set

pre ∀*p* ∈ dom *mem* · ¬ *marked*(*mem*(*p*))

post ∃*mem'* ∈ (*Oop* $\xrightarrow{m}$ *Object*) ·

             post-mark($\overleftarrow{mem}$, *roots, mem'*) ∧ *post-sweep*(*mem', roots, mem*)

As is usual in mark-sweep garbage collectors, we have stated that the mark phase must start with all objects unmarked, and the sweep phase must unmark all of the nongarbage objects.

mark

ext wr *mem* : *Oop* $\xrightarrow{m}$ *Object*

    rd *roots* : *Oop*-set

pre ∀*p* ∈ dom *mem* · ¬ *marked*(*mem*(*p*))

post *mem* = $\overleftarrow{mem}$ † {*p* ↦ μ($\overleftarrow{mem}$(*p*), *marked* ↦ true)

                          | *p* ∈ *reachable_from*(*roots,* $\overleftarrow{mem}$)}

sweep

ext wr *mem* : *Oop* $\xrightarrow{m}$ *Object*

    rd *roots* : *Oop*-set

pre ∀*p* ∈ dom *mem* · *p* ∈ *reachable_from*(*roots, mem*) ⇒ *marked*(*mem*(*p*))

post let *remaining* = {*p* ∈ dom $\overleftarrow{mem}$ | *marked*($\overleftarrow{mem}$(*p*))} in

     mem = {*p* ↦ μ($\overleftarrow{mem}$(*p*), *marked* ↦ false) | *p* ∈ *remaining*}

8.4   Reference counters

The mark-sweep algorithm was the first garbage collection technique used. It reclaims all garbage, but suffers from the problem that when invoked it takes time proportional to the number of objects in the system. (More accurately, the first phase takes time proportional to the number of nongarbage objects, while the second takes time proportional to the total number of objects.) When used in an interactive system, this can cause a disconcerting pause in activity.

The next collection scheme was introduced shortly after the mark-sweep scheme [Col60, Knu79]. It has the advantage that it reclaims some garbage as soon as it is created, but cannot reclaim all garbage (no known algorithm can do both efficiently). The technique is simple: with each object is kept a count of the number of references to it in the memory. As a reference is copied, the count is incremented; when a reference is destroyed (by being overwritten or reclaimed), the count is decremented. Should the count fall to zero then no other references to the object exist, and it can be immediately reclaimed.

A self-referential structure, that is a collection of objects with *Oops* $p_1, \ldots, p_n$ ($n > 0$) such that $refers\_to(p_{i+1}, mem(p_i))$ ($1 \le i < n$) and $refers\_to(p_1, mem(p_n))$, will always have positive reference counts, and so can never be reclaimed by the reference counting technique.

To describe a reference counting system, we extend the definition of *Object* to include a nonzero count:

$$Object :: \; body \; : \; Bag(Oop)$$
$$RC \quad : \; \mathbb{N}_1$$

The following functions increment and decrement respectively the reference count of an object:

$$inc\_rc : Object \to Object$$
$$inc\_rc(obj) \quad \triangleq \quad \mu(obj, RC \mapsto RC(obj) + 1)$$

$$dec\_rc : Object \to Object$$
$$dec\_rc(obj) \quad \triangleq \quad \mu(obj, RC \mapsto RC(obj) - 1)$$
$$\text{pre } RC(obj) > 1$$

When created, an object has a reference count of one:

$$init\_object = mk\text{-}Object(\{ \}, 1)$$

The definition of a retrieve function from a reference-counted *State$_{RC}$* to the earlier *State* is straightforward and left as an exercise for the reader. The invariant is somewhat less obvious. In addition to stating that there are no 'dangling' references, we must also state that the reference counts are accurate:

$$inv\text{-}State_{RC}(mk\text{-}State_{RC}(mem, roots)) \quad \triangleq$$
$$roots \subseteq \text{dom } mem$$
$$\wedge \, no\_dangling\_refs(mem)$$
$$\wedge \, ref\_counts\_accurate(roots, mem)$$

For each object this is determined by summing the number of occurrences of an *Oop* in all the object bodies in the memory and checking that the sum is equal to the object's reference count. Note that an extra reference is added for root objects.

$ref\_counts\_accurate(roots, mem)$ $\triangle$

   $\forall p \in \mathrm{dom}\,mem \cdot$

       $RC(mem(p)) = (\text{if } p \in roots \text{ then } 1 \text{ else } 0)$

            $+ \sum\limits_{q \in \mathrm{dom}\,mem} count(p, body(mem(q)))$

To maintain the reference counts, *add_ref* is modified to perform the appropriate increment operation:

$add\_ref\ (from, to\colon Oop)$

ext wr $mem\ :\ Oop \xrightarrow{m} Object$

   rd $roots\ :\ Oop\text{-set}$

pre $\{from, to\} \subseteq reachable\_from(roots, mem)$

post let $mem' = \overleftarrow{mem} \dagger \{from \mapsto add\_to\_obj(to, \overleftarrow{mem}(from))\}$ in

   $mem = mem' \dagger \{to \mapsto inc\_rc(mem'(to))\}$

Note that the update to the memory must be done in two stages because of the possibility that *from = to*.

Similarly, *remove_ref* performs a decrement operation. However, if the count falls to zero, then the object is freed, and the counts of all the objects referenced from the freed object are decremented. This in turn may cause further freeing and decrementing. The recursive decrement and freeing operation is captured by the *dec* function.

$remove\_ref\ (from, to\colon Oop)$

ext wr $mem\ :\ Oop \xrightarrow{m} Object$

   rd $roots\ :\ Oop\text{-set}$

pre $\{from, to\} \subseteq reachable\_from(roots, mem) \wedge refers\_to(to, mem(from))$

post $mem = dec(add(to, init\text{-}Bag),$

                    $\overleftarrow{mem} \dagger \{from \mapsto remove\_from\_obj(to, \overleftarrow{mem}(from))\})$

$$dec : Bag(Oop) \times (Oop \xrightarrow{m} Object) \to (Oop \xrightarrow{m} Object)$$

$dec(ptrs, mem) \quad \triangleq$

    if $ptrs = init\text{-}Bag$

    then mem

    else let $garbage = \{p \in set(ptrs) \mid RC(mem(p)) = count(p, ptrs)\}$,

            $left = set(ptrs) - garbage$,

            $mem' = garbage \mathbin{\unlhd\!\!\!\!-} mem$,

            $mem'' = mem' \dagger \{p \mapsto \mu(mem(p), RC \mapsto$

                          $RC(mem(p)) - count(p, ptrs)) \mid p \in left\}$ in

      $dec(\sum_{p \in garbage} body(mem(p)), mem'')$

The *dec* function requires some explanation. At each step it is passed a bag, *ptrs*, containing the *Oops* to have their counts decreased – the number of occurrences of an *Oop* in the bag is the amount by which its count is to be decreased – and a memory, *mem*. If the bag is empty, then *mem* is returned unchanged. Otherwise *garbage* is calculated to be the set of *Oops* in *mem* whose reference count will fall to zero and hence become garbage; *left* is the set of nongarbage pointers in *ptrs*. The garbage is excluded from the memory (yielding *mem'*), and the reference counts of the *Oops* in *left* are adjusted. Finally, *dec* is called recursively with the sums of the bags of *Oops* in the *garbage* objects (we use a distributed form of + between bags to perform this summation).

Using a free stack

The use of recursion in the *dec* function highlights the unbounded nature of recursive freeing in the reference count scheme. When a large structure loses its last reference, there may be a significant pause in normal processing due to the traversal of a large tree of objects. To avoid this, at the penalty of slowing down object creation slightly, a *free stack* may be used [Wei63]. When an object's reference count falls to zero, it is added to a set of objects available for reuse (known as the free stack). When an object is created, should the free stack be nonempty and an object of suitable size be found within it, then its storage is used for the new object. Before releasing the storage for reuse, all objects referenced from within it have their counts decremented, and if any fall to zero they are added to the free stack.

To model this, we modify the definition of *Object* so that objects may have reference counts of zero:

$Object ::$ $body : Bag(Oop)$

         $RC \quad : \mathbb{N}$

The free stack is then the set of objects in the memory with reference counts of zero. (A further reification might model the set as an explicit component in the state.)

The *create* operation checks the free stack for any eligible objects (note that we ignore problems of size):

create (*from*: *Oop*) *to*: *Oop*
ext wr *mem* : *Oop* $\xrightarrow{m}$ *Object*
   rd *roots* : *Oop*-set
pre *from* ∈ *reachable_from*(*roots*, *mem*)
post let *mem'* = $\overleftarrow{mem}$†{*from* ↦ *add_to_obj*(*to*, $\overleftarrow{mem}$(*from*)), *to* ↦ *init_object*} in
    if ∃*p* ∈ dom $\overleftarrow{mem}$ · *RC*($\overleftarrow{mem}$(*p*)) = 0
    then *to* ∈ dom $\overleftarrow{mem}$ ∧ *RC*($\overleftarrow{mem}$(*to*)) = 0 ∧
        mem = *mem'* † {*p* ↦ *dec_rc*(*mem'*(*p*)) | *p* ∈ *all_refs*($\overleftarrow{mem}$(*to*))}
    else *to* ∉ dom $\overleftarrow{mem}$ ∧ *mem* = *mem'*

The *remove_ref* operation now simply decrements a single reference count (addition to the free stack being implicit if the count falls to zero):

remove_ref (*from*, *to*: *Oop*)
ext wr *mem* : *Oop* $\xrightarrow{m}$ *Object*
   rd *roots* : *Oop*-set
pre {*from*, *to*} ⊆ *reachable_from*(*roots*, *mem*) ∧ *refers_to*(*to*, *mem*(*from*))
post let *mem'* = $\overleftarrow{mem}$ † {*from* ↦ *remove_from_obj*(*to*, $\overleftarrow{mem}$(*from*))} in
    mem = *mem'* † {*to* ↦ *dec_rc*(*mem'*(*to*))}

8.5   Incremental mark-sweep

The main deficiency of the mark-sweep approach is that each garbage collection takes a long time, leading to unexpected and unwelcome pauses in an interactive system. For many years the only alternative was a reference count scheme, which suffered from the problems that it could not reclaim cyclic structures, and imposed an overhead on every pointer manipulation.

In the late 1970s a number of schemes to perform mark-sweep garbage collection in parallel with mutation [Ste75, DLM+78] were proposed. These had the advantage of removing the annoying pauses, but required a parallel processor to perform the garbage collection. At about the same time Baker [Bak78] proposed a scheme for *incremental* garbage collection that did not require a parallel processor, and yet was *real-time*: it placed a small upper bound on the amount of time required for a garbage collection step.

In essence, Baker's scheme encodes one of three states into the address of an object:

Visited objects have already been traced by the collector, and are known not to be garbage.

Unvisited objects are referenced from visited objects, but have not themselves been traced. They are also known not to be garbage.

Untraced objects have not been encountered by the garbage collector at all, and may or may not be garbage.

Baker's algorithm traces all accessible objects, relocating each as it goes. When the unvisited set becomes empty, then all live objects are in the visited set, and all objects in the untraced set are garbage. Because the scheme is incremental, an object may become garbage and remain in the visited set for some time, but will be reclaimed at the next collection.

A formal description begins by adding to each object a component that describes to which set it belongs:

$Object$ :: $body$: $Bag(Oop)$
$\quad\quad\quad\quad space$: $\{$UNTRACED, UNVISITED, VISITED$\}$

The object manipulation functions are redefined to operate on the *body* part; suitable definitions can be found in Section 8.3.

When an object is created it contains no references to other objects and is known not to be garbage, and therefore is marked as visited.

$init\_object = mk\text{-}Object(\{\ \}, \text{VISITED})$

Other than this change, the *create* operation is as it was in the abstract specification. Similarly, the specification of *remove_ref* from the mark-sweep collector applies to the incremental scheme.

The major change occurs in *add_ref*. If a reference is added from a visited object, f, to an untraced object, t, then t must be recorded as unvisited. Otherwise, at the end of the marking phase the sole reference to t may occur in f, which was scanned before t was added to it.

$add\_ref\ (from, to\text{:}\ Oop)$
ext wr mem : $Oop \xrightarrow{m} Object$
$\quad$ rd $roots$: Oop-set
pre $\{from, to\} \subseteq reachable\_from(roots, mem)$
post $mem = \overleftarrow{mem}\ \dagger\ \{from \mapsto add\_to\_obj(to, \overleftarrow{mem}(from))\}$
$\quad\quad\quad\quad\quad\quad \dagger$ if $space(\overleftarrow{mem}(from)) = \text{VISITED} \wedge space(\overleftarrow{mem}(to)) = \text{UNTRACED}$
$\quad\quad\quad\quad\quad\quad$ then $\{to \mapsto \mu(\overleftarrow{mem}(to), space \mapsto \text{UNVISITED})\}$
$\quad\quad\quad\quad\quad\quad$ else $\{\ \}$

A garbage collection step chooses an unvisited object, p (it does not matter which), marks it as visited, and marks all untraced objects referenced from p as unvisited. If there are no unvisited objects left, then the untraced ones are reclaimed and the visited ones marked as untraced for the the next cycle of marking; root objects are marked as unvisited.

GCstep
ext wr *mem* : *Oop* $\xrightarrow{m}$ *Object*
   rd *roots* : *Oop*-set
post let *unvisited* = $\{p \in$ dom $\overleftarrow{mem} \mid space(\overleftarrow{mem}(p)) =$ UNVISITED$\}$ in
   if *unvisited* $\neq \{\ \}$
   then $\exists u \in$ *unvisited* ·
      let *untraced* = $\{p \in$ *all_refs*$(\overleftarrow{mem}(u)) \mid$
                      $space(\overleftarrow{mem}(p)) =$ UNTRACED$\}$ in
      mem = $\overleftarrow{mem} \dagger \{u \mapsto \mu(\overleftarrow{mem}(u), space \mapsto$ VISITED$)\}$
             $\dagger \{p \mapsto \mu(\overleftarrow{mem}(p), space \mapsto$ UNVISITED$) \mid p \in$ *untraced*$\}$
   else *mem* = $\{p \mapsto \mu(\overleftarrow{mem}(p), space \mapsto$
           if $p \in$ *roots* then UNVISITED else UNTRACED$)$
           $\mid p \in$ dom $\overleftarrow{mem} \wedge space(\overleftarrow{mem}(p)) =$ VISITED$\}$

In Baker's version of this algorithm, when an object changed from untraced to visited or unvisited it was copied into a different area of memory; the transition from unvisited to visited did not require copying. However, every complete garbage collection cycle required all accessible objects to be copied from one *semispace* to another (a beneficial side-effect of this was the compaction of storage, an issue ignored in this chapter).

8.6   Generation scavenging

A development of the Baker algorithm, due to Lieberman and Hewitt [LH81], relied on the observation that most garbage in a typical LISP system was created by the death of short-lived objects. The Lieberman–Hewitt algorithm concentrates garbage collection effort on young objects by dividing all objects into *ages*, with a semispace per age. Younger semispaces are scanned more frequently than older ones. The reader may like to try modifying the earlier definitions to incorporate these changes.

Ungar [Ung84] noticed that a typical Smalltalk-80 system suffered from the age problem even more acutely than did LISP, with the vast majority of objects becoming garbage soon after they were created. Hence, he simplified the Lieberman–Hewitt collector by dividing objects into just two ages: new and old. Old objects are not garbage collected at all, with all the activity concentrated on the new set. In order to ensure that any new objects referenced from old ones are not prematurely reclaimed, a *remembered set* records which old objects may contain references to new ones. The new and remembered sets are part of the amended state:

$$State_{GS} :: \begin{array}{ll} mem & : Oop \xrightarrow{m} Object \\ roots & : Oop\text{-set} \\ new & : Oop\text{-set} \\ remembered & : Oop\text{-set} \end{array}$$

As all garbage collection activity is concentrated on the new set, the invariant insists that no new objects are roots. Otherwise, it is a straightforward extension of the earlier invariant:

$inv\text{-}State_{GS}(mk\text{-}State_{GS}(mem, roots, new, remembered)) \quad \triangle$
$\qquad (roots \cup new \cup remembered) \subseteq \text{dom } mem$
$\qquad \wedge\ no\_dangling\_refs(mem)$
$\qquad \wedge\ is\text{-}disjoint(roots, new)$
$\qquad \wedge\ is\text{-}disjoint(new, remembered)$

The mutator operations must record the *Oops* of any old objects that may contain references to new ones. This involves a test in the *create* and *add_ref* operations, but the *remove_ref* operation does not perform any checks, as this would be expensive in an implementation. Instead, the remembered set that is part of the state is a superset of the true remembered set, which is recomputed when a garbage collection is performed:

create (*from*: *Oop*) *to*: *Oop* .
ext wr *mem*   : $Oop \xrightarrow{m} Object$
    rd *roots*   : *Oop*-set
    wr *new*   : *Oop*-set
    wr *remembered* : *Oop*-set
pre *from* $\in$ *reachable_from*(*roots, mem*)
post *to* $\notin$ dom $\overleftarrow{mem}$
$\qquad \wedge\ mem = \overleftarrow{mem} \dagger \{from \mapsto add\_to\_obj(to, \overleftarrow{mem}(from)), to \mapsto init\_object\}$
$\qquad \wedge\ new = \overleftarrow{new} \cup \{to\}$
$\qquad \wedge\ \text{if } from \in \overleftarrow{new}$

    then *remembered* = $\overleftarrow{remembered}$

    else *remembered* = $\overleftarrow{remembered} \cup \{from\}$

add_ref (*from, to*: *Oop*)
ext wr *mem*   : $Oop \xrightarrow{m} Object$
    rd *roots*   : *Oop*-set
    rd *new*   : *Oop*-set
    wr *remembered* : *Oop*-set
pre $\{from, to\} \subseteq$ *reachable_from*(*roots, mem*)

post $mem = \overleftarrow{mem} \dagger \{from \mapsto add\_to\_obj(to, \overleftarrow{mem}(from))\}$

$\wedge$ if $from \notin \overleftarrow{new} \wedge to \in \overleftarrow{new}$

then $remembered = \overleftarrow{remembered} \cup \{from\}$

else $remembered = \overleftarrow{remembered}$

The garbage collection operation finds all new objects reachable from the roots and the remembered set, and discards the rest. In addition, any objects in the remembered set which no longer refer to a new object are removed from the remembered set.

GC

ext wr *mem*	$: Oop \xrightarrow{m} Object$
rd *roots*	$: Oop\text{-set}$
wr *new*	$: Oop\text{-set}$
wr *remembered*	$: Oop\text{-set}$

post $new = \overleftarrow{new} \cap reachable\_from(roots \cup \overleftarrow{remembered}, \overleftarrow{mem})$

$\wedge remembered = \{p \in \overleftarrow{remembered} \mid \neg \textit{is-disjoint}(new, all\_refs(\overleftarrow{mem}(p)))\}$

$\wedge mem = (\overleftarrow{new} - new) \triangleleft \overleftarrow{mem}$

Because of the presence of the remembered set, the test for reachability does not require a sweep of all accessible objects – the sweep area can be confined to the new objects. This is more apparent if the first line of the post-condition is recast in the following, equivalent form:

$$new = reachable\_from_{GS}(roots \cup \overleftarrow{remembered}, \overleftarrow{new} \triangleleft \overleftarrow{mem})$$

The $reachable\_from_{GS}$ function need only take the part of the memory containing the new objects as its argument:

$reachable\_from_{GS} : Oop\text{-set} \times (Oop \xrightarrow{m} Object) \rightarrow Oop\text{-set}$

$reachable\_from_{GS}(r, m) \quad \triangleq \quad visit_{GS}(\{\,\}, m, r)$

$visit_{GS} : Oop\text{-set} \times (Oop \xrightarrow{m} Object) \times Oop\text{-set} \rightarrow Oop\text{-set}$

$visit_{GS}(visited, mem, unvisited) \quad \triangleq$

    if $unvisited = \{\,\}$

    then $visited$

    else let $visited' = visited \cup unvisited$ in

        $visit_{GS}(visited', mem,$

                $\bigcup\{all\_refs(mem(p)) \cap \text{dom } mem \mid p \in unvisited\} - visited')$

Of course, the scheme just presented suffers from the problem that the new set will increase as new, long-lived objects survive collections. Hence, the aim of generation scavenging, that is to make the collection time imperceptible, will be lost.

To keep the size of the new set down, any new objects which survive a predetermined number of collections are *tenured*: they move out of the new set and are no longer eligible for reclamation.

In this scheme, each new object has a record of its 'age':

$State_{GS}$ :: *mem*   : $Oop \xrightarrow{m} Object$
          roots   : Oop-set
          new   : $Oop \xrightarrow{m} \mathbb{N}$
          remembered : Oop-set

When created, an object has age zero:

create (*from*: Oop) *to*: Oop
ext wr *mem*   : $Oop \xrightarrow{m} Object$
     rd *roots*   : Oop-set
     wr *new*   : $Oop \xrightarrow{m} \mathbb{N}$
     wr *remembered* : Oop-set
pre *from* $\in$ *reachable_from*(*roots*, *mem*)
post *to* $\notin$ **dom** $\overleftarrow{mem}$
      $\wedge$ *mem* = $\overleftarrow{mem}$ † {*from* $\mapsto$ *add_to_obj*(*to*, $\overleftarrow{mem}$(*from*)), *to* $\mapsto$ *init_object*}
      $\wedge$ *new* = $\overleftarrow{new}$ $\cup$ {*to* $\mapsto$ 0}
      $\wedge$ **if** *from* $\in$ **dom** $\overleftarrow{new}$
        then *remembered* = $\overleftarrow{remembered}$
        else *remembered* = $\overleftarrow{remembered}$ $\cup$ {*from*}

The *add_ref* operation requires a small change to account for the modified definition of *new*; this is left as an exercise. The *GC* operation increases the age of new objects that survive collection, and tenures objects with age *threshold*.

GC
ext wr *mem*   : $Oop \xrightarrow{m} Object$
     rd *roots*   : Oop-set
     wr *new*   : $Oop \xrightarrow{m} \mathbb{N}$
     wr *remembered* : Oop-set
post let *new'* = *reachable_from*(*roots* $\cup$ $\overleftarrow{remembered}$, $\overleftarrow{mem}$) $\triangleleft$ $\overleftarrow{new}$ **in**
     new = *tenure*(*new'*)
      $\wedge$ *remembered* = {*p* $\in$ $\overleftarrow{remembered}$ |
                       $\neg$ *is-disjoint*(**dom** *new*, *all_refs*($\overleftarrow{mem}$(*p*)))}
      $\wedge$ *mem* = (**dom** $\overleftarrow{new}$ – **dom** *new'*) $\triangleleft$ $\overleftarrow{mem}$

$$tenure : (Oop \xrightarrow{m} \mathbb{N}) \to (Oop \xrightarrow{m} \mathbb{N})$$

$$tenure(new) \quad \triangle \quad \{p \mapsto new(p) + 1 \mid p \in \mathsf{dom}\ new \land new(p) < threshold\}$$

8.7   Deferred reference counting

The final scheme presented dates from before the Baker incremental collector, and is an attempt to decrease the cost of reference counting. It was noticed that, for LISP systems at least, most of the mutator activity occurs in the region of memory containing the program variables, usually known as the *stack*. Performing a reference count operation whenever a variable changes slows systems down by 20 percent, so the idea of a *deferred* reference counting scheme was invented by Deutsch and Bobrow [DB76].

The basic idea is this: any references to objects from the stack are not included in their reference counts. This enables the mutator to operate on the stack at full speed. Objects not part of the stack are mutated in the usual way, performing reference count operations. When the count of an object falls to zero, the *Oop* of the object is recorded in a zero count table (ZCT). Periodically, to reclaim garbage, the stack is swept and *Oops* in the ZCT that are not referenced from the stack are reclaimed. (The Deutsch–Bobrow scheme also includes other features optimized for LISP usage, but these are not dealt with in this chapter. One arises from the observation that most objects in a LISP system are referenced only once, and hence storing only the reference counts of multiply referenced objects saves space. The reader may like to reify the specification presented to include this feature.)

Object is defined as it was for simple reference counting. The state is extended to record which objects comprise the stack, and which are in the ZCT.[3]

$$
\begin{array}{lll}
State_{DRC} & :: & mem \;\; : \; Oop \xrightarrow{m} Object \\
& & roots \;\; : \; Oop\text{-set} \\
& & stack \;\; : \; Oop\text{-set} \\
& & zct \quad : \; Oop\text{-set}
\end{array}
$$

The invariant for this state adds the property that all *Oops* in the ZCT have reference counts of zero:

---

[3]In a typical LISP system the stack does not consist of objects, but activation records, which cannot be referenced in the usual way by pointers. However, for the purposes of this specification we shall assume that the stack is just a distinguished set of objects (as it is in a Smalltalk-80 system, for example).

$$inv\text{-}State_{DRC}(mk\text{-}State_{DRC}(mem, roots, rc)) \quad \triangle$$
$$(roots \cup stack \cup zct) \subseteq \text{dom } mem$$
$$\wedge\ no\_dangling\_refs(mem)$$
$$\wedge\ ref\_counts\_accurate_{DRC}(roots, mem, stack)$$
$$\wedge\ \forall p \in zct \cdot RC(mem(p)) = 0$$

Note that it is not necessarily the case that all objects with a reference count of zero are in the ZCT: an object that is part of the stack, but not referenced from a nonstack object, will have a count of zero, but will not be in the ZCT. Entry into the ZCT occurs primarily when the last reference to an object from a nonstack object disappears.

The accuracy of reference counts is determined by examining nonstack objects only (cf. the definition of *ref_counts_accurate* in Section 8.4).

$$ref\_counts\_accurate_{DRC}(roots, mem, stack) \quad \triangle$$
$$\forall p \in \text{dom } mem \cdot$$
$$RC(mem(p)) = (\text{if } p \in roots \text{ then } 1 \text{ else } 0)$$
$$+ \sum_{q \in ((\text{dom } mem) - stack)} count(p, body(mem(q)))$$

The *create* operation distinguishes between references from stack and nonstack objects, and installs the newly allocated *Oop* in the ZCT if appropriate:

create (*from*: *Oop*) *to*: *Oop*
ext wr *mem* : $Oop \xrightarrow{m} Object$
   rd *roots* : *Oop*-set
   rd *stack* : *Oop*-set
  wr *zct*   : *Oop*-set
pre *from* $\in$ *reachable_from*(*roots*, *mem*)
post let *rc* = if *from* $\in$ *stack* then 0 else 1 in
     $mem = \overleftarrow{mem} \dagger \{from \mapsto add\_to\_obj(to, \overleftarrow{mem}(from)), to \mapsto mk\text{-}Object(\{\ \}, rc)\}$
     $\wedge\ to \notin \text{dom } \overleftarrow{mem}$
     $\wedge\ zct = \text{if } from \in stack \text{ then } \overleftarrow{zct} \cup \{to\} \text{ else } \overleftarrow{zct}$

The *create* operation creates a new object not on the stack. In systems where it is possible to create an object on the stack a dual of this operation is required, or possibly operations to move an object to and from the stack. These are left as exercises for the reader.

The mutator operations are now defined. We have split them into two pairs, depending on whether the object being mutated is on the stack or not. We could have as easily made the test in the post-condition, but in practice the different cases can be distinguished statically and the overhead implied by the post-condition test can be avoided. Hence, *add_ref* mutates a nonstack object, *add_ref_s* mutates an object on the stack, and similarly for *remove_ref* and *remove_ref_s*.

The post-conditions of the on-stack operations are the same as the abstract operations defined in Section 8.2. This emphasizes that there is no additional overhead on these operations imposed by deferred reference counting.

add_ref_s (*from, to*: *Oop*)
  ext wr *mem* : *Oop* $\xrightarrow{m}$ *Object*
    rd *roots* : *Oop*-set
    rd *stack* : *Oop*-set
  pre {*from, to*} $\subseteq$ *reachable_from*(*roots, mem*) $\land$ *from* $\in$ *stack*
  post *mem* = $\overleftarrow{mem}$ † {*from* $\mapsto$ *add_to_obj*(*to*, $\overleftarrow{mem}$(*from*))}

remove_ref_s (*from, to*: *Oop*)
  ext wr *mem* : *Oop* $\xrightarrow{m}$ *Object*
    rd *roots* : *Oop*-set
    rd *stack* : *Oop*-set
  pre {*from, to*} $\subseteq$ *reachable_from*(*roots, mem*)
    $\land$ *refers_to*(*to, mem*(*from*)) $\land$ *from* $\in$ *stack*
  post *mem* = $\overleftarrow{mem}$ † {*from* $\mapsto$ *remove_from_obj*(*to*, $\overleftarrow{mem}$(*from*))}

The off-stack operations modify the ZCT appropriately.

add_ref (*from, to*: *Oop*)
  ext wr *mem* : *Oop* $\xrightarrow{m}$ *Object*
    rd *roots* : *Oop*-set
    rd *stack* : *Oop*-set
    wr *zct*   : *Oop*-set
  pre {*from, to*} $\subseteq$ *reachable_from*(*roots, mem*) $\land$ *from* $\notin$ *stack*
  post let *mem′* = $\overleftarrow{mem}$ † {*from* $\mapsto$ *add_to_obj*(*to*, $\overleftarrow{mem}$(*from*))} in
      mem = *mem′* † {*to* $\mapsto$ *inc_rc*(*mem′*(*to*))}
      $\land$ *zct* = $\overleftarrow{zct}$ − {*to*}

remove_ref (*from, to*: *Oop*)
  ext wr *mem* : *Oop* $\xrightarrow{m}$ *Object*
    rd *roots* : *Oop*-set
    rd *stack* : *Oop*-set
    wr *zct*   : *Oop*-set
  pre {*from, to*} $\subseteq$ *reachable_from*(*roots, mem*)
    $\land$ *refers_to*(*mem*(*from*), *to*) $\land$ *from* $\notin$ *stack*

post let $mem' = \overline{mem} \dagger \{from \mapsto remove\_from\_obj(to, \overline{mem}(from))\}$ in
$\quad mem = mem' \dagger \{to \mapsto dec\_rc(mem'(to))\}$
$\quad \wedge zct = $ if $RC(mem(to)) = 0$ then $\overleftarrow{zct} \cup \{to\}$ else $\overleftarrow{zct}$

Finally, we come to the collection operation itself. This is similar to the recursive freeing operation in Section 8.4, but has the added complexity of maintaining the ZCT and searching the stack. The first stage of the operation is to identify garbage by finding all entries in the ZCT that do not occur on the stack. The auxiliary function *on_stack* identifies whether a particular *Oop* occurs on the stack.

GC
ext wr *mem* : $Oop \xrightarrow{m} Object$
$\quad$ rd *roots* : *Oop*-set
$\quad$ wr *stack* : *Oop*-set
$\quad$ wr *zct* : *Oop*-set
post let $zct' = \{p \in \overleftarrow{zct} \mid on\_stack(p, stack, \overline{mem})\}$ in
$\quad$ let $garbage = \overleftarrow{zct} - zct'$ in
$\quad (zct, stack, mem) = free(garbage, zct', \overleftarrow{stack}, \overline{mem})$

$on\_stack : Oop \times Oop\text{-set} \times (Oop \xrightarrow{m} Object) \rightarrow \mathbb{B}$
$on\_stack(p, stack, mem) \quad \triangle \quad \exists q \in stack \cdot p \in all\_refs(mem(q))$
pre $stack \subseteq$ dom *mem*

The *free* operation takes a set of *Oops* representing the garbage objects, computes a bag of *Oops*, *dec*, representing the changes in counts of those objects referenced from the garbage, and alters the reference counts accordingly. Any objects whose counts become zero and are not on the stack are reclaimed in the next stage of the recursion. Meanwhile, garbage objects are removed from the stack and ZCT, and the ZCT is recomputed.

$$free : Oop\text{-set} \times Oop\text{-set} \times Oop\text{-set} \times (Oop \xrightarrow{m} Object) \rightarrow$$
$$Oop\text{-set} \times Oop\text{-set} \times (Oop \xrightarrow{m} Object)$$

$free(freed, zct, stack, mem) \quad \triangleq$
    if $freed = \{\ \}$
    then $(zct, stack, mem)$
    else let $dec = \sum_{p \in freed} body(mem(p))$,
        $stack' = stack - freed$,
        $mem' = (freed \vartriangleleft mem)\ \dagger$
                $\{p \mapsto \mu(mem(p), RC \mapsto$
                      $RC(mem(p)) - count(p, dec))\ |\ p \in set(dec)\}$,
        $freed' = \{p \in set(dec)\ |$
                  $RC(mem'(p)) = 0 \wedge \neg\, on\_stack(p, stack', mem')\}$,
        $zct' = zct - freed'$
             $\cup \{p \in set(dec)\ |$
                $RC(mem'(p)) = 0 \wedge on\_stack(p, stack', mem')\}$ in
    $free(freed', stack', zct', mem')$

8.8 Summary

This chapter has presented a collection of specifications that describe different types of garbage collection schemes. While by no means exhaustive, a wide variety of schemes has been covered. Each specification can serve to help explain the scheme (although it should be emphasized that many implementation issues have been glossed over) and can also serve as the first step in a series of reifications towards an implementation.

The author thanks Cliff Jones and Ifor Williams for many illuminating and thought-provoking discussions on the topic of garbage collection.

8.9 Appendix: bags

For reference, here is a complete specification of the bag operations used in this chapter.

$$Bag(X) = X \xrightarrow{m} \mathbb{N}_1$$

$$init\text{-}Bag = \{\ \}$$

$count : X \times Bag(X) \rightarrow \mathbb{N}$
$count(el, b) \quad \triangleq \quad$ if $el \in \text{dom}\, b$ then $b(el)$ else 0

$add : X \times Bag(X) \rightarrow Bag(X)$
$add(el, b) \quad \triangle \quad b \dagger \{el \mapsto count(el, b) + 1\}$

$remove : X \times Bag(X) \rightarrow Bag(X)$
$remove(el, b) \quad \triangle \quad$ if $count(el, b) = 1$
$\qquad\qquad\qquad$ then $\{el\} \lhd b$
$\qquad\qquad\qquad$ else $b \dagger \{el \mapsto count(el, b) - 1\}$
pre $count(el, b) \geq 1$

$set : Bag(X) \rightarrow X\text{-set}$
$set(b) \quad \triangle \quad$ dom b

$\_ + \_: Bag(X) \times Bag(X) \rightarrow Bag(X)$
$a + b \triangleq \{p \mapsto count(p, a) + count(p, b) \mid p \in$ dom $a \cup$ dom $b\}$

9

A Small Language Definition

Cliff B. Jones

The main stimulus for the inception of VDM was the description of programming languages. It is therefore appropriate that this book of case studies should demonstrate the use of the BSI syntax for language description. A limited amount of notation has to be introduced which has not been used in other case studies but the main emphasis is on precisely the sort of modelling which is familiar in other applications of VDM. This and the next chapter present language descriptions. Here the task is a small procedural language which could be thought of as a 'micro Pascal'. This is the conventional area of denotational semantic definitions whereas the next chapter (and to a certain extent Chapter 11) are more novel applications of denotational semantics.

9.1   Introduction

The preface of [BJMN87] explains the role played by formal descriptions of programming languages in the development of VDM. Although not covered in [Jon90], the subjects of programming language semantics, and implementations based thereon, remain of crucial importance because of the danger that errors could be introduced into correct programs by erroneous compilers. Furthermore, formal descriptions present the opportunity to define meaningful and useful reference points for programming language standards. Not only can the formality provide a precise statement, but a suitably written formal specification can also provide a useful starting point for systematic designs of implementations.

   This chapter presents a description of a small, hypothetical, procedural programming language. The language is kept simple so that the main points can be illustrated in a reasonable space. The reader is referred to [BJ82] for more realistic definitions including ALGOL 60 and Pascal or to the references in the Teacher's Notes associated with [Jon90] for, *inter alia*, work on PL/I and Ada.

   There are three more-or-less distinct approaches to fixing the semantics of a programming language. The oldest approach is to write an abstract interpreter which gives an *operational semantics*. An *axiomatic semantics* is a series of proof rules which permit all possible facts to be deduced about valid observations on a program's behavior. Except for the fact that there has been no discussion of completeness, the inference rules presented in [Jon90] are in this mould. For studying language concepts and relating implementations to specifications, it is now widely accepted that a *denotational semantics* is most useful. (A fuller discussion of these alternatives can be found in most books on semantics – see, for example, Lucas's chapter in [BJ82].)

   It is obviously not appropriate to explain the method of *denotational semantics* in any depth here. The basic idea is very simple: given a language L whose semantics is to be defined, one has to provide a way of mapping any construct of L into a language whose semantics are already understood and which, hopefully, is easy to manipulate algebraically. For standard procedural languages, the denotations are likely to be functions – in the simplest case – functions from states to states.

   A full language description would contain:

- A concrete syntax.

- An abstract syntax.

- Context conditions (restricting the class of abstract texts).

- A set of understood semantic objects.

- A mapping from objects of the abstract syntax (which also satisfy the context conditions) to semantic objects.

The issue of concrete syntax descriptions and the design of reasonable concrete syntax is clearly very important but is not considered further here since it is a separate concern.

There is a restriction on the semantic mapping known as the *denotational rule*. This requires that the mapping respects the structure of the abstract syntax: denotations of composite objects are built (only) from the denotations of their components, i.e. the mapping is homomorphic. A fuller description of the denotational method the reader is referred to [Sch86, Sto77] or, for VDM, to [BJ82].

There are several different orders in which a full language description can be presented: here some repetition is employed which should aid the reader – but would be avoided in a reference document.

9.2 Abstract syntax

This section introduces a core language to which some extensions are considered in Section 9.6. This abstract syntax describes a class of objects which are abstractions of the concrete texts of programs. The language chosen for this exercise has a simple block structure and includes standard 'structured programming' control constructs.

The abstract syntax is presented top (from *Program*) down (to variable reference). The root node of the abstract syntax is:

Program :: *Stmt*

(A list of abbreviations is given at the end of this chapter.) The fact that the content of a program is (only) a statement is deceptive; as is shown below, one of the possibilities for a *Stmt* is that it is a block.

There are six forms of statement in the language:

$Stmt = Block \cup If \cup While \cup Call \cup Assign \cup \text{NULL}$

$$
\begin{aligned}
Block \ :: \ &typem \ : \ Id \xrightarrow{m} Sctype \\
&procm \ : \ Id \xrightarrow{m} Proc \\
&body \ \ \ : \ Stmt^*
\end{aligned}
$$

$$
\begin{aligned}
If \ :: \ &test \ : \ Expr \\
&th \ \ \ : \ Stmt \\
&el \ \ \ : \ Stmt
\end{aligned}
$$

$$
\begin{aligned}
While \ :: \ &test \ \ \ : \ Expr \\
&body \ : \ Stmt
\end{aligned}
$$

Call :: *pr* : *Id*
            al : *Varref**

Assign :: *lhs* : *Varref*
               rhs : *Expr*

The NULL statements have no contents; in fact they are only there to cover situations like empty else-clauses in conditionals.

Procedures can be defined within blocks:

Proc :: *fpl*   : *Id**
             typem : $Id \xrightarrow{m} Sctype$
             body   : *Stmt*

Sctype = {INT, BOOL}

Notice that parameters can only be scalars; this language does not allow procedures to be passed as parameters.

Most of the interesting points about expressions can be made with only three simple alternative forms:

Expr = *Infix* ∪ *Rhsref* ∪ *Const*

Infix :: *l*   : *Expr*
             op : *Operator*
             r   : *Expr*

Operator = {PLUS, OR, LESSTHAN}

Rhsref :: *Varref*

Const = *Scval*

Varref :: *Id*

The set of scalar values (*Scval*) is defined in Section 9.4.

This syntax has not, of course, settled semantic questions like the parameter passing mechanism: these topics are discussed in Section 9.5.

9.3   Context conditions

The next part of a language definition should be the description of those conditions which define the subset of *Program* to which semantics must be given. Experience with denotational semantics descriptions has led to the separation of the context conditions (sometimes called 'static semantics') from the main semantic mapping. The relevant function is actually defined in Section 9.5 but this section lays the foundation.

The context conditions are very like data type invariants on objects defined by *Program*. An abstract *Program* may or may not be 'well-formed' with respect to the correct use of declared variables, etc. (The reason that these conditions can not be captured in the abstract syntax are that it is essentially a context-free syntax.) The context conditions themselves are defined by a recursive function, called *WF*, and a typing function called *TP*. It is a convention that the names of these functions – in contrast to, say, [Jon90] – are written with upper case letters. (In many definitions, the meaning functions, etc. are only given one, overloaded, name.) These functions create and use a static environment (*Senv*) which contains information derived from both the variable (*Sctype*) and procedure declarations (*Procattr*). Objects of this static environment are maps:

$$Senv = Id \xrightarrow{m} Attr$$

$$Attr = Sctype \cup Procattr$$

A *Procattr* contains a list of the types of the parameters:

$$Procattr :: Sctype^*$$

$$Sctype = \text{see abstract syntax}$$

The type of the context conditions is, in nearly all cases:

$$WF: Text \rightarrow Senv \rightarrow \mathbb{B}$$

9.4   Semantic objects

Fixing the semantic objects for this simple language is relatively straightforward. The core idea for most procedural languages is to find an appropriate abstraction of their store-like objects and then to reflect the imperative nature of the language by employing 'transformations' (i.e. functions from stores to stores) as the denotations. In a language with no block structure or procedures, it would probably be possible to abstract store as a mapping from the identifiers for variable names to their values. In the language presented in Section 9.2 there are two features which make the choice more interesting. On the one hand, the block structure makes it possible for one name to denote different variables in different scopes; on the other hand, the same variable can be denoted by different identifiers (in the same scope) because the parameter passing is by variable. The standard way of tackling this problem is to introduce – as an abstraction of machine locations – a surrogate for each variable. These surrogates are normally known as *locations* and here the set is called *Scloc* (since nonscalar locations are needed in the extensions discussed in Section 9.6). The simple idea of mapping names to values can then be broken into two maps: one from names to locations and the other from locations to values.

This is the most basic modelling decision in this definition. It remains to decide where the two maps are to be held. Because it can be changed by any assignment statement, it is natural to place the mapping from locations to values in the store. But the association from names to locations only changes between scopes and this can be clearly reflected by placing it in an environment parameter. Most meaning functions then become functions from environments to functions from stores to stores. This sort of higher-order function is very common in denotational semantic definitions.

Thus, the denotations of statements etc. are determined with respect to an environment (*Env*) which contains the denotations of all of the identifiers occurring in the text. These denotations are either scalar locations (*Scloc*) or procedure denotations (*Procden*). The parameter passing method in this section is *by variable* so the domain of the functional procedure denotations is a sequence of scalar locations; the range is a store-to-store transformation (*Tr*) which is defined below.

$$Env = Id \xrightarrow{\;m\;} (Scloc \cup Procden)$$

$$Scloc = \text{arbitrary infinite set}$$

$$Procden = Scloc^* \to Tr$$

As for most imperative languages, the denotations of the statement constructs are transformations (*Tr*) which are functions over *Stores*.

$$Tr = Store \to Store$$

Notice that when the signature of *Procden* is expanded, it is seen to be a function which yields functions as results.

The main semantic functions have the type:

$$M: Text \to Env \to Tr$$

A *Store* maps scalar locations to their values:

$$Store = Scloc \xrightarrow{\;m\;} Scval$$

$Scval = \mathbb{B} \cup \mathbb{Z}$

A number of useful auxiliary functions can be defined for a *Store*. (The parameter σ is used consistently for *Store*.) Access to, and change of, values are defined by:

$contents : Scloc \rightarrow Store \rightarrow Scval$
$contents(l) \quad \triangle \quad \lambda\sigma \cdot \sigma(l)$

Here, the functional result of *contents* is defined by the use of a lambda expression.

$assign : Scloc \times Scval \rightarrow Tr$
$assign(l, v) \quad \triangle \quad \lambda\sigma \cdot \sigma \dagger \{l \mapsto v\}$

Remember that *Tr* is a functional type which is why a lambda definition is required.

New locations are allocated and initialized by a function called *newlocs*. This function takes a mapping from names to types as an argument and yields a function which is like a transformation except that the function yields an additional result which is an association from the required identifiers to their allocated locations. The type information is required since the locations are also initialized. It is desirable not to tie *newlocs* too tightly.[1] Here, it is defined implicitly so as to under-determine which locations are actually allocated. Rather than discuss post-conditions of higher-order functions, the required properties are presented as an implication.

$newlocs: (Id \xrightarrow{m} Sctype) \rightarrow Store \rightarrow Store \times (Id \xrightarrow{m} Scloc)$
$newlocs(m)(\sigma) = (\sigma', \rho') \implies$
$\qquad \mathrm{dom}\, \rho' = \mathrm{dom}\, m \wedge \textit{is-disj}(\mathrm{rng}\, \rho', \mathrm{dom}\, \sigma) \wedge \textit{is-oneone}(\rho') \wedge$
$\qquad \sigma' = \sigma \cup \{\rho'(id) \mapsto 0 \mid m(id) = \textsc{Int}\} \cup \{\rho'(id) \mapsto \mathsf{false} \mid m(id) = \textsc{Bool}\}$

Locations are removed from store by:

$epilogue : Scloc\text{-set} \rightarrow Tr$
$epilogue(ls) \quad \triangle \quad \lambda\sigma \cdot ls \blacktriangleleft \sigma$

9.5 Mapping

The mapping from the abstract syntax to the semantic objects is the main part of the definition. Experience with writing larger definitions has resulted in the move to an order in which – rather than follow a strict separation of the parts of the definition – the abstract syntax, context conditions, and semantic mapping are presented together. This makes it possible to collect all of the relevant information about one language construct

---

[1]The reason for leaving the freedom is so that it becomes easier to prove correct various compiling strategies. It is, however, a moot point whether *newlocs* is a function at all: this point is not pursued here – see [HJ89] for further details.

together in one place. This plan is followed here even though it results in repeating the abstract syntax given in Section 9.2.

With such a recursive abstract syntax it is difficult to present the language in an order such that the whole definition can be grasped in one pass. In a reference document, a 'top-down' order is likely to yield a more convenient presentation. Here a 'bottom-up' order is taken: the reader will find the abstract syntax of Section 9.2 useful to establish the context of the low-level details until the higher-level semantic functions are encountered.

Variable references

The statement which sets the tone of procedural languages is the assignment (cf. *Assign* in Section 9.2). In a simple case like $x := y$, the variable on the left-hand side of the assignment must be evaluated to a location and that on the right to a value (ALGOL 68 'dereferencing'). In this core language, which only has scalar variables, a variable reference is just an identifier:

> *Varref* :: *Id*

The context condition requires that the identifier is known (the reference is in an appropriate scope) and that it refers to a scalar variable (not a procedure). This is done by checking the information stored in the static environment (in all of the context conditions the parameter ρ is used for *Senv*):

> $WFVarref : Varref \rightarrow Senv \rightarrow \mathbb{B}$
> $WFVarref \, [\![mk\text{-}Varref(id)]\!] \, \rho \quad \triangle \quad id \in \text{dom} \, \rho \wedge \rho(id) \in Sctype$

The use of so-called 'Strachey brackets' ($[\![\cdots]\!]$) follows a convention in semantic definitions: they set off arguments of the abstract syntax. It is also common practice to omit parentheses around short arguments: thus $WFVarref \, [\![mk\text{-}Varref(id)]\!] \, \rho$ is the way that the more familiar expression $WFVarref(mk\text{-}Varref(id))(\rho)$ is written in a denotational semantic text.

In other context conditions, it will be necessary to determine the types of variable references. This information is also obtained from the static environment:

> $TPVarref : Varref \rightarrow Senv \rightarrow Sctype$
> $TPVarref \, [\![mk\text{-}Varref(id)]\!] \, \rho \quad \triangle \quad \rho(id)$

As indicated above, the denotation of a variable reference is the scalar location which is stored in the environment (the meaning functions use *Env* – here, ρ is used for parameters of type *Env*):

> $MVarref : Varref \rightarrow Env \rightarrow Scloc$
> $MVarref \, [\![mk\text{-}Varref(id)]\!] \, \rho \quad \triangle \quad \rho(id)$

Remember that this yields the location (not the value) corresponding to an identifier.

Expressions

Checking the abstract syntax for *Assign* shows that a *Varref*, which is to occur in an expression, is embedded in an object which is a *Rhsref* (in the example above, $x := y$, the actual abstract object would be *mk-Assign(mk-Varref(x), mk-Rhsref(mk-Varref(y)))*). So, the abstract syntax of references to variables is given by:

Rhsref :: *Varref*

The context condition simply uses that for the embedded variable reference:

WFRhsref : *Rhsref* → *Senv* → $\mathbb{B}$
WFRhsref $[\![mk\text{-}Rhsref(vr)]\!]\rho$ $\triangleq$ *WFVarref* $[\![vr]\!]\rho$

The same indirection is present in the case of the *TP* function:

TPRhsref : *Rhsref* → *Senv* → *Sctype*
TPRhsref $[\![mk\text{-}Rhsref(vr)]\!]\rho$ $\triangleq$ *TPRhsref* $[\![vr]\!]\rho$

The meaning function obtains the contents of the location as computed by *MVarref*:

MRhsref : *Rhsref* → *Env* → *Store* → *Scval*
MRhsref $[\![mk\text{-}Rhsref(vr)]\!]\rho$ $\triangleq$ *contents(MVarref* $[\![vr]\!]\rho$)

This is what distinguishes a right-hand reference – whose denotation is a value – from a left-hand reference – whose denotation is a location.

An even simpler form of expression is a constant:

Const = *Scval*

Any $c \in$ *Const* is well-formed:

WFConst : *Const* → *Senv* → $\mathbb{B}$
WFConst $[\![c]\!]\rho$ $\triangleq$ true

Its type is given by:

TPConst : *Const* → *Senv* → *Sctype*
TPConst $[\![c]\!]\rho$ $\triangleq$ if $c \in \mathbb{B}$ then BOOL else INT

Its denotation (in any environment) is the value of the constant:

MConst : *Const* → *Env* → *Store* → *Scval*
MConst $[\![c]\!]\rho$ $\triangleq$ $\lambda\sigma \cdot c$

Notice that *MConst* has to be made to depend – in a trivial way – on the state, so that its signature matches that of *MExpr*.

The relevant points about infix expressions can be illustrated with:

Infix :: *l* : *Expr*
         op : *Operator*
         r : *Expr*

Operator = {PLUS, OR, LESSTHAN}

The well-formedness of infix expressions checks that the operator and operand types match:

WFInfix : *Infix* → *Senv* → $\mathbb{B}$
WFInfix [[*mk-Infix(l, op, r)*]] ρ $\triangleq$
    WFExpr [[*l*]] ρ ∧ *WFExpr* [[*r*]] ρ ∧
    (*TPExpr* [[*l*]] ρ = *TPExpr* [[*r*]] ρ = INT ∧ *op* ∈ {PLUS, LESSTHAN} ∨
    TPExpr [[*l*]] ρ = *TPExpr* [[*r*]] ρ = BOOL ∧ *op* = OR)

The type of an infix expression is governed by the operator:

TPInfix : *Infix* → *Senv* → *Sctype*
TPInfix [[*mk-Infix(l, op, r)*]] ρ $\triangleq$
    if *op* ∈ {LESSTHAN, OR} then BOOL else INT

In order to determine the meaning of an infix expression, it is assumed that the meaning of the operators is given by:

MOperator: *Operator* → (*Scval* × *Scval*) → *Scval*

Then:

MInfix : *Infix* → *Env* → *Store* → *Scval*
MInfix [[*mk-Infix(l, op, r)*]] ρ $\triangleq$
    $\lambda\sigma$ · *MOperator* [[*op*]] (*MExpr* [[*l*]] $\rho\sigma$, *MExpr* [[*r*]] $\rho\sigma$)

Notice that both operands (*l, r*) can be evaluated in the same store (σ) because there is no feature in this language which can cause side-effects in expression evaluation.

This has covered the only three forms of expression in the language:

Expr = *Infix* ∪ *Rhsref* ∪ *Const*

The overall context condition can be defined by cases:

$WFExpr : Expr \rightarrow Senv \rightarrow \mathbb{B}$

$WFExpr \llbracket e \rrbracket \rho \quad \triangle \quad$ cases e of

$\qquad\qquad\qquad mk\text{-}Infix(l, op, r) \rightarrow WFInfix \llbracket e \rrbracket \rho,$

$\qquad\qquad\qquad mk\text{-}Rhsref(vr) \quad \rightarrow WFRhsref \llbracket e \rrbracket \rho,$

$\qquad\qquad\qquad otherwise \qquad\quad\ \rightarrow WFConst \llbracket e \rrbracket \rho$

$\qquad\qquad$ end

The signatures of the other relevant functions are:

$TPExpr\text{:} Expr \rightarrow Senv \rightarrow Sctype$

$MExpr\text{:} Expr \rightarrow Env \rightarrow Store \rightarrow Scval$

Their definitions follow exactly the same case statement form and are not written out here.

Statements

The preceding subsection has prepared everything needed for the assignment statement:

$Assign \ :: \ lhs \ : \ Varref$

$\qquad\qquad\ rhs \ : \ Expr$

An assignment statement which consists of a *lhs* and a *rhs* is well-formed in a static environment ρ if, and only if: *lhs* is a well-formed *Varref* in ρ; *rhs* is a well-formed *Expr* in ρ; and the scalar types found by *TP* (also in ρ) for *lhs* and *rhs* are the same:

$WFAssign : Assign \rightarrow Senv \rightarrow \mathbb{B}$

$WFAssign \llbracket mk\text{-}Assign(lhs, rhs) \rrbracket \rho \quad \triangle$

$\qquad WFVarref \llbracket lhs \rrbracket \rho \wedge WFExpr \llbracket rhs \rrbracket \rho \wedge$

$\qquad TPVarref \llbracket lhs \rrbracket \rho \in Sctype \wedge TPVarref \llbracket lhs \rrbracket \rho = TPExpr \llbracket rhs \rrbracket \rho$

The denotation of an assignment statement which consists of a *lhs* and a *rhs* in an environment ρ is a transformation ($assign(loc, val) \in Tr$) which is determined by the denotations of its constituents in ρ. Notice that the value of an expression does rely on the *Store* while the location denoted by a variable reference does not:

$MAssign : Assign \rightarrow Env \rightarrow Tr$

$MAssign \llbracket mk\text{-}Assign(lhs, rhs) \rrbracket \rho \quad \triangle$

$\qquad \lambda \sigma \cdot assign(MVarref \llbracket lhs \rrbracket \rho, MExpr \llbracket rhs \rrbracket \rho \sigma)(\sigma)$

The simplest form of statement in the language is the null statement (there is exactly one such statement):

NULL

Such an object is always (in any environment) well-formed:

$WFNull : \text{NULL} \rightarrow Senv \rightarrow \mathbb{B}$
$WFNull\,[\![\text{NULL}]\!]\,\rho \;\;\triangleq\;\; \text{true}$

The meaning of a null statement is the identity transformation:

$MNull : \text{NULL} \rightarrow Env \rightarrow Tr$
$MNull\,[\![\text{NULL}]\!]\,\rho \;\;\triangleq\;\; I_{Store}$

Conditional statements contain other statements within them:

$If ::\ test\ :\ Expr$
$\qquad th\ \ :\ Stmt$
$\qquad el\ \ :\ Stmt$

The context condition validates the type of the test and checks the well-formedness of the constituent statements:

$WFIf : If \rightarrow Senv \rightarrow \mathbb{B}$
$WFIf\,[\![mk\text{-}If(test, th, el)]\!]\,\rho \;\;\triangleq\;\;$
$\qquad WFExpr\,[\![test]\!]\,\rho \wedge TPExpr\,[\![test]\!]\,\rho = \text{BOOL} \wedge WFStmt\,[\![th]\!]\,\rho \wedge WFStmt\,[\![el]\!]\,\rho$

The obvious way to show that the evaluation of the test precedes the execution of one or other statement is to write:

$MIf : If \rightarrow Env \rightarrow Tr$
$MIf\,[\![mk\text{-}If(test, th, el)]\!]\,\rho \;\;\triangleq\;\;$
$\qquad \lambda\sigma\cdot\text{let } b = MExpr\,[\![test]\!]\,\rho\sigma \text{ in}$
$\qquad\qquad \text{if } b \text{ then } MStmt\,[\![th]\!]\,\rho\sigma \text{ else } MStmt\,[\![el]\!]\,\rho\sigma$

But this sort of ordering and passing of states occurs so often in denotational semantics that a special def combinator has been provided in VDM which makes it possible to present this as:

$MIf\,[\![mk\text{-}If(test, th, el)]\!]\,\rho \;\;\triangleq\;\;$
$\qquad \text{def } b: MExpr\,[\![test]\!]\,\rho;$
$\qquad \text{if } b \text{ then } MStmt\,[\![th]\!]\,\rho \text{ else } MStmt\,[\![el]\!]\,\rho$

The use of such 'combinators' can significantly increase the readability of large definitions; it can also make it easier to see that the 'denotational rule' is being followed.

The abstract syntax for the repetitive construct is:

$While ::\ test\ \ :\ Expr$
$\qquad\quad body\ :\ Stmt$

Its well-formedness condition checks that the test expression has the appropriate type and that the body is well-formed:

$WFWhile : While \rightarrow Senv \rightarrow \mathbb{B}$
$WFWhile \, [\![mk\text{-}While(test, body)]\!] \, \rho \quad \triangleq$
$\qquad WFExpr \, [\![test]\!] \, \rho \wedge TPExpr \, [\![test]\!] \, \rho = \text{Bool} \wedge WFStmt \, [\![body]\!] \, \rho$

The meaning function again uses the def combinator but also needs to compute the least-fixed point of the recursive definition of *wh*.

$MWhile : While \rightarrow Env \rightarrow Tr$
$MWhile \, [\![mk\text{-}While(test, body)]\!] \, \rho \quad \triangleq$
$\qquad \text{let } wh = (\text{def } b: MExpr \, [\![test]\!] \, \rho; \text{if } b \text{ then } MStmt \, [\![body]\!] \, \rho; wh \text{ else } I_{Store})$
$\qquad \text{in } wh$

The abstract syntax of call statements is:

$Call \, :: \, pr \, : \, Id$
$\qquad\quad al \, : \, Varref^*$

The corresponding context conditions check that *pr* actually refers to a procedure and that the types of *al* match the declared parameter types (which have been stored in *Procden*):

$WFCall : Call \rightarrow Senv \rightarrow \mathbb{B}$
$WFCall \, [\![mk\text{-}Call(pr, al)]\!] \, \rho \quad \triangleq$
$\qquad pr \in \text{dom } \rho \wedge \rho(pr) \in Procattr \wedge$
$\qquad \text{let } mk\text{-}Procattr(tl) = \rho(pr) \text{ in}$
$\qquad \text{len } tl = \text{len } al \wedge \forall i \in \text{inds } tl \cdot TPVarref \, [\![al(i)]\!] \, \rho = tl(i)$

The meaning function should be considered in relation to the type of *Procden* (cf. Section 9.4) which shows that applying a *Procden* to a list of locations yields a transformation; the fact that the *al* of a *Call* is a list of variable references determines that they are evaluated to locations:

$MCall : Call \rightarrow Env \rightarrow Tr$
$MCall \, [\![mk\text{-}Call(pr, al)]\!] \, \rho \quad \triangleq$
$\qquad \text{let } ll = [MVarref \, [\![al(i)]\!] \, \rho \mid i \in \text{elems } al] \text{ in}$
$\qquad \text{let } prden = \rho(pr) \text{ in}$
$\qquad prden(ll)$

Procedures

Before considering blocks, procedure declarations must be discussed. Their abstract syntax is:

> *Proc* :: *fpl*   : *Id**
>   *typem* : *Id* $\xrightarrow{m}$ *Sctype*
>   *body*   : *Stmt*

The context condition requires that no identifier is repeated in *fpl* and that each such parameter name is given a type in *typem*; the *body* must be well-formed in a static environment which is modified to include the parameters:

> *WFProc* : *Proc* → *Senv* → $\mathbb{B}$
> *WFProc* $[\![mk\text{-}Proc(fpl, tm, s)]\!]\, \rho \quad \triangle$
>   *is-uniques*(*fpl*) ∧ elems *fpl* = dom *tm* ∧ *WFStmt* $[\![s]\!]\,(\rho \dagger tm)$

(Auxiliary functions like *is-uniques* are defined at the end of this chapter.) The context conditions for *Block* need a procedure attribute for each procedure; this is computed by:

> *TPProc* : *Proc* → *Procattr*
> *TPProc* $[\![mk\text{-}Proc(fpl, tm, s)]\!] \quad \triangle \quad mk\text{-}Procattr(tm \circ fpl)$

The meaning of a procedure declaration is a function (cf. *Procden* in Section 9.4) from a sequence of scalar locations to a transformation:

> *MProc* : *Proc* → *Env* → *Procden*
> *MProc* $[\![mk\text{-}Proc(fpl, tm, s)]\!]\, \rho \quad \triangle$
> $\lambda ll \cdot MStmt$ $[\![s]\!]\,(\rho \dagger \{fpl(i) \mapsto ll(i) \mid i \in$ inds $fpl\})$

It is essential to the normal meaning of procedures that the environment (ρ) in which their denotations are determined is that of the *declaring* block. It is this which gives languages with ALGOL-like block structure their 'lexicographic naming' idea. The parameter locations (*ll*) are derived in the *calling* environment.

Statement sequences

The body of a block is actually a sequence of statements so some extra functions are required:

> *WFSeq* : *Stmt** → *Senv* → $\mathbb{B}$
> *WFSeq* $[\![sl]\!]\, \rho \quad \triangle \quad \forall s \in$ elems *sl* · *WFStmt* $[\![s]\!]\, \rho$

The meaning of a sequence of statements is a transformation formed by composing the meanings of the component statements:

$MSeq : Stmt^* \rightarrow Env \rightarrow Tr$

$MSeq \llbracket sl \rrbracket \rho \quad \triangleq$

$\qquad \lambda \sigma \cdot$ if $sl = [\,]$ then σ else $MSeq \llbracket \text{tl } sl \rrbracket (\rho)(MStmt \llbracket \text{hd } sl \rrbracket (\rho)(\sigma))$

Blocks

The construct for declaring variables and procedures is a *Block*, its abstract syntax is:

$Block ::$ $typem$ $:$ $Id \xrightarrow{m} Sctype$

$\qquad procm$ $:$ $Id \xrightarrow{m} Proc$

$\qquad body$ $:$ $Stmt^*$

For blocks the context condition is:

$WFBlock : Block \rightarrow Senv \rightarrow \mathbb{B}$

$WFBlock \llbracket mk\text{-}Block(tm, pm, sl) \rrbracket \rho \quad \triangleq$

$\qquad is\text{-}disj(\text{dom } tm, \text{dom } pm) \wedge$

$\qquad (\forall pr \in \text{rng } pm \cdot WFProc \llbracket pr \rrbracket ((\text{dom } pm \mathbin{\lhd\!\!\!-} \rho) \dagger tm)) \wedge$

$\qquad (\text{let } prattrm = \{pid \mapsto TPProc \llbracket pm(pid) \rrbracket \mid pid \in \text{dom } pm\} \text{ in}$

$\qquad WFSeq \llbracket sl \rrbracket (\rho \dagger tm \dagger prattrm))$

This requires that the same name is not used for both a scalar variable and a procedure in the same block; it also specifies that the components of a block must be well-formed with respect to appropriate environments. The local declarations of both variables and procedures are used to form a new static environment in which the well-formedness of the body of the block is checked. Notice that this formulation prohibits recursion – direct or indirect – because the well-formedness of each *Proc* is checked in a reduced static environment.

The meaning function is:

$MBlock : Block \rightarrow Env \rightarrow Tr$

$MBlock \llbracket mk\text{-}Block(tm, pm, sl) \rrbracket \rho \quad \triangleq$

$\qquad \lambda \sigma \cdot \text{let } (\sigma', \rho') = newlocs(tm)(\sigma) \text{ in}$

$\qquad\qquad \text{let } \rho'' = \{pid \mapsto MProc \llbracket pm(pid) \rrbracket (\rho \dagger \rho') \mid pid \in \text{dom } pm\} \text{ in}$

$\qquad\qquad \text{let } \sigma'' = MSeq \llbracket sl \rrbracket (\rho \dagger \rho' \dagger \rho'')(\sigma') \text{ in}$

$\qquad\qquad epilogue(\text{rng } \rho')(\sigma'')$

The locations for the local variables (formed by *newlocs*) are put into ρ' and are thus available within procedures declared in the same block; local procedure denotations are not because there is no recursion. The denotation of a *Proc*, $pm(pid)$, is found by $MProc \llbracket pm(pid) \rrbracket (\rho \dagger \rho')$. The creation of σ' captures the initialization of the local variables and σ'' is the state after the meaning of the block body has been elaborated – this has to have the locations of the local variables removed before the meaning of the block ($\in Tr$) is complete.

The abstract syntax of *Stmt* shows that all of the cases have been defined:

Stmt = *Block* $\cup$ *If* $\cup$ *While* $\cup$ *Call* $\cup$ *Assign* $\cup$ NULL

The meaning functions and context conditions:

WFStmt: *Stmt* $\rightarrow$ *Senv* $\rightarrow$ $\mathbb{B}$
MStmt: *Stmt* $\rightarrow$ *Env* $\rightarrow$ *Tr*

can again be defined by cases in terms of the functions defined above.

Programs

The overall structure in the language is a *Program*:

Program :: *Stmt*

The context conditions are defined for all constructs by a function called *WF*. For a *Program* the definition is:

WFProgram : *Program* $\rightarrow$ $\mathbb{B}$
WFProgram $[\![mk\text{-}Program(s)]\!]$ $\;\triangleq\;$ *WFStmt* $[\![s]\!]$ ($\{in \mapsto$ INTG, $out \mapsto$ INTG$\}$)

This definition uses *WFStmt* which requires a static environment. The creation of the initial *Senv* reflects the fact that the only identifiers used within a *Program* which do not have to be declared in *Blocks*, or parameter lists, surrounding their use are *in* and *out*. Were the language to have a collection of predefined functions and constants (e.g. *maxint*), they would also be stored in the initial *Senv*.

By arranging for one input integer and one similar output value, the overall meaning of a *Program* turns out to be a function:

MProgram : *Program* $\rightarrow$ $\mathbb{Z}$ $\rightarrow$ $\mathbb{Z}$
MProgram $[\![mk\text{-}Program(s)]\!]$ (in_0) $\;\triangleq\;$
    let $(\sigma_0, \rho_0) = newlocs(\{in \mapsto$ INTG, $out \mapsto$ INTG$\})\{\ \}$ in
    let $\sigma' = MStmt [\![s]\!] (\rho_0)(\sigma_0 \dagger \{\rho_0(in) \mapsto in_0\})$ in
    $\sigma'(\rho_0(out))$

This represents a rather primitive view of communication with the outside world but, clearly, more powerful input and output statements could be added to the language.

9.6 Language extensions

This section describes how the language definition given above might be modified or extended to cope with other language features.

Parameter passing

It is easy to change the language so as to make all parameter passing work by value. The abstract syntax (cf. Section 9.2) need not be changed at all. (If – as in Pascal – the programmer is to be given the choice between 'by value' and 'by variable' parameter mechanisms, the abstract syntax of procedures must be extended to show which parameters are to be passed in which way.) The modified procedure denotations reflect the type of the object to be passed at call time:

$$Procden = Scval^* \rightarrow Tr$$

Although one *need not* change call statements, it is now possible to generalize the arguments so that:

$$Call :: pr : Id$$
$$al : Expr^*$$

The context condition for call statements (*WFCall*) need only be changed so that the expressions in *al* are handled. The changes necessary to the meaning function for *Call* show the store explicitly since it is needed for expression evaluation:

$MCall \llbracket mk\text{-}Call(pr, al) \rrbracket (\rho)(\sigma) \quad \triangle$
  let $vl = [MExpr \llbracket al(i) \rrbracket \rho\sigma \mid i \in \text{inds } al]$ in
  let $prden = \rho(pr)$ in
  $prden(vl)(\sigma)$

The final change involves the semantics (*Procden*) of procedure declarations. Unlike the by-variable case, locations must now be found for the *fpl* when the procedure is invoked (and removed after execution of the body):

$MProc : Proc \rightarrow Env \rightarrow Procden$
$MProc \llbracket mk\text{-}Proc(fpl, tm, s) \rrbracket (\rho)(vl)(\sigma) \quad \triangle$
  let $(\sigma', \rho') = newlocs(tm)(\sigma)$ in
  let $\sigma'' = \sigma' \dagger \{\rho'(fpl(i)) \mapsto vl(i) \mid i \in \text{inds } fpl\}$ in
  let $\sigma''' = MStmt \llbracket s \rrbracket (\rho \dagger \rho')(\sigma'')$ in
  $epilogue(\text{rng } \rho')(\sigma''')$

Parameter passing by value/result is interesting because it provides a way for a procedure to change the values of its arguments without creating the aliasing which complicates reasoning in the case of parameter passing by variable. The syntax of *Call* statements reverts (i.e. arguments can only be variable references) to that in Section 9.2. Procedure denotations also revert to:

$$Procden = Scloc^* \rightarrow Tr$$

The meaning of call statements is identical with that in Section 9.5. The whole effect is seen in the change to:

$MProc : Proc \rightarrow Env \rightarrow Procden$
$MProc \llbracket mk\text{-}Proc(fpl, tm, s) \rrbracket (\rho)(ll)(\sigma) \quad \triangle$
       let $(\sigma', \rho') = newlocs(tm)(\sigma)$ in
       let $\sigma'' = \sigma' \dagger \{\rho'(fpl(i)) \mapsto \sigma(ll(i)) \mid i \in$ inds $fpl\}$ in
       let $\sigma''' = MStmt \llbracket s \rrbracket (\rho \dagger \rho')(\sigma'')$ in
       $(\text{rng}\,\rho') \triangleleft (\sigma''' \dagger \{ll(i) \mapsto \sigma'''(\rho'(fpl(i))) \mid i \in$ inds $fpl\})$

Here, the key point is the copy back of the results after execution of the procedure body.

Multiple assignment

Suppose the language were extended to include a multiple assignment statement:

$Stmt = \ldots \cup Massign$

$Massign :: lhs : Varref^*$
$\qquad\qquad\;\; rhs : Bexpr^*$

This is a place where, if the 'wrong' choices are made, the semantics (i.e. language) would become messy. Obviously the left-/right-hand sides want to be the same length. The case for avoiding repeated identifiers (e.g. $v1, v1' := \text{true}, \text{false}$) is strong. So a reasonable context condition is:

$WFMassign : Massign \rightarrow Senv \rightarrow \mathbb{B}$
$WFMassign \llbracket mk\text{-}Massign(lhs, rhs) \rrbracket \rho \quad \triangle$
       len $lhs = $ len $rhs \land is\text{-}uniques(lhs) \land$
       $\forall i \in$ inds $lhs \cdot$
              $WFVarref \llbracket lhs(i) \rrbracket \rho \land WFExpr \llbracket rhs(i) \rrbracket \rho \land$
              $TPVarref \llbracket lhs(i) \rrbracket \rho = TPExpr \llbracket rhs(i) \rrbracket \rho$

But there is still the open issue of when expressions are evaluated in relation to the assignments. Does:

$v1 := \text{true};$
$v1, v2 := \text{false}, v1$

set $v2$ to true or to false? Here a semantics which evaluates all of the right-hand side in the same store and then makes all of the assignments is given (but the alternative is not wrong, it just represents a different language):

$MMassign : Massign \rightarrow Env \rightarrow Tr$

$MMassign \, [\![mk\text{-}Massign(lhs, rhs)]\!] \, (\rho)(\sigma) \quad \triangle$

    let $locs = [MVarref \, [\![lhs(i)]\!] \, \rho \mid i \in$ inds $lhs]$ in

    let $vals = [MExpr \, [\![rhs(i)]\!] \, \rho\sigma \mid i \in$ inds $rhs]$ in

    $\sigma \dagger \{locs(i) \mapsto vals(i) \mid i \in$ inds $lhs\}$

Composite types

Pascal-like records provide one example of composite types. It is easy to extend the syntax of Section 9.2 to cope with records whose fields are selected by identifiers:

$Block$ :: $typem$: $Id \xrightarrow{m} Type$

          $procm$: $Id \xrightarrow{m} Proc$

          $body$: $Stmt^*$

$Type = Sctype \cup Rectype$

$Rectype = Id \xrightarrow{m} Type$

Notice that, because *Rectype* recurses back to *Type*, records can be nested to arbitrary level. No context condition is given so that it is possible to use the same field selector at different levels in the same record (e.g. $\{a \mapsto \{a \mapsto \text{INT}\}\}$).

If records are only manipulable via their scalar components, it is easy to make the requisite changes to the abstract syntax and context conditions. The interesting decision relates to the handling of the record structure in *Store/Env*. If scalar elements of records are to be passable as (by variable) parameters, it is much easier to construct a definition in which the structure of records is shown in the locations (rather than in the values). Thus the environment is changed so as to make it possible to find scalar locations and *Store* is kept as a map whose domain is *Scloc*.

$Senv = Id \xrightarrow{m} Attr$

$Attr = Type \cup Procattr$

$Env = Id \xrightarrow{m} (Loc \cup Procden)$

$Loc = Scloc \cup Recloc$

$Recloc = Id \xrightarrow{m} Loc$

$Store = Scloc \xrightarrow{m} Scval$

There is no need to change the context condition for *Block* (*WFBlock*) given in Section 9.5. The major changes come with variable references:

$Varref = Scvarref \cup Fldref$

$Scvarref \; :: \; Id$

$WFScvarref \, \llbracket mk\text{-}Scvarref(id) \rrbracket \, \rho \quad \triangle \quad id \in \mathrm{dom} \, \rho \wedge \rho(id) \in Sctype$

$TPScvarref \, \llbracket mk\text{-}Scvarref(id) \rrbracket \, \rho \quad \triangle \quad \rho(id)$

$MScvarref : Scvarref \rightarrow Env \rightarrow Scloc$
$MScvarref \, \llbracket mk\text{-}Scvarref(id) \rrbracket \, \rho \quad \triangle \quad \rho(id)$

$Fldref \; :: \; rec \; : \; Id$
$\qquad\qquad flds \; : \; Id^*$

$WFFldref : Fldref \rightarrow Senv \rightarrow \mathbb{B}$
$WFFldref \, \llbracket mk\text{-}Fldref(rec, flds) \rrbracket \, \rho \quad \triangle$
$\qquad rec \in \mathrm{dom} \, \rho \wedge \rho(rec) \in Rectype \wedge match(flds, \rho(rec))$

$match : Id^* \times Type \rightarrow \mathbb{B}$
$match(flds, rtp) \quad \triangle$
$\qquad \text{if } flds = [\,]$
$\qquad \text{then } rtp \in Sctype$
$\qquad \text{else } rtp \in Rectype \wedge \mathrm{hd}\,flds \in \mathrm{dom}\,rtp \wedge match(\mathrm{tl}\,flds, rtp(\mathrm{hd}\,flds))$

$TPFldref : Fldref \rightarrow Senv \rightarrow Sctype$
$TPFldref \, \llbracket mk\text{-}Fldref(rec, flds) \rrbracket \, \rho \quad \triangle \quad select(flds, \rho(rec))$

$select : Id^* \times Type \rightarrow Type$
$select(flds, rtp) \quad \triangle \quad \text{if } flds = [\,] \text{ then } rtp \text{ else } select(\mathrm{tl}\,flds, rtp(\mathrm{hd}\,flds))$

$MFldref : Fldref \rightarrow Env \rightarrow Scloc$
$MFldref \, \llbracket mk\text{-}Fldref(rec, flds) \rrbracket \, \rho \quad \triangle \quad select_d(flds, \rho(rec))$

The function $select_d$ is identical in definition to *select*: some ML-like polymorphism would allow one function to be used for both tasks. Notice that the meaning of a right-hand-side reference is as before ($M \, \llbracket mk\text{-}Rhsref(vr) \rrbracket \, \rho\sigma$).

It is now possible to sketch a semantic model for one-dimensional *Arrays*. The first part is easy:

Varref = Scvarref ∪ Arrayvarref

Scvarref :: *Id*

Arrayvarref :: *arr* : *Id*
         ssc : *Expr*

Senv = Id $\xrightarrow{m}$ *Varattr ∪ Procattr*

Varattr = Sctype ∪ Arrayattr

Arrayattr :: *Sctype*

WFArrayvarref : *Arrayvarref* → *Senv* → $\mathbb{B}$
WFArrayvarref [*mk-Arrayvarref*(*arr*, *ssc*)] *ρ*   △
     ρ(*arr*) ∈ *Arrayattr* ∧ *TPExpr* [*ssc*] *ρ* = INT

It is important that the component relation (of the arrays) is placed in the *Env* so that sublocations (or even ALGOL 68 style slices) can be passed as (by variable) arguments. Thus:

Env = Id $\xrightarrow{m}$ (*Loc* ∪ ...)

Loc = Scloc ∪ Arrayloc

Arrayloc = Scloc*

Notice that this model assumes that arrays are indexed from 1. Further generalizations are not difficult but one must think about the (normal) regularity constraints on the shape of *Arrays*.

9.7 Appendix

Auxiliary functions

In common with other uses of VDM, it has been convenient to extract some auxiliary functions whose definitions are given here.

is-disj : *X*-set × *X*-set → $\mathbb{B}$
is-disj(s_1, s_2)   △   ∀*e* ∈ s_1 · *e* ∉ s_2

$is\text{-}uniques : X^* \to \mathbb{B}$

$is\text{-}uniques(l) \quad \triangle \quad \forall i,j \in \mathsf{inds}\, l \cdot i \neq j \;\Rightarrow\; l(i) \neq l(j)$

Abbreviations

Arrayloc	array location
Attr	attribute
ATTR	attribute (of a procedure)
Const	constant
disj	disjoint
Env	environment
Expr	expression
Fldref	field (of a record) reference
Id	identifier
Loc	location
Massign	multiple assign
Proc	procedure
Procattr	procedure attribute
Procden	procedure denotation
Recloc	record location
Rectype	record type
Rhsref	reference (to a variable)
Scloc	scalar location
Scval	scalar value
Scvarref	scalar variable reference
Sctype	scalar type
Senv	static environment
Stmt	statement
Tr	transformation
TP	type (function)
Varref	variable reference
WF	well-formed (function)

10

Object-oriented Languages

Mario I. Wolczko

Continuing with the language specification theme introduced in the last chapter, Mario Wolczko examines what is meant by the term 'object oriented'. Firstly he identifies the essential features of these languages namely the ideas of object, message, method and class. Following this an abstract syntax for a hypothetical language is introduced and the semantics specified in the conventional denotational style. Lastly, the notion of inheritance is briefly discussed and a specific model specified. The material in this chapter shows how formal specification techniques can be used, at an early stage in the language design process, to investigate the meaning of novel language features. Once the meaning of these features has been decided upon a fuller language definition exercise can be undertaken with some degree of confidence that the essential structure of the language is well founded.

10.1   Introduction

One of the earliest applications of VDM was to the formalization of programming language semantics. The VDM approach to denotational semantics has been used to describe a wide variety of programming language features, and a substantial number of real languages. In [BJ82], for example, can be found complete denotational descriptions of Pascal and ALGOL-60.

In this chapter, VDM is used to investigate the semantics of object-oriented languages. Although the object-oriented approach has been around for two decades, it is only recently that it has gained widespread attention and popularity. Moreover, there is much confusion as to what exactly characterizes an object-oriented language. The aim of this chapter is to present a semantic model of the core features of object-oriented languages, so that any comparison between object-oriented and conventional languages may be based on firmer foundations.

10.2   What is object-oriented programming?

Rather unsurprisingly, the most important thing about object-oriented programming is the idea of an *object*. An object is a computational entity that can encapsulate both behavior and state, and interacts by sending and receiving messages. Let us examine the various facets of this statement in more detail.

First, objects encapsulate behavior. In most object-oriented languages a message to an object will result in the invocation of a procedure. The particular procedure to be executed will be determined by the object receiving the message, and not the sender of the message. The message conveys intent, whilst the object determines how that intention should be satisfied.

Second, objects encapsulate state. The only way to interact with an object is to send it a message – there is no way to covertly manipulate the object's state. An object may choose to make some of its state visible in the way it responds to messages, but it need not. It is worth emphasizing that the state of an object, i.e. its internal data, is independent of its identity. Different objects can have the same internal state, and interactions with one object need not affect any other.

How are these properties realized in object-oriented programming languages?[1] The state of an object is captured by the values of its internal variables, known as *instance variables*. Every instance variable can refer to an object. Some, *primitive* objects, do not have any instance variables, and are immutable, e.g. objects representing the integers.

---

[1] In this chapter we shall address mainstream object-oriented languages, such as Smalltalk, Simula and Eiffel, and ignore the more unusual object-oriented models such as actor systems. For a more detailed survey, see [Wol88].

The behavior of an object is described by its response to a message. For each different sort of message, a *method* is defined – this is the procedure that will be activated in response to that sort of message. A collection of methods can define completely the behavior of an object. Usually such collections are named, and referred to as classes. All objects instantiated from a class, and therefore having behavior defined by the class, are known as *instances* of the class.

These, therefore, are the core concepts we need to describe: objects (including primitive objects and those with instance variables), messages, methods and classes. We shall do this by inventing a small and simple object-oriented language, and specifying its semantics.

Modelling objects

The first stage is to model objects. We shall divide objects into two categories, primitive and nonprimitive (or 'plain'), and place them in an 'object store.' Each object will be identified by a unique 'handle' known as an *Oop* (short for 'object pointer'). These are the keys to the object memory; indexing the store with an *Oop* will return the associated object:

$$Object\_memory = Oop \xrightarrow{m} Object$$

Every object has two parts: a body for the 'data part', and a class identifier for the behavior. We shall assume that classes are immutable, so that we need not represent them directly in the object memory:

$$Object :: class : Class\_name$$
$$body : Object\_body$$

$$Class\_name :: Id$$

Plain objects associate a value with each instance variable; this value can refer to any other object. Primitive objects stand for themselves. In our simple language, the only sort of primitive object is an integer. In real languages, other objects, such as characters and real numbers, might be primitives.

$$Object\_body = Plain\_object \cup Primitive\_object$$

$$Plain\_object = Id \xrightarrow{m} Oop$$

$$Primitive\_object = \mathbb{Z} \cup \ldots$$

The following auxiliary functions are used to access and modify a plain object's instance variables:

$$inst\_var : Id \times Oop \times Object\_memory \rightarrow Oop$$
$$inst\_var(iv, oop, \sigma) \quad \triangleq \quad body(\sigma(oop))(iv)$$

$$update\_inst\_var : Id \times Oop \times Oop \times Object\_memory \rightarrow Object\_memory$$
$$update\_inst\_var(inst\_var, oop, value, \sigma) \quad \triangleq$$
$$\sigma \dagger \{oop \mapsto \mu(\sigma(oop), body \mapsto body(\sigma(oop)) \dagger \{inst\_var \mapsto value\})\}$$

Methods and classes

The denotation of a method is a function that transforms the object memory. It takes as parameters an *Oop* referring to the receiver of the associated message, a list of *Oops* representing the arguments to the message, and an object memory, and returns a (possibly modified) object memory and result *Oop*.

$$Method\_den = Oop \times Oop^* \times Object\_memory \rightarrow Oop \times Object\_memory$$

The denotation of a class is a collection of method denotations, indexed by message name. The name of a message is usually termed a *selector*.

$$Class\_den = Selector \xrightarrow{m} Method\_den$$

Computation proceeds by objects sending messages to each other. In response to a message, an object will invoke a method, which in turn can access the instance variables of that object, or send messages to other objects. Let us now examine the abstract syntax of our simple language.

10.3   Abstract syntax

We will assume that at the commencement of execution the object memory is empty. A single object of a designated class, known as the *root class*, will be created, and an initiating expression will be evaluated. Normally, this expression will send a message to the root object, which will in turn create more objects.

Thus, a program consists of a set of classes, one of which is nominated as the root class, and an initiating expression:

$$
\begin{array}{lll}
Program :: & Root & : Class\_name \\
& Init & : Expression \\
& Classes & : Class\_map
\end{array}
$$

Each class consists of a set of method definitions. Some methods are 'primitive' (such as the addition method between integer objects):

$$Class\_map = Class\_name \xrightarrow{m} Class\_body$$

$$Class\_body = Selector \xrightarrow{m} (Method \cup Primitive\_method)$$

However, most methods contain a body, which is a single expression, and a declaration of the parameters to the method:

$$Method = Method\_body$$

$$Method\_body :: Params : Ulist(Id)$$
$$Expr \quad : Expression$$

The parameter list is a sequence of identifiers, no identifier appearing more than once in the sequence:

$$Ulist(X) = X^*$$

where

$$inv\text{-}Ulist(X)(l) \quad \triangle \quad \text{card inds } l = \text{card elems } l$$

There are five basic types of expression, in addition to expressions which are the sequential composition of subexpressions:

$$Expression = Expression\_list \cup Assignment \cup Object\_name$$
$$\cup Message \cup New\_expr \cup Literal\_object$$

$$Expression\_list :: Expression^*$$

Note that this is an expression-oriented, rather than statement-oriented language. Every expression returns a value, but the value can be ignored.

An assignment evaluates an expression and assigns the result to a variable.

$$Assignment :: LHS : AVar\_id$$
$$RHS : Expression$$

There are three types of identifier accessible within a method:

Instance variables are used to access the mutable state of the object processing the current message (the *receiver*)

Argument identifiers refer to the *Oops* passed with the current message

Temporary variables provide working store within a method.

Only instance and temporary variables can be assigned to within a method.

$$Arg\_id :: Id$$

$$Temp\_id :: Id$$

Inst_var_id :: *Id*

AVar_id = *Temp_id* ∪ *Inst_var_id*

In addition, the self keyword refers to the receiver.

Object_name = *Var_id* ∪ {SELF}

Var_id = *Arg_id* ∪ *Temp_id* ∪ *Inst_var_id*

When sending a message, one expression is evaluated to determine which object will receive the message, and other expressions can be evaluated to pass arguments to the message. The message selector itself is determined from the program text.

Message :: *Rcvr* : *Expression*
        Sel : *Selector*
        Args : *Expression*[*]

To create a new object, a 'new-expression' is evaluated, naming the class of object to be created. The values of the instance variables of the new object will be undefined initially.

New_expr :: *Class* : *Class_name*

Primitive objects cannot be created via a new-expression; they are created by being named by a literal.

Literal_object = *Int_literal* ∪ ...

Int_literal :: ℤ

10.4 Semantics

Having described the syntax of the language, we can proceed to specify its semantics. (For brevity, we shall omit a formal description of the context conditions, stating them informally where appropriate.)

We require a collection of semantic functions that take the appropriate syntactic elements, together with any relevant context, and map them to their denotations.

The denotation of the entire program will be the denotation of the initiating expression, in the context of the other classes. Supplying this expression with an initial, empty store will yield the result of the program, which we will choose to be the final store, together with the result of the expression.

Answer = *Oop* × *Object_memory*

MProgram : *Program* → *Answer*
MProgram ⟦*mk-Program*(*rootc*, *init*, *classes*)⟧   △
    let ρ_0 = {*c* ↦ *MClass_body* ⟦*classes*(*c*)⟧ ρ_0 | *c* ∈ dom *classes*} in
    let (*root_oop*, σ_0) = *create*(*mk-Object*(*rootc*, { }), { }),
        δ_0 = *mk-DEnv*(*root_oop*, { }, { }),
        (*result*, δ_r, σ_r) = *MExpression* ⟦*init*⟧ (ρ_0)(δ_0)(σ_0) in
    (*result*, σ_r)

SEnv = *Class_name* $\xrightarrow{m}$ *Class_den*

The first line establishes the relevant context for the initiating expression. This is a map containing the denotations of all the classes in the program, and is known as the *static environment*. The use of ρ_0 on the right-hand side indicates that we are taking the least fixed point of this expression [BJ82]. The second line creates the root object and adds it to the empty store, and the last two lines evaluate the denotation of the initiating expression in the initial store and return the result (the meaning of the δ_0 expression will become clear below).

The denotation of a class is the composition of the denotations of its individual methods:

MClass_body : *Class_body* → *SEnv* → *Class_den*
MClass_body ⟦*meths*⟧ ρ △
    {*sel* ↦ *MMethod* ⟦*meths*(*sel*)⟧ (*sel*)(ρ) | *sel* ∈ dom *meths*}

The denotation of a primitive method is itself; *MMethod_body* is used to describe the denotation of a nonprimitive method.

MMethod : (*Method* ∪ *Primitive_method*) → *Selector* → *SEnv* → *Method_den*
MMethod ⟦*m*⟧ (*sel*)(ρ)   △   if *m* ∈ *Primitive_method*
                                        then *m*
                                        else *MMethod_body* ⟦*m*⟧ (*sel*)(ρ)

Primitive_method = *Method_den*

Within the execution of a method we need to record the values of the variables local to that method (arguments and temporaries), as well as the receiver of the method. These are collected together into a *dynamic environment*, and this is passed from expression to expression within the method.

DEnv :: *Rcvr*   : *Oop*
         Params : *Id* $\xrightarrow{m}$ *Oop*
         Temps : *Id* $\xrightarrow{m}$ *Oop*

The following function can be used to set or update the value of a temporary:

$update\_temp : Id \times Oop \times DEnv \to DEnv$
$update\_temp(id, value, \delta) \quad \triangle \quad \mu(\delta, Temps \mapsto Temps(\delta) \dagger \{id \mapsto value\})$

The denotation of a nonprimitive method is a function that creates an initial dynamic environment (binding formal to actual parameters), and evaluates the body of the method in that environment. The environment is discarded when the method returns.

$MMethod\_body : Method\_body \to Selector \to SEnv \to Method\_den$
$MMethod\_body[\![mk\text{-}Method\_body(formals, expr)]\!](sel)(\rho) \quad \triangle$
$\quad\quad \lambda rcvr, actuals, \sigma \cdot$
$\quad\quad\quad\quad \text{let } \delta = mk\text{-}DEnv(rcvr, bind\_args(formals, actuals), \{\ \}),$
$\quad\quad\quad\quad\quad\quad (result, \delta', \sigma') = MExpression[\![expr]\!](\rho)(\delta)(\sigma) \text{ in}$
$\quad\quad\quad\quad (result, \sigma')$

$bind\_args : Ulist(Id) \times Oop^* \to (Id \xrightarrow{m} Oop)$
$bind\_args(formals, actuals) \quad \triangle \quad \{formals(i) \mapsto actuals(i) \mid i \in \text{inds } formals\}$

The denotations of the various types of expression are similar functions, but they also take an environment parameter, and return a (possibly modified) environment in addition to the result *Oop* and object memory.

The denotation of an *Expression_list* is straightforward:[2]

$MExpression : Expression \to SEnv \to DEnv \to Object\_memory \to$
$\quad\quad\quad\quad\quad\quad\quad\quad\quad\quad\quad\quad\quad\quad Oop \times DEnv \times Object\_memory$
$MExpression[\![mk\text{-}Expression\_list(exprs)]\!](\rho)(\delta)(\sigma) \quad \triangle$
$\quad\quad \text{let } (oop, \delta', \sigma') = MExpression[\![hd\ exprs]\!](\rho)(\delta)(\sigma) \text{ in}$
$\quad\quad \text{if len } exprs = 1 \text{ then } (oop, \delta', \sigma')$
$\quad\quad \text{else } MExpression[\![mk\text{-}Expression\_list(tl\ exprs)]\!](\rho)(\delta')(\sigma')$

An assignment expression updates either an instance variable of the receiver, or a temporary in the dynamic environment:

$MExpression[\![mk\text{-}Assignment(id, rhs)]\!](\rho)(\delta)(\sigma) \quad \triangle$
$\quad\quad \text{let } (result, \delta', \sigma') = MExpression[\![rhs]\!](\rho)(\delta)(\sigma) \text{ in}$
$\quad\quad \text{cases } id \text{ of}$
$\quad\quad mk\text{-}Temp\_id(t) \quad\quad \to (result, update\_temp(t, result, \delta'), \sigma')$
$\quad\quad mk\text{-}Inst\_var\_id(iv) \to (result, \delta', update\_inst\_var(iv, Rcvr(\delta), result, \sigma'))$
$\quad\quad \text{end}$

---

[2]Most of these definitions could be shortened by the use of combinators [BJ82], but for simplicity the explicit forms have been used.

The various forms of object name extract values from the receiver or the dynamic environment:

$$MExpression \llbracket mk\text{-}Arg\_id(id) \rrbracket (\rho)(\delta)(\sigma) \quad \triangleq \quad (Params(\delta)(id), \delta, \sigma)$$

$$MExpression \llbracket mk\text{-}Temp\_id(id) \rrbracket (\rho)(\delta)(\sigma) \quad \triangleq \quad (Temps(\delta)(id), \delta, \sigma)$$

$$MExpression \llbracket mk\text{-}Inst\_var\_id(id) \rrbracket (\rho)(\delta)(\sigma) \quad \triangleq$$
$$(inst\_var(id, Rcvr(\delta), \sigma), \delta, \sigma)$$

$$MExpression \llbracket \text{SELF} \rrbracket (\rho)(\delta)(\sigma) \quad \triangleq \quad (Rcvr(\delta), \delta, \sigma)$$

Note that the value of an uninitialized temporary is undefined.

The crucial part of the definition is the semantics of message-sending. First, the receiver and arguments must be determined:

$$MExpression \llbracket mk\text{-}Message(rcvr, sel, arglist) \rrbracket (\rho)(\delta)(\sigma) \quad \triangleq$$
$$\text{let } (rcvr\_oop, \delta', \sigma') = MExpression \llbracket rcvr \rrbracket (\rho)(\delta)(\sigma),$$
$$(actuals, \delta'', \sigma'') = MExpression\_list \llbracket arglist \rrbracket (\rho)(\delta')(\sigma'),$$
$$(result, \sigma''') = perform(sel, \rho, rcvr\_oop, actuals, \sigma'') \text{ in}$$
$$(result, \delta'', \sigma''')$$

The following function evaluates a list of expressions, returning a list of results:

$$MExpression\_list : Expression^* \rightarrow SEnv \rightarrow DEnv \rightarrow Object\_memory \rightarrow$$
$$Oop^* \times DEnv \times Object\_memory$$
$$MExpression\_list \llbracket el \rrbracket (\rho)(\delta)(\sigma) \quad \triangleq$$
$$\text{if } el = [\,]$$
$$\text{then } ([\,], \delta, \sigma)$$
$$\text{else let } (val, \delta', \sigma') = MExpression \llbracket \text{hd } el \rrbracket (\rho)(\delta)(\sigma),$$
$$(val\_list, \delta'', \sigma'') = MExpression\_list \llbracket \text{tl } el \rrbracket (\rho)(\delta')(\sigma') \text{ in}$$
$$([val]^\frown val\_list, \delta'', \sigma'')$$

Next, the *perform* function is given the receiver and argument *Oops*, and evaluates the message by:

1. determining the class of the receiver;

2. looking up the denotation of that class in the static environment;

3. applying the denotation of the class to a selector to yield the denotation of the appropriate method;

4. applying the denotation of the method to the relevant *Oops* and object memory.

perform : *Selector* × *SEnv* × *Oop* × *Oop** × *Object_memory* →
                                                                    Oop × *Object_memory*
perform(*sel*, ρ, *rcvr*, *args*, σ) $\triangleq$ ρ(*class*(σ(*rcvr*)))(*sel*)(*rcvr*, *args*, σ)

Creating a new object is straightforward. We use a nondeterministic specification for the *create* function, because it does not matter which particular *Oop* is allocated to the new object, only that it has not already been allocated.

MExpression ⟦*mk-New_expr*(*class*)⟧ (ρ)(δ)(σ) $\triangleq$
    let (*new_oop*, σ′) = *create*(*mk-Object*(*class*, { }), σ) in
    (*new_oop*, δ, σ′)

create (*obj*: *Object*) *new_oop*: *Oop*
ext wr σ : *Object_memory*
post (*new_oop* ∉ dom $\overleftarrow{σ}$) ∧ (σ = $\overleftarrow{σ}$ ∪ {*new_oop* ↦ *obj*})

The only unusual aspect of the semantics of literals is that the implementation can choose to make a new object for the literal, or find an existing object with the same value. Because literals are immutable, these options are equivalent.

MExpression ⟦*mk-Int_literal*(*int*)⟧ (ρ)(δ)(σ) $\triangleq$
    let (*oop*, σ′) = *find_or_make_immutable*(*int*, Integer, σ) in
    (*oop*, δ, σ′)

find_or_make_immutable:
    Primitive_object × *Class_name* × *Object_memory* → *Oop* × *Object_memory*

find_or_make_immutable (*value*: *Primitive_object*,
                    class: *Class_name*) *obj*: *Oop*
ext wr σ : *Object_memory*
post σ(*obj*) = *mk-Object*(*class*, *value*) ∧ (σ = $\overleftarrow{σ}$ ∨ {*obj*} ◁ σ = $\overleftarrow{σ}$)

Finally, we give an example of a primitive method: integer addition. This function simply finds or creates an integer object with the value that is the sum of its operands.

plus_primitive : *Primitive_method*
plus_primitive $\triangleq$
    λ*rcvr_oop*, [*arg_oop*], σ ·
        find_or_make_immutable(*body*(σ(*rcvr_oop*)) + *body*(σ(*arg_oop*)),
                                                                    Integer, σ)

10.5 Inheritance

Inheritance is an important feature in object-oriented languages. However, it not an *essential* feature, as some have argued [Str87]. For example, the simple language just described is most certainly object-oriented, but does not have any form of inheritance.

There are many different inheritance schemes, but most seem to fall into one of two camps: class-based or object-based. In class-based inheritance, a class may have a number of parent classes from which it inherits method definitions and instance structure. An instance of such a class responds to the methods defined in that class, plus any inherited from parent classes (or, in turn, their parents, and so on). Similarly, such an instance will have the instance variables defined by the class in addition to any defined by ancestor classes. Interesting variations in design are used to resolve name clashes between instance variables and method names in different ancestor classes [Wol88].

In object-based inheritance, an object can inherit directly from other objects. In some languages, the pattern of inheritance can even be changed at run-time, whereas inheritance between classes is usually static. In most languages with object-based inheritance a special form of message-sending, known as *delegation*, is used. As Lieberman has shown [Lie86], delegation can be used to emulate class-based inheritance, but the converse is not true.

To conclude this chapter, we will extend our tiny object-oriented language to include delegation. This will give us a simple yet flexible form of inheritance.

10.6 Semantics of delegation

When one object delegates a message to another, it passes on the whole message, including selector and arguments. Also passed, implicitly, is the identity of the delegating object, known as the *client*. In responding to the message, the object being delegated to can behave as if it were being sent the message in the normal way, but it can also send a message to the client, asking for some sort of assistance. Delegation implies that responsibility for completing the task is shared between the objects; they cooperate in their response.

We shall distinguish between ordinary methods and delegating methods at the syntactic level. A delegating method simply passes the entire message on to the object named by one of the instance variables.

Method = Method_body $\cup$ Delegated_method

Delegated_method :: *Id*

The denotation of a method will have to take an extra argument, representing the *Oop* of the client. This will also be stored in the dynamic environment, and will be accessible via a keyword, client, analogous to the keyword self.

$$Method\_den = Oop \times Oop \times Oop^* \times Object\_memory \rightarrow Oop \times Object\_memory$$

$$
\begin{aligned}
DEnv :: \ &Rcvr \quad : Oop \\
&Client \quad : Oop \\
&Params : Id \xrightarrow{\ m\ } Oop \\
&Temps \quad : Id \xrightarrow{\ m\ } Oop
\end{aligned}
$$

$$Object\_name = Var\_id \cup \{\text{SELF, CLIENT}\}$$

$$MExpression\,[\![\text{CLIENT}]\!]\,(\rho)(\delta)(\sigma) \quad \triangleq \quad (Client(\delta), \delta, \sigma)$$

A conventional message send sets self and client to be the same object; this requires a small modification to *MExpression*, and a further change to *perform* to pass the client *Oop* to the method denotation:

$$
\begin{aligned}
&MExpression\,[\![mk\text{-}Message(rcvr, sel, arglist)]\!]\,(\rho)(\delta)(\sigma) \quad \triangleq \\
&\quad \textsf{let}\ (rcvr\_oop, \delta', \sigma') = MExpression\,[\![rcvr]\!]\,(\rho)(\delta)(\sigma), \\
&\qquad (actuals, \delta'', \sigma'') = MExpression\_list\,[\![arglist]\!]\,(\rho)(\delta')(\sigma'), \\
&\qquad (result, \sigma''') = perform(sel, \rho, rcvr\_oop, rcvr\_oop, actuals, \sigma'')\ \textsf{in} \\
&\quad (result, \delta'', \sigma''')
\end{aligned}
$$

$$
\begin{aligned}
perform : &Selector \times SEnv \times Oop \times Oop \times Oop^* \times Object\_memory \rightarrow \\
&\qquad\qquad\qquad\qquad\qquad\qquad\qquad\qquad Oop \times Object\_memory
\end{aligned}
$$
$$
\begin{aligned}
&perform(sel, \rho, rcvr, client, args, \sigma) \quad \triangleq \\
&\quad \rho(class(\sigma(rcvr)))(sel)(rcvr, client, args, \sigma)
\end{aligned}
$$

Additionally, *MMethod_body* is altered to save the client *Oop* in the dynamic environment:

$$
\begin{aligned}
&MMethod\_body : Method\_body \rightarrow Selector \rightarrow SEnv \rightarrow Method\_den \\
&MMethod\_body\,[\![mk\text{-}Method\_body(formals, expr)]\!]\,(sel)(\rho) \quad \triangleq \\
&\quad \lambda rcvr, client, actuals, \sigma \cdot \\
&\qquad \textsf{let}\ \delta = mk\text{-}DEnv(rcvr, client, bind\_args(formals, actuals), \{\ \}), \\
&\qquad\quad (result, \delta', \sigma') = MExpression\,[\![expr]\!]\,(\rho)(\delta)(\sigma)\ \textsf{in} \\
&\qquad (result, \sigma')
\end{aligned}
$$

Finally, a meaning function for delegating methods is required. This simply evaluates the message for the object being delegated to, passing on the client *Oop*:

$$MMethod\_body : Delegated\_method \rightarrow Selector \rightarrow SEnv \rightarrow Method\_den$$
$$MMethod\_body \llbracket mk\text{-}Delegated\_method(id) \rrbracket (sel)(\rho) \quad \triangle$$
$$\quad \lambda rcvr, client, actuals, \sigma \cdot$$
$$\quad\quad perform(sel, \rho, inst\_var(id, rcvr, \sigma), client, actuals, \sigma)$$

10.7 Other forms of inheritance

Extending the basic model to include delegation is not difficult. However, the description of class-based inheritance poses other problems. There are at least two approaches:

- In general, class-based object-oriented languages possess the property that any class constructed using inheritance can be equivalently constructed without using inheritance. Hence one approach is to convert any class that uses inheritance into an equivalent class that does not, and then apply the simpler semantic function that does not have to cope with inheritance [Wol88]. However, this approach cannot be said to be truly denotational.

- A second approach is to attempt to determine the meaning of a class by composing the meanings of its ancestor classes [Kam88, Coo88]. However, at the time of writing (1989), nobody had successfully applied this technique to a language with multiple inheritance.

10.8 Summary

In this chapter we have illustrated how the basic mechanisms of object-oriented languages can be described using VDM:

- Objects require a particular memory structure, based on two-level map (from *Oop* to objects, and thence to *Oops* again).

- Message-sending requires that the binding of messages to method denotations take place on every message send.

- Classes can be described as functions that interpret messages.

In addition we have shown how the simplest form of inheritance, namely delegation, can be added to the basic model.

11

Specification of a Dataflow Architecture

Kevin D. Jones

This chapter introduces two interesting aspects of VDM specifications. Ostensibly, the paper describes a machine architecture and, as such, is the first excursion into hardware description presented in this book. In spite of the use of the word 'software' in the title of this book, this chapter fits the overall style of contributions. In fact, it illustrates well the fact that a VDM specification – written at the right level of abstraction – could be reified to either hardware or software implementations. The particular machine discussed is the 'tagged dataflow' architecture developed at Manchester University. The machine exhibits a form of parallelism but this is reduced in the formal specification to nondeterminism. The description strongly resembles the denotational semantics descriptions in the two preceding chapters, but here the denotations have to be relations in order to encompass the nondeterminism.

11.1 Introduction

This chapter presents an outline of a semantic description of the Manchester Dataflow Machine (MDFM) written in VDM with some extensions. The full description can be found in [Jon86b], which includes the design of a nondeterminate applicative programming language and the development of an associated compiler.

This work can be taken as illustrative of the extension of 'traditional' VDM methods to parallel – or, more generally, nondeterminate – environments. Dataflow machines would seem to serve as a good example in this situation since they are inherently nondeterministic and seem likely to be of importance in the future due to commercial interest.

The rest of Section 11.1 provides an introduction to the ideas behind dataflow machines, in general, and the Manchester Dataflow Machine in particular. Section 11.2 describes the development of a denotational semantics for this machine. The complete version is discussed in Section 11.3. Section 11.4 draws together some comments on this work.

Dataflow machines

In order to understand the formal model that follows, this section gives some background to the concepts involved in dataflow computing. For a more complete description, see the publications of the Dataflow Group at Manchester University (e.g. [GW83]).

All dataflow machines are based on the theoretical concept of a dataflow graph. Such a graph is a structure consisting of nodes and arcs. These represent operations and data paths, respectively. Graphs are represented pictorially as shown in Figure 11.1.

When all the input tokens to some nodes are present, action can occur. This action, called *firing*, consists of the 'consumption' of the input tokens, followed by the computation and 'production' of the corresponding output tokens. In Figure 11.1 nodes 1 and 4 are in a position to fire since their input tokens are present.

More formally, dataflow graphs are considered to be two-dimensional descriptions of a partial ordering on computational events. They are structured by data dependency. Nodes represent indivisible atomic actions. Arcs connect dependent nodes unidirectionally, showing the direction of dependency. They are connected to the input/output points of nodes. Tokens are items of data passed along arcs. A node may execute only if all of its inputs are available. This is referred to as the *firing rule*. It will, at some time in the future, consume the tokens on the input arcs. Later, a result token is produced on the output arc. This is the only constraint on execution, so it can be seen that all sequencing is implicit in the model. This means that a central controller, such as the program counter of the von Neumann model, is unnecessary. Variations on the model exist which affect the exact definition of the firing rule, but all follow the above description to some extent.

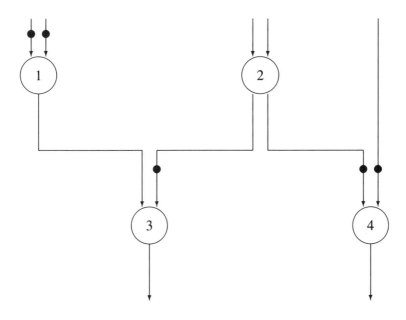

Figure 11.1 An example of a dataflow graph

The concept of a dataflow machine arose from considering direct execution of these graphs. Data are represented as tokens actually moving along arcs. An architecture that uses (a representation of) these graphs as its basic programs forms the basis of a dataflow machine. The graph showing data dependencies does not enforce a linear ordering. It can be seen how this partial order leads naturally to a parallel architecture. At any point in time, more than one node may be in a position to fire. Any (or all) ready nodes may be activated in parallel (since they are independent) provided there are sufficient processors available.

The major difference between various implementations of the dataflow model can be found in the way code reusability is dealt with. Reusable code causes a problem, since it is necessary to preserve the context of tokens in order to ensure correct tokens are matched together. One approach is to make all arcs first in first out (FIFO) queues. In the extreme case, these queues are limited to a maximum length of one. This gives the static approach to dataflow (using the terminology of [GW83]). This is capable of handling re-usability in an iterative sense but does not naturally extend to recursion, since multiple re-entry would cause difficulties. Recursion can be simulated by 'copying' portions of the graph.

Alternatives to the queuing strategy have been proposed, usually in an attempt to increase asyncronicity. In the Manchester Dataflow Machine [GW80], code is made truly re-entrant by forcing tokens to carry tagging information, to preserve matchings. From a pragmatic point of view, the dynamic tagged approach seems to give certain advantages in terms of available parallelism and quantity of code held. There is no proliferation of program code by copying, and reuse is limited only by the number of tags (sometimes called 'colors') available.

The Manchester Dataflow Machine

For a complete description of the MDFM, the reader is referred to the various papers published by the Manchester Dataflow Group (e.g. [GW80]). The following is intended to be a general introduction sufficient to enable the reader to understand the intention of the formal semantics presented in the next section.

The MDFM is an example of a strongly-typed, tagged token architecture with multiple processors. It permits re-entrant code and allows dynamic generation of graphs (i.e. arcs can be created during execution changing the structure of the graph). The theoretical concept of a dataflow graph has been described above, so here we examine the way in which the machine implements such graphs.

A graph is represented by storing its nodes, and sufficient information (at each node) to define the arcs. Just as for the abstract graphs, nodes are considered to be the basic entities. They are taken as basic operations of the machine and are represented by a structure of the form:

> *Node* :: *Operator*
> *Destination*

An *operator* is a primitive operation of the machine e.g. DUP, BRA.[1] A *destination* is the 'arc' of the dataflow graph, i.e. it defines where output is to go.

The data items (*tokens*) within the machine are represented as:

> *Token* :: *Data*
> *Label*
> *Destination*

The meaning of these fields is given below:

data gives the value (and type) of the token, e.g. an integer, a character, etc. See [Kir81] for full list of types and values.

label is the tag used to identify the token uniquely. This actually consists of three subfields which are used as:

---

[1] See [Kir81] for a complete list.

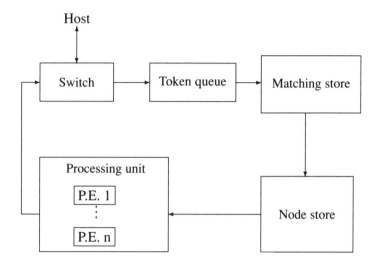

Figure 11.2 The configuration of the Manchester DataFlow Machine

1. *activation_name* – separates instantiations of re-entrant code in the case of functions;

2. *iteration_level* – used for iterative code;[2]

3. *index* – used for data structuring.

destination is used to identify the node to which the token is being sent, i.e. it implicitly defines the data arcs. This field also includes other information which is described below.

The machine is physically based on a ring structure. This is composed of a number of independent units around which the data tokens (and composite structures) circulate. The ring has the configuration shown in Figure 11.2.

Specific details such as number of bits in a token, catalog number of processing elements, length of wire between units and other information vital to engineers will not be given. Anyone interested to this level should consult [Gur82]. Next, each unit on the ring is looked at in more detail.

1. The switch

   This routes information to and from the host machine. It can be ignored if input

---

[2]Fields 1 and 2 are grouped together under the name *color*.

is taken to be present in the ring and that output remains there. It is also used to load the graph into the node store, using special instructions that identify tokens as node store data, but this is not considered further.

2. The token queue

This unit is present for purely pragmatic reasons. It is used to buffer tokens. The actual representation strategy has no effect and both a FIFO queue and a stack are used interchangeably. This has no effect beyond some difference in processing speed for particular sorts of programs. [3]

3. Matching store

This is a unique feature of the MDFM and gives the architecture a flexibility that would not be found in a 'pure' dataflow machine. Assuming all nodes are binary, a simplified description of the function of the matching store can be given as follows. When a token enters the matching store, a search is made within the store for the matching token. A token matches if it has the same destination (i.e. is going to the same node) and the labels are identical. If such a match is made, the pair are packaged together into a *group package* and passed along the ring to the node store. If no match is found then the incoming token is placed in the store to await the arrival of its matching token. More complex matching facilities are available and these are described later.

4. The node store

This unit holds the representation of the dataflow graph and can be taken to be equivalent to the program store of a conventional machine. Each node of the graph is stored, according to the representation described above, in a uniquely addressed location. This representation, actually consisting of an operator code and a node store address representing the arc to the next node, is loaded into the store from the host. This is similar to the loading of a program in a conventional machine. When a group package arrives from the token store, the relevant node is selected according to the destination field of the incoming tokens. A copy of the operator and the result destination are added to the package. This is known as an *executable package*. It is then sent to the processing unit.

5. The processing unit

This is the actual computing unit of the machine. It consists of a number (up to twenty in the current machine) of independent processing elements. Each is capable of accepting an executable package, performing the specified operation

---

[3]That is not completely true. Changing the queue/stack switch could sometimes have an interesting effect, since some local 'wizards' have been known to depend on properties of the queue to make 'unsafe' programs execute.

and producing the result token with the appropriate destination field. This is then passed on round the ring. It is in this area of the machine that true parallel processing is found. Since the processing elements operate independently, they accept incoming packages on an availability basis, in parallel.

In summary, the action of the MDFM (after initialization) is:

- A token enters the matching store.

- If the matching partner is not present within the store, the incoming token is placed in the store to wait.

- If the matching token is found, then all inputs to a particular node are present and that node is eligible to fire. The tokens are grouped together and sent to the node store.

- The relevant operator and the result destination are picked up.

- This package goes to the processing unit where it is executed by one of the processing elements, producing a result. This is sent back around the ring to continue the process.

The termination of a program, executed on this machine can occur in one of two ways. The first way is *clean termination*. In this case, all tokens have left the ring (i.e. have been given destinations in the host and so are switched out). Termination occurs when there are no tokens left anywhere in the ring and the host machine has received all expected output. In the second case,[4] output is handled as above but the difference is that tokens are still present in the ring. As will be seen below, use of special matching functions can cause tokens to be left in the matching store with no possibility of a matching token ever arriving. In this case, the program is said to terminate when all tokens left in the ring are stored in the matching store (i.e. there is no chance of a match, and so no possibility of any further action). It is intended that good examples of dataflow programs leave the store empty. A dataflow program which does so is said to be well-formed.

As was mentioned earlier, one interesting feature of the MDFM is the fact that dataflow arcs can be generated dynamically, i.e. during execution. The mechanism for handling this is the provision of primitive operations to extract and set the destination fields of tokens. In fact, destinations, colors, etc. can generally be handled as data values. (For precise details, see [Kir81].)

The above description of the operation and structure of the MDFM is sufficient for a general understanding of the machine. However, it does contain one major simplification. In reality, the matching store may be used in a more complex manner.

---

[4]I suppose this could be called *unclean termination* – but usually it is politely ignored.

Matching

The matching process described above is the default action of the store. This is known as extract wait (*EW*) since its function is to extract a token if there is a match and to cause a token to wait otherwise. This is sufficient for almost all 'normal' programming and represents pure dataflow. However, there are cases, such as explicit nondeterminate programming, where other actions may be desirable. To facilitate this, the action of the matching store can be controlled explicitly by use of a *matching function* carried by the incoming token. This matching function specifies the action to be taken by the matching store, both in the case of a match and a failure to match. These are usually denoted by a two-letter code, the first denoting the match action and the second denotes the fail action (as in *EW* above). This code is carried in the token's destination field, along with the (previously described) node address.

Before going into the detail of matching, it is necessary to give a more complete description of a token. In fact, the destination field contains a further subfield known as the *input point*. This specifies whether the token is the right or left operand of the node to which it is sent. This also explains the many–one matching situation mentioned in defer, below, in that two tokens with the same input point could arrive before the matching token with the opposite input point. The situation where two tokens with identical destination fields are both present in the store is forbidden in the MDFM (since a true matching token would have the opposite input point) and is known as a *matching store clash*. The matching function defer exists to avoid such a clash. In dataflow terminology, a program is said to be *unsafe* if there is the possibility of store clashes and *safe* if there is no such possibility.

In the current implementation, there are four possible match actions and four possible fail actions. These are listed below.

Match action

1. Extract

    The matching token is removed from the store, combined with the incoming token to form a group package and passed on to the node store.

2. Preserve

    A copy of the matching token (present in the store) is taken to form the group package but the stored token is not removed from the store.

3. Increment

    As preserve, except the token in store has its value field increased by one.

4. Decrement

    As increment, except the field is decreased as opposed to being increased.

Fail action

1. Wait
   The incoming token is placed in the store to wait for a match. This is the normal way of placing a token in the matching store.

2. Defer
   The incoming token is not stored but is passed back to the token queue (via the rest of the ring but in transparent fashion) to be resubmitted. This is used to avoid store clashes when many tokens could potentially match.

3. Abort
   The incoming token is not stored but it is grouped with a special EMPTY token and passed on. This is usually used to control explicit nondeterminacy.

4. Generate
   The action of generate is identical to abort except that a copy of the incoming token with its input point is stored. This means future tokens with identical destinations to the original incoming token will find a match. This again finds its main usage in situations involving nondeterminacy.

There is also a further matching function, bypass (*BY*), which simply allows the token to pass through the store unaffected. This is used for input to unary nodes where no matching is required.

Not all possible combinations of available matching functions are implemented. The currently available combinations are:

1. Extract wait (*EW*)

2. Bypass (*BY*)

3. Extract defer (*ED*)

4. Preserve defer (*PD*)

5. Increment defer (*ID*)

6. Decrement defer (*DD*)

7. Extract abort (*EA*)

8. Preserve generate (*PG*)

For a more complete description of the function and usage of matching functions on the MDFM, the reader is referred to [Bus83].

By the use of special matching functions, it is possible to deviate considerably from the model of pure dataflow. As Section 11.3 illustrates, this causes increased complexity in the formal semantics of the architecture.

11.2   The development of a denotational semantics

One of the goals of the work reported here is to produce a denotational semantics of the MDFM at a sufficiently low level to capture all the relevant detail of the machine, including matching functions.

The semantics of a simple dataflow machine

The most suitable approach was deemed to be the production of a denotational semantics, giving meaning at the level of a program within the machine (i.e. a *Node_store*).

It is necessary to decide on a suitable denotation, since the nondeterminism inherent in the machine means the usual denotation of continuous functions cannot be used. It was decided that the extension to powerdomains [Plo76] was unnecessary in this case. An adequate semantics could be given using relations as denotations, following [Par80]. So the basic approach is to define the semantics of the machine in terms of a fixed point over a relation on a set of tokens, characterizing the state of the machine.[5]

In order to facilitate the understanding of the formal semantics, a greatly simplified version of the machine is taken as a starting point. Additional complexity is added in stages, eventually leading to the complete MDFM. The presentation below follows that development.[6]

The first machine is greatly simplified. Its programs consist of pure, loop-free dataflow graphs with all nodes being binary input/unary output.[7]

The basic computation is performed by a *Node* – representing the basic program elements of the machine. Each *Node* consists of an *Operator*, which is a function describing the computation, and a *Destination* specifying to where the result should be sent:

---

[5]See [Sch86] for details on fixed points.

[6]The set constructor is taken to denote the powerset and is not restricted to the finite cases. Any extra notation used to deal with relational concepts, generally follows [Jon81]. To avoid confusion due to the use of μ as both a fixed point operator and record update operator in previous VDM related work, the former is represented as **fix** .

[7]For convenience, the term 'program' will be used to refer to the graph representation held in the node store.

Node :: *O* : *Operator*
  D : *Destination*

Operator = *Value* × *Value* → *Value*

A *Destination* contains the *Node_address* to which the value is to be sent plus an *Input_point*. [8]

Destination :: *NA* : *Node_address*
      IP : *Input_point*

The meaning of an individual *Node* is defined (by the function $\mathcal{M}_N$) in terms of the application of its operator to the values in a set of appropriate input *Tokens* and the creation of a new *Token* containing the result sent to the given *Destination*.

$\mathcal{M}_N$: *Node* → *Token*-set → *Token*
$\mathcal{M}_N$ [[*mk-Node(o,d)*]] {*mk-Token*(v_1,d_1), *mk-Token*(v_2,d_2)} $\triangle$
  mk-Token($o(v_1,v_2),d$)

A program is represented by a *Node_store*, which is a collection of *Nodes* indexed by their addresses.

Node_store = *Node_address* $\xrightarrow{m}$ *Node*

A subsidiary function *ips* is used to identify the *Tokens* destined for a particular *Node*.

ips : *Node_address* × *Token*-set → *Token*-set
ips(*d,ts*) $\triangle$ {$t \in ts \mid NA(D(t)) = d$}

The meaning of a 'program' is defined as the fixed point of a relation over token sets. The basis of this expression are those sets of *Tokens* in which no further computation is possible. [9] Any *Node* which has two input *Tokens* can be 'fired', i.e. the $\mathcal{M}_N$ function can apply. To allow for the parallelism in the machine (which is 'side-effect' free), all such *Nodes* can fire at once. This is modelled by use of a distributed union:

$\mathcal{M}_P$: *Node_store* → (*Token*-set × *Token*-set)-set
$\mathcal{M}_P$ [[*ns*]] $\triangle$
    fix $\mathcal{R}$ · ({(*ts,ts*) | ¬∃$d \in$ **dom** *ns* · **card** *ips*(*d,ts*) = 2} ∪
    $\bigcup$ {{(*ts,ts'*) | (*ts* − *fs* ∪ $\mathcal{M}_N$ [[*ns*(*d*)]] (*fs*), *ts'*) ∈ $\mathcal{R}$ }
        | $d \in$ **dom** *ns* ∧ *fs* = *ips*(*d,ts*) ∧ **card** *fs* = 2})

---

[8]At this level of simplicity, input points are not checked. However, if they were not included, two tokens with identical values input to a node would be coalesced by the set construction, preventing valid firings occurring. Since the set construction is required in later definitions, it does not seem appropriate to use (say) a pair construct here.

[9]In this simple case, that means there are no *Nodes* which have two input *Tokens*.

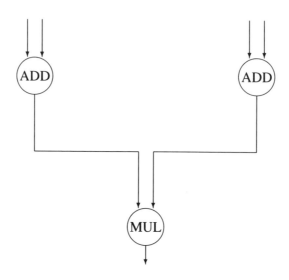

Figure 11.3 A simple example

The above formulae can be interpreted as follows. A meaning function ($\mathcal{M}_\text{P}$) is given from a program to a relation on token sets. The meaning of a program is found by building a fixed point, backwards from terminated states. The basis for the construction is the set of states that do not change (i.e. have no nodes that could possibly fire). States that can be arrived at by an eligible node firing are added at each step. This is done for all eligible nodes and the distributed union is taken.

The firing of a node is represented by the removing of its input tokens from, and adding its result tokens to, the state. The result of a particular node firing is given by the meaning function $\mathcal{M}_\text{N}$ on given node address. This is defined to be the construction of a result token which has the result destination and a value given by the node operator being applied to the input values. The input set (*ips*) of the node is generated, giving the candidates for firing.

This gives the general idea of the way in which the semantics is developed. In order to gain a better grasp of the formalism, and the way it 'works' on a dataflow program, it is worth examining a small example.

Consider the graph to calculate $(a + b) * (c + d)$, as shown in Figure 11.3. If we look at how this graph would be represented, we get to following node store:[10]

$$ns = \{1 \mapsto (+,3), 2 \mapsto (+,3), 3 \mapsto (*, out)\}$$

where 1, 2 and 3 are destinations (representing the node store addresses). *out* is just meant to represent a destination that is not within the graph being considered.

Assume the initial token set is:

$$ts_0 = \{(val_a, 1), (val_b, 1), (val_c, 2), (val_d, 2)\}$$

The construction of the relation is based on the 'final' states (i.e. those which will not transform further). It can be seen that the relation must allow the following actions. At the first step, either node 1 or node 2 could fire giving:

$$\mathcal{R}^1 = \{(ts_0, ts_1), (ts_o, ts_2)\}$$

where ts_1 results from node 1 firing, i.e.:

$$ts_1 = \{(val_{a+b}, 3), (val_c, 2), (val_d, 2)\}$$

and ts_2 results from node 2 firing, i.e.:

$$ts_2 = \{(val_a, 1), (val_b, 1), (val_{c+d}, 3)\}$$

derived from the $\mathcal{M}_N$ function on the + operator in each case.

At the next step only 1 or 2, depending on which has not already fired, is eligible to fire, and so on.

So, it can be seen why the meaning is given as a distributed union within a fixed-point construction. The fixed point builds the sequences of token sets produced as each action takes place in time. Each future action is enabled by the tokens produced at the current step. The starting point for the construction is the set of tokens for which no action takes place. This undergoes the identity transformation. Each step in the construction represents a firing action taking place. The union operation allows for many nondeterministic choices of which of the eligible nodes actually fires at any particular step. In other words, all possible computation paths are included in the expression.

This should enable an intuitive grasp of the semantics. More complex examples are not presented in detail as they very quickly become tedious.

The semantics of a more general dataflow machine

For this version of the machine, some of the restrictions are removed. Specifically, labels are added to tokens and nodes are generalized to n-input, n-output.

The major modification needed is a more complex means of checking if a node is eligible to fire. It is now possible to have more than one set of inputs to a node. There

---

[10]For clarity, constructors and input points are ignored.

needs to be a means of keeping these sets distinct. To deal with this, a label field is added to tokens:

Token :: *V* : *Value*
           D : *Destination*
           L : *Label*

A *Node* is extended to contain information about the number of expected inputs and the output *Destination* is generalized to a set:

Node :: *O* : *Operator*
          D : *Destination*-set

Operators now contain details of their arity in addition to the *Function*.

Operator :: *F*   : *Function*
             NIP : $\mathbb{N}$

Function: *Token*-set $\times$ *Destination*-set $\rightarrow$ *Token*-set

Since the definitions are seen to be becoming longer, a slightly different style of definition is used for $\mathcal{M}_\mathrm{P}$. The identity relation over the set s is written as $\mathcal{E}_s$, following [Jon81]. The relation is now defined in terms of relational composition ($\,\mathring{,}\,$) over $\mathcal{R}$. This combinator has the following type:

$\mathring{,}$: (*Token*-set $\times$ *Token*-set)-set $\times$ (*Token*-set $\times$ *Token*-set)-set
$\rightarrow$ (*Token*-set $\times$ *Token*-set)-set

is normally used in an infix form and has the usual meaning for composition. Using the following operators:

$\mathcal{M}_\mathrm{P}$: *Node_store* $\rightarrow$ (*Token*-set $\times$ *Token*-set)-set
$\mathcal{M}_\mathrm{P}\,[\![ns]\!]$ $\quad\triangle\quad$ **fix** $\mathcal{R} \cdot \mathcal{E}_s \cup \bigcup\{\mathcal{M}_\mathrm{N}\,[\![ns(d),d]\!]\,\mathring{,}\,\mathcal{R} \mid d \in \mathrm{dom}\,ns\}$
    where
    let $n = NIP(o)$ in
        $s = \{ts \in Token\text{-set} \mid \forall d \in \mathrm{dom}\,ns \cdot rdys(d,ts,n) = \{\,\}\}$

the meaning of a single node firing is extended to the relational type to allow use of composition:

$\mathcal{M}_N : Node \times Node\_address \rightarrow (Token\text{-set} \times Token\text{-set})\text{-set}$

$\mathcal{M}_N \, [\![mk\text{-}Node(o, nd), d]\!] \quad \triangle$

  let $f = F(o)$

   and

   $n = NIP(o)$ in

  $\mathcal{E}_s \cup \bigcup \{ \{ (ts, (ts - rs) \cup f(rs, nd)) \mid rs \in rdys(d, ts, n) \} \mid ts \in Token\text{-set} \}$

  where

    $s = \{ ts \in Token\text{-set} \mid rdys(d, ts, n) = \{ \} \}$

The function *rdys* extracts those sets of *Tokens* which constitute complete input sets to the given *Node*:

$rdys : Nodeaddress \times Token\text{-set} \times \mathbb{N} \rightarrow (Token\text{-set})\text{-set}$

$rdys(d, ts, nip) \quad \triangle$

   $\{ rts \subseteq ts \mid \forall t_1, t_2 \in rts \cdot (L(t_1) = L(t_2) \wedge NA(D(t_1)) = d) \wedge \mathsf{card}\, rts = nip \}$

Most of this definition should be easily understood since it does not differ very much from the earlier definition above. The noticeable additions are the checking for a given cardinality on a nodes input set as opposed to the default of two in a binary case and the multiple level of choice on the *rdys* function. This is due to the fact that it is necessary, in the first instance, to select all possible ready sets to the given node and to take the distributed union of the result of any of these being used. This gives the desired result at the $\mathcal{M}_N$ level.

The use of $\mathcal{M}_N$ and $\,;\,$ (relational composition) within the definition of $\mathcal{M}_P$ make it easier to see how the composition is used to build fixed point. This notation is maintained for the later definitions.

Termination

Before increasing the complexity of the machine any further, a significant technical difficulty needs to be considered. It is well known that problems are encountered when using relations as a denotation (see [Jon73] for example), particularly due to relational composition. This is most easily illustrated by the case of distinguishing between $\{(a, b)\}$ and $\{(a, b), (a, \perp)\}$, when nontermination is a possible result. (The symbol for bottom $\perp$ is used in its traditional sense to represent nontermination, i.e. undefined result.) To solve this problem, the approach of [Par80] is followed, where the denotation of a program is given as a pair of functions:

1. The meaning function as before.

2. A second function giving the set of inputs over which termination is guaranteed.

The termination function appropriate to the previous definition is:[11]

$\mathcal{T}_P$: *Node_store* → (*Token*-set)-set
$\mathcal{T}_P$ [*ns*] △ **fix** $\mathcal{S}$ · *termset*(*ns*) ∪
      {*ts* | ∀*na* ∈ dom *ns* · ∀*ts*′ · *ts*$\mathcal{M}_N$ [*ns*(*na*), *na*] *ts*′ ⇒ *ts*′ ∈ $\mathcal{S}$ }

The function *termset* generates sets of *Tokens* which are all terminated:

termset : *Node_store* → (*Token*-set)-set
termset(*ns*) △ {*ts* | ∀*t* ∈ *ts* · *D*(*t*) ∉ dom *ns*}

The termination function ($\mathcal{T}_P$) is also defined in terms of a fixed point. This is built over the possible token sets. An informal explanation of the derivation of this function can be given as follows. The starting point is given by the function *termset* (i.e. those states containing only tokens that can not be modified further since they have destinations that do not apply to any nodes in the node store). The fixed point is then built by adding all states which must yield one of these states whichever node fires, and so on.

This definition is as far as it is reasonable to progress using an abstract machine. Further steps are necessary to consider the precise details found in the MDFM.

11.3   The formal semantics of the MDFM

To give the semantics of the complete machine, it is necessary to work at a slightly less abstract level. Some of the abstractions used previously need to be removed as they hide information important at this level. For example, previous definitions used a function from *Token*-set to *Token*-set to represent primitive operators. This is not sufficiently detailed to characterize the machine exactly and so is replaced by enumeration of available operators. These operators do not conform exactly to those present in the Manchester hardware but represent a somewhat idealized representation of them. This decision is justified on the grounds of simplicity. [12] Most of the modifications made are of this nature.

As before, the new definition is built by expanding the previous definition where possible. However, due to the increasing length, a slightly different style of definition, making use of more subsidiary functions is adopted making it necessary to modify some of the earlier work.

More significantly, matching functions and associated matching actions are introduced. As can be seen below, this causes some increase in the complexity of the defi-

---

[11]The following conventions simplify considerations of input/output: tokens which are addressed to a destination not within the node store (i.e. *NA*(*D*(*t*)) ∉ dom *ns*) are assumed to be output; it is assumed that any program which has a state composed entirely of output tokens has terminated.

[12]Given that the actual instruction set is microcodable, this is reasonable even from a practical viewpoint.

nition. This is caused by the fact that it is no longer possible to represent nonmatching as the identity relation. Previously, nonmatching was equivalent to nothing happening and firing meant tokens were consumed. Special matching may introduce extra tokens, both for success and fail cases. This means further checking of the state and additional processes for firing have to be added.

However, a simplification is also possible. Since the MDFM is restricted to either unary or binary nodes, it is no longer necessary for nodes to hold information about the number of expected inputs as this is deducible from inspection of the matching function of the incoming token (unary if *BY*; binary otherwise (remembering Section 11.1)).

A list of differences from the previous definition is given below along with an indication of the reason for the modification.

1. Type checking and error detail are added – these use the extra information carried by tokens to perform some error checking.

2. Tokens carry type information – this is necessary to reflect the 'strong typing' present in the machine.

3. Labels are expanded – this is to allow labels to be used both to separate tokens in multiple instantiations of a piece of graph and to separate elements of a data structure. [13]

4. Matching functions are included in destinations to enable matching actions to be considered.

5. Operators are made explicit – this is done to allow a more precise characterization of the actual machine. Not all implemented operators are included.

6. Alternative result destinations are included – this addition is necessary to deal with branching and switching nodes. In fact, the hardware only gives a restricted version of this facility but it can be achieved using *DUP* nodes.

7. Literals are added to nodes – that is, constant values could be attached to one input of a binary node removing the need to pass in fixed constants.

8. The identity relation used in previous definitions to represent 'no firing' is replaced by an operator allowing for deferred failures – this is forced by the fact that defer and wait have a slightly different action. The matching functions of waiting tokens are not considered again (they are within the store). On the other hand, a deferred token is represented as if the defer had not occurred.

---

[13]Only two fields are given since the third field is used in practice to separate a special case of multiple instantiation.

9. The test of a node's readiness to fire is more complex. It is no longer enough to simply test if the cardinality of the ready set is equal to the number of expected inputs since action is also required in the case of some failures involving special matching functions.

10. The meaning function for nodes ($\mathcal{M}_N$) is rewritten – this is again made necessary by the possibility of failure actions.

11. An additional meaning function is included ($\mathcal{M}_{OP}$) – this is used in conjunction with the enumerated set to define the available primitive operations.

12. Test and special action functions are added – to deal with matching functions.

13. One further complexity is introduced by the use of the *GCL* node. This node returns a unique identifier (color) each time it fires. In the machine, this is possible by the use of a global variable containing a set of unused colors. Given the applicative style of the definition, this is difficult to reflect here without the extra complexity of passing an extra parameter through all levels of the definition. In order to avoid this, the notation is abused and an external variable is used, following the operation definition style of VDM.

As can be seen most of the above present no particular difficulties. The exception is the treatment of matching functions, which is explained in detail below.

It is not feasible to present the full definition here, it can be found in [Jon86b]. The following is a skeleton of the complete definition which serves to illustrate the structure.

The complete definition

The basic types are extended to contain complete information.

$Token$ :: V : *Value*
$\quad\quad\quad$ TY : *Type*
$\quad\quad\quad$ L : *Label*
$\quad\quad\quad$ D : *Destination*

Type = **Machine types e.g.** INT,COLOR

$Label$ :: C : *Color*
$\quad\quad\quad$ I : *Index*

$Destination$ :: NA : *Node_address*
$\quad\quad\quad\quad\quad$ MF : *Matching_function*
$\quad\quad\quad\quad\quad$ IP : *Input_point*

Matching_function = {EW,...,EA}

$$\vdots$$

Node :: *O*   : *Operator*
          D   : *Nextdestinations*
          LIT : *Literal*

Operator = **Primitive Machine Operations**

$$\vdots$$

The meaning of a program is largely as before. The extension is to allow a more general test for an action occurring, to allow for special matching functions:

$\mathcal{M}_P$: *Node_store* → (*Token*-set × *Token*-set)-set
$\mathcal{M}_P$ [ns] $\triangleq$ **fix** $\mathcal{R} \cdot nfail(s) \cup \bigcup \{\mathcal{M}_N$ [$ns(na), na$]$;\; \mathcal{R} \mid na \in$ dom $ns\}$
   where
   $s = \{ts \in Token\text{-set} \mid \neg\, \exists na \in$ dom $ns \cdot is\_action(ts, na)\}$

The termination function is also similar to the previous definition:

$\mathcal{T}_P$: *Node_store* → (*Token*-set)-set
$\mathcal{T}_P$ [ns] $\triangleq$ **fix** $\mathcal{S} \cdot baseset(ns) \cup$
       $\bigcup \{\{ts \in$ dom $\mathcal{M}_N$ [$ns(na), na$] $\mid \forall ts' \cdot ts\mathcal{M}_N$ [$ns(na), na$] ts'
           $\Rightarrow ts' \in \mathcal{S}\} \mid na \in$ dom $ns\}$

The $\mathcal{M}_N$ function now has to allow for special failures as well as normal firing:

$\mathcal{M}_N$: *Node* × *Node_address* → (*Token*-set × *Token*-set)-set
$\mathcal{M}_N$ [$mk\text{-}Node(op, nd, l), na$] $\triangleq$
   $ident(na) \cup fireaction(na, op, nd, l) \cup failaction(na, op, nd)$

The meaning of an *Operator* is given by $\mathcal{M}_{OP}$. This function also generates any extra tokens caused by special success matching:

$\mathcal{M}_{OP}$: *Operator* × *Token*-set × *Nextdestinations* × *Literal* → *Token*-set
$\mathcal{M}_{OP}$ [op, ts, ds, l] $\triangleq$
     the result of performing the operation plus extra match tokens

The rest of the definition consists of subsidiary functions handing the details of this scheme.

As was mentioned above, most of the extra complexity in this definition is caused by the mechanisms added to handle matching functions. To facilitate the understanding of this, an informal explanation of the way in which matching is modelled is given below.

In the previous definitions, matching was implicitly extract wait, i.e. pure dataflow. This resulted in the simple mechanism of removing tokens from the state when finding matches, and performing an identity transformation in the case of waiting. In the complete definition, the matching functions are divided into three general cases:

1. Successful matching actions.

2. Normal failing actions, i.e. wait and defer.

3. Special fail actions.

The first case, that of successful matching, is dealt with by an extra section to the $\mathcal{M}_{OP}$ function. (In some sense, successful matching and firing could legitimately be regarded as closely linked since all tokens succeeding in matching immediately proceed to fire.) Extra tokens are generated and added to the state to represent the effect of special matchings. In the case of extract, no extra tokens are generated. (Firing tokens are consumed in the *fireaction* function.) Preserve causes a copy of the waiting token (identified by the *NIL* matching function) to be added to the state. Increment and decrement cause a token with the appropriately adjusted value to be generated.

Normal failing, i.e. failures that do not 'change' the state, is handled by the *nfail* operator. The reason for the quotes in the previous sentence is the fact that wait does require a slight modification to the state. It is necessary to identify the token as having undergone a failed matching, i.e. being resident in the store, for subsequent successful matchings. To enable this, the matching function of the waiting token is replaced with *NIL*. This is necessary to avoid the selection of the wrong token's succeed function on subsequent matches. The defer action leaves the state completely unchanged. This would be expected since it is primarily an 'engineering' solution to a problem and could be imagined to have the meaning 'forget that ever happened and try again later'.

The final case, that the fail matching functions requiring special action, is a little more complex. This condition is detected by the test function *failaction*. This uses the function *specialfail* to examine the state for incomplete input sets containing a token which has a matching function that is a member of the *Failmf* set. The function *failres* uses the subsidiary function *ft* to generate the appropriate new token, i.e. an *EMPTY* token for abort and an inverted token for generate.

This completes the record of the derivation of the formal semantics for the MDFM. The full definition contains some simplifications of the actual machine but these were simply to reduce the length of the definitions to a manageable size. All of the important characteristics have been described and the complete detail could be included at the cost of increased bulk. It should be noted that the definition is, in some sense, parameterized on certain features to the level of the $\mathcal{M}_{OP}$ function. To give a semantics for a different version of the same machine, e.g. with different matching functions, the same general definition could be used. To make this definition fully parameterized on these sets, it would be necessary to add another level of function below $\mathcal{M}_{OP}$ to deal with matching separately.

11.4   Conclusions

This work shows a complete model for an existing piece of hardware. This is, of course, not the ideal way to proceed: it would have been better to have designed the 'implementation' from the 'specification'. However, working from a real example brings out some interesting points.

As can be seen from [Jon86b], a model which deals with the intricacies of the 'real world' is far from ideal from the point of view of reasoning about the system. It would have been convenient to have a more abstract model (of which the model in Section 11.3 was a verified refinement) to reason about.

As can be seen from the above, there is not a great deal of difference between the model of a parallel machine given here and the more common sequential machines seen previously. The major differences come at the level of the structure required to model the parallelism: relations in place of functions. The other modification made to the specification language in this work is to allow explicit use of the fixed point operator **fix** since this made to construction of the proofs (in [Jon86b]) easier. It should still be recognizable as VDM.

Acknowledgements

Thanks are due to: Cliff Jones, who supervised this work; the Dataflow Group at Manchester for providing necessary information, and the SERC, for providing financial support.

12

Formally Describing Interactive Systems

Lynn S. Marshall

The specification and design of user interfaces is an extremely challenging subject area. Not only does it involve the difficult aesthetic and human factor issues associated with layout, use of color, information display, structure hierarchy, ease of use, learning efficiency, etc. but it also requires the precise specification of the dialog structure between the user and the system. Dialog specification is important because it provides an abstract representation of the legal set of interactions between the user and the system allowing properties such as dialog consistency, safety, liveness and security to be analyzed. This chapter addresses the development of a formal system for the specification of user interfaces. Its first part discusses the use of VDM and statecharts for this purpose. Interaction between a user and a system may be viewed as a flow of control between operations. Operations are specified in VDM and the flow of control is specified using statecharts. To prove properties about the dialog, the meaning of statecharts must be established and proof rules derived. These issues are tackled in the second half of the paper and a number of proofs demonstrated. The VDM used in this chapter does not conform strictly to the standard. The semantics of pre-conditions have been changed, statechart labels have been introduced and are used within the VDM operation specifications. In addition a number of abbreviations have been introduced; for instance only abbreviated ext clauses are used. This study should be viewed as showing how a formal system may be extended rather than as an example of the use of standard VDM.

12.1 Introduction

Computer science is a relatively young field. Just a few decades ago there were only a few computers in existence. They were very expensive, owned by large companies, and used only by specially trained personnel. Today, smaller computers are generally available and the use of computers of all sizes is widespread. As the number of applications for computers grows, the need for hardware and software to function correctly becomes critical. **Formal methods** have emerged to assist in this area. The term 'formal methods' encompasses both formal description and verified design. Formal description involves the use of a mathematical notation to define the function of a system, while verified designs use formal reification techniques for developing systems in a way which can be proved correct with respect to the formal description. Since computer systems are used by workers in all disciplines, the area of **user interface** design has become very important. Not only must computer users get the correct results, it should also be easy for them to obtain these results. The area of user interface design is in its infancy and few concrete guidelines exist. Perhaps the application of formal description methods to user interface design will provide new insights into both fields.

The user interface

Many computer systems are of an interactive nature. At each stage of the interaction the user enters some input and the computer responds to it. The component of the interactive system which acts as an interpreter between the user and the underlying application program is the **user interface**:

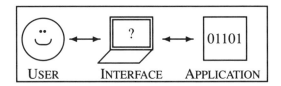

The user interface controls who has the initiative at any stage in the dialog. It translates the user's request into a form the application will accept and the application's reply into a form that the user can understand. The role of the interface is to allow the user to utilize software with a minimum of effort.

The user interface is given many different names in the literature. These include user computer interface, human/computer interface (HCI), computer/human interface (CHI), human/computer dialog, human/machine interface, man/machine interface (MMI), and interactive dialog. The term **user interface** was chosen for brevity. It is understood that the user is interfacing with a computer. Also, this name does not unnecessarily restrict the users of the system to humans and/or males.

By any name, a good interface is an essential part of any system. Even an excellent system will be useless without an adequate interface. The user interface should be easy to learn and easy to use. It should be simple and reliable, yet flexible and transparent to the user. The interface should also be consistent and efficient, and as independent of the application as is feasible. Clear documentation and diagnostics are vital. However, these qualities are hard to define and measure. Also, many design choices are unclear. The user's reaction to various user interfaces is difficult to appraise. User interface design may need to take into account the different users of the system, the applications that the users need to access, and the input and output devices available. The fact that the user interface is dependent on so many system-specific details adds to the difficulty in proposing design guidelines.

Due to these problems, user interface design is not an exact science. There remains much disagreement and many unknown quantities. Currently, user interface design remains an iterative procedure utilizing social scientists and psychologists in an attempt to develop systems acceptable to the user community. See Section 12.2 for a further discussion of user interface design.

Formal description methods

Describing a system formally involves the use of a mathematical notation. In this way a precise description of a system's function can be given. A formal description is abstract. It describes **what** a system does without stating **how** this should be accomplished. Given a formal description, properties of the system can be formally stated and, provided the notation has a sound mathematical basis, proved. Once the system designer is satisfied with the description he can have confidence in any system constructed from it. A formal description of a system is valuable to both system designers and users. It is a precise standard for an implementation. It provides useful documentation for the user, and it can be used as a tool in system analysis and design. A formal description is a functional or semantic definition in that it describes what a system does.

A formal description is often referred to in the literature as a formal specification. This term is avoided as it can be misleading. Although a particular formal description may be adopted as the specification of a system, not all formal descriptions are necessarily specifications. Note that while it may be possible to prove that a system satisfies a formal description, no formal comparison can be made between this description and the original informal system specification.

A formal description should be understandable, testable and maintainable, but not necessarily optimal. It should be complete, consistent, unambiguous and nonredundant. The method should be concise and readable, but capable of coping with new technology and radical principles.

Some authors argue that a system description can benefit from being slightly informal. Informal descriptions may be easier to write and understand, and can be useful in some instances, but, for a description notation to be used for analyzing properties of the proposed system, a formal mathematical basis is necessary.

Many researchers feel that an executable description method is best as it allows rapid prototyping of the description and iterative system design. However, an executable description language leads to 'program-like' thinking and discourages abstractness, the major aim of a formal description.

Formal methods are currently employed mainly for describing and proving properties of noninteractive, or static, systems. Error handling is not as vital in a static system as in an interactive system. Due to this, the formal description usually deals only with valid input, leaving the interception of invalid input and production of error messages to the implementor. Even if an interactive system is considered, the formal description usually considers only the application, ignoring the user interface along with key issues like error handling, on-line help information, and interrupts.

Formal methods and the user interface

The aim of this chapter is to discover a formal technique which meets the requirements outlined below and is suitable for describing the user interface of an interactive system. The user interface introduces new challenges to the area of formal description. The interactive nature of the interface makes the flow of control a vital aspect. Error handling, on-line assistance, interrupts, and response time are issues not dealt with in the formal description of a static system or application. While some portion of the user interface description may need to be dependent on the input device, interface style, and/or application, it would be ideal if a large part of the interface description was standard.

A formal description of an interactive system and its user interface will be most helpful if it is a tool both for the user interface designer or design team, and for the users of the proposed system. To be of use to both these groups the notation must be both rigorous and easy to understand. The user wants a general feel for how the system and its operations can be used, while the designer must know what capabilities he must build into the system.

To both the user and designer, questions such as 'what happens next?' and 'what happens after X?' are of vital importance. This flow of control within the system should be determined by a glance at the user interface description. To allow the user interface designer to consider only the user interface or a portion thereof, a split of the formal description into manageable sections will be necessary, especially in a large and complex system. Dividing the description into various levels, each giving more and more detail, would be appropriate, as would be a modular presentation of the description which separates the various components of the system and the user interface.

At the same time the notation should be simple, concise and understandable. It should not be necessary to have much special training to follow the description. Also, the formal description must be abstract. While the flow of control is important for illustrating the overall effects of the user interface, the description should not impose order when it is unnecessary. Finally, a sound basis in mathematics is needed for the notation to be rigorous enough for claims concerning properties of the user interface to be formally verified.

Introducing a formal notation will not suddenly cause all user interfaces which have been described using this technique to be ideal. However, a formal description technique which can easily express the user interface of an interactive system should reduce the need for iterative user interface design. If the use of formal methods can help in the construction of user interfaces or in the determination of what makes a good user interface, research in this area is worthwhile.

Synopsis

Section 12.2 describes the current research in user interface design and examines ways in which formal methods can be of use. Section 12.3 describes the adopted approach, while an example using the proposed approach is presented in Section 12.4. The semantics of the method and sample proofs are given in Sections 12.5 and 12.6. Section 12.7 gives the conclusions and suggestions for further work. Further details, additional examples and many more references are contained in [Mar86].

12.2 Formal methods and the user interface

This section examines how formal methods can best be applied to assist in the design of user interfaces.

User interface design

Many researchers are attempting to find ways of improving user interface design. Currently, however, most interfaces are designed in a haphazard manner. Many authors lament the lack of methods and tools to aid in user interface design, or claim that much of the research is too philosophical to be of any help. Some researchers set extremely optimistic goals involving analyzing the communication facilities of the human brain and applying the findings to user interface design.

As discussed in Section 12.1, researchers have not yet reached agreement over the necessary characteristics of a user interface. An abundance of adjectives appear in the literature containing user interface guidelines. These include considerate, courteous, respectful, and helpful; reliable, adaptable, and easy to use; compatible and brief; efficient; flexible, transparent, and easy to learn; and understandable, simple, consistent, clear, and versatile. The term 'user-friendly' is often mentioned though numerous researchers agree that its meaning is unclear. How 'friendly' an interface is depends on the task and the user. The ease of use of a system depends on various factors. Also, there is a trade-off between ease of learning and ease of use. Recommendations for user interface design often conflict thus making the user interface designer's task a difficult one.

Formal description of user interface properties

Many of the issues arising in interactive computer graphics are related to those of user interface design. One area examined in Chapter 13 is that of describing the representation of a straight line on a raster device. It is possible to formally describe various properties which must be met by any reasonable approximation to such a straight line. A description such as this is ideal in that it is abstract, very general, easy to understand, and useful. Formal verification techniques can be applied to any line drawing algorithm to ensure that it satisfies the required properties.

Often, a formal description supplies constraints on a system, rather than giving a complete definition [GH86]. Unfortunately, research in user interface design has not yet reached the stage where this technique can be successfully applied. [GHW82] recommends formally stating as many constraints as possible and the generative user engineering principles (gueps) proposed in [HT85] aim to do this. However, due to disagreement over various features and the informality of properties proposed for the user interface, formalizing a complete set of guidelines is not currently feasible.

Considering the user interface in isolation

Since it is not appropriate to try to describe the desirable properties of any user interface perhaps a technique for describing the user interface of a particular interactive system would be helpful. If formal descriptions were formulated for each of the user, application, and user interface they could then be considered separately or together to prove properties concerning the system. However, when designing the user interface it is not always possible to consider the interface independently of the particular interactive system. Often the application, user, devices, and required interface style are major considerations in design decisions. The designer often wants to exploit these characteristics to get the best interface possible. Current research in the area of user interface management systems (UIMSs) [BLSS83, GE84] encourages separation of the user interface from the application. However, researchers often admit that this is not always attainable and a UIMS is usually only partially independent of the rest of the system.

Discussions of user interface dependence and independence occur frequently in the literature. One paper [BLSS83] suggests that the user interface should be as independent as possible of the input and output devices, language, machine, and interaction technique. [OD83] opts for application independence and device dependence. Some authors also recommend device dependence [Bae80, NS81], while another [HT85] suggests that the user interface should be user dependent. It is possible that these discrepancies can be explained by considering the amount of detail in each author's view of the user interface. However, a technique for describing the user interface alone could well prove inadequate to aid in user interface design.

Formal description of an interactive system

Thus neither describing a list of properties of the ideal user interface, nor developing a technique to describe just the user interface of a system seems profitable. It was finally decided that the best way to advance the use of formal methods in user interface design would be to discover or develop a formal description notation appropriate for the entire interactive system, with emphasis on the user interface.

12.3 Approach

The required properties of the formal description technique are the following:

flow of control. The user interface governs the flow of control within an interactive system. The formal description should clearly illustrate this general, or top level, view of the interactive system.

levels. To allow the system designer or user to look at the formal description in as much or as little detail as desired, the description should be split into levels ranging from the top level flow of control discussed above, to the details of each operation within the system.

modular. All but the top level of the formal description should be modular. This will enable the design of each operation to be considered in isolation.

concise. The notation should allow the necessary concepts to be expressed in a concise manner. A notation which is clumsy or verbose will unnecessarily lengthen the description.

understandable. The formal description technique should be easy to understand. As well as satisfying the points above, the notation should be as clear and simple as possible.

abstract. While a user interface may be partially dependent on the particular interactive system, the description should still remain abstract. The formal description should not dictate any issues which need not be resolved until the implementation stage.

Although the top level flow of control is vital to the design of the system, it is often the case that, at lower levels, the ordering of certain events is immaterial at the description stage.

sound. To allow formal proofs of correctness to be carried out, the description technique should have a sound mathematical basis.

VDM [Jon90] uses **pre**- and **post**-conditions for the abstract description of operations. This method satisfies all of the requirements except that it is inadequate for illustrating the flow of control. The best formal description method for showing the top level flow of control are transition-state diagrams (TSDs). In fact, statecharts [Har84], a form of extended TSD, seem to be the best choice. The chosen approach is a combination of statecharts and VDM operations. A statechart describes the toplevel flow of control between the operations of the system, while each operation is described by a **pre**- and a **post**-condition. The details of the approach are described below. Note that a restricted form of statechart is used to enable the semantics of the method to be fully described.

Statecharts

A statechart shows the flow of control of a system. A statechart can be any one of the following.

Operation. A simple operation is illustrated:

Composition. A sequential composition of two statecharts, $S = S_1; S_2$, is illustrated:

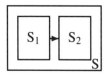

Selection. The selection of at most one statechart from a list.
IF = **if** c_1 **then** S_1 | c_2 **then** S_2 | $\cdots$ | c_n **then** S_n **fi**:

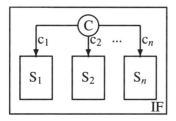

Loop. A looping construct, LP = **loop** S_1 **if** c **exit** S_2 **pool**:

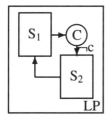

Wait. Wait for a condition to become true. The wait construct assumes that there is something outside the system which can effect the state. This construction is normally used to wait for the user to enter input before attempting to read it in. The need for this construct is explained later in this section. **wait** c **tiaw** is illustrated:

A statechart must not attempt to force an operation to occur when its **pre**-condition is not satisfied. Any labels on the statechart (e.g. 'c' above) must be defined in terms of the data types in the state. It is often convenient to use these labels in the **pre**-condition of the corresponding operations.

Logon example

Basic logon

This example involves a user attempting to logon to a computer system. The user can type ahead but the input queue is restricted and if he exceeds the queue length his input is discarded. If the entered user name is invalid a message is printed. The logon terminates when the user enters a valid name.

User interface statechart

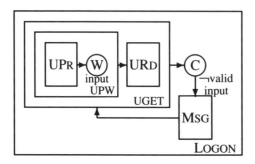

LOGON = **loop** UGET **if** valid input **exit** MSG **pool**
UGET = UPW ; UREAD
UPW   = UPRMT ; **wait** input **tiaw**

User statechart

USER = **loop** INPT **pool**

State

State ::	uprompt	: String	prompt for user name (cn)
	invmsg	: String	invalid message (cn)
	users	: Word-set	valid users (cn)
	qlen	: $\mathbb{N}_1$	maximum input queue length (cn)
	input	: String	input queue
	curuser	: Word	current user name
	screen	: Text	output to screen

$Text = String^*$

$String = Word^*$

$Word = Letter^*$

$Char = Letter \cup Space$

Invariant

len *input* $\leq$ *qlen*

Statechart label definitions

valid input $\equiv$ *curuser* $\in$ *users*
input $\equiv$ *input* $\neq$ [ ]
tr $\equiv$ true

Operations

Set the initial values of the state. Note that the constant (cn) portion of the state is dependent on the system and the values given below illustrate one possible choice:

INIT
ext cn *uprompt, invmsg, users, qlen*
   wr *input, curuser, screen*
post *uprompt* = [Login:] $\wedge$ *invmsg* = [Invalid, login] $\wedge$
   users = {Tom, Dick, Harriet} $\wedge$ *qlen* = 50 $\wedge$ *input* = [ ] $\wedge$
   curuser = '' $\wedge$ *screen* = [ ]

The prompt is displayed on the screen:

UPRMT
ext cn *uprompt*
   wr *screen*
post *screen* = *addstr* $\left(\overleftarrow{screen}, uprompt \right)$

The user can enter a word at any time. The word is displayed and, provided the input queue is not full, added to the input queue:

> INPT
> ext cn *qlen*
>   wr *input, screen*
> post $\exists w \in$ *Word* ·
>
> $$input = \text{if len } \overleftarrow{input} < qlen$$
> $$\text{then } \overleftarrow{input} \ \hat{} \ [w]$$
> $$\text{else } \overleftarrow{input}$$
> $$\wedge \ screen = addstr\left(\overleftarrow{screen}, w\right)$$

If there is input it is moved to the current user field:

> UREAD
> ext wr *input, curuser*
> pre input
> post $curuser = \text{hd } \overleftarrow{input} \wedge input = \text{tl } \overleftarrow{input}$

If the user name entered is invalid a message is printed:

> MSG
> ext cn *invmsg, users*
>   rd *curuser*
>   wr *screen*
> pre ¬valid input
> post $screen = addstr\left(\overleftarrow{screen}, invmsg\right)$

Function

Add a string to some text:

> $addstr : Text \times String \rightarrow Text$
> $addstr(t, s) \quad \triangle \quad t \ \hat{} \ [s]$

Quoting operation example

If the screen in the preceding example may be optionally cleared whenever a new string is added, then the *addstr* function would no longer be adequate. Instead, a DISP operation could be defined as follows.

Display information on the screen. The screen may be cleared first:

DISP *(S: String)*

ext wr *screen*

post *screen* = $\left(\overleftarrow{screen} \,\hat{}\, [s] \right) \vee [s]$

The operations using *addstr* would be redefined to quote DISP. For example, the prompt is displayed on the screen:

UPRMT

ext cn *uprompt*

   wr *screen*

post **post**-DISP$\left(uprompt, \overleftarrow{screen}, screen \right)$

Splitting the formal description

When splitting the description into levels, statecharts seem suited only to the outmost level, with **pre**- and **post**-conditions for the second level and, if necessary, functions giving even more detail. In splitting the formal description between the top two layers the major consideration is how the flow of control can best be illustrated. If the user interface wants to display a prompt and then read in a value entered by the user the interface must PRMT then READ. However, if the interface must store a value (for future use) and display a message, then STORE and DISP is more appropriate as the order is immaterial.

In the former case, PRMT then READ, it is best to use a statechart:

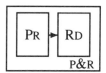

However, for STORE and DISP a single operation is appropriate. Store and display the input:

STORE & DISP

ext rd *input, message*

   wr *save, disp*

pre *input* ≠ nil

post *save* = *input* ∧ *disp* = $\overleftarrow{disp} \,\hat{}\, message$

Applying this type of reasoning allows each notation to be employed when it is most suitable.

Discussion of wait

The LOGON example shows the user and user interface as separate processes (each has its own statechart) while the application is tied in with the user interface. This representation is chosen since it is realistic. The user interface can control the application program but it is not always possible or desirable for the user interface to control the user. Neither is it plausible for the user to have complete control over the user interface.

The wait construct described is a tie between the user and interface:

input

It is employed when it is necessary for the user interface to wait for input. This construct was chosen as it indicates that there may be a time delay, and because it keeps the user and interface as independent as possible.

Other representations exist. For example, since INPT is the only operation which can make 'input' true, another statechart is:

However, this statechart obscures any time delay that may occur, and there is no clear indication that the INPT operation may also occur at any other time.

12.4   Example

The LOGON example of Section 12.3 can quite easily be extended.

Add password

The user must enter a password after entering his user name. The password is not displayed on the screen, and any input entered before the password prompt appears is discarded. The interface statechart is updated. The user's statechart does not change. *users* becomes a map. *pprompt*, *echo* and *curpswd* are added to the state, and the definition of 'valid input' changes. The operations INIT and MSG are updated, and PPRMT and PREAD are added.

Statechart

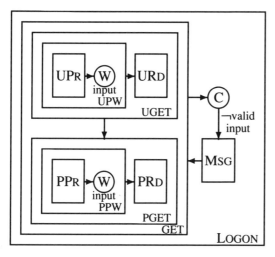

State

$$
\begin{array}{lll}
State & :: & uprompt & : & String \\
& & pprompt & : & String \\
& & invmsg & : & String \\
& & users & : & Word \xrightarrow{m} Word \\
& & qlen & : & \mathbb{N}_1 \\
& & input & : & String \\
& & echo & : & \mathbb{B} \\
& & curuser & : & Word \\
& & curpswd & : & Word \\
& & screen & : & Text
\end{array}
$$

     prompt for password (cn)

     valid user/passwords (cn)

     echo flag

     current password

Invariant

len *input* ≤ *qlen*

Statechart label

valid input ≡ *curuser* ∈ dom *users* ∧ *curpswd* = *users*(*curuser*)

Operations

Set the initial values of the state. Note that the constant (cn) portion of the state is dependent on the system and the values given below illustrate one possible choice:

INIT
ext cn *uprompt, pprompt, invmsg, users, qlen*
    wr *input, echo, curuser, curpswd, screen*
post *uprompt* = [Login:] ∧ *pprompt* = [Password:] ∧
    invmsg = [Invalid, login., Try, again.] ∧
    users = {Tom ↦ se3cx, Dick ↦ fred, Harriet ↦ hello} ∧
    qlen = 50 ∧ *input* = [ ] ∧ *echo* ∧ *curuser* = '' ∧
    curpswd = '' ∧ *screen* = [ ]

The password prompt is displayed on the screen, input is flushed, and echoing is turned off:

PPRMT
ext cn *pprompt*
    wr *input, echo, screen*
post ¬*echo* ∧ *input* = [ ] ∧ *screen* = $addstr\left(\overleftarrow{screen}, pprompt\right)$

If there is input it is moved to the current password field and echoing is turned on:

PREAD
ext wr *input, echo, curpswd*
pre *input*
post *echo* ∧ *curpswd* = hd $\overleftarrow{input}$ ∧ *input* = tl $\overleftarrow{input}$

If the user name and/or password entered are invalid a message is printed:

MSG
ext cn *invmsg, users*
    rd *curuser, curpswd*
    wr *screen*
pre ¬*valid input*
post *screen* = $addstr\left(\overleftarrow{screen}, invmsg\right)$

Add limit

The user has only a certain number of tries to login. Once this limit is exceeded the keyboard is locked for a certain length of time. The interface statechart is updated. A clock which ticks continuously is introduced. This is another process illustrated by the

CLOCK statechart. The user's statechart does not change. *trylimit*, *locktime*, *trynum*, and *time* are added to the state. The definitions of 'limit' and 'unlock' are given. The operations INIT and MSG change, while LOCK and TICK are added.

Interface statechart

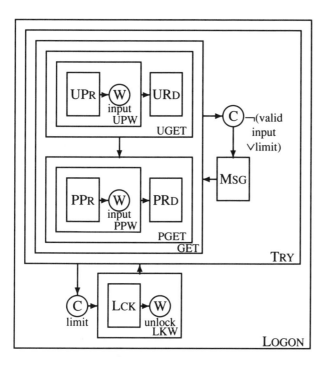

Clock statechart

State

$$
\begin{array}{rll}
State \ :: & uprompt & : String \\
& pprompt & : String \\
& invmsg & : String \\
& users & : Word \xrightarrow{m} Word \\
& echo & : \mathbb{B} \\
& trylimit & : \mathbb{N}_1 \\
& locktime & : \mathbb{N}_1 \\
& qlen & : \mathbb{N}_1 \\
& input & : String \\
& curuser & : Word \\
& curpswd & : Word \\
& screen & : Text \\
& trynum & : \mathbb{N}_1 \\
& time & : \mathbb{N}
\end{array}
$$

maximum number of tries (cn)
length of time of keyboard lock (cn)

number of tries
time since last reset

Statechart labels

limit $\equiv trynum \geq trylimit$
unlock $\equiv time \geq locktime$

Operations

Set the initial values of the state. Again, the constant (cn) portion of the state is dependent on the system and the values given below are just an example:

INIT
ext cn *uprompt, pprompt, invmsg, users, trylimit, locktime, qlen*
    wr *input, echo, curuser, curpswd, screen, trynum, time*
post *uprompt* = [Login:] $\wedge$ *pprompt* = [Password:] $\wedge$
    invmsg = [Invalid,login.,Try,again.] $\wedge$
    users = {Tom $\mapsto$ se3cx, Dick $\mapsto$ fred, Harriet $\mapsto$ hello} $\wedge$
    trylimit = 5 $\wedge$ *locktime* = 1800 $\wedge$ *qlen* = 50 $\wedge$ *input* = [ ] $\wedge$ *echo* $\wedge$
    curuser = '' $\wedge$ *curpswd* = '' $\wedge$ *screen* = [ ] $\wedge$ *trynum* = 1 $\wedge$ *time* = 0

If the user name and/or password entered are invalid a message is printed:

MSG
ext cn *invmsg, users*
    rd *curuser, curpswd*
    wr *screen, trynum*
pre $\neg\big(\text{valid input} \vee \text{limit}\big)$
post $screen = addstr\big(\overleftarrow{screen}, invmsg\big) \wedge trynum = \overleftarrow{trynum} + 1$

Reset the time to indicate the beginning of keyboard lock, and reset the try number:

LOCK
ext cn *trylimit*
    wr *trynum, time*
pre limit
post $trynum = 1 \wedge time = 0$

Clock ticks continuously:

TICK
ext wr *time*
post $time = \overleftarrow{time} + 1$

Add timeout

If the user pauses too long between typing his user name and password he must re-enter his user name. The interface statechart changes accordingly. It is illustrated in two parts to make it easier to read. The user and clock statecharts do not change. *timelimit* is added to the state. The definition of 'timeout' is given. The operations INIT and PPRMT change.

Statecharts

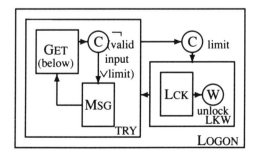

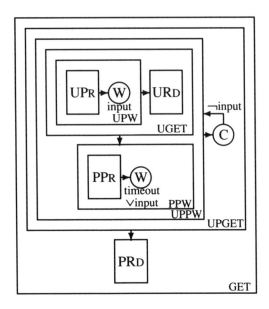

State

$$State :: uprompt : String$$
$$pprompt : String$$
$$invmsg : String$$
$$users : Word \xrightarrow{m} Word$$
$$echo : \mathbb{B}$$
$$trylimit : \mathbb{N}_1$$
$$timelimit : \mathbb{N}_1 \qquad\qquad \text{time limit for entering password (cn)}$$
$$locktime : \mathbb{N}_1$$
$$qlen : \mathbb{N}_1$$
$$input : String$$
$$curuser : Word$$
$$curpswd : Word$$
$$screen : Text$$
$$trynum : \mathbb{N}_1$$
$$time : \mathbb{N}$$

Statechart label

$$\text{timeout} \equiv time \geq timelimit$$

Operations

Set the initial values of the state. Again, the constant (cn) portion of the state is dependent on the system and the values given below are just an example:

INIT
ext cn *uprompt, pprompt, invmsg, users, trylimit, timelimit, locktime, qlen*
    wr *input, echo, curuser, curpswd, screen, trynum, time*
post *uprompt* = [Login:] ∧ *pprompt* = [Password:] ∧
    invmsg = [Invalid,login.,Try,again.] ∧
    users = {Tom ↦ se3cx, Dick ↦ fred, Harriet ↦ hello} ∧
    trylimit = 5 ∧ *timelimit* = 30 ∧ *locktime* = 1800 ∧ *qlen* = 50 ∧
    input = [ ] ∧ *echo* ∧ *curuser* = '' ∧ *curpswd* = '' ∧
    screen = [ ] ∧ *trynum* = 1 ∧ *time* = 0

The password prompt is displayed on the screen, the time reset, input flushed, and echoing turned off:

PPRMT
ext cn *pprompt*
    wr *input, echo, screen, time*
post ¬*echo* ∧ *input* = [ ] ∧ *screen* = *addstr*($\overleftarrow{screen}$, *pprompt*) ∧ *time* = 0

12.5 Semantics

Definitions

Let S be a set and R be a relation. Then:

$S \triangleleft R \triangleq \{(\overleftarrow{s},s) \in R \mid \overleftarrow{s} \in S\}$ $S \triangleleft\!\!\!- R \triangleq \{(\overleftarrow{s},s) \in R \mid \overleftarrow{s} \notin S\}$

$R \triangleright S \triangleq \{(\overleftarrow{s},s) \in R \mid s \in S\}$ $R -\!\!\!\triangleright S \triangleq \{(\overleftarrow{s},s) \in R \mid s \notin S\}$

$R^2 = R; R$ $R^+ = \bigcup_{i>0} R^i$

$R^* = \bigcup_{i\geq 0} R^i = I \cup R^+$ $\mathcal{I} = \{(s,s) \mid s \in \Sigma\}$

Semantic model

The underlying semantic model of the formal description notation assumes a global state, Σ. The semantics of a description are given by a function defining the termination set:

$$\mathcal{T}[\![\,]\!] : Desc \rightarrow \mathcal{P}(\Sigma)$$

giving all states in which the given description can be sensibly applied, and by a function describing the meaning relation:

$$\mathcal{M}[\![\,]\!] : Desc \rightarrow \mathcal{P}(\Sigma \times \Sigma)$$

giving pairs of initial and final states related to each other by the description. For a description to be implementable it is necessary that:

(1) $TS \subseteq \text{dom } \mathcal{M}[\![S]\!]$

Note that $\mathcal{T}[\![\mathcal{I}]\!] = \Sigma$ and $\mathcal{M}[\![\mathcal{I}]\!] = \mathcal{I}$.
The termination and meaning functions can also be applied to expressions:

$$\mathcal{T}[\![\,]\!] : Expr \rightarrow \mathcal{P}(\Sigma)$$

gives all states in which the given expression can be evaluated.

$$\mathcal{M}[\![\,]\!] : Expr \rightarrow (\Sigma \mapsto \mathbb{B})$$

gives the value of the expression in the states for which it is defined. Again it is necessary that:

$$\mathcal{T}[\![e]\!] \subseteq \text{dom } \mathcal{M}[\![e]\!]$$

Let c be a boolean expression. Then we can define:

$$C = \text{dom}(\mathcal{T}[\![c]\!] \triangleleft \mathcal{M}[\![c]\!] \triangleright \{true\})$$
$$\neg C = \text{dom}(\mathcal{T}[\![\neg c]\!] \triangleleft \mathcal{M}[\![\neg c]\!] \triangleright \{true\})$$
$$\bar{C} = \Sigma - C$$

For the description to be implementable it must be the case that:

$$C \cap \neg C = \{\}$$

For the operations described by **pre**- and **post**-conditions, any state allowed by the **pre**-condition should be described in the **post**-condition:

$$\forall op \in description, \forall \overleftarrow{\sigma} \in \Sigma \cdot (\textbf{pre-}op(\overleftarrow{\sigma}) \Rightarrow \exists \sigma \in \Sigma \cdot \textbf{post-}op(\overleftarrow{\sigma}, \sigma))$$

To allow for systematic program development from the description a method of reifying the description is needed. A reification, $[[S']]$, of a description, $[[S]]$, is said to satisfy the description provided:

> (2) $[[S']]$ sat $[[S]]$
> i.e. $\mathcal{T}[[S]] \subseteq \mathcal{T}[[S']]$
> > (S' terminates whenever S does)
> and $\mathcal{T}[[S]] \lhd \mathcal{M}[[S']] \subseteq \mathcal{M}[[S]]$
> > (over the termination set of S the meaning of S' is contained in the meaning of S)

So if we claim to have found the meaning relation and termination set for a statechart construct we need to show that:

> (I) $\mathcal{T}[[cons]] \subseteq$ dom $\mathcal{M}[[cons]]$
> (II) $[[cons']]$ sat $[[cons]]$

provided these two clauses are true for each statechart within the construct.

The following sections present the termination sets and meaning relations for the statechart constructs.

Concatenation

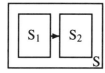

Written:

$$S_1; S_2$$

Claim:

The meaning relation and termination set for concatenation are:

$$\mathcal{M}[[S_1; S_2]] \triangleq \mathcal{M}[[S_1]]; \mathcal{M}[[S_2]]$$
$$\mathcal{T}[[S_1; S_2]] \triangleq \mathcal{T}[[S_1]] - \text{dom}\,(\mathcal{M}[[S_1]] \triangleright \mathcal{T}[[S_2]])$$

Have:

Here the substatecharts are S_1 and S_2, so we assume that (1) and (2) are true for these two statecharts:

A. $\mathcal{T}[\![S_1]\!] \subseteq \mathrm{dom}\,\mathcal{M}[\![S_1]\!]$ and
B. $\mathcal{T}[\![S_2]\!] \subseteq \mathrm{dom}\,\mathcal{M}[\![S_2]\!]$ by (1)

$[\![S_1']\!]$ sat $[\![S_1]\!]$ by (2) i.e.:
C. $\mathcal{T}[\![S_1]\!] \subseteq \mathcal{T}[\![S_1']\!]$ and
D. $\mathcal{T}[\![S_1]\!] \vartriangleleft \mathcal{M}[\![S_1']\!] \subseteq \mathcal{M}[\![S_1]\!]$

$[\![S_2']\!]$ sat $[\![S_2]\!]$ by (2) i.e.:
E. $\mathcal{T}[\![S_2]\!] \subseteq \mathcal{T}[\![S_2']\!]$ and
F. $\mathcal{T}[\![S_2]\!] \vartriangleleft \mathcal{M}[\![S_2']\!] \subseteq \mathcal{M}[\![S_2]\!]$

Prove:

Now we can prove (I) and (II) by proving 1., 2., and 3.:

(I) $\mathcal{T}[\![S_1; S_2]\!] \subseteq \mathrm{dom}\,\mathcal{M}[\![S_1; S_2]\!]$ or:
1. $\mathcal{T}[\![S_1]\!] - \mathrm{dom}\,(\mathcal{M}[\![S_1]\!] \vartriangleright \mathcal{T}[\![S_2]\!]) \subseteq \mathrm{dom}\,(\mathcal{M}[\![S_1]\!]; \mathcal{M}[\![S_2]\!])$
(II) $[\![S_1'; S_2']\!]$ sat $[\![S_1; S_2]\!]$ i.e.:
   $\mathcal{T}[\![S_1; S_2]\!] \subseteq \mathcal{T}[\![S_1'; S_2']\!]$ and $\mathcal{T}[\![S_1; S_2]\!] \vartriangleleft \mathcal{M}[\![S_1'; S_2']\!] \subseteq \mathcal{M}[\![S_1; S_2]\!]$ or:
2. $\mathcal{T}[\![S_1]\!] - \mathrm{dom}\,(\mathcal{M}[\![S_1]\!] \vartriangleright \mathcal{T}[\![S_2]\!]) \subseteq \mathcal{T}[\![S_1']\!] - \mathrm{dom}\,(\mathcal{M}[\![S_1']\!] \vartriangleright \mathcal{T}[\![S_2']\!])$ and
3. $\mathcal{T}[\![S_1]\!] - \mathrm{dom}\,(\mathcal{M}[\![S_1]\!] \vartriangleright \mathcal{T}[\![S_2]\!]) \vartriangleleft \mathcal{M}[\![S_1']\!]; \mathcal{M}[\![S_2']\!] \subseteq \mathcal{M}[\![S_1]\!]; \mathcal{M}[\![S_2]\!]$

Note 1:

Proving this here will simplify proof 1.

$$\mathcal{T}[\![S_1]\!] - \mathrm{dom}\,(\mathcal{M}[\![S_1]\!] \vartriangleright \mathcal{T}[\![S_2]\!]) \subseteq \mathrm{dom}\,(\mathcal{T}[\![S_1]\!] \vartriangleleft \mathcal{M}[\![S_1]\!] \vartriangleright \mathcal{T}[\![S_2]\!])$$

Intuitively, the set of initial states for which $S_1; S_2$ always terminates is contained in the set of initial states for which $S_1; S_2$ could terminate:

Note 1 proof:

$\mathcal{T}[\![S_1]\!] - \mathrm{dom}\,(\mathcal{M}[\![S_1]\!] \vartriangleright \mathcal{T}[\![S_2]\!])$
a. $= \mathcal{T}[\![S_1]\!] - \mathrm{dom}\,(\mathcal{T}[\![S_1]\!] \vartriangleleft \mathcal{M}[\![S_1]\!] \vartriangleright \mathcal{T}[\![S_2]\!])$ by defn. $-$.
b. $= \mathrm{dom}\,(\mathcal{T}[\![S_1]\!] \vartriangleleft \mathcal{M}[\![S_1]\!]) - \mathrm{dom}\,(\mathcal{T}[\![S_1]\!] \vartriangleleft \mathcal{M}[\![S_1]\!] \vartriangleright \mathcal{T}[\![S_2]\!])$ by A.
c. $\subseteq \mathrm{dom}\,\left((\mathcal{T}[\![S_1]\!] \vartriangleleft \mathcal{M}[\![S_1]\!]) - (\mathcal{T}[\![S_1]\!] \vartriangleleft \mathcal{M}[\![S_1]\!] \vartriangleright \mathcal{T}[\![S_2]\!])\right)$ by defn. dom .
d. $= \mathrm{dom}\,(\mathcal{T}[\![S_1]\!] \vartriangleleft \mathcal{M}[\![S_1]\!] \vartriangleright \mathcal{T}[\![S_2]\!])$ by defn. $-, \vartriangleright$.

Proof 1:

$\mathcal{T}\,[\![S_1]\!] - \mathsf{dom}\,(\mathcal{M}[\![S_1]\!] \, \triangleright \, \mathcal{T}\,[\![S_2]\!]) \subseteq \mathsf{dom}\,(\mathcal{M}[\![S_1]\!]; \mathcal{M}[\![S_2]\!])$:

$\mathcal{T}\,[\![S_1]\!] - \mathsf{dom}\,(\mathcal{M}[\![S_1]\!] \, \triangleright \, \mathcal{T}\,[\![S_2]\!])$

a. $\subseteq \mathsf{dom}\,(\mathcal{T}\,[\![S_1]\!] \, \triangleleft \, \mathcal{M}[\![S_1]\!] \, \triangleright \, \mathcal{T}\,[\![S_2]\!])$ by Note 1.

b. $\subseteq \mathsf{dom}\,(\mathcal{M}[\![S_1]\!] \, \triangleright \, \mathcal{T}\,[\![S_2]\!])$ by defn. $\triangleleft$.

c. $\subseteq \mathsf{dom}\,(\mathcal{M}[\![S_1]\!] \, \triangleright \, \mathsf{dom}\,\mathcal{M}[\![S_2]\!])$ by *B*.

d. $= \mathsf{dom}\,(\mathcal{M}[\![S_1]\!]; \mathcal{M}[\![S_2]\!])$ by defn. $\triangleright$.

Proof 2:

$\mathcal{T}\,[\![S_1]\!] - \mathsf{dom}\,(\mathcal{M}[\![S_1]\!] \, \triangleright \, \mathcal{T}\,[\![S_2]\!]) \subseteq \mathcal{T}\,[\![S_1']\!] - \mathsf{dom}\,(\mathcal{M}[\![S_1']\!] \, \triangleright \, \mathcal{T}\,[\![S_2']\!])$:

$\mathcal{T}\,[\![S_1]\!] - \mathsf{dom}\,(\mathcal{M}[\![S_1]\!] \, \triangleright \, \mathcal{T}\,[\![S_2]\!])$

a. $\subseteq \mathcal{T}\,[\![S_1]\!] - \mathsf{dom}\,(\mathcal{M}[\![S_1']\!] \, \triangleright \, \mathcal{T}\,[\![S_2]\!])$ by defn. $-$, and *D*.

b. $\subseteq \mathcal{T}\,[\![S_1]\!] - \mathsf{dom}\,(\mathcal{M}[\![S_1']\!] \, \triangleright \, \mathcal{T}\,[\![S_2']\!])$ by defn. $\triangleright, -$, and *E*.

c. $\subseteq \mathcal{T}\,[\![S_1']\!] - \mathsf{dom}\,(\mathcal{M}[\![S_1']\!] \, \triangleright \, \mathcal{T}\,[\![S_2']\!])$ by *C*.

Proof 3:

$(\mathcal{T}\,[\![S_1]\!] - \mathsf{dom}\,(\mathcal{M}[\![S_1]\!] \, \triangleright \, \mathcal{T}\,[\![S_2]\!])) \, \triangleleft \, \mathcal{M}[\![S_1']\!]; \mathcal{M}[\![S_2']\!] \subseteq \mathcal{M}[\![S_1]\!]; \mathcal{M}[\![S_2]\!]$:

$(\mathcal{T}\,[\![S_1]\!] - \mathsf{dom}\,(\mathcal{M}[\![S_1]\!] \, \triangleright \, \mathcal{T}\,[\![S_2]\!])) \, \triangleleft \, \mathcal{M}[\![S_1']\!]; \mathcal{M}[\![S_2']\!]$

a. $= (\mathcal{T}\,[\![S_1]\!] - \mathsf{dom}\,(\mathcal{M}[\![S_1]\!] \, \triangleright \, \mathcal{T}\,[\![S_2]\!])) \, \triangleleft \, (\mathcal{T}\,[\![S_1]\!] \, \triangleleft \, \mathcal{M}[\![S_1']\!]); \mathcal{M}[\![S_2']\!]$

by defn. $\triangleleft$.

b. $\subseteq (\mathcal{T}\,[\![S_1]\!] - \mathsf{dom}\,(\mathcal{M}[\![S_1]\!] \, \triangleright \, \mathcal{T}\,[\![S_2]\!])) \, \triangleleft \, \mathcal{M}[\![S_1]\!]; \mathcal{M}[\![S_2']\!]$ by *D*.

c. $= (\mathcal{T}\,[\![S_1]\!] - \mathsf{dom}\,(\mathcal{M}[\![S_1]\!] \, \triangleright \, \mathcal{T}\,[\![S_2]\!])) \, \triangleleft \, \mathcal{M}[\![S_1]\!] \, \triangleright \, \mathcal{T}\,[\![S_2]\!]; \mathcal{M}[\![S_2']\!]$

by defn. $-, \triangleright, \triangleright$.

d. $= (\mathcal{T}\,[\![S_1]\!] - \mathsf{dom}\,(\mathcal{M}[\![S_1]\!] \, \triangleright \, \mathcal{T}\,[\![S_2]\!])) \, \triangleleft \, \mathcal{M}[\![S_1]\!]; \mathcal{T}\,[\![S_2]\!] \, \triangleleft \, \mathcal{M}[\![S_2']\!]$

by defn. $\triangleleft, \triangleright$.

e. $\subseteq (\mathcal{T}\,[\![S_1]\!] - \mathsf{dom}\,(\mathcal{M}[\![S_1]\!] \, \triangleright \, \mathcal{T}\,[\![S_2]\!])) \, \triangleleft \, \mathcal{M}[\![S_1]\!]; \mathcal{M}[\![S_2]\!]$ by *F*.

f. $\subseteq \mathcal{M}[\![S_1]\!]; \mathcal{M}[\![S_2]\!]$ by defn. $\triangleleft$.

If

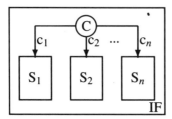

Written:

$IF = $ if c_1 then S_1; c_2 then S_2; ...; c_n then S_n fi
$IF' = $ if c_1 then S_1'; c_2 then S_2'; ...; c_n then S_n' fi

Claim:

$\mathcal{M}[\![IF]\!] \triangleq \bigcup(C_i \blacktriangleleft \mathcal{M}[\![S_i]\!]) \cup (\bigcup C_i \blacktriangleleft \mathcal{I})$
$\mathcal{T}[\![IF]\!] \triangleq \overline{\bigcup(C_i - \mathcal{T}[\![S_i]\!])} \cap (\bigcap \mathcal{T}[\![c_i]\!])$

Have:

A. $\mathcal{T}[\![S_i]\!] \subseteq \mathrm{dom}\,\mathcal{M}[\![S_i]\!]$
$[\![S_i']\!]$ sat $[\![S_i]\!]$ i.e.:
B. $\mathcal{T}[\![S_i]\!] \subseteq \mathcal{T}[\![S_i']\!]$ and
C. $\mathcal{T}[\![S_i]\!] \blacktriangleleft \mathcal{M}[\![S_i']\!] \subseteq \mathcal{M}[\![S_i]\!]$

Prove:

(I) $\mathcal{T}[\![IF]\!] \subseteq \mathrm{dom}\,\mathcal{M}[\![IF]\!]$ or:
1. $\overline{\bigcup(C_i - \mathcal{T}[\![S_i]\!])} \cap (\bigcap \mathcal{T}[\![c_i]\!]) \subseteq \mathrm{dom}\left(\bigcup(C_i \blacktriangleleft \mathcal{M}[\![S_i]\!]) \cup (\bigcup C_i \blacktriangleleft \mathcal{I})\right)$
(II) $[\![IF']\!]$ sat $[\![IF]\!]$ i.e.:
    $\mathcal{T}[\![IF]\!] \subseteq \mathcal{T}[\![IF']\!]$ and $\mathcal{T}[\![IF]\!] \blacktriangleleft \mathcal{M}[\![IF']\!] \subseteq \mathcal{M}[\![IF]\!]$ or:
2. $\overline{\bigcup(C_i - \mathcal{T}[\![S_i]\!])} \cap (\bigcap \mathcal{T}[\![c_i]\!]) \subseteq \overline{\bigcup(C_i - \mathcal{T}[\![S_i']\!])} \cap (\bigcap \mathcal{T}[\![c_i]\!])$ and
3. $(\overline{\bigcup(C_i - \mathcal{T}[\![S_i]\!])} \cap (\bigcap \mathcal{T}[\![c_i]\!])) \blacktriangleleft \left(\bigcup(C_i \blacktriangleleft \mathcal{M}[\![S_i']\!]) \cup (\bigcup C_i \blacktriangleleft \mathcal{I})\right) \subseteq$
    $\bigcup(C_i \blacktriangleleft \mathcal{M}[\![S_i]\!]) \cup (\bigcup C_i \blacktriangleleft \mathcal{I})$

Note 2:

$$\overline{\bigcup(C_i - \mathcal{T}[\![S_i]\!])} \cap (\bigcap \mathcal{T}[\![c_i]\!]) \subseteq \bigcup(C_i \cap \mathcal{T}[\![S_i]\!]) \cup (\bigcup \overline{C_i})$$

Intuitively, the set of states in which all the conditions can be evaluated and the branches corresponding to all true conditions terminate is contained in the set of states in which some true branch will terminate or no condition is true.

Note 2 proof:

$$\overline{\bigcup(C_i - \mathcal{T}[\![S_i]\!])} \cap (\bigcap \mathcal{T}[\![c_i]\!])$$

   a. $\subseteq \overline{\bigcup(C_i - \mathcal{T}[\![S_i]\!])}$ by defn. $\cap$.
   b. $= \bigcup(\Sigma - (C_i - \mathcal{T}[\![S_i]\!]))$ by defn. $-$.
   c. $= \bigcup(\Sigma - (C_i - (C_i \cap \mathcal{T}[\![S_i]\!])))$ by defn. $-$.
   d. $= \bigcup((\Sigma - C_i) \cup (C_i \cap \mathcal{T}[\![S_i]\!]))$ by defn. $-$.
   e. $= \bigcup((C_i \cap \mathcal{T}[\![S_i]\!]) \cup \overline{C_i})$ by defn. $-$.
   f. $= \bigcup(C_i \cap \mathcal{T}[\![S_i]\!]) \cup (\bigcup \overline{C_i})$ by defn. $\bigcup$.

Proof 1:

$$\overline{\bigcup(C_i - \mathcal{T}[\![S_i]\!])} \cap (\bigcap \mathcal{T}[\![c_i]\!]) \subseteq \mathrm{dom}\,(\bigcup(C_i \triangleleft \mathcal{M}[\![S_i]\!]) \cup (\bigcup C_i \triangleleft \mathcal{I})) :$$

$$\overline{\bigcup(C_i - \mathcal{T}[\![S_i]\!])} \cap (\bigcap \mathcal{T}[\![c_i]\!])$$
   a. $\subseteq \bigcup(C_i \cap \mathcal{T}[\![S_i]\!]) \cup (\bigcup \overline{C_i})$ by Note 2.
   b. $\subseteq \bigcup(C_i \cap \mathrm{dom}\,\mathcal{M}[\![S_i]\!]) \cup (\bigcup \overline{C_i})$ by A.
   c. $= \bigcup(\mathrm{dom}\,C_i \triangleleft \mathcal{M}[\![S_i]\!]) \cup (\bigcup \overline{C_i})$ by defn. dom , $\triangleleft$.
   d. $= \bigcup(\mathrm{dom}\,C_i \triangleleft \mathcal{M}[\![S_i]\!]) \cup (\bigcup \mathrm{dom}\,C_i \triangleleft \mathcal{I})$ by defn. dom , $\triangleleft$.
   e. $= \mathrm{dom}\,\Big(\bigcup(C_i \triangleleft \mathcal{M}[\![S_i]\!]) \cup (\bigcup C_i \triangleleft \mathcal{I})\Big)$ by defn. dom .

Proof 2:

$$\overline{\bigcup(C_i - \mathcal{T}[\![S_i]\!])} \cap (\bigcap \mathcal{T}[\![c_i]\!]) \subseteq \overline{\bigcup(C_i - \mathcal{T}[\![S_i']\!])} \cap (\bigcap \mathcal{T}[\![c_i]\!]) :$$

$$\overline{\bigcup(C_i - \mathcal{T}[\![S_i]\!])} \cap (\bigcap \mathcal{T}[\![c_i]\!])$$
      $\subseteq \overline{\bigcup(C_i - \mathcal{T}[\![S_i']\!])} \cap (\bigcap \mathcal{T}[\![c_i]\!])$ by defn.$-,\overline{}$, and B.

Proof 3:

$$\left(\overline{\bigcup(C_i - T[\![S_i]\!])} \cap (\bigcap T[\![c_i]\!])\right) \triangleleft \left(\bigcup(C_i \triangleleft M[\![S_i']\!]) \cup (\bigcup C_i \triangleleft I)\right) \subseteq$$
$$\bigcup(C_i \triangleleft M[\![S_i]\!]) \cup (\bigcup C_i \triangleleft I):$$

$$\left(\overline{\bigcup(C_i - T[\![S_i]\!])} \cap (\bigcap T[\![c_i]\!])\right) \triangleleft \left(\bigcup(C_i \triangleleft M[\![S_i']\!]) \cup (\bigcup C_i \triangleleft I)\right)$$

a. $\subseteq \left(\bigcup(C_i \cap T[\![S_i]\!]) \cup (\bigcup \overline{C_i})\right) \triangleleft \left(\bigcup(C_i \triangleleft M[\![S_i']\!]) \cup (\bigcup C_i \triangleleft I)\right)$ by Note 2.

b. $= \left(\bigcup(C_i \cap T[\![S_i]\!]) \triangleleft \bigcup(C_i \triangleleft M[\![S_i']\!])\right) \cup \left((\bigcup \overline{C_i}) \triangleleft (\bigcup C_i \triangleleft I)\right)$

                                         by defn. $\triangleleft, \cup$.

c. $\subseteq \bigcup(C_i \triangleleft M[\![S_i]\!]) \cup \left((\bigcup \overline{C_i}) \triangleleft (\bigcup C_i \triangleleft I)\right)$ by *C*.

d. $= \bigcup(C_i \triangleleft M[\![S_i]\!]) \cup (\bigcup C_i \triangleleft I)$ by defn. $\triangleleft$.

While

Written:

    $WH = $ while c do S
    $WH' = $ while c do S'

Claim:

    $M[\![WH]\!] \triangleq fix\left(\lambda r \cdot (\neg C \triangleleft I) \cup (C \triangleleft M[\![S]\!]; r)\right)$
    $T[\![WH]\!] \triangleq fix\left(\lambda s \cdot \neg C \cup \left((C \cap T[\![S]\!]) - \text{dom}(M[\![S]\!] \triangleright s)\right)\right)$

    Note that $T[\![WH]\!]$ is not ω-continuous. Also, C is total (i.e. $\neg C = \Sigma - C = \tilde{C}$).

Have:

    A. $T[\![S]\!] \subseteq \text{dom} \, M[\![S]\!]$
    $[\![S']\!]$ sat $[\![S]\!]$ i.e.:
    B. $T[\![S]\!] \subseteq T[\![S']\!]$ and
    C. $T[\![S]\!] \triangleleft M[\![S']\!] \subseteq M[\![S]\!]$

Prove:

(I) & 1. $\mathcal{T}[\![WH]\!] \subseteq \text{dom } \mathcal{M}[\![WH]\!]$

(II) $[\![WH']\!]$ sat $[\![WH]\!]$ i.e.:

$\mathcal{T}[\![WH]\!] \subseteq \mathcal{T}[\![WH']\!]$ or

2. $fix\left(\lambda s \cdot \neg C \cup \left((C \cap \mathcal{T}[\![S]\!]) - \text{dom}\left(\mathcal{M}[\![S]\!] \triangleright s\right)\right)\right) \subseteq$

$\qquad fix\left(\lambda s \cdot \neg C \cup \left((C \cap \mathcal{T}[\![S']\!]) - \text{dom}\left(\mathcal{M}[\![S']\!] \triangleright s\right)\right)\right)$ and

3. $\mathcal{T}[\![WH]\!] \triangleleft \mathcal{M}[\![WH']\!] \subseteq \mathcal{M}[\![WH]\!]$

Proof 1:

$\mathcal{T}[\![WH]\!] \subseteq \text{dom } \mathcal{M}[\![WH]\!]$:

Let: $\mathcal{F}(s) = \neg C \cup \text{dom}(C \triangleleft \mathcal{M}[\![S]\!] \triangleright s)$

then: $\mathcal{F}(\{\,\}) = \neg C$

and: $\mathcal{F}^{n+1}(\{\,\}) = \mathcal{F}(\mathcal{F}^n(\{\,\})) = \neg C \cup \text{dom}(C \triangleleft \mathcal{M}[\![S]\!] \triangleright \mathcal{F}^n(\{\,\}))$

Let: $\mathcal{G}(r) = (\neg C \triangleleft \mathcal{I}) \cup (C \triangleleft \mathcal{M}[\![S]\!]; r)$

then: $\mathcal{G}(\{\,\}) = \neg C \triangleleft \mathcal{I}$

and: $\mathcal{G}^{n+1}(\{\,\}) = \mathcal{G}(\mathcal{G}^n(\{\,\})) = (\neg C \triangleleft \mathcal{I}) \cup (C \triangleleft \mathcal{M}[\![S]\!]; \mathcal{G}^n(\{\,\}))$

Claim: $\bigcup_{n \geq 0} \mathcal{F}^n(\{\,\}) \subseteq \text{dom} \bigcup_{n \geq 0} \mathcal{G}^n(\{\,\})$

To prove this we will use induction:

Show: $\mathcal{F}^n(\{\,\}) \subseteq \text{dom } \mathcal{G}^n(\{\,\}) \; \forall n \geq 0$

By induction on n:

Case $n = 0$: $\mathcal{F}^0(\{\,\}) = \{\,\} \subseteq \{\,\} = \text{dom } \mathcal{G}^0(\{\,\})$

Case $n = 1$: $\mathcal{F}(\{\,\}) = \neg C \subseteq \text{dom}(\neg C \triangleleft \mathcal{I}) = \text{dom } \mathcal{G}(\{\,\})$

Assume true for n and prove for $n + 1$:

$\mathcal{F}^n(\{\,\}) \subseteq \text{dom } \mathcal{G}^n(\{\,\})$ and Prove: $\mathcal{F}^{n+1}(\{\,\}) \subseteq \text{dom } \mathcal{G}^{n+1}(\{\,\})$

$\mathcal{F}^{n+1}(\{\,\}) = \neg C \cup \text{dom}(C \triangleleft \mathcal{M}[\![S]\!] \triangleright \mathcal{F}^n(\{\,\}))$

a. $\subseteq \neg C \cup \text{dom}(C \triangleleft \mathcal{M}[\![S]\!] \triangleright \text{dom } \mathcal{G}^n(\{\,\}))$ by induction hypothesis.

b. $= \neg C \cup \text{dom}(C \triangleleft \mathcal{M}[\![S]\!]; \mathcal{G}^n(\{\,\}))$ by defn. $\triangleright$, dom .

c. $= \text{dom}\left((\neg C \triangleleft \mathcal{I}) \cup (C \triangleleft \mathcal{M}[\![S]\!]; \mathcal{G}^n(\{\,\}))\right)$ by defn. $\triangleleft$, dom .

d. $= \text{dom } \mathcal{G}^{n+1}(\{\,\})$

So: $\mathcal{F}^n(\{\,\}) \subseteq \text{dom } \mathcal{G}^n(\{\,\}) \; \forall n \geq 0$

thus: $\bigcup_{n \geq 0} \mathcal{F}^n(\{\,\}) \subseteq \text{dom} \bigcup_{n \geq 0} \mathcal{G}^n(\{\,\})$

Now: $\mathcal{T}[\![WH]\!]$

a. $= fix\Big(\lambda s \cdot \neg C \cup \big((C \cap \mathcal{T}[\![S]\!]) - \mathrm{dom}\,(\mathcal{M}[\![S]\!] \triangleright s)\big)\Big)$

b. $\subseteq fix\Big(\lambda s \cdot \neg C \cup \dot{\mathrm{dom}}\,\big((C \cap \mathcal{T}[\![S]\!]) \triangleleft \mathcal{M}[\![S]\!] \triangleright s)\big)\Big)$ by Note 1.

c. $\subseteq fix\Big(\lambda s \cdot \neg C \cup \mathrm{dom}\,(C \triangleleft \mathcal{M}[\![S]\!] \triangleright s)\Big)$ by defn. $\cap, A$.

d. $= \bigcup_{n \geq 0} \mathcal{F}^n(\{\,\})$ by defn. *fix*.

e. $\subseteq \mathrm{dom}\, \bigcup_{n \geq 0} \mathcal{G}^n(\{\,\})$ by Claim.

f. $= \mathrm{dom}\, \mathcal{M}[\![WH]\!]$ by defn. *fix*.

Proof 2:

$$fix\Big(\lambda s \cdot \neg C \cup \big((C \cap \mathcal{T}[\![S]\!]) - \mathrm{dom}\,(\mathcal{M}[\![S]\!] \triangleright s)\big)\Big) \subseteq$$
$$\qquad fix\Big(\lambda s \cdot \neg C \cup \big((C \cap \mathcal{T}[\![S']\!]) - \mathrm{dom}\,(\mathcal{M}[\![S']\!] \triangleright s)\big)\Big) :$$

$$fix\Big(\lambda s \cdot \neg C \cup \big((C \cap \mathcal{T}[\![S]\!]) - \mathrm{dom}\,(\mathcal{M}[\![S]\!] \triangleright s)\big)\Big)$$

a. $\subseteq fix(\lambda s \cdot \neg C \cup \big((C \cap \mathcal{T}[\![S]\!]) - \mathrm{dom}\,(\mathcal{M}[\![S']\!] \triangleright s)\big)\Big)$ by C.

b. $\subseteq fix(\lambda s \cdot \neg C \cup \big((C \cap \mathcal{T}[\![S']\!]) - \mathrm{dom}\,(\mathcal{M}[\![S']\!] \triangleright s)\big)\Big)$ by B.

Proof 3:

$\mathcal{T}[\![WH]\!] \triangleleft \mathcal{M}[\![WH']\!] \subseteq \mathcal{M}[\![WH]\!] :$

Now: $\mathcal{T}[\![WH]\!] = fix\Big(\lambda s \cdot \neg C \cup \big((C \cap \mathcal{T}[\![S]\!]) - \mathrm{dom}\,(\mathcal{M}[\![S]\!] \triangleright s)\big)\Big) \subseteq$
$\qquad \neg C \cup \mathcal{T}[\![S]\!]$ by defn. *fix*,

and: $C \cap \neg C = \{\,\}$ by assumption.

So: $\mathcal{T}[\![WH]\!] \triangleleft \big((\neg C \triangleleft \mathcal{I}) \cup (C \triangleleft \mathcal{M}[\![S]\!]; r)\big) \subseteq$
$\qquad \mathcal{T}[\![WH]\!] \triangleleft \big((\neg C \triangleleft \mathcal{I}) \cup (C \triangleleft \mathcal{M}[\![S']\!]; r)\big)$ by C.

And: $\mathcal{T}[\![WH]\!] \triangleleft \mathcal{M}[\![WH']\!] \subseteq \mathcal{T}[\![WH]\!] \triangleleft \mathcal{M}[\![WH]\!]$ by defn. *fix*, $\mathcal{M}[\![\,]\!]$.

Thus: $\mathcal{T}[\![WH]\!] \triangleleft \mathcal{M}[\![WH']\!] \subseteq \mathcal{M}[\![WH]\!]$ by A.

Loop

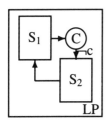

Written:

$LP =$ loop S_1 if c exit S_2 pool
$LP' =$ loop S_1' if c exit S_2' pool

Define:

Here is the definition of *LP* in terms of concatenation and while:

$LP \triangleq S_1;$ while $\neg c$ do $(S_2; S_1)$
$LP' \triangleq S_1';$ while $\neg c$ do $(S_2'; S_1')$

Have:

The meaning relation and the termination set for loop are determined from those for concatenation and while.

$$\mathcal{M}[\![LP]\!] = \mathcal{M}[\![S_1]\!]; fix\Big(\lambda r \cdot (C \triangleleft \mathcal{I}) \cup (\neg C \triangleleft \mathcal{M}[\![S_2]\!]; \mathcal{M}[\![S_1]\!]; r)\Big) :$$

$\mathcal{M}[\![LP]\!]$
a. $= \mathcal{M}[\![S_1;$ while $\neg c$ do $(S_2; S_1)]\!]$ by defn. above.
b. $= \mathcal{M}[\![S_1]\!]; \mathcal{M}[\![$ while $\neg c$ do $(S_2; S_1)]\!]$ by defn. $\mathcal{M}[\![S_1; S_2]\!]$.
c. $= \mathcal{M}[\![S_1]\!]; fix\Big(\lambda r \cdot (C \triangleleft \mathcal{I}) \cup (\neg C \triangleleft \mathcal{M}[\![S_2; S_1]\!]; r)\Big)$ by defn. $\mathcal{M}[\![WH]\!]$.
d. $= \mathcal{M}[\![S_1]\!]; fix\Big(\lambda r \cdot (C \triangleleft \mathcal{I}) \cup (\neg C \triangleleft \mathcal{M}[\![S_2]\!]; \mathcal{M}[\![S_1]\!]; r)\Big)$ by defn. $\mathcal{M}[\![S_1; S_2]\!]$.

$$\mathcal{T}[\![LP]\!] = \mathcal{T}[\![S_1]\!] - \mathrm{dom}\left(\mathcal{M}[\![S_1]\!] \triangleright fix\left(\lambda s \cdot C \cup \right.\right.$$

$$\left.\left.\left((\neg C \cap \mathcal{T}[\![S_2]\!]) - \mathrm{dom}\left(\mathcal{M}[\![S_2]\!] \triangleright \mathcal{T}[\![S_1]\!] \cup \mathcal{M}[\![S_2]\!]; \mathcal{M}[\![S_1]\!] \triangleright s\right)\right)\right)\right) :$$

$\mathcal{T}[\![LP]\!]$

a. $= \mathcal{T}[\![S_1; \text{ while } \neg c \text{ do } (S_2; S_1)]\!]$ by defn. above.

b. $= \mathcal{T}[\![S_1]\!] - \mathrm{dom}\left(\mathcal{M}[\![S_1]\!] \triangleright \mathcal{T}[\![\text{ while } \neg c \text{ do } (S_2; S_1)]\!]\right)$ by defn. $\mathcal{T}[\![S_1; S_2]\!]$.

c. $= \mathcal{T}[\![S_1]\!] - \mathrm{dom}\left(\mathcal{M}[\![S_1]\!] \triangleright fix\left(\lambda s \cdot C \cup \right.\right.$

$$\left.\left.\left((\neg C \cap \mathcal{T}[\![S_2; S_1]\!]) - \mathrm{dom}\left(\mathcal{M}[\![S_2; S_1]\!] \triangleright s\right)\right)\right)\right) \text{ by defn. } \mathcal{T}[\![WH]\!].$$

d. $= \mathcal{T}[\![S_1]\!] - \mathrm{dom}\left(\mathcal{M}[\![S_1]\!] \triangleright fix\left(\lambda s \cdot C \cup \right.\right.$

$$\left.\left.\left((\neg C \cap (\mathcal{T}[\![S_2]\!] - \mathrm{dom}(\mathcal{M}[\![S_2]\!] \triangleright \mathcal{T}[\![S_1]\!]))) - \mathrm{dom}(\mathcal{M}[\![S_2]\!]; \mathcal{M}[\![S_1]\!] \triangleright s)\right)\right)\right)$$
      by defn. $\mathcal{T}[\![S_1; S_2]\!], \mathcal{M}[\![S_1; S_2]\!]$.

e. $= \mathcal{T}[\![S_1]\!] - \mathrm{dom}\left(\mathcal{M}[\![S_1]\!] \triangleright fix\left(\lambda s \cdot C \cup \right.\right.$

$$\left.\left.\left((\neg C \cap \mathcal{T}[\![S_2]\!]) - \mathrm{dom}(\mathcal{M}[\![S_2]\!] \triangleright \mathcal{T}[\![S_1]\!])) - \mathrm{dom}(\mathcal{M}[\![S_2]\!]; \mathcal{M}[\![S_1]\!] \triangleright s)\right)\right)\right)$$
      by defn. $\cap, -$.

f. $= \mathcal{T}[\![S_1]\!] - \mathrm{dom}\left(\mathcal{M}[\![S_1]\!] \triangleright fix\left(R\lambda s \cdot C \cup \right.\right.$

$$\left.\left.\left((\neg C \cap \mathcal{T}[\![S_2]\!]) - (\mathrm{dom}(\mathcal{M}[\![S_2]\!] \triangleright \mathcal{T}[\![S_1]\!]) \cup \mathrm{dom}(\mathcal{M}[\![S_2]\!]; \mathcal{M}[\![S_1]\!] \triangleright s))\right)\right)\right)$$
      by defn. $\cup, -$.

g. $= \mathcal{T}[\![S_1]\!] - \mathrm{dom}\left(\mathcal{M}[\![S_1]\!] \triangleright fix\left(\lambda s \cdot C \cup \right.\right.$

$$\left.\left.\left((\neg C \cap \mathcal{T}[\![S_2]\!]) - \mathrm{dom}(\mathcal{M}[\![S_2]\!] \triangleright \mathcal{T}[\![S_1]\!] \cup \mathcal{M}[\![S_2]\!]; \mathcal{M}[\![S_1]\!] \triangleright s)\right)\right)\right)$$
      by defn. $\cup, \mathrm{dom}$.

Now:

Since we have already completed the necessary proofs:

1. $\mathcal{T}[\![LP]\!] \subseteq \mathrm{dom}\, \mathcal{M}[\![LP]\!]$ and
2. $[\![LP']\!] \text{ sat } [\![LP]\!]$

follow from the proofs for concatenation and while.

Wait

Written:

    WT = wait c tiaw

We assume that C is total and that there is a unique user action, U, which will make C become true. We also assume that the user eventually performs U.

Define:

Based on the assumption we can define WT in terms of if:

$WT \triangleq$ if $\neg c$ then U fi
$WT' \triangleq$ if $\neg c$ then U' fi

Have:

$\mathcal{M}[\![WT]\!] = (\neg C \triangleleft \mathcal{M}[\![U]\!]) \cup (C \triangleleft \mathcal{I})$:

$\mathcal{M}[\![WT]\!]$
a. $= \mathcal{M}[\![$ if $\neg c$ then U fi $]\!]$ by defn. above.
b. $= (\neg C \triangleleft \mathcal{M}[\![U]\!]) \cup (C \triangleleft \mathcal{I})$ by defn. $\mathcal{M}[\![IF]\!]$.

$\mathcal{T}[\![WT]\!] = C \cup \mathcal{T}[\![U]\!]$:

$\mathcal{T}[\![WT]\!]$
a. $= \mathcal{T}[\![$ if $\neg c$ then U fi $]\!]$ by defn. above.
b. $= \overline{(\neg C - \mathcal{T}[\![U]\!])} \cap \mathcal{T}[\![\neg C]\!]$ by defn. $\mathcal{T}[\![IF]\!]$.
c. $= \overline{(\neg C - \mathcal{T}[\![U]\!])}$ by defn. c.
d. $= C \cup (\neg C \cap \mathcal{T}[\![U]\!])$ by defn. $-$, $\overline{}$.
e. $= C \cup \mathcal{T}[\![U]\!]$ by defn. $\cup$, $\cap$.

Now:

1. $\mathcal{T}[\![WT]\!] \subseteq$ dom $\mathcal{M}[\![WT]\!]$ and
2. $[\![WT']\!]$ sat $[\![WT]\!]$
follow from the proofs for if.

Proof rules

$$\{P\}S\{R\}$$

means: if $\overleftarrow{\sigma} \in P$ and S is performed on $\overleftarrow{\sigma}$ then S will terminate, and if the resulting state is σ then $(\overleftarrow{\sigma}, \sigma) \in R$.
Alternatively this can be read as:

> If the predicate P is true then S will terminate and when S terminates the predicate R will be true. i.e. S satisfies (P,R).

This can also be written:

$$S \text{ sat } (P,R)$$

Note that, although the same notation is used to represent both the predicate and the set of values which satisfy the predicate, no confusion should arise.
$\{P\}S\{R\}$ can be taken to mean:

$$P \subseteq \mathcal{T}[\![S]\!] \wedge P \triangleleft \mathcal{M}[\![S]\!] \subseteq R$$

If a further condition is placed on the final state as in $\{P\}S\{R \wedge P'\}$ there is then an additional requirement:

$$\text{rng}\,(P \triangleleft \mathcal{M}[\![S]\!]) \subseteq P' \text{ or: } P \triangleleft \mathcal{M}[\![S]\!] = P \triangleleft \mathcal{M}[\![S]\!] \triangleright P'$$

The following sections give the proof rules for the statechart constructs.

Concatenation rule

Claim:

> Here we claim that if the first two clauses are true then the third is also true:

$$\{P_1\}S_1\{R_1 \wedge P_2\} ; \{P_2\}S_2\{R_2\} \implies \{P_1\}S_1; S_2\{R_1; R_2\}$$

Have:

> Here the first two clauses are expanded using the definitions above:

$$\{P_1\}S_1\{R_1 \wedge P_2\} \triangleq (a)\, P_1 \subseteq \mathcal{T}[\![S_1]\!] \wedge (b)\, P_1 \triangleleft \mathcal{M}[\![S_1]\!] \subseteq R_1 \wedge$$
$$(c)\, P_1 \triangleleft \mathcal{M}[\![S_1]\!] = P_1 \triangleleft \mathcal{M}[\![S_1]\!] \triangleright P_2$$
$$\{P_2\}S_2\{R_2\} \triangleq (d)\, P_2 \subseteq \mathcal{T}[\![S_2]\!] \wedge (e)\, P_2 \triangleleft \mathcal{M}[\![S_2]\!] \subseteq R_2$$

Show:

The third clause is expanded showing the two parts we must prove:

$$\{P_1\}S_1;S_2\{R_1;R_2\} \triangleq P_1 \subseteq \mathcal{T}\,[\![S_1;S_2]\!] \wedge P_1 \triangleleft \mathcal{M}[\![S_1;S_2]\!] \subseteq R_1;R_2 =$$
$$(1).\ P_1 \subseteq \mathcal{T}\,[\![S_1]\!] - \mathrm{dom}\,(\mathcal{M}[\![S_1]\!] \triangleright \mathcal{T}\,[\![S_2]\!]) \wedge$$
$$(2).\ P_1 \triangleleft \mathcal{M}[\![S_1]\!]; \mathcal{M}[\![S_2]\!] \subseteq R_1;R_2$$

Proofs:

(1). $P_1 \subseteq \mathcal{T}\,[\![S_1]\!] - \mathrm{dom}\,(\mathcal{M}[\![S_1]\!] \triangleright \mathcal{T}\,[\![S_2]\!])$:

Now: $\mathcal{M}[\![S_1]\!] \triangleright \mathcal{T}\,[\![S_2]\!]$
a. $\subseteq \mathcal{M}[\![S_1]\!] \triangleright P_2$ by (d).
b. $\subseteq (P_1 \triangleleft \mathcal{M}[\![S_1]\!]) \triangleright P_2$ by defn. $\triangleleft$.
c. $\subseteq (P_1 \triangleleft \mathcal{M}[\![S_1]\!] \triangleright P_2) \triangleright P_2$ by (c).
d. $= \{\,\}$ by defn. $\triangleright, \triangleright$.
So: $\mathcal{T}\,[\![S_1]\!] = \mathcal{T}\,[\![S_1]\!] - \mathrm{dom}\,(\mathcal{M}[\![S_1]\!] \triangleright \mathcal{T}\,[\![S_2]\!])$
Thus: $P_1 \subseteq \mathcal{T}\,[\![S_1]\!] - \mathrm{dom}\,(\mathcal{M}[\![S_1]\!] \triangleright \mathcal{T}\,[\![S_2]\!])$ by (a).

(2). $P_1 \triangleleft \mathcal{M}[\![S_1]\!]; \mathcal{M}[\![S_2]\!] \subseteq R_1;R_2$:

$P_1 \triangleleft \mathcal{M}[\![S_1]\!]; \mathcal{M}[\![S_2]\!]$
a. $\subseteq R_1 \triangleright P_2; \mathcal{M}[\![S_2]\!]$ by (b).
b. $= R_1; P_2 \triangleleft \mathcal{M}[\![S_2]\!]$ by defn. $;, \triangleleft$.
c. $\subseteq R_1;R_2$ by (e).

If rule

Claim:

$$\{P \wedge C_i\}S_i\{R\} \ ; \ \{P \wedge \forall i \cdot \neg C_i\}I\{R\} \ ; \ P \subseteq \bigcap \mathcal{T}\,[\![c_i]\!] \ \Rightarrow \ \{P\}\ \text{if } c_i \text{ then } S_i \text{ fi } \{R\}$$

Have:

$$\{P \wedge C_i\}S_i\{R\} \triangleq (a)\ P \cap C_i \subseteq \mathcal{T}\,[\![S_i]\!] \wedge \ (b)\ (P \cap C_i) \triangleleft \mathcal{M}[\![S_i]\!] \subseteq R$$
$$\{P \wedge \forall i \cdot \neg C_i\}I\{R\} \triangleq (c)\ (P \cap \overline{\bigcup C_i}) \triangleleft \mathcal{M}[\![I]\!] \subseteq R$$
$$(d)\ P \subseteq \bigcap \mathcal{T}\,[\![c_i]\!]$$

Show:

$$\{P\}\ \text{if } c_i \text{ then } S_i \text{ fi } \{R\} \triangleq P \subseteq \mathcal{T}\,[\![IF]\!] \wedge P \triangleleft \mathcal{M}[\![IF]\!] \subseteq R =$$
$$(1).\ P \subseteq \overline{\bigcup(C_i - \mathcal{T}\,[\![S_i]\!])} \cap (\bigcap \mathcal{T}\,[\![c_i]\!]) \wedge$$
$$(2).\ P \triangleleft (\bigcup(C_i \triangleleft \mathcal{M}[\![S_i]\!]) \cup (\bigcup C_i \triangleleft I)) \subseteq R$$

Proofs:

(1). $P \subseteq \overline{\bigcup(C_i - \mathcal{T}[\![S_i]\!])} \cap (\bigcap \mathcal{T}[\![c_i]\!])$:

Now: $\bigcup(C_i - \mathcal{T}[\![S_i]\!])$
a. $\subseteq \bigcup(C_i - (P \cap C_i))$ by (a).
b. $\subseteq \bigcup(C_i - P)$ by defn. $-$.
c. $\subseteq \overline{P}$ by defn. $\overline{}$.
So: $P \subseteq \overline{\bigcup(C_i - \mathcal{T}[\![S_i]\!])}$ by defn. $\subseteq, \overline{}$.
Now: $P \subseteq \bigcap \mathcal{T}[\![c_i]\!]$ by (d).
Thus: $P \subseteq \overline{\bigcup(C_i - \mathcal{T}[\![S_i]\!])} \cap (\bigcap \mathcal{T}[\![c_i]\!])$

(2). $P \triangleleft ((\bigcup(C_i \triangleleft \mathcal{M}[\![S_i]\!])) \cup (\bigcup C_i \triangleleft I)) \subseteq R$:

$P \triangleleft ((\bigcup(C_i \triangleleft \mathcal{M}[\![S_i]\!])) \cup (\bigcup C_i \triangleleft I))$
a. $= P \triangleleft (\bigcup(C_i \triangleleft \mathcal{M}[\![S_i]\!])) \cup P \triangleleft (\bigcup C_i \triangleleft I)$ by defn. $\triangleleft, \cup$.
b. $= \bigcup((P \cap C_i) \triangleleft \mathcal{M}[\![S_i]\!]) \cup P \triangleleft (\bigcup C_i \triangleleft I)$ by defn. $\triangleleft, \cup$.
c. $= \bigcup((P \cap C_i) \triangleleft \mathcal{M}[\![S_i]\!]) \cup (P \cap \overline{\bigcup C_i}) \triangleleft I)$ by defn. $\triangleleft, \triangleleft, \overline{}$.
d. $\subseteq R \cup (P \cap \overline{\bigcup C_i}) \triangleleft I)$ by (b).
e. $\subseteq R \cup R$ by (c).
f. $= R$ by defn. $\cup$.

While rule

Claim:

$\{P \wedge C\}S\{R \wedge P\}$; R transitive and well-founded
$\Rightarrow \{P\}$ while c do $S\{R^* \wedge (P \wedge \neg C)\}$

Have:

$\{P \wedge C\}S\{R \wedge P\} \triangleq (a)\ P \cap C \subseteq \mathcal{T}[\![S]\!] \ \wedge \ (b)\ (P \cap C) \triangleleft \mathcal{M}[\![S]\!] \subseteq R \ \wedge$
$\quad (c)\ (P \cap C) \triangleleft \mathcal{M}[\![S]\!] = (P \cap C) \triangleleft \mathcal{M}[\![S]\!] \triangleright P$
R transitive $\triangleq (d)\ R; R = R$
R well-founded $\triangleq$ no infinite chains.
$\qquad\qquad\qquad$ This allows a special type of induction (see (1). below).

Show:

$\{P\}$ while c do $S\{R^* \wedge (P \wedge \neg C)\} \triangleq (1).\ P \subseteq \mathcal{T}[\![WH]\!] \ \wedge$
$\quad (2).\ P \triangleleft \mathcal{M}[\![WH]\!] \subseteq R^* \ \wedge (3).\ P \triangleleft \mathcal{M}[\![WH]\!] \subseteq P \triangleleft \mathcal{M}[\![WH]\!] \triangleright (P \cap \neg C)$

Proofs:

(1). $P \subseteq T \, [\![WH]\!]$

By induction on R (well-founded and transitive).
Prove:
A. $P - \text{dom} \, R \subseteq T \, [\![WH]\!]$
B. $R = R \triangleright T \, [\![WH]\!] \Rightarrow$
$$P \cap \text{dom} \, R \subseteq \neg C \cup \left((C \cap T \, [\![S]\!]) - \text{dom} \, (M[\![S]\!] \triangleright T \, [\![WH]\!]) \right)$$

A. $P - \text{dom} \, R \subseteq T \, [\![WH]\!]$:
Note: $(P - \text{dom} \, R) \cap C = \{ \}$
Proof:
$(P - \text{dom} \, R) \cap C$
a. $= (P \cap C) - \text{dom} \, R$ by defn. $\cap, -$.
b. $= \text{dom} \, (P \cap C) \triangleleft M[\![S]\!] - \text{dom} \, R$ by (a).
c. $\subseteq \text{dom} \, R - \text{dom} \, R$ by (b).
d. $= \{ \}$ by defn. $-$.
So: $P - \text{dom} \, R \subseteq \neg C$ since C total.
$\subseteq T \, [\![WH]\!]$ by defn. $T \, [\![WH]\!]$.
as desired.

B. Assume: $R = R \triangleright T \, [\![WH]\!]$
Prove: $P \cap \text{dom} \, R \subseteq \neg C \cup \left((C \cap T \, [\![S]\!]) - \text{dom} \, (M[\![S]\!] \triangleright T \, [\![WH]\!]) \right)$
Case B(i) Assume: $\neg C \, (= \Sigma - C)$:
$P \cap \text{dom} \, R$
a. $= P \cap \text{dom} \, R \cap \neg C$ by assumption.
b. $\subseteq \neg C$ defn. $\cap$.
c. $\subseteq \neg C \cup \left((C \cap T \, [\![S]\!]) - \text{dom} \, (M[\![S]\!] \triangleright T \, [\![WH]\!]) \right)$ by defn. $\cup$.
as desired.

Case B(ii) Assume: C :

Claim 1: $P \cap \text{dom}\, R \cap C \subseteq T\, [\![S]\!]$:

$\quad P \cap \text{dom}\, R \cap C$

$\quad$ *a.* $\subseteq P \cap C$ by defn. $\cap$.

$\quad$ *b.* $\subseteq T\, [\![S]\!]$ by (a).

Claim 2: $\text{dom}\, (T\, [\![S]\!] \triangleleft M[\![S]\!] \triangleright T\, [\![WH]\!]) = \{\,\}$:

$\quad$ Have: $(P \cap C) \triangleleft M[\![S]\!] \subseteq R$ by (b).

$\quad$ and: $R = R \triangleright T\, [\![WH]\!]$ by assumption.

$\quad$ Thus: $(P \cap C) \triangleleft M[\![S]\!] = (P \cap C) \triangleleft M[\![S]\!] \triangleright T\, [\![WH]\!]$ by defn. $\subseteq, \triangleright$.

$\quad$ and: $T\, [\![S]\!] \triangleleft M[\![S]\!] = T\, [\![S]\!] \triangleleft M[\![S]\!] \triangleright T\, [\![WH]\!]$ by Claim 1.

$\quad$ or: $T\, [\![S]\!] \triangleleft M[\![S]\!] \triangleright T\, [\![WH]\!] = \{\,\}$ by defn. $\triangleright$.

$\quad$ Therefore: $\text{dom}\, (T\, [\![S]\!] \triangleleft M[\![S]\!] \triangleright T\, [\![WH]\!]) = \{\,\}$ by defn. dom.

$P \cap \text{dom}\, R \cap C$

a. $\subseteq T\, [\![S]\!]$ by Claim 1.

b. $\subseteq C \cap T\, [\![S]\!]$ by defn. $\cap$.

c. $= (C \cap T\, [\![S]\!]) - \text{dom}\, (T\, [\![S]\!] \triangleleft M[\![S]\!] \triangleright T\, [\![WH]\!])$ by Claim 2.

d. $= (C \cap T\, [\![S]\!]) - \text{dom}\, (M[\![S]\!] \triangleright T\, [\![WH]\!])$ by defn. $\triangleleft$.

e. $\subseteq \neg C \cup \big((C \cap T\, [\![S]\!]) - \text{dom}\, (M[\![S]\!] \triangleright T\, [\![WH]\!])\big)$ by defn. $\cup$.

as desired.

(2). $P \triangleleft fix\Big(\lambda r \cdot (\neg C \triangleleft I) \cup (C \triangleleft M[\![S]\!]; r)\Big) \subseteq R^*$:

Proof by Scott induction on r since $M[\![\ ]\!]$ is continuous.

Assume: $P \triangleleft r \subseteq R^*$

Prove:

A. $P \triangleleft \{\,\} \subseteq R^*$

B. $P \triangleleft ((\neg C \triangleleft I) \cup (C \triangleleft M[\![S]\!]; r)) \subseteq R^*$

A. $P \triangleleft \{\,\} \subseteq R^*$:

$\quad P \triangleleft \{\,\} = \{\,\} \subseteq R^*$

B. $P \triangleleft ((\neg C \triangleleft \mathcal{I}) \cup (C \triangleleft \mathcal{M}[\![S]\!]; r)) \subseteq R^*$:

$P \triangleleft ((\neg C \triangleleft \mathcal{I}) \cup (C \triangleleft \mathcal{M}[\![S]\!]; r))$

a. $= P \triangleleft (\neg C \triangleleft \mathcal{I}) \cup P \triangleleft (C \triangleleft \mathcal{M}[\![S]\!]; r)$ by defn. $\triangleleft, \cup$.

b. $= (P \cap \neg C) \triangleleft \mathcal{I} \cup P \triangleleft (C \triangleleft \mathcal{M}[\![S]\!]; r)$ by defn. $\triangleleft, \cap$.

c. $= (P \cap \neg C) \triangleleft \mathcal{I} \cup (P \cap C) \triangleleft \mathcal{M}[\![S]\!]; r$ by defn. $\triangleleft, \cap$.

d. $\subseteq \mathcal{I} \cup (P \cap C) \triangleleft \mathcal{M}[\![S]\!]; r$ by defn. $\triangleleft$.

e. $\subseteq \mathcal{I} \cup R \triangleright P; r$ by (b).

f. $= \mathcal{I} \cup R; P \triangleleft r$ by defn. $\triangleright, ;, \triangleleft$.

g. $\subseteq \mathcal{I} \cup R; R^*$ by assumption.

h. $= \mathcal{I} \cup R^+$ by defn. R^+.

i. $= R^*$ by defn. R^*.

as desired.

(3). $P \triangleleft \mathcal{M}[\![WH]\!] = P \triangleleft \mathcal{M}[\![WH]\!] \triangleright (P \cap \neg C)$:

Proof by Scott induction on r since $\mathcal{M}[\![\,]\!]$ is continuous.

Assume: $P \triangleleft r = P \triangleleft r \triangleright (P \cap \neg C)$

Prove:

A. $P \triangleleft \{\} \subseteq P \triangleleft \{\} \triangleright (P \cap \neg C)$

B. $P \triangleleft ((\neg C \triangleleft \mathcal{I}) \cup (C \triangleleft \mathcal{M}[\![S]\!]; r)) =$
$\qquad P \triangleleft ((\neg C \triangleleft \mathcal{I}) \cup (C \triangleleft \mathcal{M}[\![S]\!]; r)) \triangleright (P \cap \neg C)$

A. $P \triangleleft \{\} \subseteq P \triangleleft \{\} \triangleright (P \cap \neg C)$:

$P \triangleleft \{\} = \{\} = P \triangleleft \{\} \triangleright (P \cap \neg C)$

B. $P \triangleleft ((\neg C \triangleleft \mathcal{I}) \cup (C \triangleleft \mathcal{M}[\![S]\!]; r)) =$
$\qquad P \triangleleft ((\neg C \triangleleft \mathcal{I}) \cup (C \triangleleft \mathcal{M}[\![S]\!]; r)) \triangleright (P \cap \neg C) :$
$P \triangleleft ((\neg C \triangleleft \mathcal{I}) \cup (C \triangleleft \mathcal{M}[\![S]\!]; r))$

a. $= P \triangleleft (\neg C \triangleleft \mathcal{I}) \cup P \triangleleft (C \triangleleft \mathcal{M}[\![S]\!]; r)$ by defn. $\triangleleft, \cup$.

b. $= (P \cap \neg C) \triangleleft \mathcal{I} \cup P \triangleleft (C \triangleleft \mathcal{M}[\![S]\!]; r)$ by defn. $\triangleleft, \cap$.

c. $= (P \cap \neg C) \triangleleft \mathcal{I} \cup (P \cap C) \triangleleft \mathcal{M}[\![S]\!]; r$ by defn. $\triangleleft, \cap$.

d. $= (P \cap \neg C) \triangleleft \mathcal{I} \triangleright (P \cap \neg C) \cup (P \cap C) \triangleleft \mathcal{M}[\![S]\!]; r$ by defn. $\triangleleft, \triangleright, \mathcal{I}$.

e. $= (P \cap \neg C) \triangleleft \mathcal{I} \triangleright (P \cap \neg C) \cup (P \cap C) \triangleleft \mathcal{M}[\![S]\!] \triangleright P; r$ by (c).

f. $= (P \cap \neg C) \triangleleft \mathcal{I} \triangleright (P \cap \neg C) \cup (P \cap C) \triangleleft \mathcal{M}[\![S]\!]; P \triangleleft r$ by defn. ;, $\triangleright, \triangleleft$.

g. $= (P \cap \neg C) \triangleleft \mathcal{I} \triangleright (P \cap \neg C) \cup (P \cap C) \triangleleft \mathcal{M}[\![S]\!]; P \triangleleft r \triangleright (P \cap \neg C)$
$\qquad\qquad\qquad\qquad\qquad\qquad\qquad\qquad\qquad\qquad$ by assumption.

h. $= ((P \cap \neg C) \triangleleft \mathcal{I} \cup (P \cap C) \triangleleft \mathcal{M}[\![S]\!]; P \triangleleft r) \triangleright (P \cap \neg C)$ by defn. $\triangleright$.

i. $= (P \triangleleft (\neg C \triangleleft \mathcal{I}) \cup P \triangleleft (C \triangleleft \mathcal{M}[\![S]\!]; P \triangleleft r)) \triangleright (P \cap \neg C)$ by defn. $\triangleleft$.

j. $= P \triangleleft (\neg C \triangleleft \mathcal{I} \cup C \triangleleft \mathcal{M}[\![S]\!]; P \triangleleft r) \triangleright (P \cap \neg C)$ by defn. $\triangleleft$.

k. $= P \triangleleft (\neg C \triangleleft \mathcal{I} \cup C \triangleleft \mathcal{M}[\![S]\!]; r) \triangleright (P \cap \neg C)$ by (c).

as desired.

Loop rule

Claim:

$\{P_1\} S_1 \{R_1 \wedge P_2\} \, ; \ \{P_2 \wedge \neg C\} S_2 \{R_2 \wedge P_1\} \, ;$
$R_2; R_1$ transitive and well founded
$\qquad\qquad \Rightarrow \ \{P_1\} \text{ loop } S_1 \text{ if } c \text{ exit } S_2 \text{ pool } \{R_1; (R_2; R_1)^* \wedge (P_2 \wedge C)\}$

Proof:

$\{P_1\} S_1 \{R_1 \wedge P_2\} \, ; \ \{P_2 \wedge \neg C\} S_2 \{R_2 \wedge P_1\}$

a. $\Rightarrow \ \{P_1\} S_1 \{R_1 \wedge P_2\} \, ; \ \{P_2 \wedge \neg C\} S_2; S_1 \{R_2; R_1 \wedge P_2\}$
$\qquad\qquad\qquad\qquad\qquad\qquad\qquad\qquad\qquad\qquad$ by concatenation rule.

b. $\Rightarrow \ \{P_1\} S_1 \{R_1 \wedge P_2\} \, ; \ \{P_2\} \text{ while } \neg c \text{ do } (S_2; S_1) \{(R_2; R_1)^* \wedge (P_2 \wedge C)\}$
$\qquad\qquad\qquad\qquad\qquad\qquad\qquad\qquad\qquad\qquad$ by while rule.

c. $\Rightarrow \ \{P_1\} S_1; \text{ while } \neg c \text{ do } (S_2; S_1) \{R_1; (R_2; R_1)^* \wedge (P_2 \wedge C)\}$
$\qquad\qquad\qquad\qquad\qquad\qquad\qquad\qquad\qquad\qquad$ by concatenation rule.

d. $\Rightarrow \ \{P_1\} \text{ loop } S_1 \text{ if } c \text{ exit } S_2 \text{ pool } \{R_1; (R_2; R_1)^* \wedge (P_2 \wedge C)\}$ by defn. loop.

Wait rule

Claim:

$\{P \wedge C\} I \{R \wedge C\} \, ; \ \{P \wedge \neg C\} U \{R \wedge C\} \, ; \ \mathcal{T}[\![c]\!] = \Sigma \ \Rightarrow \ \{P\} \text{ wait } c \text{ tiaw } \{R \wedge C\}$

Proof:

$\{P \wedge C\}I\{R \wedge C\}$; $\{P \wedge \neg C\}U\{R \wedge C\}$; $\mathcal{T}[\![c]\!] = \Sigma$

a. $\Rightarrow$ $\{P \wedge C\}I\{R \wedge C\}$; $\{P \wedge \neg C\}U\{R \wedge C\}$; $P \subseteq \mathcal{T}[\![c]\!]$ by defn. Σ.

b. $\Rightarrow$ $\{P\}$ if $\neg c$ then U fi $\{R \wedge C\}$ by if rule.

c. $\Rightarrow$ $\{P\}$ wait c tiaw $\{R \wedge C\}$ by defn. wait.

12.6 Proofs

A major advantage of the use of a formal technique for describing the user interface, as opposed to an informal design method, is that properties of the interface can be formally stated and proved. It is difficult to design and assess experiments to evaluate an interface, though some researchers suggest or attempt this [BK82, Pen82, Rei83, SR82]. Other researchers have attempted proofs using a formal description method [And85, Fol81, Jac84, Rei82], but little work has been done in this area, mainly due to the problems in formally representing general user interface properties.

This chapter presents a few examples of proofs that can be carried out using the suggested formal description method.

Simple properties of the interface

While exactly what comprises a 'good' user interface is unknown, there are many simple properties that a designer might want to look for in his formal description. Due to the nature of the description method, many simple properties which could be hidden in other methods and require a complicated proof become quite obvious here. Many properties of the example of Section 12.4 are apparent from the formal description. These properties include such things as:

1. The user is always prompted for input.

2. However, the user can type ahead.

3. An error message is printed if and only if invalid input is encountered.

4. The user must give a valid user name and password to successfully login.

A quick glance at the statechart and operation **pre**- and **post**-conditions will show the validity of claims such as these. The fact that many of these properties are very easy to check indicates that this method is wellsuited to the description of user interfaces.

Other properties of the interface

There are many other, more complicated, properties that a designer may want to look for in an interface. The following are examples.

Queue length proof

A designer may want to ensure that the input queue will never overflow the space allocated to it. Here is a proof that the input queue in the LOGON example of Section 12.3 never exceeds *qlen*.

Show len *inq* $\leq$ *qlen*

Now: *qlen* $\in$ $\mathbb{N}_1$ so $1 \leq$ *qlen*

    Initially *inq* = [ ] so len *inq* = $0 < 1 \leq$ *qlen*

Only the user can add things to the input queue; this is done using the operation INPT. Now the **pre**-condition of INPT requires that len *inq* < *qlen*. The **post**-condition of INPT contains:

$\exists w \in Word \cdot inq = \overleftarrow{inq} \frown [w]$

so len *inq*

   a. = len $\overleftarrow{inq}$ + len [*w*]
   b. = len $\overleftarrow{inq}$ + 1
   c. < *qlen* + 1
   d. $\leq$ *qlen* as required.

Termination

Logon termination

In the verification of application programs many proofs are concerned with the successful termination of looping constructs. In a secure user interface, part of the interface may be concerned with preventing unauthorized users from completing the logon procedure.

   The LOGON example presented in Section 12.3 is an example of a case where a user may never successfully complete the logon task, and thus the logon 'loop' will never terminate.

   However, it is interesting to note that under certain restrictions it is possible to prove that the user will eventually enter a valid user name. The conditions require that there is some measure of the user, such as his knowledge, which will increase each time an error message is presented. Provided that there is a limit to how knowledgeable the user can become, he must eventually enter a correct user name (otherwise he would become infinitely knowledgeable). While this may not be a very realistic example, it illustrates a type of proof that may be carried out.

Loop proof

Section 12.4 contains an extension to the original LOGON example in which the user has only a given number of tries before the keyboard is locked for a period of time. In this case it is possible to prove that if a user attempts to logon either he will successfully logon or the keyboard will eventually be locked, i.e., the TRY statechart always terminates.

From the VDM presented it is easy to see that:
$\{$true$\}$UPRMT$\{$true$\}$ and $\{$input$\}$UREAD$\{$true$\}$.

From the definition of **wait**, and the existence of the INPT operation:
$\{$true$\}$ wait input tiaw $\{$input$\}$.

Now: UPW = UPRMT ; wait input tiaw
So: $\{$true$\}$UPW$\{$input$\}$ by the concatenation rule.

Also: UGET = UPW ; UREAD.
So: $\{$true$\}$UGET$\{$true$\}$ by the concatenation rule.

Similarly: $\{$true$\}$PGET$\{$true$\}$.

Now: GET = UGET ; PGET.
And: $\{$true$\}$GET$\{$true$\}$ by the concatenation rule.

From the VDM:
$\{\neg($valid input $\vee$ limit$)\}$MSG$\{\overleftarrow{trynum} < trynum \leq trylimit\}$,
$\qquad$ and $\{\overleftarrow{trynum} < trynum \leq trylimit\}$ is transitive and well-founded.

Applying the **while** rule to GET and MSG gives:
$\{$true$\}$ loop GET if (valid input $\vee$ limit) exit MSG pool
$\qquad\qquad\qquad \{(\overleftarrow{trynum} < trynum \leq trylimit) \wedge ($valid input $\vee$ limit$)\}$.

Now: TRY = loop GET if (valid input $\vee$ limit) exit MSG pool .
And: limit $\equiv trynum \geq trylimit$.
So: $\{$true$\}$TRY$\{(\overleftarrow{trynum} < trynum \leq trylimit) \wedge ($valid input $\vee trynum \geq trylimit)\}$.
Or: $\{$true$\}$TRY$\{\big((trynum \leq trylimit \wedge$ valid input$) \vee (trynum = trylimit)\big)\}$.

Thus TRY always terminates. From the proof it is easy to see that when TRY terminates, either the user has entered valid input before exceeding the permitted number of attempts, or he has exceeded the limit.

12.7   Conclusions

Formal description and user interface design are both new and rapidly changing fields in which there is much ongoing research. This study aims to show how formal description methods can be used to aid in user interface design. It is argued that it is not currently feasible to formally describe the set of properties that any user interface should have. User interface research has not yet reached a stage where this approach is fruitful. Also, it is not often possible to define the user interface totally independently of the other components of the interactive system. Usually the user interface designer wants to take advantage of various characteristics peculiar to the particular interactive system for which the user interface is intended. Thus a formal technique has been developed for the description of interactive systems with emphasis on the user interface.

The proposed method is a new hybrid formal notation which combines statecharts with **pre-** and **post**-conditions. A statechart outlines the flow of control between the operations within the system, and each operation is described using **pre-** and **post**-conditions. This formal description technique meets the criteria outlined at the beginning of Section 12.3. It deals with those parts of a system which are crucial in an interactive environment: error handling, help information, and interrupts. It emphasizes the top level flow of control and describes the system in levels. (The method does not dictate a level of abstraction, and ground rules for suitable levels are a subject for research.) Each operation is described separately in a modular fashion. The notation used is concise and abstract, yet easy to understand. The technique is also mathematically sound, enabling it to be used to prove various properties of the interactive system.

Since this method has only been applied to a few examples, exploration of further examples is needed. Perhaps timing considerations could be added to allow for the description of concepts such as response time. More research is also needed to perfect and possibly extend the suggested formal description technique to deal with all possible interfaces and interface styles.

13

Line Representations on Graphics Devices

Lynn S. Marshall

This chapter contains an unusual specification. The task is to describe the output which is required on a raster graphics device when lines are to be projected. As the author relates, the starting point was an informal specification which represented nothing more precise than wishful thinking. An interesting aspect of the specification is the need to underspecify the result because of the range of devices which have to be covered. The chapter contains both the specification and a discussion of implementations. These latter are justified (with respect to the specification) at a level closer to normal mathematical reasoning (rather than the formal proofs of steps of reification).

13.1   Introduction

Formal description is a useful tool in many areas of computer science since it allows the aims of a computer system to be clearly and unambiguously expressed and statements concerning the system to be formally proven. The formal description of computer graphics systems is in its infancy. Research in this field has been pioneered by Carson [Car74], Gnatz [Gna], and Mallgren [Mal83] and is of great potential help.

Graphical data are usually in the form of images composed of various drawing primitives such as points, lines and text. Most graphical devices are unable to represent drawing primitives exactly and thus must produce an approximation to the ideal. This makes the use of conventional program verification tools, such as a test driver, very difficult. The Graphical Kernel System (GKS) is the new international standard for twodimensional interactive computer graphics (ISO 7942). Work in designing test suites for GKS implementations is certainly not straightforward, and work on a formal description of GKS is under way [DFM84, DFM88, Mar84b, Rug88].

A formal description of the approximation to an image that a given computer graphics device should display will be useful in proving that the various devices in a computer graphics system function correctly. The idea of specifying what comprises a valid approximation to some ideal picture on a given graphics device has been deliberately ignored in previous research in the formal description of graphics. Mallgren [Mal83] says, 'The display system is assumed to provide a recognizable approximation to this representative picture', while Carson [Car74] admits, 'Of course, someone must eventually describe how a line should look but we could treat this as a binding issue, not a specification issue.' However, it seems meaningless to maintain that a graphics program is functioning correctly unless it produces recognizable output. Carson [Car74] notes the following:

> At one extreme, nothing at all is said about the actual effects on a display surface when an output primitive is drawn. This would enable any vendor to claim that almost any implementation conformed to the standard, since it would be impossible to test implementations. At the other extreme, the … specification could completely describe the effects of output primitives in terms of parameters such as addressability, color, hardware, text fonts, etc. that apply to typical display devices. Unfortunately, any parameter set considered by the specifiers places unfair restrictions on manufacturers of certain classes of display devices. Furthermore, fixed parameters would inhibit the degree of technological flexibility available to implementors.

Thus, it is necessary to devise a formal description that will permit the display of any one of a range of approximation to a picture thus allowing **any** reasonable output, but **only** reasonable output.

Section 13.2 of this chapter discusses graphics devices and their capabilities, and Section 13.3 describes line and their attributes. In Section 13.4 a formal description of thin solid lines is given, while Section 13.5 describes various line drawing algorithms, and Section 13.6 is a proof that Bresenham's line drawing algorithm satisfies this description. Section 13.7 suggests some extensions and Section 13.8 gives an extended formal description for thick solid lines. A proof that a sample thick line drawing algorithm satisfies the formal description is presented in Section 13.9, and a discussion of ideas for further research and conclusions follow in Sections 13.10 and 13.11. The appendix, shows a sample line plotted by various line drawing algorithms. Further references can be found in [Mar84a, Mar85].

13.2   Graphics devices

The two major graphical display device types are the vector device and the raster device. A picture on a vector device is composed of straight line segments, while on a raster device the picture is made up of picture elements, or pixels, at fixed positions. Vector drawing displays and pen plotters are examples of vector devices. Raster devices include raster displays, laser printers, and electrostatic plotters. The graphics device model to be used initially is that of a raster device since drawing lines on vector devices is simpler.

A graphics device displays images in a number of colors. It may be capable of depicting thousands of colors, a range from black to white, or possibly just two colors (binary). For simplicity the initial model of a raster device is limited to two colors: a background color (OFF) and a foreground color (ON). The display surface is composed of pixels, each one unit square with its centre having integer coordinates. Each pixel on the screen of the device may be either ON or OFF, and the pixels approximating the line are those to which the foreground color is assigned.

13.3   Lines

A straight line to be displayed on a graphical device usually has a number of associated parameters. It must have a startpoint, an endpoint, a width, a line-type, and a color. The line can be any length, have any slope, be thick or thin, solid or broken, and can be drawn in any available color. Since the pixels of the raster device lie in a grid formation, the device must produce an approximation to the line to be displayed. Thus, the representation of a line on a raster device is nontrivial. The initial description defines thin solid lines having integral endpoints.

13.4   Straight solid thin lines with integral endpoints on a two-color raster device

What properties should the approximation to a line on a raster device have? As stated earlier, the properties given should be specific enough to allow **only** reasonable approximations but general enough to allow **any** reasonable approximation. Thus it is inappropriate to specify an exact algorithm since a range of approximations is permitted. Neither is it appropriate for the representation to be entirely implementation-dependent as the role of the formal description is to limit the implementor.

Properties

The following are some intuitive ideas concerning the approximation to a straight line on a raster device:

1. If a pixel is ON it must be 'close' to the line (i.e. no pixel that is very far from the line should be ON).

2. If a pixel is 'very close' to the line it must be ON (i.e. no pixel that is very close to the line should be OFF).

3. If two pixels are in the same row or column, on the same side of the line, and the further of the two from the line is ON then the closer of the two must also be ON.

4. The pixels which are ON form a connected region with no holes or bends.

Formal description

Data types

A line on the screen with integral endpoints:

$Line$ :: P_1 : $Pixel$
         P_2 : $Pixel$
inv $(mk\text{-}Line(p_1, p_2)) \triangleq p_1 \neq p_2$

A pixel on the screen:

$Pixel$ :: X : $\mathbb{Z}_x$
           Y : $\mathbb{Z}_y$

$\mathbb{Z}_x$: where integral x-range of screen $\subset \mathbb{Z}$
$\mathbb{Z}_y$: where integral y-range of screen $\subset \mathbb{Z}$

The set of pixels turned on when approximating a line:

> *Pixel_set*: *Pixel*-set

A line $\in \mathbb{R}^2$:

> *Realline* :: P_1 : *Point*
> P_2 : *Point*
> inv $(mk\text{-}Realline(p_1, p_2)) \triangleq p_1 \neq p_2$

A point $\in \mathbb{R}^2$:

> *Point* :: X : $\mathbb{R}$
> Y : $\mathbb{R}$

where:

$\mathbb{R}$: reals
$\mathbb{R}^*$: reals ≥ 0 $\mathbb{R}^2$: Cartesian plane
$\mathbb{R}_{[0,1]}$: reals $\in [0, 1]$ $\mathbb{R}_{(0,1)}$: reals $\in (0, 1)$
$\mathbb{Z}$: integers $\mathbb{B}$: Booleans

Note that *Pixel* is treated as a subset of *Point*. Thus any function accepting a *Point* as a parameter will also accept a *Pixel* (but not vice versa).

Make functions

Make functions are used to form instances of all multiple component data types, except the form (x, y) is always assumed to be of type *Point* (or *Pixel*).

Point functions

The following are functions defined with points as one or more of the parameters.
Addition:

> $\_ +_p \_$: *Point* $\times$ *Point* $\rightarrow$ *Point*
> $p_1 +_p p_2 \triangleq (X(p_1) + X(p_2), Y(p_1) + Y(p_2))$

Subtraction:

> $\_ -_p \_$: *Point* $\times$ *Point* $\rightarrow$ *Point*
> $p_1 -_p p_2 \triangleq (X(p_1) - X(p_2), Y(p_1) - Y(p_2))$

Multiplication:

$$\_ \bullet_p \_ : \mathbb{R} \times Point \rightarrow Point$$
$$c \bullet_p p \;\triangleq\; (c \bullet X(p), c \bullet Y(\dot{p}))$$

$$\_ \times_p \_ : Point \times Point \rightarrow Point$$
$$p_1 \times_p p_2 \;\triangleq\; (X(p_1) \bullet X(p_2), Y(p_1) \bullet Y(p_2))$$

Less than:

$$\_ <_p \_ : Point \times Point \rightarrow \mathbb{B}$$
$$p_1 <_p p_2 \;\triangleq\; X(p_1) < X(p_2) \wedge Y(p_1) < Y(p_2)$$

Less than or equal to:

$$\_ \leq_p \_ : Point \times Point \rightarrow \mathbb{B}$$
$$p_1 \leq_p p_2 \;\triangleq\; X(p_1) \leq X(p_2) \wedge Y(p_1) \leq Y(p_2)$$

Summation:

$$\sum_{i=1}^{n}{}_{p-i} : Point \times Point \times \ldots \times Point \rightarrow Point$$
$$\sum_{i=1}^{n}{}_{p}p_i \;\triangleq\; \left(\textstyle\sum_{i=1}^{n} X(p_i), \sum_{i=1}^{n} Y(p_i)\right)$$

Absolute value:

$$|\_|_p : Point \rightarrow Point$$
$$|p|_p \;\triangleq\; (|X(p)|, |Y(p)|)$$

Line function

Equality:

$$\_ =_l \_ : Realline \times Realline \rightarrow \mathbb{B}$$
$$l_1 =_l l_2 \;\triangleq\; (P_1(l_1) = P_1(l_2) \wedge P_2(l_1) = P_2(l_2)) \vee$$
$$(P_1(l_1) = P_2(l_2) \wedge P_2(l_1) = P_1(l_2))$$

Function descriptions

Is the approximation to the given line valid and within a tolerance of δ?

> $validapprox : Pixel\_set \times Line \times \mathbb{R}^* \to \mathbb{B}$
> $validapprox(pixset, line, \delta) \quad \triangle$
> > $(\forall pix \in pixset \cdot withintol(pix, line, \delta)) \wedge$
> > > if a pixel in ON it is 'close' to the line
> > $(\forall pix \in Pixel \cdot nearline(pix, line) \implies pix \in pixset) \wedge$
> > > if a pixel is 'very near' the line it is ON
> > $closrptson(pixset, line) \wedge$
> > > any pixel closer to the line than a pixel that is ON is ON
> > $validpic(pixset)$
> > > the pixel formation is valid

Is the pixel within the given tolerance of the line?

> $withintol : Pixel \times Line \times \mathbb{R}^* \to \mathbb{B}$
> $withintol(pix, line, \delta) \quad \triangle \quad \exists p \in Point \cdot onlineseg(p, line) \wedge maxdist(pix, p) \leq \delta$

Is the point on the line segment?

> $onlineseg : Point \times Line \to \mathbb{B}$
> $onlineseg(p, line) \quad \triangle \quad \exists \delta \in \mathbb{R}_{[0,1]} \cdot p = P_1(line) +_p (\delta \bullet_p \Delta(line))$

What is the difference between the endpoints of the line?

> $\Delta : Line \to Point$
> $\Delta(line) \quad \triangle \quad P_2(line) -_p P_1(line)$

What is the maximum horizontal or vertical distance between the two points?

> $maxdist : Point \times Point \to \mathbb{R}^*$
> $maxdist(p_1, p_2) \quad \triangle \quad max(\{|X(p_1) - X(p_2)|, |Y(p_1) - Y(p_2)|\})$

What is the maximum of the set?

> $max : \mathbb{R}\text{-set} \to \mathbb{R}$
> $max(s) \quad \triangle \quad \iota a \in s \cdot \forall b \in s \cdot a \geq b$
> pre $s \neq \{\}$

Is the pixel very close to the line?

> $nearline : Pixel \times Line \to \mathbb{B}$
> $nearline(pix, line) \quad \triangle \quad endpt(pix, line) \vee linethru(pix, line)$

Is the pixel an endpoint of the line?

> $endpt : Pixel \times Line \rightarrow \mathbb{B}$
> $endpt(pix, line) \quad \triangle \quad pix = P_1(line) \lor pix = P_2(line)$

Does the line run right through the pixel?

> $linethru : Pixel \times Line \rightarrow \mathbb{B}$
> $linethru(pix, line) \quad \triangle$
> $\exists p_1, p_2 \in Point \cdot onlineseg(p_1, line) \land onlineseg(p_2, line) \land$
> $\neg adjcorn(p_1, p_2, pix) \land$
> $((onreallineseg(p_1, leftbord(pix)) \land onreallineseg(p_2, rightbord(pix)))$
> $\lor (onreallineseg(p_1, botbord(pix)) \land onreallineseg(p_2, topbord(pix))))$

Are the two points adjacent corners of the pixel?

> $adjcorn : Point \times Point \times Pixel \rightarrow \mathbb{B}$
> $adjcorn(p_1, p_2, pix) \quad \triangle$
>   let $rline = mk\_Realline(p_1, p_2)$ in
> $rline =_l leftbord(pix) \lor rline =_l rightbord(pix) \lor$
> $rline =_l botbord(pix) \lor rline =_l topbord(pix)$

What is the left border of the pixel?

> $leftbord : Pixel \rightarrow Realline$
> $leftbord(pix) \quad \triangle \quad mk\_Realline(pix +_p (-\frac{1}{2}, -\frac{1}{2}), pix +_p (-\frac{1}{2}, \frac{1}{2}))$

What is the right border of the pixel?

> $rightbord : Pixel \rightarrow Realline$
> $rightbord(pix) \quad \triangle \quad mk\_Realline(pix +_p (\frac{1}{2}, -\frac{1}{2}), pix +_p (\frac{1}{2}, \frac{1}{2}))$

What is the bottom border of the pixel?

> $botbord : Pixel \rightarrow Realline$
> $botbord(pix) \quad \triangle \quad mk\_Realline(pix +_p (-\frac{1}{2}, -\frac{1}{2}), pix +_p (\frac{1}{2}, -\frac{1}{2}))$

What is the top border of the pixel?

> $topbord : Pixel \rightarrow Realline$
> $topbord(pix) \quad \triangle \quad mk\_Realline(pix +_p (-\frac{1}{2}, \frac{1}{2}), pix +_p (\frac{1}{2}, \frac{1}{2}))$

Is the point on the given real line segment?

> $onreallineseg : Point \times Realline \rightarrow \mathbb{B}$
> $onreallineseg(p, rline) \quad \triangle \quad \exists \delta \in \mathbb{R}_{[0,1]} \cdot p = P_1(rline) +_p (\delta \bullet_p \Delta_r(rline))$

What is the difference between the endpoints of the real line?

$\Delta_r : Realline \rightarrow Point$

$\Delta_r(rline) \quad \underline{\triangle} \quad P_2(rline) -_p P_1(rline)$

Are all pixels closer to the line that an ON pixel ON?

closrptson : $Pixel\_set \times Line \rightarrow \mathbb{B}$

closrptson(*pixset*, *line*) $\quad \underline{\triangle}$

$\forall pix_1, pix_2 \in Pixel \cdot samexory(pix_1, pix_2) \wedge \neg oppsides(pix_1, pix_2, line) \wedge$
$closrl(pix_1, pix_2, line) \wedge pix_2 \in pixset \Rightarrow pix_1 \in pixset$

Are the two pixels in the same row or column?

samexory : $Pixel \times Pixel \rightarrow \mathbb{B}$

samexory(pix_1, pix_2) $\quad \underline{\triangle} \quad mindist(pix_1, pix_2) = 0$

What is the minimum horizontal or vertical distance between the two points?

mindist : $Point \times Point \rightarrow \mathbb{R}^*$

mindist(p_1, p_2) $\quad \underline{\triangle} \quad min(\{|X(p_1) - X(p_2)|, |Y(p_1) - Y(p_2)|\})$

What is the minimum of the set?

min : $\mathbb{R}\text{-set} \rightarrow \mathbb{R}$

min(*s*) $\quad \underline{\triangle} \quad \iota a \in s \cdot \forall b \in s \cdot a \le b$

pre $s \ne \{\,\}$

Are the pixels on opposite sides of the line?

oppsides : $Pixel \times Pixel \times Line \rightarrow \mathbb{B}$

oppsides($pix_1, pix_2, line$) $\quad \underline{\triangle} \quad pix_1 \ne pix_2 \wedge$
$\exists p \in Point \cdot inlineseg(p, mk\_Line(pix_1, pix_2)) \wedge online(p, line)$

Is the point a nonendpoint of the line segment?

inlineseg : $Point \times Line \rightarrow \mathbb{B}$

inlineseg($p, line$) $\quad \underline{\triangle} \quad \exists \delta \in \mathbb{R}_{(0,1)} \cdot p = P_1(line) +_p (\delta \bullet_p \Delta(line))$

Is the point on the line?

online : $Point \times Line \rightarrow \mathbb{B}$

online($p, line$) $\quad \underline{\triangle} \quad \exists \delta \in \mathbb{R} \cdot p = P_1(line) +_p (\delta \bullet_p \Delta(line))$

Is the first pixel closer to the line than the second?

$closrl : Pixel \times Pixel \times Line \rightarrow \mathbb{B}$
$closrl(pix_1, pix_2, line) \quad \triangleq$
$\quad \exists \delta \in \mathbb{R}^* \cdot withintol(pix_1, line, \delta) \wedge \neg withintol(pix_2, line, \delta)$

Is the pixel formation valid?

$validpic : Pixel\_set \rightarrow \mathbb{B}$
$validpic(pixset) \quad \triangleq \quad validrows(pixset) \wedge validcols(pixset)$

Are the rows of the display valid?
(i.e. do only rows in a continuous range contain ON pixels and is each of these rows valid?)

$validrows : Pixel\_set \rightarrow \mathbb{B}$
$validrows(pixset) \quad \triangleq \quad \exists y_1, y_2 \in \mathbb{Z}_y \cdot y_1 \leq y_2 \wedge$
$\quad (\forall y \in \mathbb{Z}_y - \{y_1, ..., y_2\} \cdot \forall x \in \mathbb{Z}_x \cdot (x, y) \notin pixset) \wedge$
$\quad (\forall y \in \{y_1, ..., y_2\} \cdot validrow(pixset, y))$

Is this row of the display valid?
(i.e. does this row have only one continuous range of pixels ON?)

$validrow : Pixel\_set \times \mathbb{Z}_y \rightarrow \mathbb{B}$
$validrow(pixset, y) \quad \triangleq \quad \exists x_1, x_2 \in \mathbb{Z}_x \cdot x_1 \leq x_2 \wedge$
$\quad (\forall x \in \mathbb{Z}_x - \{x_1, ..., x_2\} \cdot (x, y) \notin pixset) \wedge$
$\quad (\forall x \in \{x_1, ..., x_2\} \cdot (x, y) \in pixset)$

Are the columns of the display valid?
(i.e. do only columns in a continuous range contain ON pixels and is each of these columns valid?)

$validcols : Pixel\_set \rightarrow \mathbb{B}$
$validcols(pixset) \quad \triangleq \quad \exists x_1, x_2 \in \mathbb{Z}_x \cdot x_1 \leq x_2 \wedge$
$\quad (\forall x \in \mathbb{Z}_x - \{x_1, ..., x_2\} \cdot \forall y \in \mathbb{Z}_y \cdot (x, y) \notin pixset) \wedge$
$\quad (\forall x \in \{x_1, ..., x_2\} \cdot validcol(pixset, x))$

Is this column of the display valid?
(i.e. does this column have only one continuous range of pixels ON?)

$validcol : Pixel\_set \times \mathbb{Z}_x \rightarrow \mathbb{B}$
$validcol(pixset, x) \quad \triangleq \quad \exists y_1, y_2 \in \mathbb{Z}_y \cdot y_1 \leq y_2 \wedge$
$\quad (\forall y \in \mathbb{Z}_y - \{y_1, ..., y_2\} \cdot (x, y) \notin pixset) \wedge$
$\quad (\forall y \in \{y_1, ..., y_2\} \cdot (x, y) \in pixset)$

13.5 Thin line drawing algorithms

If the formal description is reasonable, any of the common line drawing algorithms should satisfy it. Also, the description should be easy to extend. An outline of a variety of thin line drawing algorithms follows. Each of these algorithms satisfies the above description. The pixel set for each algorithm and the appropriate tolerance is given.

Bresenham's simple digital differential analysis (DDA) and chain code algorithms

For any given line these three algorithms produce the same approximation by sampling the line once per row or column and turning on the closest pixel to the sampled point. Whether the line is sampled by row or by column is based on the slope of the line and selected so that the maximum number of points will be sampled. The simple DDA algorithm [NS81] is the most straightforward. Bresenham's algorithm [Bre65] is optimized to use only integer arithmetic, and the chain code algorithm [RW76] stores the resulting line as a series of integers modulo 7, representing the eight different directions to an adjacent pixel.

The line is related to the pixel set by:

let $N = maxdist(P_1(line), P_2(line))$ in
$$pix \in pixset \iff \exists n \in \{0, ..., N\} \cdot pix = P_1(line) +_p round_p(\tfrac{n}{N} \bullet_p \Delta(line))$$

$round_p : Point \rightarrow Pixel$
$round_p(p) \triangleq (round(X(p)), round(Y(p)))$

$round : \mathbb{R} \rightarrow \mathbb{Z}$
$round(r) \triangleq \iota i \in \mathbb{Z} \cdot (r - \tfrac{1}{2} < i \leq r + \tfrac{1}{2})$

These algorithms always turn on pixels which the line at least touches, and thus have a tolerance of $\tfrac{1}{2}$.

Symmetric DDA algorithm

The Symmetric DDA algorithm [NS81] is similar to the simple DDA algorithm, but samples the line more frequently. The length of the line determines the number of times the line is sampled. To make the notation simpler the following abbreviations are used:

Δx for $X(\Delta(line))$ and Δy for $Y(\Delta(line))$

The length of the line is usually approximated by:

$$max(|\Delta x|, |\Delta y|) + \tfrac{1}{2} \bullet min(|\Delta x|, |\Delta y|)$$

since $\sqrt{\Delta x^2 + \Delta y^2}$ is expensive to compute. Also, for efficiency reasons, the number of steps is chosen to be a power of two. Thus the number of sampled points is $2^n + 1$, where n is the smallest n such that:

$$2^n > max(|\Delta x|, |\Delta y|) + \tfrac{1}{2} \bullet min(|\Delta x|, |\Delta y|)$$

The Symmetric DDA algorithm gives a more equal density to approximations to lines of different slopes than the Simple DDA.

The line is related to the pixel set by:

let $N = minvalidn(line)$ in
$pix \in pixset \iff \exists n \in \{0, ..., N\} \cdot pix = P_1(line) +_p round_p(\tfrac{n}{N} \bullet_p \Delta(line))$

$minvalidn : Line \rightarrow \mathbb{N}$
$minvalidn(line) \quad \triangle$
$\qquad \iota n \in \mathbb{N} \cdot valid n(n, line) \wedge \forall m \in \mathbb{N} \cdot valid n(m, line) \implies n \leq m$

$valid n : \mathbb{N} \times Line \rightarrow \mathbb{B}$
$valid n(n, line) \quad \triangle \quad \exists k \in \mathbb{N} \cdot n = 2^k \wedge$
$\qquad n > maxdist(P_1(line), P_2(line)) + \tfrac{1}{2} \bullet mindist(P_1(line), P_2(line))$

The Symmetric DDA algorithm always turn on pixels touched by the line and thus has a tolerance of $\tfrac{1}{2}$.

All pixels touched algorithm

It is easy, theoretically, to imagine a line drawing algorithm which samples the line 'everywhere' thus turning on all pixels touched by the line. Of course, this could only be implemented approximately and would be inefficient.

The line is related to the pixel set by:

$$pix \in pixset \iff \exists p \in Point \cdot onlineseg(p, line) \wedge pix = round_p(p)$$

This algorithm also has a tolerance of $\tfrac{1}{2}$.

Brons' chain code algorithm

The chain code algorithm presented by Brons [Bro74] produces a line similar but not identical to the chain code algorithm discussed earlier. The chain code is produced in a recursive manner, giving successive approximations to the line until the 'best' approximation is achieved.

It is not possible to give a simple nonrecursive description of this algorithm! Brons' chain code algorithm is often identical to the standard Chain Code algorithm. However, in cases with $|\Delta x| = n$, and $|\Delta y| = 1$, it gives approximations with a tolerance approaching 1.

Binary rate multiplier (BRM) algorithm

The BRM algorithm [NS73] was once a popular line drawing algorithm due to its speed. However, it tends to produce rather inaccurate approximations and thus, with the advent of more accurate and fast algorithms it is now rarely used. It is based on binary arithmetic. Both $|\Delta x|$ and $|\Delta y|$ are expressed in binary notation using n bits. The point (x_1, y_1) is turned ON and a binary clock then counts from 0 to $2^n - 1$. At each stage, x is incremented if and only if the bit changing from 0 to 1 in the counter is 1 in the binary representation of $|\Delta x|$. The same applies to y. Each time x, y or both change the new pixel is turned ON.

The line is related to the pixel set by:

let $n = minvalidn(line)$,

$$\forall i \in \{1, ..., n\} \cdot c_i \in \{(0,0), (0,1), (1,0), (1,1)\} \cdot (|\Delta(line)|_p = \sum_{i=1}^{n} {}_p 2^{i-1} \bullet_p c_i) \text{ in}$$

$$pix \in pixset \iff \exists d \in \{0, ..., 2^n - 1\} \cdot$$

$$pix = P_1(line) +_p signp(line) \times_p \sum_{i=1}^{n} {}_p round_p(\tfrac{d}{2^{n+1-i}} \bullet_p c_i)$$

$validn : \mathbb{N} \times Line \to \mathbb{B}$
$validn(n, line) \quad \triangle \quad 2^n > maxdist(P_1(line), P_2(line))$

$signp : Line \to Point$
$signp(line) \quad \triangle \quad (sign(X(\Delta(line))), sign(X(\Delta(line))))$

$sign : \mathbb{N} \to \mathbb{N}$
$sign(a) \quad \triangle \quad \text{if } a = |a| \text{ then } 1 \text{ else } -1$

The BRM algorithm can be very inaccurate, especially for lines with $|\Delta x|$ equal to the reflection of $|\Delta y|$ in binary notation. The tolerance for this algorithm is approximately 2.

See the appendix to this chapter for a sample line and the approximations produced by these line drawing algorithms.

13.6   Proof for Bresenham's algorithm

Note that throughout this section the following abbreviations are used:

P_1 for $P_1(line)$
X_1 for $X(P_1(line))$ Y_1 for $Y(P_1(line))$
Δ for $\Delta(line)$
Δx for $X(\Delta(line))$ Δy for $Y(\Delta(line))$
R for *round* R_p for *round$_p$*
N for $max\{|\Delta x|, |\Delta y|\}$

Part 1

$\forall pix \in pixset \cdot withintol(pix, line, \frac{1}{2})$:

$pix \in pixset \iff \exists n \in \{0, ..., N\} \cdot pix = P_1 +_p R_p(\frac{n}{N} \bullet_p \Delta)$

Now,

$p = P_1 +_p (\frac{n}{N} \bullet_p \Delta)$

is on the line segment, since $0 \leq \frac{n}{N} \leq 1$. And either $\frac{\Delta x}{N}$ or $\frac{\Delta y}{N}$ is an integer, as $N = |\Delta x|$ or $|\Delta y|$. Thus:

$maxdist(pix, p) = |R(X(p)) - X(p)|$ or $|R(Y(p)) - Y(p)|$

and so $maxdist(pix, p) \leq \frac{1}{2}$, and the ON pixel is within $\frac{1}{2}$ of the line as desired.

Part 2

$\forall pix \in Pixel \cdot nearline(pix, line) \implies pix \in pixset$:

$nearline(pix, line) \iff endpt(pix, line) \vee linethru(pix, line)$

Now if the pixel is an endpoint of the line, it will be ON (cases $n = 0$ and $n = N$). If the line runs right through the pixel, there are two cases:

Case 1

$N = |\Delta x|$:

The line runs through the pixel in a horizontal direction, and we have that the point:

$(X(pix), Y(pix) + \delta)$ for $\delta \in (-\frac{1}{2}, \frac{1}{2})$

is on the line. Since $N = |\Delta x|$ this column will be sampled, and this pixel will be turned ON since:

$R(Y(pix) + \delta) = Y(pix) + R(\delta) = Y(pix)$

Case 2

$N = |\Delta y|$:

The line runs through the pixel in a vertical direction, and the point:

$(X(pix) + \delta, Y(pix))$ for $\delta \in (-\frac{1}{2}, \frac{1}{2})$

is on the line. This row will be sampled, and since:

$R(X(pix) + \delta) = X(pix)$

this pixel will be turned ON.

Part 3

$closrptson(pixset, line)$:

$closrptson(pixset, line) \iff \neg \exists pix_1, pix_2 \in Pixel \cdot$
$samexory(pix_1, pix_2) \wedge \neg oppsides(pix_1, pix_2, line) \wedge$
$closrl(pix_1, pix_2, line) \wedge pix_2 \in pixset \wedge pix_1 \notin pixset$

Assume such pix_1 and pix_2 do exist:

Case 1

$N = |\Delta x|, \; samexory(pix_1, pix_2)$:

Since $N = |\Delta x|$, only one pixel is turned ON in each column, so we can assume that pix_1 and pix_2 are in the same row. Without loss of generality, assume that Δx is positive and that pix_1 and pix_2 are adjacent. Then since pix_2 is ON:

$$X(pix_2) = X_1 + n \text{ and } Y(pix_2) = Y_1 + R(n \bullet \tfrac{\Delta y}{\Delta x})$$

And thus:

$$X(pix_1) = X_1 + n + 1 \text{ and } Y(pix_1) = Y_1 + R(n \bullet \tfrac{\Delta y}{\Delta x})$$

Now pix_1 and pix_2 are on the same side of the line and pix_1 is closer to the line than pix_2. So, the line must cross the line $x = X(pix_1)$ between:

$$Y(pix_1) \text{ and } Y(pix_1) - \tfrac{1}{2}, \text{ or } Y(pix_1) \text{ and } Y(pix_1) + \tfrac{1}{2}$$

So:

$$R((n + 1) \bullet \tfrac{\Delta y}{\Delta x}) = R(n \bullet \tfrac{\Delta y}{\Delta x})$$

and pix_1 will be ON. Thus it is true that no such pix_1 and pix_2 exist, and the above is satisfied.

Case 2

$N = |\Delta y|, \; samexory(pix_1, pix_2)$:

Similar to Case 1, with the rows and columns interchanged.

Part 4

$validpic(pixset)$:

$$validpic(pixset) \iff validrows(pixset) \land validcols(pixset)$$

Bresenham's algorithm only turns on pixels in rows and columns between p_1 and p_2, and it turns on at least one pixel in each of these, due to the choice of N. Thus, it is necessary only to check that each of these rows and columns is valid.

Case 1

$$N = |\Delta x| :$$

Only one pixel will be turned on in each column, so the columns are valid. Assume we have an invalid row, i.e. two pixels in a row are ON, but one in between them is OFF. So:

$$\exists n, m \in \mathbb{N} \cdot p_1 = P_1 +_p R_p(\tfrac{n}{|\Delta x|} \bullet_p \Delta line) \wedge p_2 = P_1 +_p R_p(\tfrac{(n+m)}{|\Delta x|} \bullet_p \Delta line)$$

Since p_1 and p_2 are in the same row:

$$R(n \bullet \tfrac{\Delta y}{|\Delta x|}) = R((n+m) \bullet \tfrac{\Delta y}{|\Delta x|})$$

and thus:

$$\forall i \in \{0, ..., m\} \cdot R((n+i) \bullet \tfrac{\Delta y}{|\Delta x|}) = R(n \bullet \tfrac{\Delta y}{|\Delta x|})$$

So all pixels in the row between p_1 and p_2 will be ON, and the row must be valid.

Case 2

$$N = |\Delta y| :$$

The argument is the same as in Case 1, with the roles of the rows and columns reversed.

Thus Bresenham's algorithm satisfies this formal description of thin solid lines.

13.7 Extensions to the formal description

Vector devices

Although the drawing primitive on a vector device is a line, a vector device is still not able to reproduce all lines exactly. The lines that it can produce are limited by the addressing resolution of the device. Thus, if the pixel size is set equal to the resolution of the vector device the model presented will also be appropriate for vector devices. There may be some parts of the description that are redundant for a vector device. For example, *closrptson* should always be true. But the description will still suffice.

Lines with nonintegral endpoints

The formal description can easily be changed to allow for lines with nonintegral endpoints by using *Realline* everywhere instead of *Line*. It might be desirable to impose an additional condition on *validapprox* to ensure that the pixels containing the endpoints are turned on under certain conditions, but this is probably unnecessary.

Thick lines

It is quite easy to extend the thin solid line description to one for solid lines of thickness *t*. One question that arises is how the endpoints of the thick line should be treated, as both round-end and square-end models for thick lines exist. Another requirement that should be added to the description is that any pixel entirely covered by the thick line should be ON.

A formal description including these extensions is presented in the next section.

13.8   Straight solid thick lines on a two-color device

This is an extension of Section 13.4 to cover vector devices, lines with nonintegral endpoints, and thick lines. Changes from the thin line description include replacing *Line* with *Realline* to avoid the integral endpoint restriction, and introducing thick lines. The list of properties to specify, the make functions, and the point and line operations are unchanged. New data types are added, some existing functions are modified, and additional functions are introduced.

Formal description

New data types

A thick line:

$$Thkline :: LIN \ : Realline$$
$$THK \ : R^*$$

A circle:

$$Circle :: CEN : Point$$
$$RAD : R^*$$

New and changed function definitions

Is the approximation to the given thick line valid and within a tolerance of δ?

> $validapprox : Pixel\_set \times Thkline \times \mathbb{R}^* \to \mathbb{B}$
> $validapprox(pixset, thkline, \delta) \quad \triangleq$
>> $(\forall pix \in pixset \cdot withintol(pix, thkline, \delta)) \wedge$
>>> if a pixel in ON it is 'close' to the line
>>
>> $(\forall pix \in Pixel \cdot nearline(pix, thkline) \ \Rightarrow \ pix \in pixset) \wedge$
>>> if a pixel is 'very near' the line it is ON
>>
>> $closrptson(pixset, LIN(thkline)) \wedge$
>>> any pixel closer to the line than a pixel that is ON is ON
>>
>> $validpic(pixset)$
>>> the pixel formation is valid

Is the pixel within the given tolerance of the line?

> $withintol : Pixel \times Thkline \times \mathbb{R}^* \to \mathbb{B}$
> $withintol(pix, thkline, \delta) \quad \triangleq$
>> $\exists p \in Point \cdot onthklineseg(p, thkline) \wedge maxdist(pix, p) \le \delta$

Is the point on the thick line segment?

> $onthklineseg : Point \times Thkline \to \mathbb{B}$
> $onthklineseg(p, thkline) \quad \triangleq$
>> Square Ends Model:
>>> $\exists line \in Realline \cdot parline(line, thkline) \wedge onreallineseg(p, line)$
>>
>> Round Ends Model:
>>> $inter(mk\_circle(p, \frac{THK(thkline)}{2}), LIN(thkline))$

Is the real line a stroke of the thick line?

> $parline : Realline \times Thkline \to \mathbb{B}$
> $parline(line, thkline) \quad \triangleq$
>> $eucldist(P_1(line), P_1(LIN(thkline))) = eucldist(P_2(line), P_2(LIN(thkline)) \wedge$
>> $eucldist(P_1(line), P_1(LIN(thkline))) \le \frac{THK(thkline)}{2} \wedge$
>> $eucldist(P_1(line), P_2(line)) = eucldist(P_1(LIN(thkline)), P_2(LIN(thkline)))$

What is the Euclidean distance between the two points?

> $eucldist : Point \times Point \to R^*$
> $eucldist(p_1, p_2) \quad \triangleq \quad \sqrt{((X(p_1) - X(p_2))^2 + (Y(p_1) - Y(p_2)))^2)}$

Do the circle and line intersect?

$inter : Circle \times Realline \rightarrow \mathbb{B}$
$inter(circle, line) \quad \triangle \quad \exists p \in Point \cdot oncircle(p, circle) \wedge onreallineseg(p, line)$

Is the point on the circle?

$oncircle : Point \times Circle \rightarrow \mathbb{B}$
$oncircle(p, circle) \quad \triangle \quad eucldist(p, CEN(circle)) = RAD(circle)$

Is the pixel very close to the thick line?

$nearline : Pixel \times Thkline \rightarrow \mathbb{B}$
$nearline(pix, thkline) \quad \triangle$
$\qquad endpt(pix, LIN(thkline)) \vee linethru(pix, LIN(thkline)) \vee$
$\qquad thklinecov(pix, thkline)$

Is the pixel an endpoint of the line?

$endpt : Pixel \times Realline \rightarrow \mathbb{B}$
$endpt(pix, line) \quad \triangle \quad pix = P_1(line) \vee pix = P_2(line)$

Does the line run right through the pixel?

$linethru : Pixel \times Realline \rightarrow \mathbb{B}$
$linethru(pix, line) \quad \triangle$
$\qquad \exists p_1, p_2 \in Point \cdot onreallineseg(p_1, line) \wedge onreallineseg(p_2, line) \wedge$
$\qquad \neg adjcorn(p_1, p_2, pix) \wedge$
$\qquad ((onreallineseg(p_1, leftbord(pix)) \wedge onreallineseg(p_2, rightbord(pix)))$
$\qquad \vee (onreallineseg(p_1, botbord(pix)) \wedge onreallineseg(p_2, topbord(pix))))$

Is the pixel covered by the thick line?

$thklinecov : Pixel \times Thkline \rightarrow \mathbb{B}$
$thklinecov(pix, thkline) \quad \triangle \quad \forall p \in pixcorners(pix) \cdot onthklineseg(p, thkline)$

What are the corners of the pixel?

$pixcorners : Pixel \rightarrow Point\text{-set}$
$pixcorners(pix) \quad \triangle \quad \{(X(pix) - \frac{1}{2}, Y(pix) - \frac{1}{2}), (X(pix) - \frac{1}{2}, Y(pix) + \frac{1}{2}),$
$\qquad (X(pix) + \frac{1}{2}, Y(pix) - \frac{1}{2}), (X(pix) + \frac{1}{2}, Y(pix) + \frac{1}{2})\}$

Are the pixels on opposite sides of the line?

$oppsides : Pixel \times Pixel \times Realline \rightarrow \mathbb{B}$
$oppsides(pix_1, pix_2, line) \quad \triangle \quad pix_1 \neq pix_2 \wedge$
$\qquad \exists p \in Point \cdot inreallineseg(p, mk\_Realline(pix_1, pix_2)) \wedge onrealline(p, line)$

Is the point a nonendpoint of the real line segment?

$inreallineseg : Point \times Realline \rightarrow \mathbb{B}$
$inreallineseg(p, line) \quad \triangle \quad \exists \delta \in \mathbb{R}_{(0,1)} \cdot p = P_1(line) +_p (\delta \bullet_p \Delta_r(line))$

Is the point on the real line?

$onrealline : Point \times Realline \rightarrow \mathbb{B}$
$onrealline(p, line) \quad \triangle \quad \exists \delta \in \mathbb{R} \cdot p = P_1(line) +_p (\delta \bullet_p \Delta_r(line))$

Is the first pixel closer to the real line than the second?

$closrl : Pixel \times Pixel \times Realline \rightarrow \mathbb{B}$
$closrl(pix_1, pix_2, line) \quad \triangle$
$\qquad \exists \delta \in \mathbb{R}^* \cdot withintol(pix_1, line, \delta) \wedge \neg withintol(pix_2, line, \delta)$

13.9 Proof for a thick line drawing algorithm

Any reasonable thick solid line drawing algorithm should satisfy the above formal description. Although most computer graphics textbooks present algorithms only for thin line drawing, it should be possible to devise a fairly simple thick line drawing algorithm and show that it satisfies the given description.

A thick line drawing algorithm

A possible thick line drawing algorithm is one which turns on all pixels touched, similar to the thin line drawing algorithm described in Section 13.5. The model of the thick line to be used in this example is the round-end model. Like its thick line counterpart, this is an inefficient algorithm and would have to be implemented approximately.

Pixels turned ON by the algorithm

The line is related to the pixel set by:

$pix \in pixset \Leftrightarrow \exists p \in Point \cdot onthklineseg(p, thkline) \wedge pix = round_p(p)$

Algorithm tolerance

Since this algorithm turns on only pixels containing a point of the line, its tolerance, like that of many of the thin line drawing algorithms discussed, is $\frac{1}{2}$.

Proof for the algorithm

Part 1

$\forall pix \in pixset \cdot withintol(pix, thkline, \frac{1}{2})$:

In fact, $pix \in pixset \iff withintol(pix, thkline, \frac{1}{2})$:

$pix \in pixset$

$\iff \exists p \in Point \cdot onthklineseg(p, thkline) \land pix = R_p(p)$

$\iff \exists p \in Point \cdot onthklineseg(p, thkline) \land X(pix) = R(X(p)) \land Y(pix) = R(Y(p))$

$\iff \exists p \in Point \cdot onthklineseg(p, thkline) \land$
$\quad |X(pix) - X(p)| \leq \frac{1}{2} \land |Y(pix) - Y(p)| \leq \frac{1}{2}$

$\iff \exists p \in Point \cdot onthklineseg(p, thkline) \land$
$\quad max(\{|X(pix) - X(p)|, |Y(pix) - Y(p)|\}) \leq \frac{1}{2}$

$\iff \exists p \in Point \cdot onthklineseg(p, thkline) \land maxdist(pix, p) \leq \frac{1}{2}$

$\iff withintol(pix, thkline, \frac{1}{2})$

Thus a pixel is ON iff it is within a tolerance of $\frac{1}{2}$ as desired.

Part 2

$\forall pix \in Pixel \cdot (nearline(pix, thkline) \implies pix \in pixset)$:

$nearline(pix, thkline) \iff endpt(pix, LIN(thkline)) \lor$
$\qquad\qquad\qquad\qquad linethru(pix, LIN(thkline)) \lor thklinecov(pix, thkline)$

If the pixel is the endpoint of the line, or if the line passes through or covers the pixel, then the pixel must contain a point of the line and is therefore ON as shown in part 1, above.

Part 3

$closrptson(pixset, thkline)$:

No pixel closer to the line than an ON pixel can be OFF, since a pixel is ON iff it is no more than $\frac{1}{2}$ away from the line.

Part 4

$validpic(pixset)$:

Since all the pixels touched by the line are ON, these will form a totally connected pattern, and thus a valid picture (no holes).

Thus this simple thick line drawing algorithm satisfies the formal description for thick lines.

13.10 Ideas for further research

Related research

Although none of the recent formal description of computer graphics systems research has discussed the properties of the approximation to a line on a graphics device, work was carried out in the 1960s and 1970s concerning the representation of solid thin lines on raster or incremental plotter devices [Fre70]. The model used to describe a line is to number the eight pixels adjacent to a given pixel from 0 to 7 in a counterclockwise direction starting with the pixel on the right. An approximation to a thin line, called the chain code, is then given by a sequence of numbers indicating the direction to proceed from each pixel of the approximation. Freeman [Fre70] notes:

> All chains of straight lines must possess the following three specific properties:
>
> 1. The code is made up of at most two elements differing by 1 modulo 8.
> 2. One of the two elements always appears singly.
> 3. The occurrences of the singly occurring element are as uniformly spaced as possible.

Rosenfeld [Ros74] proves that the above is satisfied if and only if the chain code has the chord property. That is, if and only if for every point, p, of a line segment between two pixels which are ON, there is an ON pixel, pix, such that $maxdist(p, pix) < 1$. No extensions are given for thick lines.

While this area has been ignored for some time, raster displays and operations on them are again being researched. Guibas and Stolfi [GS82] explain that it has been believed that 'the graphics programmer should be spared the pain' of dealing with raster images, but it is now being realized that raster images 'should be given full citizenship in the world of computer science'. They discuss a function, $LINE[p_1, p_2, w]$, which draws a line of thickness w from p_1 to p_2, but note that, 'the exact definition of this shape, particularly at the two endpoints, is … application-dependent'.

Alternative approaches

The work presented in this chapter is all based on the model introduced in Section 13.2. If a different model from that of the square pixel is used, new insight into the properties of output primitives on graphics devices might be obtained. One idea is to look at different tessellations of the Cartesian plane. What would the description look like if hexagonal pixels, for example, were used? The concepts of rows, columns, and adjacent pixels would need to be examined.

Another approach might involve the splitting of the description into two parts; the local and global properties of the line. Local and global properties are discussed by Guibas and Stolfi [GS82]. A local property is one that can be checked for each pixel or small piece of the approximation. Such as:

> If a pixel is ON it is 'close' to the line.

On the other hand, a global property is one requiring the entire approximation to be considered as a whole. For example:

> The line 'looks' straight.

Examining the formal description in this way may present new ideas.

The choice of distance function can also influence the description. Although the maximum horizontal or vertical distance between two points conforms to the square pixel model, the Euclidean distance function is introduced when thick lines are considered. A different choice of distance function may simplify the description or suggest a new model.

Further properties of solid straight lines

There are many additional properties of a solid straight line that could supplement or replace some of those given in the description. It is desirable to come up with a simple formal description and, at the same time, keep it both specific and general enough to encompass all reasonable approximations. One property that the approximation should have is that the line should *look straight*. This idea is incorporated in the *validpic* portion of the description. However, perhaps a better formulation of this notion can be given. For example, for a device with a very high precision, it may not be necessary to require that there are no 'holes' in the approximation, as a small hole would be undetectable to the human eye.

Other properties which are desirable in line drawing algorithms are:

- A line produced has constant density.

- All lines produced have the same density.

- The line from p_1 to p_2 is identical to the line from p_2 to p_1.

However, these properties are not possessed by some of the commonly used algorithms. A line produced by the BRM algorithm may not be of constant density. For Bresenham's algorithm, the density of the line depends on its slope, and, unless the algorithm is adjusted slightly, lines drawn in opposite directions may differ. It may be desirable to try to incorporate relaxations of these conditions into the description. For example:

- A line produced has 'nearly' constant density.

- All lines produced have 'approximately' the same density.

- The line from p_1 to p_2 is 'close' to the line from p_2 to p_1.

Further extensions to the formal description

It would be interesting to give a formal description for a dashed line. Dashed lines are usually defined as sections of ink and space. One approach would be to split the line up into a collection of short lines, each specified as a solid line. However, as the part of the ink-space pattern to start with may be implementation dependent, this becomes quite complicated.

Another extension would include the description of gray-scale lines on a gray-scale or multicolor device. In a gray-scale algorithm, each pixel is set to an appropriate shade depending on the portion of it covered by the line. Anti-aliasing is even more complicated as a filtering pattern is used, along with a selection of colors, to smooth the edges of the line and preventing them from appearing to be jagged.

Once the description of a line on a graphics device is complete there are many other drawing primitives to consider, including marker, filled area, and text. Furthermore since a picture is rarely composed of a single primitive, it is necessary to look at all the primitives within a picture and decide how to deal with those that overlap, especially on a device with many colors. This problem is discussed by Carson [Car74], and Mallgren [Mal83]. These so-called combining functions should be specified in a formal description of the properties of a graphics device, thus giving an allowable range for the appearance of the final picture, as well as for each primitive within the picture.

Another area for research is the formal description of the behavior of graphics input devices.

13.11   Conclusions

When a new graphics device is produced, it is necessary to be certain that it functions correctly. Although the formal descriptions presented here are only the tip of the iceberg with regards to that of a complete graphics device, it is encouraging that such descriptions can be produced, and actually used, to prove that algorithms for drawing graphical primitives produce reasonable results.

13.12   Appendix: sample line

The following diagrams show how the various thin line drawing algorithms discussed
in Section 13.5 approximate the line from $(0,0)$ to $(21,10)$. This line was chosen since
it accentuates the differences between the line drawing algorithms.

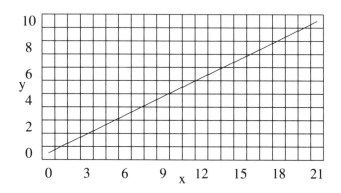

The line to be approximated, running from (0,0) to (21,10).

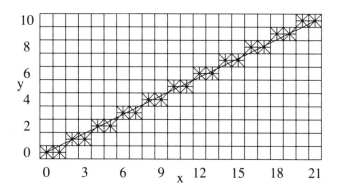

Approximation produced by Bresenham's, the simple DDA, and chain code algorithms.

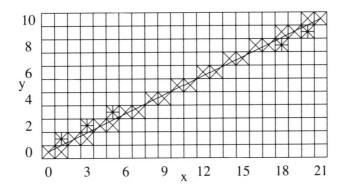

The symmetric DDA algorithm turns on all the pixels turned on by the simple DDA, and some additional ones.

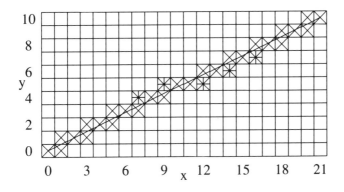

The all pixels touched algorithm turns on all the pixels turned on by the symmetric DDA, and more.

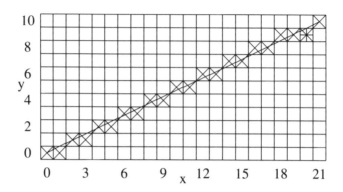

Brons' chain code algorithm is identical to the chain code algorithm except in column 20.

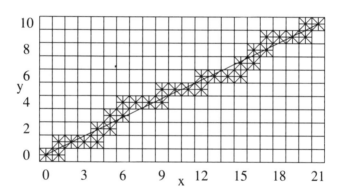

The BRM algorithm is quite inaccurate when approximating this line, since in binary form $\Delta x = \neg(\Delta y)$.

A

Glossary of Notation

The following sections provide a brief summary of the VDM notation. A detailed text book description of the language may be found in [Jon90].

A.1 Lexical conventions

The specifications collected together in this book have been written over the last six years and thus embody a variety of styles and conventions. While the editors have endeavored to impose a consistent lexical and notational style on the specifications, considerable variations still remain as it has not been practicable for these to be completely removed. In order to provide some help to the reader various of these conventions are discussed below.

1. **Operation names.** Operation names are given as either upper case or lower case letters. The first character should be a letter which may then be followed by one or more letters, digits, dashes or underscores. For example, the following are examples of operation names: *NEW*, *create*, *GC*, *remove_ref*, *ADD-VALUE*.

2. **Function names.** Three broad conventions may be discerned:

   (a) The names of functions are usually given as sequences of lower case letters, digits, underscores or dashes; names should start with a lower case character. Subscripting may be employed at the end of a function name. The following examples illustrate this convention: $inv\text{-}State_{DRC}$, *circular*, *get_name*, f_2, g.

   (b) The second form of naming functions involves an infix or mixfix notation. For example $\_ \circ \_$, $\_divides\_,\_ \bullet_p \_$. This form is described in Jones [Jon90].

   (c) The final naming form appears in those case studies involving the denotational definition of language constructs. Here functions are defined over the types of particular language constructs and the specification style requires the construction of functions which determine if a particular construct is **Well**

Formed and, for well-formed constructs, yield its **TyPe**. In these, and similar, cases we find functions of the following form being defined: *WFConst*, *TPConst*, *MProgram*, etc.

3. **Type names.** Two conventions may be identified:

   (a) Standard built-in types are shown as expected, thus $\mathbb{N}$, $\mathbb{B}$, $x \xrightarrow{m} y$, etc.

   (b) User defined types start with an upper case letter which is followed by one or more lower case letters, digits, underscores, dashes, etc.; subscripts may be used at the end of a type name. The following are examples of type names: *Student_name*, Tp_1.

4. **Variable names.** Variable names start with a lower case letter which may then be followed by zero or more lower case letters, digits, underscores, dashes, etc. Subscripts may once again be used at the end of a variable name. For example: x_1, *y*, *partitions*, *student_name*.

5. **Selector names.** Selector names follow the same rules as for function names: remember they are sometimes refered to a *selector functions* or *projection functions*. However, they are sometimes expressed using sequences of upper case characters. For example:

$$Object :: body : Bag(Oop)$$
$$RC \quad : \mathbb{N}$$

A.2 Functions

The D_i and R are types $E_R \in R$	
$f : D_1 \times D_2 \ldots \to R$	Function definition signature
$f(d_1, d_2, \ldots) \triangleq E_R$	Function definition
$f(d_1 : D_1, d_2 : D_2, \ldots)r : R$	Function specification
pre$\ldots d_1 \ldots d_2$	Pre-condition
post$\ldots d_1 \ldots d_2 \ldots r$	Post-condition
$f(d)$	Application
$f_1 \circ f_2$	Function composition
$f \uparrow n$	Function iteration

A.3 Operation specification

State – a specification state type $\Sigma = \{\sigma \mid \sigma \in State \wedge \textit{inv-State}(\sigma)\}$ – set of states $\overleftarrow{\sigma}, \sigma \in \Sigma$ – initial and final state values The T_i are types.	
$OP(p_1 : T_1, p_2 : T_2, \ldots)r : T_r$	Signature
ext rd $e_1 : T_1$	Read/write state
wr $e_2 : T_2$	Access declarations
pre $\ldots p_1 \ldots p_2 \ldots e_1 \ldots e_2 \ldots$	Pre-condition
post $\ldots p_1 \ldots p_2 \ldots e_1 \ldots e_2 \ldots \overleftarrow{e_2} \ldots r \ldots$	Post-condition
$\textit{pre-OP}(p_1, p_2, \sigma)$	Operation Quotation
$\textit{post-OP}(p_1, p_2, \overleftarrow{\sigma}, \sigma, r)$	

A.4 Logic

E, E_1, E_2 are truth valued expressions S is a set, T is a type $x \in S$	
$\mathbb{B}$	$\{\mathsf{true}, \mathsf{false}\}$
$\neg E_1$	Negation
$E_1 \wedge E_2$	Conjunction
$E_1 \vee E_2$	Disjunction
$E_1 \Rightarrow E_2$	Implication
$E_1 \Leftrightarrow E_2$	Equivalence
$E_1 = E_2$	Equals
$E_1 \neq E_2$	Not Equals
$\forall x \in S \cdot E$ $\forall x : T \cdot E$	Universal quantification
$\exists x \in S \cdot E$ $\exists x : T \cdot E$	Existential quantification
$\exists! x \in S \cdot E$ $\exists! x : T \cdot E$	Unique existence

A.5 Trivial types

not yet defined	Set of distinguished values
$=$	Equals
$\neq$	Not Equals

A.6 Union type

[*Type*]	*Type* $\cup$ {nil}
Type | nil	as above

A.7 Numbers

n, n_1, n_2 – numeric expressions or terms	
$\mathbb{N}$	$\{0, 1, 2, \ldots\}$
$\mathbb{N}_1$	$\{1, 2, \ldots\}$
$\mathbb{Z}$	$\{\ldots, -1, 0, 1, \ldots\}$
$\mathbb{Q}$	Rational Numbers
$\mathbb{R}$	Real Numbers
$+n$	Unary Plus
$-n$	Unary Minus
$n_1 + n_2$	Binary Plus
$n_1 - n_2$	Binary Minus
$n_1 \times n_2$	Multiplication
n_1/n_2	Division
$n_1 < n_2$	Less Than
$n_1 \leq n_2$	Less Than or Equals
$n_1 = n_2$	Equals
$n_1 \neq n_2$	Not Equals
$n_1 \geq n_2$	Greater Than or Equals
$n_1 > n_2$	Greater Than
n_1 rem n_2	Remainder
n_1 mod n_2	Modulus
abs n	Absolute Value
$n_1 \uparrow n_2$	Exponentiation
n_1 divides n_2	Integer Division

A.8   Sets

The table below lists the operators appropriate to the set data type. Figure A.1 shows the signatures of the operatorss using what is called an ADJ diagram. In these diagrams the ovals denote data types, in most cases *generic* in some type, while the arcs associate operators with argument and result data types.

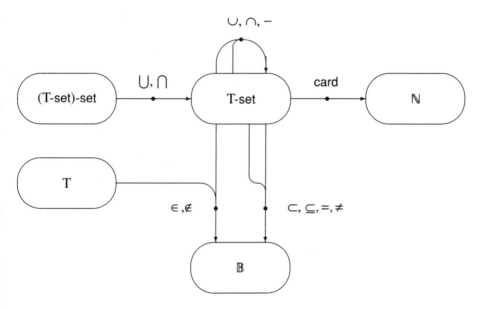

Figure A.1 ADJ diagram for the set operators.

T-set	Finite Power Set
$\{a, b, c\}$	Set Enumeration
$\{x \in S \mid p(x)\}$	Set Comprehension
$\{i, \dots, j\}$	Subset of Integers
$\{\}$	Empty set
$x \in S$	Element of
$x \notin S$	Not an Element of
$S_1 = S_2$	Equals
$S_1 \neq S_2$	Not Equals
$S_1 \cup S_2$	Union
$S_1 \cap S_2$	Intersection
$\bigcup SS$	Distributive Union
$\bigcap SS$	Distributive Intersection
$S_1 - S_2$	Difference
$S_1 \subset S_2$	Strict Subset
$S_1 \subseteq S_2$	Subset
card S	Cardinality of a set
$\iota x \in S \cdot p(x)$	Iota function

Above the table:

T is the type over which the set is defined
S, S_1, S_2 are sets
SS is a set of sets
$x \in S$
$p(x)$ is a predicate involving x
$i, j \in \mathbb{Z}$

A.9 Records

$t, x \in Type_s$
$r, r_1, r_2 \in R\_type$
s is a selector function

$R\_type::s:Type_s$	Composite Object
$mk\text{-}R\_type(x, y, z, \dots)$	Constructor
$s(r)$	Selector Function
$\mu(r, s \mapsto t)$	Modify a Composite Object
$r_1 = r_2$	Equals
$r_1 \neq r_2$	Not Equals

A.10 Maps

The map operators are recorded in the following table and the ADJ diagram is shown in Figure A.2.

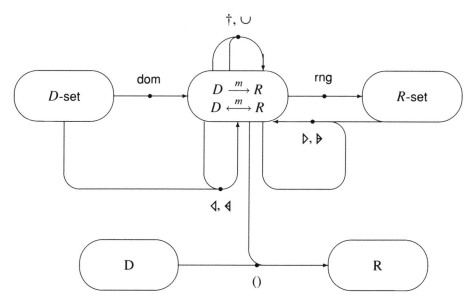

Figure A.2 ADJ diagram for the map operators.

D is the **D**omain type	
R is the **R**ange type	
$d, d_1, d_2 \in R$	
$m(d), f(d), r_1, r_2 \in R$	
M, M_1, M_2 are maps	
$S_d \in D, S_r \in R$	
$n \in \mathbb{N}_1$	
$D \xrightarrow{m} R$	Finite Maps
$D \xleftarrow{m} R$	Bi-directional Finite Maps
$\{d_1 \mapsto r_1, d_2 \mapsto r_2\}$	Map Enumeration
$\{d \mapsto f(d) \in D \times R \mid p(d)\}$	Map Comprehension
$\{\,\}$	Empty Map
$M_1 = M_2$	Equals
$M_1 \neq M_2$	Not Equals
$M(d)$	Map Application
M^{-1}	Map Inverse
$\text{dom } M$	Domain, $\text{dom } M \subseteq D$
$\text{rng } M$	Range, $\text{rng } M \subseteq R$
$S_d \lhd M$	Domain Restriction
$S_d \ntriangleleft M$	Domain Subtraction
$M \rhd S_r$	Range Restriction
$M \ntriangleright S_r$	Range Subtraction
$M_1 \dagger M_2$	Overwriting
$M_1 \cup M_2$	Union
$M_1 \circ M_2$	Composition
$M \uparrow n$	Iteration

A.11 Sequences

The table below shows the sequence operators and the ADJ diagram for these operators is given in Figure A.3.

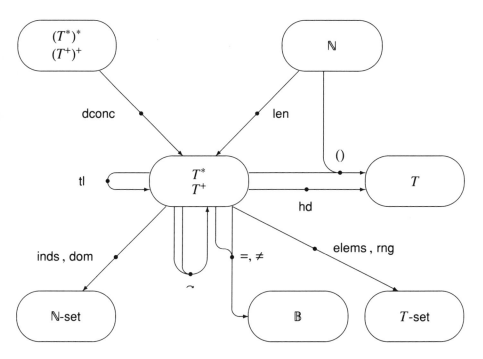

Figure A.3 ADJ diagram for the sequence operators.

T is the type over which the sequence is defined	
L, L_1, L_2 are sequences	
$n \in \mathbb{N}_1 \wedge n \in \operatorname{dom} L$	
$i, j \in \mathbb{N}$	
T^*	Finite Sequence
T^+	Non-empty Finite Sequence
$[a, b, c, d]$	Sequence Enumeration
$[\,]$	Empty Sequence
$L_1 = L_2$	Equals
$L_1 \neq L_2$	Not Equals
$L(n)$	Sequence Application
$\operatorname{len} L$	Length
$L_1 \,\widehat{}\, L_2$	Concatentation
$\operatorname{dconc} L_2$	Distributed Concatenation
$\operatorname{hd} L$	Head
$\operatorname{tl} L$	Tail
$\operatorname{dom} L$	Domain
$\operatorname{rng} L$	Range
$\operatorname{inds} L$	Indices. Same as $\operatorname{dom} L$
$\operatorname{elems} L$	Elements. Same as $\operatorname{rng} L$
$L(i, \dots, j)$	Sub-sequence

A.12   Conditional expressions

E_1 is a truth valued expression	
E_2, E_3 – expressions of the same type	
if E_1 then E_2 else E_3	Conditional Expression
cases $select(x)$ of $\qquad$ nil $\to \{\,\}$ $\qquad$ otherwise x $\qquad$ end	Cases Construct

A.13   Local definition

$y \in T$
let $x = E_1$ in E_2
let $mk\text{-}T(\dots) = y$ in E
let $z \in S$ in E

A.14   Lambda expressions

λ-notation is derived from the λ-calculus, a formal system used for studying the definition of functions and their application. We have already seen how function definitions are produced. For example:

> *double* : $\mathbb{N} \to \mathbb{N}$
> *double*(x) $\triangleq$ $2 \times x$

λ-notation allows us to keep distinct the ideas of defining a function, as an object which can be manipulated directly, and the naming of the function. For instance we can define an unnamed instance of the *double* function using λ-notation as follows:

> $\lambda x \cdot 2 \times x$

Given this definition we can then name the function as follows:

> let *double* = $\lambda x \cdot 2 \times x$ in
>
> ...

Application involves applying a function to an argument. Using *double* again we can apply the function to the value 2 as follows *double*(2) which clearly yields 4. Similarly we can apply the λ-expression as follows:

> $\lambda x \cdot 2 \times x(2)$

which once again yields the value 4.

The form of a λ-expression is as follows:

> $\lambda variable\_list \cdot Expression$

where the variables declared in *variable_list* should appear within *Expression*.

Consider the simple function which takes two integer arguments and produces the sum as a result. This function may be specified as follows:

> $\lambda x, y \cdot x + y$

As mentioned above λ-notation allows us to introduce unnamed functions which can then be manipulated in their own right. Clearly we can define functions which accept functions as arguments and can yield functions as results. For example, the function *apply* accepts a function as an argument and yields a function. This resultant function can, in turn, be applied to an appropriately typed value to yield a result.

> let *apply* = $\lambda f \cdot \lambda x \cdot f(x)$ in
>
> ...

Applying *apply* to *double* results in the following manipulations:

$apply(double) = \lambda x \cdot double(x)$
$apply(double)4 = \lambda x \cdot double(x)4 = double(4) = 8$

Alternatively, the *apply* function may be defined in the following manner using the more conventional function definition style. As we are not using polymorphic types in the book the type of the function *apply* has to be declared fully so that *apply(double)* is correctly typed:

$apply : (\mathbb{N} \to \mathbb{N}) \to (\mathbb{N} \to \mathbb{N})$
$apply(f) \quad \triangleq \quad \lambda x \cdot f$

An appropriate discussion of λ-notation and the λ-calculus may be found in Schmidt [Sch86].

A.15   Development proof obligations

Implementability proof obligation

$$\forall \overleftarrow{\sigma} \in \Sigma \cdot$$
$$pre\text{-}OP(\overleftarrow{\sigma}) \;\Rightarrow\; \exists \sigma \in \Sigma \cdot post\text{-}OP(\overleftarrow{\sigma}, \sigma)$$

The check that we need to make for each individual operation is that it can be implemented: Thus, there must exist a final state (which satisfies the invariant) such that the post condition of the operation can be satisfied. This proof obligation, known as the implementability (or satisfiability) proof obligation, has to be discharged for each operation.

Adequacy proof obligation

$$\forall a \in A \cdot$$
$$\exists r \in R \cdot ret(r) = a$$

The adequacy proof obligation asserts that every possible state value in our abstract model has at least one representation in our reified model. The function *ret* (retrieve function) is provided to transform representations of type R to representations of type A.

Operation modelling proof obligation – domain rule

$$
\forall r \in R \cdot \\
\quad pre\text{-}OPA(ret(r)) \implies pre\text{-}OPR(r)
$$

The **domain rule** states that every reified state that satisfies the pre-condition of the abstract operation, when viewed through the retrieve function, should also satisfy the pre-condition of the reified operation, i.e. the reified operation must not be more restrictive, that is defined on fewer states, than the abstract operation.

Operation modelling proof obligation – result rule

$$
\forall \overleftarrow{r}, r \in R \cdot \\
\quad pre\text{-}OPA(ret(\overleftarrow{r})) \wedge post\text{-}OPR(\overleftarrow{r}, r) \implies post\text{-}OPA(ret(\overleftarrow{r}), retr(r))
$$

The second operation modelling proof obligation, called the **result rule**, derives from an analysis of final states (states arising from the invocation of an operation). Here we will talk about state pairs $(\overleftarrow{r}, r)$ (initial and final states respectively) at the reified state level. Given that the initial state, when viewed through the retrieve function, satisfies the pre-condition of the abstract operation and that the state pair satisfy the post-condition of the the reified operation then the two states, when viewed through the retrieve function, will produce a state pair that will satisfy the post-condition of the abstract operation. In this case the reified operation specifications are being restricted to producing final states which have abstract representations, that is, no final states should be produced at the reified level which do not have abstract representations.

Bibliography

[And85]   S. O. Anderson. Proving properties about interactive systems. Technical report, Heriot-Watt University, Edinburgh, October 1985.

[ASU86]   A. Aho, R. Sethi, and J.D. Ullman. *Compilers – Principles, Techniques and Tools*. Addison-Wesley, 1986.

[Bae80]   R. Baecker. Towards an effective characterization of graphical interaction. In R. A. Guedj, P. J. W. ten Hagen, F. R. A. Hopgood, H. A. Tucker, and D. A. Duce, editors, *Methodology of Interaction*. North-Holland, 1980.

[Bak78]   H. G. Baker. List processing in real time on a serial computer. *Comm. ACM*, 21(4):280–294, 1978.

[BCJ83]   H. Barringer, J. H. Cheng, and C. B. Jones. A logic covering undefined in program proofs. *Acta Informatica*, 21:251–269, 1983.

[BJ82]   D. Bjørner and C. B. Jones. *Formal Specification and Software Development*. Prentice Hall International, 1982.

[BJM88]   R. Bloomfield, R. B. Jones, and L. S. Marshall, editors. *VDM '88: VDM – The Way Ahead*, volume 328 of *Lecture Notes in Computer Science*. Springer-Verlag, Berlin, 1988.

[BJMN87]   D. Bjørner, C. B. Jones, M. Mac an Airchinnigh, and E. J. Neuhold, editors. *VDM – A Formal Definition at Work*, volume 252 of *Lecture Notes in Computer Science*. Springer-Verlag, 1987.

[BK82]   L. Borman and R. Karr. Evaluating the 'friendliness' of a timesharing system. *ACM SIGSOC Bulletin*, 13(2–3):31–34, 1982.

[BLSS83]   W. Buxton, M. R. Lamb, D. Sherman, and K. C. Smith. Towards a comprehensive user interface management system. *ACM Computer Graphics*, 17(3):35–42, 1983.

[BM72]   R. S. Boyer and J. S. Moore. The sharing of structure in theorem-proving programs. In B. Meltzer and D. Michie, editors, *Machine Intelligence, Vol. 7*, pages 101–116. Edinburgh University Press, 1972.

[Bre65]   J. E. Bresenham. Algorithm for computer control of a digital plotter. *IBM Systems Journal*, 4(1):25–30, 1965.

[Bro74]   R. Brons. Linguistic methods for the description of a straight line on a grid. *Computer Graphics and Image Processing*, 3:48–62, 1974.

[Bun83]   A. Bundy. *The Computer Modelling of Mathematical Reasoning*. Academic Press, 1983.

[Bus83]   V. J. Bush. A survey of the use of matching functions. Private Communication, 1983.

[C$^+$86]   R. L. Constable et al. *Implementing Mathematics with the Nuprl Proof Development System*. Prentice Hall, 1986.

[Cam86]   J. Cameron. An overview of JSD. *IEEE Transactions on Software Engineering*, SE-12(2):222–242, 1986.

[Car74]   G. S. Carson. The specification of computer graphics systems. *IEEE Computer Graphics and Applications*, 3(6):27–41, 1974.

[CB83]   J. Corbin and M. Bidoit. A rehabilitation of Robinson's unification algorithm. In R. E. A. Mason, editor, *Information Processing '83*, pages 909–914. Elsevier Science Publishers (North-Holland), 1983.

[CM84]   W. F. Clocksin and C. S. Mellish. *Programming in Prolog*. Springer-Verlag, second edition, 1984.

[Coh81]   J. Cohen. Garbage collection of linked data structures. *ACM Computing Surveys*, 13(3):341–367, 1981.

[Coh89]   B. Cohen. Justification of formal methods for system specification. *Software Engineering Journal*, 4(1):26–35, 1989.

[Col60]   G. E. Collins. A method for overlapping and erasure of lists. *Comm. ACM*, 3(12):655–657, 1960.

[Coo88]   W. R. Cook. The semantics of inheritance. Private Communication, 1988.

[Dat81]   C. J. Date. *An Introduction to Data Base Systems*. Addison-Wesley, 1981.

[DB76]   L. P. Deutsch and D. G. Bobrow. An efficient, incremental, automatic garbage collector. *Comm. ACM*, 19(9):522–526, 1976.

[DFM84]   D. A. Duce, E. V. C. Fielding, and L. S. Marshall. Formal specification and graphics software. Technical Report RAL-84-068, Rutherford Appleton Laboratory, August 1984.

[DFM88]   D. A. Duce, E. V. C. Fielding, and L. S. Marshall. Formal specification of a small example based on GKS. *ACM Transactions on Graphics*, 7(3):180–197, 1988.

[DLM⁺78] E. W. Dijkstra, L. Lamport, A. J. Martin, C. S. Scholten, and E. F. M. Steffens. On-the-fly garbage collection: An exercise in cooperation. *Comm. ACM*, 21(11):966–975, 1978.

[Ede85]   E. Eder. Properties of substitutions and unifications. *Journal of Symbolic Computation*, 1:31–46, 1985.

[Eva86]   A. J. Evans. Heap storage specification and refinement to a target language. Technical Report RAISE/STC/AJE/1, STC Technology, 1986.

[Fil84]   M. Filgueiras. A Prolog interpreter working with infinite terms. In J. A. Campbell, editor, *Implementations of Prolog*, pages 250–258. Ellis Horwood, 1984.

[Fol81]   J. D. Foley. Tools for the designers of user interfaces. Technical report, George Washington University, March 1981.

[Fre70]   H. Freeman. Boundary encoding and processing. In B. S. Lipkin and A. Rosenfeld, editors, *Picture Processing and Psychopictorics*, pages 241–266. Academic Press, 1970.

[GE84]   S. Guest and E. Edmonds. Graphical support in a user interface management system. Technical report, Human–Computer Interface Research Unit, Leicester, Polytechnic, 1984.

[GH86]   J. V. Guttag and J. J. Horning. A Larch shared language handbook. *Science of Computer Programming*, 6(2):135–158, 1986.

[GHW82]   J. Guttag, J. Horning, and J. Wing. Some notes on putting formal specifications to productive use. Technical report, DEC, Palo Alto, CA, June 1982.

[Gna]   R. Gnatz. *Approaching a Formal Framework for Graphics Software Standards*. Technical University of Munich.

[GS82]   L. J. Guibas and J. Stolfi. A language for bitmap manipulation. *ACM Transactions on Graphics*, 1(3):191–214, 1982.

[Gur82]   J. R. Gurd. Manchester prototype dataflow system description. Private Communication, 1982.

[GW80]   J. R. Gurd and I. Watson. A data driven system for high speed parallel computing. *Computer Design*, 19(6/7), 1980.

[GW83]   J. R. Gurd and I. Watson. Preliminary evaluation of a prototype dataflow computer. In *Proc. IFIP 83*. North-Holland, 1983.

[Har84]   D. Harel. Statecharts: A visual approach to complex systems. Technical report, Department of Applied Mathematics, The Weizmann Institute of Science, December 1984.

[Hay85]   I. Hayes. Specification directed module testing. Technical Report PRG-49, Programming Research Group, Oxford University Computing Laboratory, Oxford, England, 1985.

[Her67]   J. Herbrand. Researches in the theory of demonstration. In J. van Heijenoort, editor, *From Frege to Gödel: A Source Book in Mathematical Logic 1879 – 1931*. Harvard University Press, 1967.

[HHS87]   J. F. He, C. A. R. Hoare, and J. W. Sanders. Data refinement refined. Technical report, Programming Research Group, Oxford University Computing Laboratory, 1987.

[HJ89]   I. J. Hayes and C.B. Jones. Specifications are not (necessarily) executable. *Software Engineering Journal*, November 1989.

[HO80]   G. Huet and D. Oppen. Equations and rewrite rules; a survey. In R.V. Book, editor, *Formal Language Theory: Perspectives and Open Problems*, pages 349–405. Academic Press, 1980.

[How83]   D. R. Howe. *Data Analysis for Data Base Design*. Edward Arnold, 1983.

[HT85]   M. D. Harrison and H. W. Thimbleby. Formalising guidelines for the design of interactive systems. In P. Johnson and S. Cook, editors, *People and Computers: Designing the Interface*, pages 161–171. Cambridge University Press, 1985.

[Hue75]   G. Huet. A unification algorithm for typed λ-calculus. *Theoretical Computer Science*, 1:27–57, 1975.

[IST85]   IST. *Database System Interface - IST 1021/2*, third edition, October 1985.

[Jac84]   R. J. K. Jacob. Designing a human – computer interface with software spec-
           ification techniques. Technical report, Naval Research Laboratory, Wash-
           ington, DC, 1984.

[JL88]   C.B. Jones and P.A. Lindsay. A support system for formal reasoning: Re-
           quirements and status. In *[BJM88]*, pages 139–152, 1988.

[JM88]   C.B. Jones and R. Moore. Muffin: A user interface design experiment for a
           theorem proving assistant. In *[BJM88]*, pages 337–375, 1988.

[Jon73]   C. B. Jones. Formal development of programs. Technical Report TR12.117,
           IBM Hursley, 1973.

[Jon80]   C. B. Jones. *Software Development: A Rigorous Approach*. Prentice Hall
           International, 1980.

[Jon81]   C. B. Jones. *Development Methods for Computer Programs – including a
           Notion of Interference*. PhD thesis, University of Oxford, 1981.

[Jon86a]   C. B. Jones. *Systematic Software Development using VDM*. Prentice Hall
           International, 1986.

[Jon86b]   K. D. Jones. *The Application of a Formal Development Method to a Parallel
           Machine Environment*. PhD thesis, The University of Manchester, 1986.

[Jon90]   C. B. Jones. *Systematic Software Development using VDM*. Prentice Hall
           International, second edition, 1990.

[Kam88]   S. Kamin. Inheritance in SMALLTALK-80: A denotational definition. In *Pro-
           ceedings of the Fifteenth ACM Symposium on the Principles of Program-
           ming Languages*, pages 80–87, San Diego, California, January 1988.

[Kir81]   C. C. Kirkham. The basic programmers manual. Private Communication,
           1981.

[Knu79]   D. E. Knuth. *Fundamental Algorithms*, volume 1 of *The Art of Computer
           Programming*. Addison-Wesley, 1979.

[LH81]   H. Lieberman and C. Hewitt. A real-time garbage collector based on the
           lifetimes of objects. *Comm. ACM*, 26(6):419–429, 1981.

[Lie86]   H. Lieberman. Using prototypical objects to implement shared behavior in
           object oriented systems. *ACM SIGPLAN Notices*, 21(11):214–223, Novem-
           ber 1986.

[Lin88]   P. A. Lindsay. A survey of mechanical support for formal reasoning. *Software Engineering Journal*, 3(1), 1988.

[Mal83]   W. R. Mallgren. *Formal Specification of Interactive Graphics Programming Languages*. ACM Distinguished Dissertations – 1982. MIT Press, 1983.

[Mar84a]   L. S. Marshall. A formal specification of line representations on graphics devices. Technical report, Department of Computer Science, University of Manchester, September 1984.

[Mar84b]   L. S. Marshall. *GKS Workstations: Formal Specification and Proofs of Correctness for Specific Devices*. University of Manchester, England, September 1984. Transfer Report.

[Mar85]   L. S. Marshall. A formal specification of line representations on graphics devices. In *Lecture Notes in Computer Science – 186*, pages 129–147. Springer Verlag, 1985.

[Mar86]   L. S. Marshall. *A Formal Description Method for User Interfaces*. PhD thesis, University of Manchester, 1986.

[MM82]   A. Martelli and U. Montanari. An efficient unification algorithm. *ACM Transactions on Programming Languages and Systems*, 4(2):258–282, April 1982.

[Moo87]   R. Moore. *Towards a Generic Muffin*. Ipse document 060/00140/2.1, 1987. University of Manchester.

[MRG88]   C. Morgan, K. Robinson, and P. Gardiner. On the refinement calculus. Technical Report PRG-70, Programming Research Group, Oxford University Computing Laboratory, 1988.

[MW80]   Z. Manna and R. Waldinger. A deductive approach to program synthesis. *ACM Transactions on Programming Languages and Systems*, 2:90–121, 1980.

[MW81]   Z. Manna and R. Waldinger. Deductive synthesis of the unification algorithm. *Science of Computer Programming*, 1:5–48, 1981.

[NCC86]   NCC, National Computing Centre Limited. *SSADM*, 1986.

[Nil84]   J. F. Nilsson. Formal Vienna Definition Method models of Prolog. In J. A. Campbell, editor, *Implementations of Prolog*, pages 218–308. Ellis Horwood, 1984.

[Nip86]   T. Nipkow. Non-deterministic data types. *Acta Informatica*, 22:629–661, 1986.

[NS73]   W. M. Newman and R. F. Sproull. *Principles of Interactive Computer Graphics*. McGraw-Hill/Kogakuska Limited, 1973.

[NS81]   W. M. Newman and R. F. Sproull. *Principles of Interactive Computer Graphics*. McGraw Hill, second edition, 1981.

[OD83]   D. R. Olsen Jr. and E. Dempsey. Syntax directed graphical interaction. *ACM Sigplan Notices*, 18(6):112–119, 1983.

[Par80]   D. M. R. Park. On the semantics of fair parallelism. In D. Bjørner, editor, *Abstract Software Specifications*. Springer-Verlag, 1980. Lecture Notes in Computer Science, 98.

[Pau85]   L. Paulson. Verifying the unification algorithm in LCF. *Science of Computer Programming*, 5:143–170, 1985.

[Pen82]   W. D. Penniman. The need for quantitative measurement of on-line user behavior. *ACM SIGSOC Bulletin*, 13(2/3):42–45, 1982.

[Plo76]   G. D. Plotkin. A powerdomain construction. *SIAM Journal of Computing*, 5(3), 1976.

[Pre87]   R. Pressman. *Software Engineering: A Practitioner's Approach*. McGraw-Hill, second edition, 1987.

[PW78]   M. S. Paterson and M. N. Wegman. Linear unification. *Journal of Computer and System Sciences*, 16:158–167, 1978.

[Rat87]   B. Ratcliff. *Software Engineering: Principles and Methods*. Blackwell, 1987.

[Rei82]   P. Reisner. Formal grammar as a tool for analyzing ease of use: Some fundamental concepts. Technical report, IBM Research Laboratory, San Jose, December 1982.

[Rei83]   P. Reisner. Analytic tools for human factors of software. Technical report, IBM Research Laboratory, San Jose, March 1983.

[Rob65]   J. A. Robinson. A machine-oriented logic based on the resolution principle. *Journal of the ACM*, 12(1):23–41, 1965.

[Rob71]   J. A. Robinson. Computational logic – the unification computation. In
            B. Meltzer and D. Michie, editors, *Machine Intelligence, Vol. 6*. Edinburgh
            University Press, 1971.

[Ros74]   A. Rosenfeld. Digital straight line segments. *IEEE Transactions on Com-
            puters*, C-23(12):1264–1269, 1974.

[Rug88]   C. Ruggles. Towards a formal definition of GKS and other graphics stan-
            dards. In *[BJM88]*, pages 64–73, 1988.

[RW76]   J. Rothstein and C. Weiman. Parallel and sequential specification of a con-
            text sensitive language for straight lines on grids. *Computer Graphics and
            Image Processing*, 5:106–124, 1976.

[SA77]   R. C. Schank and R. D. Abelson. *Scripts, Plans, and Understanding*.
            Lawrence Erlbaum, 1977.

[Sch86]   D. A. Schmidt. *Denotational Semantics: A Methodology for Language De-
            velopment*. Allyn and Bacon, Inc., Boston, 1986.

[Sho83]   M. L. Shooman. *Software Engineering: Design, Reliability and Manage-
            ment*. McGraw-Hill, New York, 1983.

[Sie84]   J. H. Siekmann. Universal unification. In *Lecture Notes in Computer Sci-
            ence*, volume 170, pages 1–42. Springer-Verlag, 1984.

[Som88]   I. Sommerville. *Software Engineering*. Addison-Wesley, third edition, 1988.

[SR82]   N. K. Sondheimer and N. Relles. Human factors and user assistance in inter-
            active computing systems: an introduction. *IEEE Transactions on Systems,
            Man, and Cybernetics*, SMC-12(2):102–107, 1982.

[SR88]   J. Staples and P. J. Robinson. Efficient unification of quantified terms. *Jour-
            nal of Logic Programming*, 5(2):133–149, 1988.

[Ste75]   G. L. Steele Jr. Multiprocessing compactifying garbage collection. *Comm.
            ACM*, 18(9):495–508, 1975.

[Ste86]   V. Stenning. An introduction to ISTAR. In I. Sommerville, editor, *Software
            Engineering Environments*. Peter Peregrinus, 1986.

[Sto77]   J. E. Stoy. *Denotational Semantics: The Scott-Strachey Approach to Pro-
            gramming Language Theory*. MIT Press, 1977.

[Str87]   B. Stroustrup. What is "object-oriented programming"? In J. Bézivin, J.-M. Hullot, P. Cointe, and H. Lieberman, editors, *Proceedings of the 1987 European Conference on Object-Oriented Programming*, pages 51–70. Springer-Verlag, June 1987. Lecture Notes in Computer Science, 276.

[Ung84]   D. Ungar. Generation scavenging: A non-disruptive, high performance storage reclamation algorithm. In *Proceedings of the Software Engineering Symposium on Practical Software Development Environments*, pages 157–167, Pittsburgh, PA, 1984. ACM SIGSOFT/SIGPLAN.

[Vad86]   S. Vadera. A theory of unification. Master's thesis, University of Manchester, 1986.

[VS86]   J. S. Vitter and R. A. Simons. New classes for parallel complexity: A study of unification and other complete problems for $\mathcal{P}$. *IEEE Transactions on Computers*, 35(5), 1986.

[War89]   B. Warboys. The IPSE 2.5 project: Process modelling as the basis for a support environment. In *Proceedings of the International Conference on System Development Environments and Factories – Berlin, May 1989*, 1989.

[Wei63]   J. Weizenbaum. Symmetric list processor. *Comm. ACM*, 6(9):524–544, 1963.

[Wel82]   A. Welsh. The specification, design and implementation of NDB. Master's thesis, Manchester University, October 1982.

[Wol88]   M. I. Wolczko. *Semantics of Object-Oriented Languages*. PhD thesis, Department of Computer Science, University of Manchester, May 1988. Technical Report UMCS–88–6–1.

[WS79]   N. Winterbottom and G. C. H. Sharman. NDB: Non-programmer data base facility. Technical Report TR.12.179, IBM Hursley, September 1979.